Proceedings of the Seventh
West Coast Conference
on Formal Linguistics

Proceedings of the Seventh
West Coast Conference on Formal Linguistics
1988

Edited by Hagit Borer

Published for
THE STANFORD LINGUISTICS ASSOCIATION
by
The Center for the Study of Language and Information
Ventura Hall, Stanford University
Stanford, California

Preface

The seventh West Coast Conference on Formal Linguistics (WCCFL 7) was hosted by the Cognitive Science Department and the Linguistics Program at the University of California in Irvine from February 26 to February 28, 1988. Thirty-five papers were presented on diverse topics, including semantics, phonology, and syntax, as well as language acquisition and parsing. Twenty-eight of these papers are printed in this volume. Not included are papers presented by Lee Bickmore, Ewa Czawkowski-Higgins, Mark Johnson, Juliette Levin, Elaine McNulty, William Poser, and Juan Uriagereka and Stan Vikner.

Special thanks go to Mary-Louise Kean and Robert May, whose skillfull organization made the conference possible. WCCFL 7 was supported by generous grants from the UC Irvine School of Humanities, the School of Social Sciences, The Office of Research, Irvine Campus, and the Sloan Foundation. Finally, thanks to Pat Adams, Betty Simmes and Barbara Kupferberg for assisting with many of the details of the conference and with the preparation of this volume.

Contents

Sequence of Tense, Intensionality and Scope
Dorit   Abusch
Center for Cognitive Science, University of Texas, Austin.

1. Introduction

The purpose of this paper is to present a theory of tense interpretation for English in main and embedded clauses. We claim the temporal interpretation of sentences can be predicted from:
(a) Their logical form, a constraint on which incorporates the notion of a transposing context. By logical forms we mean the LF level in Government - Binding theory or derivation trees in Montague Grammar.
(b) The semantics we give for tenses.
In the current study we restrict ourselves to simple tense forms.

2. SQT-Theory vs. the Independent Theory

In this section we compare two theories which try to account for the interpretation of past tense clauses embedded to past tense matrix (PAST UNDER PAST SENTENCES). Each will be challenged by a counterexample which we believe raises a genuine difficulty.

The first suggestion is one version of SEQUENCE OF TENSE THEORY (SQT-theory). It assumes the existence of a morphological SEQUENCE OF TENSE RULE (SQT-R) responsible for the shift of present tense morphology into past tense in complements of matrix clauses which have past tense morphology. An argument for this version of SQT may go as follows: Sentences (1) and (2)

(1)   John said that Mary was pregnant.
(2)   Tim claimed that Bill lived in Hells Kitchen.

are ambiguous. (1) has a shifted reading in which John said at a past time that Mary was pregnant at an earlier time, and a simultaneous reading in which John said at some past time that Mary was pregnant at the same time. We will label those two readings, described in Costa (1972) and further discussed in Enç (1987), as the BACKWARD SHIFTED and the SIMULTANEOUS reading respectively.

Assuming past tense is a semantic operator shifting evaluation time, the simultaneous reading should obtain only with present tense complements. This is so since the present tense rule introduces a time overlapping the evaluation time, which in (1)-(2) lies in the past. However, the complements of (1)-(2) have past tense morphology. To obtain the simultaneous reading for the Past under Past sentences (1)-(2), it is suggested that at the interpretive level the complement has present tense, and that SQT-R converts present tense into the past tense of the surface string.

The counterevidence against this theory is presented by Enç (1987). Consider (3) and (4):

(3)   John said that Mary is pregnant.
(4)   Julia testified that her husband is insane.

Enc argues that the time of Mary's pregnancy in (3) must include both the utterance time and John's saying time. Given this, she continues, it is not clear why (1)-(2) have the simultaneous reading, while (3)-(4) have the special one mentioned above. If as assumed by SQT-theory, (1)-(2) have present tense at the interpretive level, in principle they should have the same meaning as (3)-(4).

1

The second theory we present is THE INDEPENDENT THEORY OF TENSE,[1] which is a no SQT one. One version of it, simplified here, is Dowty's (1982). Only two points, it is claimed, are needed for temporal reference, one for event- and the other for utterance time. Each verb has a separate event time index.[2] The event times for the three verbs in (5)

(5) The child who stole the cat saw the man who washed his car.

are freely ordered with respect to each other. The only restriction on their interpretation is that each event-time should precede the utterance time. For instance, the child could have stolen the cat before, at the same time or after the man washed his car. The free ordering among the events agrees with the backward shifted and the simultaneous readings of (1)-(2) with no appeal to SQT-theory in the latter case.

The evidence against no-SQT-theory is derived from Kamp and Rohrer (1984). They employ the term TRANSPOSITION in their study of temporal interpretation of French embedded discourse, where a transposed tense form is one which underwent SQT-R. The term transposition might be preferable to sequence of tense, since it refers directly to the shift from one tense form to another when certain conditions are met. The English example we present below illustrates a similar point to the one they make.[3] Consider (6)

(6) John decided a week ago that in ten days at breakfast he would say to his mother that they were having their last meal together.

The preferred interpretation of the doubly embedded clause in (6) is that in which John's saying time is co-temporal with the time of having his last meal with his mother.[4]

Dowty's no SQT-theory treats the future as an operator shifting both the utterance time and the evaluation time in the double time indexed model. would, which has past tense, must precede the utterance time. would in (6) shifts the utterance and evaluation time of John's saying to the future as illustrated in (6'):

(6') $[[\text{would } \phi]]_{i, u} = 1$ iff $\exists k \, (k > i) \; [[\phi]]_{k, k} = 1$

were having has past tense, so it must be evaluated at some time i' preceding the local utterance time as illustrated in (6"). It follows from this that the meal time in (6) must precede the saying time, contrary to what we said above about their co-temporality.

(6")

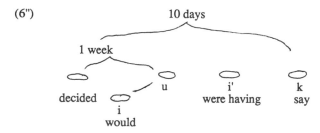

Choosing the utterance time as the evaluation time for the meal does not yield the correct reading for (6) either. This is so since the meal time in (6) follows rather than precedes the utterance time. (6) appears to be a counterexample not only to Dowty's theory, but to any theory which claims that a past tense always expresses precedence with respect to something (real utterance time, local utterance time or evaluation time, etc). For in the intended reading, the were having time precedes no time referred to in the sentence.

3. Embedded Relative Clauses and Complements

We have already seen example (5) with an embedded RC where the event described by the past tense RC can take any temporal ordering in relation to the event depicted by the past tense matrix. This, we saw, suggested that RCs are interpreted relative to the utterance time, as though they are not embedded. Complements , it seems, are more restricted in their temporal interpretation. The complement sentence in (1) does not have the reading in which Mary's pregnancy is later than John's saying time. When the event in the embedded clause is later than the event of the past tense matrix, we say the sentence has a FORWARD SHIFTED READING. Below are more examples which demonstrate the contrast between complements and embedded RC. Assume (7)-(8) were uttered on Thursday, and all mentioned days are part of a single week.

(7) John talked on Tuesday to a mechanic who repaired his car
   a. on Monday.
   b. the same day.
   c. on Wednesday.

(8) John heard on Tuesday that a mechanic repaired his car
   a. on Monday.
   b. the same day.
   c. on Wednesday.

Then (7a)-(7c) with the embedded RC are all fine, but with the complement, when (8c) is assigned a forward shifted reading, it is bad. Enç (1987) provided a syntactic explanation for this contrast using constraints similar to GB binding theory, e.g., using the concept of governing category, applying at D-structure. We will show that the proper generalization instead has to do with function/argument and scope relations which in GB would not be captured at D-structure. Consider example (9)

(9) John suspected$_j$ that $\begin{cases} \text{a. a man who killed}_k \text{ him} \\ \text{b. a man who would kill}_k \text{ him} \end{cases}$ was$_j$ behind the door.

and focus on the simultaneous reading- that in which the man being behind the door is co-temporal with John's suspicion. Given this, sentence (9a) is acceptable only when the RC is taken as a piece of information contributed by the speaker. When the RC reports a suspicion of John, (9a) is odd, presumably for the following reasons:

(a). The backward shifted and simultaneous readings in which John had suspicions about a man who has already killed him, or is killing him,[5] is pragmatically excluded.

(b). The remaining reading, which is consistent with our beliefs about the world, is the forward shifted one, in which the killing of John is later than his suspicion. But the forward shifted reading is ruled out in (9a) for the same reason it is not available in the complements of (1)-(2) and in (8c), all of which have an attitude verb in their matrix. What distinguishes the RC in (9a) from those in (5) and (7c), which permit the forward shifted reading, is that it is embedded to an attitude verb. When the RC describes John's attitude, (9b) and not (9a) , must be used.

(9a) is a counterevidence to the claim made by Enç that the contrast between the interpretation of complements and embedded RCs follows from their deep structure syntax.[6] We must look for a new generalization to account for the facts. So far it seems that when the past tense matrix contains an attitude verb, then whether the past tense embedded clause is a complement or a RC, the sentence can not have the forward shifted reading.

4. The Temporal Interpretation of Sentences with Matrix Intensional Verbs

The tense in NPs which are arguments of intensional transitive verbs are subject to the same temporal restriction as tenses in an S' embedded to attitude verbs. Consider

(10) John looked for a woman who married him.

which is ambiguous between an extensional (de-re) reading at which John looked for a specific woman who married him) and an intensional (de-dicto) reading at which John looked for a woman, but not a particular one, who married him). The forward shifted reading is not available with the intensional reading. Enç would predict no difference between the intensional reading of (10) and a corresponding example with an extensional verb, since the deep structures would be isomorphic. Enç's analysis is a no SQT one, in which the constraints on tense anchoring and the binding possibilities at D-structure account for the temporal interpretation of tenses. It also fails to predict the right reading for (6), which we suggested was counterevidence to any no SQT-theory.

We will examine sentences with three kinds of embedding matrix verbs and show they obey the following generalization (G):

(G) A sentence with a past tense embedding verb V_1, and a past tense embedded verb V_2, may have a shifted forward interpretation iff in the logical form of that sentence, V_2 does not appear within an intensional argument of V_1.

The three kinds of verbs are:
(a). Intensional attitude verbs (say, suspect, believe ...).
(b). Intensional transitive verbs (look for, need ...).
(c). Extensional transitive verbs (steal, talk to, bite ...).
In the de re reading of (10) with the forward shifted reading, the verb marry is outside the intensional argument of the embedding verb look for

(11) $\exists x(\text{woman}' (x) \ \& \ \text{marry}'(j, x) \ \& \ \text{look-for}' (j, \hat{}\lambda P (P(x))))$.

In the de-dicto reading, which lacks the forward shifted interpretation, the RC verb V_2 is inside the intensional argument of the verb look for as in (12)

(12) look for' (j, $\hat{}\lambda P \exists x (P (x) \ \& \ \text{woman}' (x) \ \& \ \text{marry}' (x, j)))$.

As is evident from the representation of (1) given below

(13) say' (j, ^pregnant' (m))

pregnant is inside the intensional argument of say. Assuming that S' can not be quantified in, this will be true in all semantic representations for the sentence, which lacks the forward shifted reading.

In (9a), the verb of the RC can have either narrow or wide scope relative to the attitude verb suspect. When the verb of the RC (kill) is outside suspect (d= the door)

(14) $\exists x$ (man' (x) & kill' (x, j) & suspect' (j, ^behind (x, d))).

the forward shifted reading is available. This is the case where the RC is contributed by the speaker. When the RC describes an attitude of John, the verb kill is inside the intensional argument of the attitude verb and like in example (1)-(2), the shifted forward reading is not available.

Our last example of embedded sentences is of an extensional transitive verb in the matrix, like steal in (5) and talked to in (7). In (15) below,

(15) John bit a donkey which kicked him.

the verb kick in the embedded RC is outside bit as is evident from (16), and moreover that argument is not intensional.

(16) $\exists x$ (donkey' (x) & bit' (j, x) & kick' (x, j)).

So as expected, (15) can have the forward shifted reading.

5. Transposing contexts and the Semantics of Tenses

5.1. The Definition of a Transposing Context

The semantics our theory provides for English simple tense forms, together with the definition of transposing contexts, aims to account for three major facts: (1) the simultaneous reading of Past under Past sentences, (2) the special meaning of Present under Past, and (3) the interpretation of embedded RCs and complements.

We view example (6), where the past tense in the most deeply embedded clause does not denote a time prior to its evaluation or local utterance time, but co-temporal with it, as strong evidence in favour of a theory along the lines of SQT. While the simultaneous reading of Past under Past can be explained by no-SQT-theories like Enç's or the Independent Theory, we do not see how they can account for example (6).

In our system, unlike in SQT-theories, tenses are not transposed from one another, but instead their distribution depends on whether they occur in transposing contexts, or not. We presume a mechanism which ensures that some tenses occur only in transposing contexts, while others in both transposing and non-transposing ones.[7] Here is the definition of transposing contexts:

(G') In sentences with an embedded Tns_2, Tns_2 is in a transposing context iff it is within an intensional argument of a past tense verb V_1.

5.2. The Simple Past Tense

We distinguish between two past tenses: $Past_1$ which can be found in any context and is marked in the lexicon as [Trans ?], and $Past_2$ which can occur only in transposing contexts and is marked as [Trans +]. The meaning of Past$_1$ is the precedence relation, while Past$_2$ contributes the overlapping relation. Consider (1) again

(1)   John said that Mary was pregnant.
(1')   [$_s$ past John say [$_{s'}$ that past Mary be pregnant]].

The embedded past tense is in a transposing context, so it can be either Past$_1$ or Past$_2$.[8] We assume the evaluation time for the argument of the intensional verb is the "now" of the experiencer subject of the verb. When the embedded tense is Past$_1$, which is associated with the precedence relation, the backward shifted reading is generated, in which the pregnancy precedes John's saying time. When the embedded tense is Past$_2$, which occurs only in transposing contexts and denotes the overlapping relation, the simultaneous reading is produced. The forward shifted reading is simply not generated.

Unlike the complement in (1), the embedded RC can have the forward shifted reading due to its scope ambiguity. Consider again example (7)

(7) John talked on Tuesday to a mechanic who repaired his car
      a. on Monday.
      b. the same day.
      c. on Wednesday.

Since there is no intensional verb, the embedded tense must be past$_1$. If it is within the scope of the matrix tense, we derive a shifted backward reading. (7) can have the forward shifted or simultaneous reading as an independent reading (see fn. 1). This is so since when its second past tense has maximal scope, as in (7'),

(7')   [[$_{NP}$ a mechanic [$_{s'}$ who past repair his car]]$_6$ [past John talk to e$_6$]].

it is evaluated with respect to the utterance time, and can bear any order relative to the event described in the main clause. Unlike Enç, we predict that the RC in (9a)

(9a) John suspected that a man who killed him was behind the door.

does not have the forward shifted interpretation on the intensional reading. Since killed is enclosed in a transposing context, its tense can be either Past$_1$ or Past$_2$. Then the time of killing either precedes (Past$_1$) or overlaps (Past$_2$) the "now" of the experiencer subject. Again, a forward shifted reading is not generated.[9] The same is true for NPs which are object of intensional verbs (example 10).

5.3. The Present Tense

We have already presented Enç's claim that the time of Mary's pregnancy in (3) must include both the utterance time and John's saying time, or as she puts it ' ... in order to interpret the complement correctly, we must have access to both evaluation times introduced previously' (Enc 1987: 637). To convince the reader of the special meaning of Present under Past, Enç provides the following example:

(17) John heard two years ago that Mary is pregnant.

and claims its anomaly can be explained by the fact that human pregnancies can not last for a period encompassing two years. Our example (18)

(18)   Yesterday at noon John pointed out that the sun is straight overhead.

is on the same lines, and indicates that the event described in the complement must be a continuous event spanning the utterance time and the time of the higher verb. Assume that (18) is uttered at noon in Central Park, with the sun straight overhead. Furthermore, assume that at the previous day at noon, John uttered (18') in Central Park:

(18')   The sun is straight overhead.

Sentence (18) is odd, presumably because it contemplates the sun being overhead for a continuous 24-hour period.

Something more specific than that the semantics should have access to both times has to be said about the interpretation of Present under Past sentences and the semantics of present tense. (19) indicates that the embedded present tense sentence need not be actually true either at the believing time or at the utterance time:

(19)   John believed that Mary is pregnant but actually she has just been overeating.

We assume that the argument of the believed proposition is the "now" of the believer, John. John believed a proposition, which is the set of world-time pairs $<w,t>$ in which Mary is pregnant. If the speaker utters (a) at t_1 in the presence of John,

(a)   John believed that Mary is pregnant.

it seems to us that John may object that he only believed Mary was pregnant at his saying time, but not necessarily at t_1. He might, in effect, ask the speaker not to misrepresent his believed proposition by constraining its argument (i.e., the interval t in the pair $<w, t>$) to overlap t_1. John's objection seems to be defensible: It is the simultaneous reading of the Past under Past version of (a) which describes what he actually believed.

Nevertheless, we have strong intuitions that present complements of past tense matrix require accessibility to both utterance and evaluation time. We suggest that under special circumstances, the speaker is allowed to misrepresent John's proposition by assigning it a different time interval argument. We want to incorporate this intuition in the semantics for the present tense, and at the same time be able to predict when a mismatch between John's proposition and the one ascribed to him is acceptable. We also do not want to force the believed proposition to be actually true at the time of John's belief (t_0), since in (19) the speaker denies Mary's pregnancy at t_0 (and also at the utterance time). Our semantics for the present tense is (where e is the evaluation time and u the utterance time):[10]

(20) $[[\text{Pres } \emptyset]]_{w,e,u}$ True iff $[[\emptyset]]_{w,e,u}$ True and e overlaps u.

Now we will figure out what (a) means:

(a') $[[\text{believe (John, } {}^{\wedge}\text{Pres pregnant (Mary)}]]_{w_0, t_0, u} =$ True iff

$<j, \{<w,t>| m \in [[\text{pregnant}]]_{w, t}$ and $t \; 0 \; u\}> \in [[\text{believe}]]_{w_0, t_0}.$

(a') is true with respect to a world w_O and times t_O, u iff the ordered pair whose first element is an individual John, and the second the proposition with the arguments w, t where t overlaps u, and Mary is in the extension of <u>pregnant</u> at w, t (let's call it proposition p), are in the extension of <u>believe</u> at w_O, t_O.

Since proposition p does not include any reference to the time and world of John's belief (i.e. $<w_O$, $t_O >$), but only to w and t, (a') does not imply that the pregnancy must pertain at t_O or u in w_O. This takes care of example (19).

It is proposition p that the speaker ascribes to John. We claim the speaker is interested in p as an explanation for the symptoms which Mary had throughout the extended period $[t_O, t_1]$ i.e., Mary's big belly, and mentions John only to support, or dismiss the pregnancy diagnosis- whatever is suggested by the circumstance of utterance. Since the speaker has good reason to be interested in p, the mismatch between John's proposition and the one the speaker ascribes to him is justified.

But what happens when Mary's symptoms ceased sometimes between John's believing time and the utterance time? In that case, we are no longer sure the speaker would use the Present under Past. An explanation may be that since the symptoms indicating Mary's pregnancy at the utterance time no longer exist, the speaker is not interested in p as a possible explanation for the symptoms. Under what circumstances the mismatch is allowed seems to be a matter of pragmatics.

The proposition ascribed to John in (18) suggests that the sun may remain in the center of the Manhattan sky for twenty four hours, and the one ascribed in (17) that human pregnancies last for two years.[11] Given our background belief about human pregnancies and our solar system, these two propositions could not be true. Since we assume the speaker is also convinced of this, it is unlikely that he will be interested in them as explanations for any symptoms. This is perhaps the reason for judging (17)-(18) as odd. Notice that the oddity of (17)-(18) is not quite the same as that of (a) when Mary's symptoms no longer exist at the utterance time. This is so since in principle, Mary's pregnancy could have continued up to the utterance time.[12]

We claim the present tense retains the same meaning in all contexts, both transposing and non-transposing ones. The special meaning is derived in Present under Past complements and the intensional reading of embedded RCs. In (3) and the intensional reading of (21)

(3) John said that Mary is pregnant.
(21) John looked for a student who understands the Incompleteness Theorem.

the present tense is inside an intensional argument as in example (a). Notice that the meaning of the present tense is independent of the notion of a transposing context. Instead, it places a constraint on the evaluation time of the intensional argument as discussed above. When the intensional matrix verb in (21) is replaced by an extensional one,

(22) John found a student who understands the Incompleteness Theorem.

we have a wide scope derivation where the present tense has maximal scope, and the time of understanding the Incompleteness Theorem is deictic to the utterance time only. We said the present tense denotes a time overlapping both the evaluation time and the utterance time, but in the wide scope reading of (22) , these two are redundant, since the evaluation time is the utterance time. Exactly the same takes place in the extensional reading of (21).

5.4. The Future

Consider (23)-(26):

(23) John said that he will feed the squirrels in Gramercy Park.
(24) Jeffery looked for a studio which will go Co-Op.

(25) John said that he would feed the squirrels in Gramercy Park.
(26) Jeffery looked for a studio that would go Co-Op.

In (23) with will in the complement, the time of the feeding of the squirrels is interpreted as later than the utterance time (and hence also the saying time), while in (25) with would in the complement, as later than the saying time, but not necessarily the utterance time.

SQT-theory predicts that when the matrix is past, will transposes into would. However, in (23)-(24), will is not transposed. Our treatment accounts for the different interpretations of (23)-(24) and (25)-(26) and also for the occurrence of will in transposing contexts.

We claim the simple future tense will incorporates in it a present tense element which we said occurs in all contexts, and must overlap both e and u. Thus, will feed is analyzed as [Pres [woll [feed]]] where woll is the tenseless form of will and would. Then by the meaning of the future element woll and by the fact that complements can not be quantified in, the time of the feeding of the squirrels in (23) must follow both the saying time and the utterance time which the present tense singles out. The same is true for (24) on the narrow scope derivation. When the embedded NP of (24) has wide scope, its present tense is deictic to the utterance time. The meaning of woll guarantees the time the studio is going Co-Op is later than the utterance time.

would feed on the other hand, has a past tense element and is analyzed as [Past [woll [feed]]]. The past element can either be $Past_1$ or $Past_2$. In a transposing context $Past_2$ overlaps the saying time, so the time of the feeding of the squirrels is later than it. Thus, the difference between will and would in transposing contexts is predicted, as well as the occurrence of will in transposing contexts.[13]

In the wide scope derivation of (26), $Past_1$ precedes the utterance time, so the two events of a studio going Co-Op and the looking for a studio are freely ordered relative to each other.[14]

6. Remaining Puzzles

We have not yet said what we take tenses to be. Should they be treated as sentential operators in formal theories, or as referential expression as first suggested in Partee (1973) and further discussed in her (1984). Enç (1986) takes the latter view and criticizes the classical sentential operator analysis. Example (27), she says,

(27) Every fugitive is now in jail.

illustrates the empirical inadequacy of the sentential analysis. Since the sentence has present tense, the NP is evaluated with respect to the utterance time whether it is in the scope of the tense, or outside it. The sentential analysis predicts only the reading involving individuals which are fugitives now. However, (27) has a non-contradictory reading involving individuals who were fugitives and are now in jail. Although (27) has no past tense, the subject seems to be interpreted at a past time.

Enç suggests that nouns as well as verbs are provided with temporal arguments. That of the verb is the syntactic tense, and the temporal argument of the NP, which is not represented in the syntax, is supplied in the course of interpretation. She claims only nouns and verbs, which are predicates of individuals, are sensitive to times.

Irene Heim[15] and Mark Liberman (personal communication) have given examples where NPs seem to trigger transposition. Consider (28)-(29)

(28) Mary's announcement that she was pregnant is irrelevant now.
(29) Everybody knows John's earlier claim that Mary would win the prize.

(29) suggests would win could only be seen as a transposed tense in relation to John's earlier claim, for the main verb has present tense. Similarly in (28), where the NP Mary's announcement is the only candidate for triggering transposition in was pregnant. Those examples suggest, along the lines of Enç, that the NP has a temporal argument which is responsible for the transposition of the complement verb. For examples like (28)-(29), where the NP is assumed to bear a temporal argument, the context of transposition should be extended to include cases where the embedded verb is in the scope of the past tense temporal argument of the NP.[16]

Notice that when we talked about Tns_2 being in the scope of an intensional argument of V_1, we were not necessarily assuming a sentential analysis of tense, since any constituent can be in the scope of another one. However, a sentential analysis of tense can probably also account for (28)-(29) by assuming that NPs provide temporal operators which have scope over the predicates coming from an N or N'.

Ladusaw argued that the interaction of SQT-R and quantifying in is responsible for the different interpretations of RCs embedded to past and non past matrix (Ladusaw 1977). Consider (30)-(31):

(30) John found a unicorn that (is) walk(ing).
(31) John will find a unicorn that (is) walk(ing).

The unicorn walking time in (31) can be interpreted as either overlapping the finding time or the utterance time. Ladusaw says that if the NP a unicorn that is walking is introduced via the quantifying in rule S14 in PTQ, the translation of the subordinate clause is outside the scope of the future operator (31a). But when the NP is introduced directly, its translation is in the scope of the future operator (31b):

(31a) $\exists x[\text{unicorn}'(x)\ \&\ \text{walk}'(x)\ \&\ F[\text{find}'(j, x)]]$.
(31b) $F[\exists x[\text{unicorn}'(x)\ \&\ \text{walk}'(x)\ \&\ \text{find}'(j, x)]]$.

When the matrix has past tense, SQT-R is obligatory. In the wide scope derivation of (30), the NP is in the higher position in the deep structure, and is inserted by quantifier lowering, so in this case SQT-R can not apply. The embedded clause has present tense in the output sentence, and the walking time is interpreted as overlapping the utterance time. (30) has no narrow scope derivation because if the subordinate present tense has narrow scope it undergoes transposition, changing present tense into past tense.

For Ladusaw, it is the scope relation between the tenses of the matrix and embedded RC which determines the interpretation of the embedded RC. For us, it is the configuration in (G') and the assumption that the evaluation time of the argument of the intensional verb is the time of the verb. (G') and Ladusaw's analysis are not the same, as is illustrated by (32) with the LF (32')

(32)   John looked for a woman who loved him.
(32')   [$_s$ Tns$_1$ [$_s$ [$_{NP}$ a woman   [$_{s'}$ who Tns$_2$ love him]]$_4$ [$_s$ John look
for e$_4$]]].

For Ladusaw, the complement tense is in the scope of the matrix one, so it could
have been transposed from underlying present, or be an underlying past. For (G'),
Tns$_2$ is not inside an argument of V$_1$ (look for in (32)), so Tns$_2$ is not in a
transposing context and can only be Past$_1$, which yields the backward shifted
reading. This shows that the transposing contexts specified by (G') are a subset of
those specified by Ladusaw. However both generate all the readings of (32).
Ladusaw generates the forward shifted reading of (32) by quantifying in, and (G')
generates the simultaneous and forward shifted readings as independent ones. Since
the two theories generate all the readings of Past under Past sentences, although
through different derivations, it is hard to decide between them. However,
Ladusaw's transposition theory does not account for the special meaning of Present
under Past, nor for the appearance of will in complements (and in embedded RC
with narrow scope) of past tense verbs (example (23)-(24)).
      In the definition of a transposing context we required the matrix V$_1$ to be past
and Tns$_2$ within an intensional argument of V$_1$. To find out whether intensionality
is a necessary condition for transposition, we must look at sentences which do not
have intensional verbs in their matrix, but where the embedded tense is inside the
matrix verb like in (33)

(33)   John found a woman who loved him.

Whether we incorporate intensionality into our definition of transposing contexts or
not, all the readings of (33) can be generated. When the matrix is extensional, Tns$_2$
is not in a transposing context, and the embedded tense in (33) can only be Past$_1$
which gives the backward shifted reading. The other two are covered by the
independent reading. If we exclude the intensionality requirement from (G'),
Tns$_2$ is in a transposing context, and may be either Past$_1$ or Past$_2$, which yield the
backward shifted and simultaneous reading respectively. For Ladusaw, Tns$_2$ is in
the scope of Tns$_1$, which generates the backward shifted and simultaneous
readings as illustrated in (33'):

(33')   [$_s$ Tns$_1$ John find [$_{NP}$ a woman [$_{s'}$ who Tns$_2$ love him]]]

The forward shifted reading is generated by Ladusaw and (G') without
intensionality on the wide scope reading of (33).
      Although we can not show that intensionality plays a necessary role in
transposition, intensionality does seem to explain the special meaning of Present
under Past complements discussed in 5.3. It is also intensionality which enables us
to check whether at the level where scope is represented, transposition has occurred
or not, by reference to the de-re/ de-dicto distinction.

Acknowledgements:
      I would like to thank Christian Rohrer for his invitation to be involved in a
Grant from Deutsche Forschungs Gemeinschaft which enabled me to develop the
ideas pursued in this paper. Its final version was written while I was a postdoctoral
fellow at the Center for Cognitive Sciences, University of Texas, Austin. I have
benefited a lot from discussions with Mats Rooth and from his insightful
comments. Thanks to Hans Kamp who went carefully over my draft, improving it,

and to Toshiyuki Ogihara for helpful comments. The responsibility for mistakes and errors is solely mine. Earlier versions of this work were presented at AT&T Bell Laboratories, and the conference 'The Structure of Events and Natural Language Metaphysics', organized by the Center for Cognitive Science, University of Texas, Austin.

Notes

1. The term 'the independent theory of tense' indicates that the embedded tense is always evaluated with respect to the utterance time, independently of the evaluation time introduced by the higher verb. We will refer to the reading generated that way as THE INDEPENDENT READING.

2. In our discussion of Dowty (1982), 'event time', 'reference time', and 'evaluation time' will be synonymous.

3. Here is Kamp and Rohrer's example:
   (a) Hier il decida enfin ce qu'il allait faire. Dans trois jours il
       Yesterday he decided finally what he was going to do. In three days he
       dirait à ses parents qu'il allait quiter la maison.
       would say to his parents that he was going to leave home.
They note '... it is clear that the saying event to which the second sentence refers is to take place after the utterance time of the discourse' (Kamp & Rohrer, 1984:3).

4. Toshiyuki Ogihara has informed me that Lee Baker came up with the same kind of example: (a) I told Bill that you would say that you only had three magic tricks to do, but it looks as if you have bought enough equipment to do six or seven (from Ogihara (1988)). In Baker's example, like in mine, the time of doing the magic tricks is interpreted as co-temporal with the saying time, despite the past tense morpheme in you only had three magic tricks to do.

5. Pragmatics aside, (9a) can not have the simultaneous reading, since the verb of its RC is an event one, (kill), and as observed by Costa (1972), Past under Past constructions with embedded event sentences can not have the simultaneous reading. To see the contrast compare (a) John said that Mary was sick to (b) John claimed that Bill failed the test. With the event verb fail in the complement of (b), only the backward shifted reading is available, but with the stative be sick both the backward shifted and simultaneous readings are obtained.

6. According to Enç, in the complement (a) John heard that Mary was pregnant, the lower past tense can be anchored by being bound in its governing category. The matrix tense is a possible antecedent and this anchoring yields the simultaneous reading:
   (a') [Comp$_0$ [NP [Pst$_i$ [V [Comp [NP [Pst$_i$ ...
The lower past tense can also be anchored through its local comp which yields the backward shifted reading:
   (a") [Comp$_0$ [NP [Past$_i$ [V[Comp$_i$ [NP [Pst$_j$ ...
In the case of an embedded RC (b) John saw the man who was crying, like in (a'), the lower tense can be bound in its governing category, which yields the simultaneous reading:
   (b') [Comp$_0$ [NP [Pst$_i$ [V [NP [Comp... Pst$_i$ ...
However, the NP the man prevents the complement local comp from being

governed, and hence from being bound in its governing category. Enç's definitions require that in this case it denotes the speech time. Since the seeing must precede the speech time, the two events can be freely ordered relative to each other, which is consistent with the forward shifted reading:

(b") $[\text{Comp}_0 [\text{NP} [\text{Past}_i [V [\text{NP} [\text{Comp}_0 [.... \text{Pst}_j ...$

7. This is similar to the enterprise in Kamp and Rohrer (1984). In their study of temporal reference in French, they analyzed French tense forms by a set of features, and introduced a mechanism which determines which feature combination is allowed when transposition occurs.

8. Enc's theory also excludes transposition of present into past. Unlike us, she assumes a single past tense in D-structure, and predicts the meaning of embedded sentences by her anchoring strategy.

9. In their study of temporal reference in French, Kamp and Rohrer (1984:6) came up with an example of a tensed RC inside an S' of an intensional verb:

(a). Jeanne m'a dit samedi dernier que le physicien que tu allait recontrer
Last Saturday Jeanne told me that the physicist that you were going to meet
venait de faire une découverte importante.
(had) just made an important discovery.

(b). Jeanne m'a dit samedi dernier que le physicien que tu as recontré lundi
Last Saturday Jeanne told me that the physicist that you met on Monday
venait de faire une découverte importante.
(had) just made an important discovery.

They note that with an Imparfait in the tensed RC in (a), there is an ambiguity in whether the RC is a contribution of the speaker, or part of the reported attitude. With a Passé Simple in the RC of (b), it is only interpreted as a contribution of the speaker. This contrast is predicted by the DRS construction algorithm. While Kamp and Rohrer are mainly interested in the question where an Imparfait and Passé Simple can occur, we are interested in the question where the shifted forward reading can not occur.

10. This is like Dowty's (1982) and Enç's (1987) rule for the Present Tense.

11. There is a problem with this implication. The time adverbial two years ago in (17) and yesterday at noon in (18) put restrictions on the hearing time and the pointing out time. But from what we have said so far, it does not follow that two years and twenty four hours separate the utterance time from the "now" of John, i.e. t. If w_0 is allowed to be one of the worlds w, perhaps we can derive this implication. To put it differently, there is no interaction between the higher verb time and the time of the embedded proposition, so we can not derive the desired implication of the two years pregnancy and the sun staying for twenty four hours in the center of Manhattan sky.

12. For further analysis of the contexts where the Present under Past can be used see Ogihara (1987).

13. We claimed that would VP can also be analyzed as having Past₁. This implies that in (25), Past₁ must precede the saying time. By the meaning of woll, the feeding of the squirrels is required to be later than Past₁, but not necessarily later than the saying time. We believe that there are contexts which give rise to such an interpretation of would VP. Consider (a)

(a) Sitting at his office at Princeton, Gödel remembered how confidently he had read for the first time Hilbert's list of problems. Although he of course also remembered that he would solve several of them, he could not help but be amazed at his youthful brashness.

Gödel remembering (remembered) occurs at the time of his sitting in his office at Princeton when he is famous. Past$_1$ in would solve is anaphoric to the time when young Gödel read Hilbert's problems. The solving of several of them occurs after the reading time and before the remembering time.

14. Toshiyuki Ogihara suggested to me that in (a) John met a woman two years ago who would become his wife, would must have past$_2$, since it is interpreted as simultaneous with the time of the meeting, and the time of the woman becoming John's wife is later than it. Since we claimed Past$_2$ can only occur in transposing contexts, and the main verb of (a) is an extensional one, it is not clear how we derive the correct meaning for (a). Our response is that when would in (a) has Past$_1$, and the NP has wide scope, the three possible orderings between the matrix past tense and the past tense in would are possible. When they are co-temporal, (a) is assigned the predicted interpretation.

15. Toshiyuki Ogihara told me Heim suggested examples like (28)-(29). (29) is taken from Ogihara (1988).

16. Mats Rooth has suggested to me the following example (a) Every obnoxious child was a rich man where the time of being a rich man can not be interpreted as later than the time of being a child, exactly like in Past under Past complements in which the forward shifted reading is blocked. Rooth has also pointed out that with the time adverbial later, the time of being rich can follow that of being an obnoxious child (b) Every obnoxious child was later a rich man.

References

Costa, Rachel. 1972. Sequence of Tense in That-Clause. Papers from the Eight Regional meeting. P. Peramteau, J. Levi and G. Phares. eds., 41-51. Chicago Linguistic Society, University of Chicago, Chicago, Illinois.
Dowty David. 1982. Tenses, Time Adverbs and Compositional Semantics Theory. Linguistics and Philosophy 5. 23-55.
Enç, Mürvet. 1986. Toward a Referential Analysis of Temporal Expressions. Linguistic and Philosophy 9. 405-426.
Enç, Mürvet. 1987. Anchoring Condition for Tense. Linguistic Inquiry 18. 633-657.
Kamp, Hans and Rohrer, Christian. 1984. Indirect Discourse. Manuscript. University of Texas, Austin and University of Stuttgart.
Ladusaw, William. 1977. Some Problems with Tense in PTQ. Texas Linguistic Forum 6. 89-102. University of Texas, Austin.
Ogihara, Toshiyuki. 1987. A Present Tense Embedded under a Past Tense. A paper presented at the LSA meeting.
Ogihara, Toshiyuki.1988 . Draft Chapter of Dissertation. Univ. of Texas, Austin.
Partee, Barbara. 1973. Some Structural Analogies between Tenses and Pronouns in English. Journal of Philosophy 70. 601-609.
Partee, Barbara.1984. Nominal and Temporal Anaphora, Linguistics and Philosophy 7.3. 243-286.

Type-shifting and Variable-Introducing Disjunction
in English and Japanese[*]
Chinatsu Aone
The University of Texas at Austin

0. Introduction

In this paper, I first discuss an approach to the semantics of disjunction in English, which uses generalized disjunction and type-shifting. Then, I elaborate and generalize another approach, so-called variable-introducing disjunction, which is first discussed in Rooth and Partee (1982) (henceforth R & P (1982)) as a solution to the problems found in generalized conjunction. Finally, I will extend this latter approach to several forms of disjunction which appear in questions, negation, and concessive clauses in Japanese.

1. Disjunction in English
1.1 Generalized conjunction and the problems with it

Generalized conjunction, discussed in Keenan and Faltz (1978), R & P (1982) and Partee and Rooth (1983) (henceforce P & R (1983)), is an attempt to treat all types of conjoined constituents as being directly generated syntactically (i.e. they assume there is no such operation as syntactic conjunction reduction) and give a single meaning for $\underline{and}$ and a single meaning for $\underline{or}$ that appear in various types of conjunction. The definitions of "conjoinable type" and "generalezed conjunction" from R & P (1982) are given in (1) and (2).

(1) Recursive definition of $\underline{conjoinable \; type}$:
   (i) t is a conjoinable type.
   (ii) if b is a conjoinable type, then for any a, < a, b> is a conjoinable type.

(2) Recursive definition of generalized $\sqcap$ and $\sqcup$:
   (i) In D_t , $\sqcap$ and $\sqcup$ are equivalent to $\land$ and $\lor$ respectively (defined by standard truth tables.)

   (ii) Let f, g be arbitary functions in $D_{<a,b>}$. Then $f \sqcap g$ is that function in $D_{<a,b>}$ which maps any element x of D_a onto the element $f(x) \sqcap g(x)$ of D_b. (Similarly for $\sqcup$.)

     $f \sqcap g: x \rightarrow f(x) \sqcap g(x)$ $f \sqcup g: x \rightarrow f(x) \sqcup g(x)$

The following are some equivalences for conjunction and disjunction in intensional logic (IL) which are drived from (2). (The verifications are also given in P & R (1983).)

(3) a. $\phi \sqcap \psi = \lambda z [\phi(z) \sqcap \psi(z)]$, where ϕ and ψ are a (single) functional type, and z is a variable of appropriate type not occuring free in ϕ or ψ.

   b. $[\phi \sqcap \psi] (x) = \phi(x) \sqcap \psi(x)$

   c. $\lambda v \phi \sqcap \lambda v \psi = \lambda v[\phi \sqcap \psi]$ (Symilarly for $\sqcup$.)

Now if we assume the type of the translation of all transitive verbs is $<< s, type (T)>$, type(IV)> (i.e. $<< s, << s,< e, t>>, t>>, < e, t>>$) as in PTQ, then the interpretaion of [TV$_1$ and TV$_2$] would be :

(4) $\lambda \wp \lambda x [TV_1'(\wp)(x) \land TV_2'(\wp)(x)]$[1]

where $\wp$ is of type $< s,<< s,< e, t>>, t>>$. However, P & R (1982, 1983) argue, this translation gives the wrong results for (5a) and (5b), but the right results for (5c) and (5d).

(5) a. John caught and ate a fish.   ($\neq$ caught a fish and ate a fish)
   b. John hugged and kissed three women.
   c. John wants and needs two secretaries.

---

[*] Many thanks to Nicholas Asher, Jim Barnett, Barbara Partee, Mats Rooth and especially Irene Heim for their useful comments. However, any responsibility for deficiencies must rest with me.

[1] I am assuming that the type of CN and IV is $< e, t >$, instead of $<< s, e >, t>$, as Dowty el.al. do.

15

d. John needed and bought a new coat.

On the other hand, if the type of TV were < e, type(IV)>, then the interpretaion of [TV$_1$ and TV$_2$] would be as in (6):

(6) $\lambda y \lambda x$ [TV$_1$' (y)(x) $\wedge$ TV$_2$' (y)(x)]

This time, (6) gives the right results for (5a) and (5b), and the wrong results for (5c) and (5d). Because of these, P & R suggest that we give up Montague's strategy of assigning to all members of a given syntactic category the "highest" type needed for any of them, but instead we interpret all expressions as having their most "basic" meaning at the lowest type pssible. So, for (5a) and (5b), the type of TV is < e, type(IV) >, but for (5c) it is << s, type(T)>, type(IV) >. As for (5d), the type of 'need' is << s, type(T)>, type(IV)> and that of 'buy' is lifted from < e, type(IV) > to << s, type(T)>, type(IV)> P & R give a "typo ambiguity principle" for TV's. (A similar principle can be made for term phrases, which have type e as their minimal type for proper nouns and pronouns, and type << s, < e, t>>, t> for quantified noun phrases>) :

(7) Type ambiguity principles
   a. Each verb is entered in the lexicon in its minimal type.
   b. A phrasal rule promotes lower-type TV's to higher-type homonyms.
   c. Processing strategy: interpret all expressions at the lowest type possible; in particular, interpret conjoined expressions at the lowest type they both have.

        In this treatment of conjunctions, then, there is no 1-to-1 correspondence between syntactic categories and their types. Rather, each syntactic category has expressions of different types although these types are all predictable from type ambiguity principles. Now, if we set up a new category for and and or , whose name is, say, CONJ, we get as many "categorial definitions" (i.e. definitions in terms of more fundamental categories) of CONJ as there are categories, e.g. (t/t)/t, (IV/IV)/IV, and so on. The categorial definition and the type for or are given by the following rule:

(8) If α and β are of category A, and have translations α', β' of type a, and or is of category (A/A)/A
    and has a translation $\sqcup$ of type < a, < a, a>>, then [α or β] is of category A and has a translation
    [α' $\sqcup$ β'] of type a.

In treating conjunction in this way, we get the following semantics for a maid or a cook, for example:

(9) a. a maid or a cook
    b. $\lambda P \exists x$ [maid'(x) $\wedge$ P{x}] $\sqcup$ $\lambda P \exists x$ [cook'(x) $\wedge$ P{x}]
       = $\lambda P[\exists x$ [maid'(x) $\wedge$ P{x}] $\sqcup$ $\exists x$ [cook'(x) $\wedge$ P{x}]] (by (3c))
       = $\lambda P[\exists x$ [maid'(x) $\wedge$ P{x}] $\vee$ $\exists x$ [cook'(x) $\wedge$ P{x}]] (by (2i))
       = $\lambda P \exists x$ [[maid'(x) $\wedge$ P{x}] $\vee$ [cook'(x) $\wedge$ P{x}]]
       = $\lambda P \exists x$ [[maid'(x) $\vee$ cook'(x)] $\wedge$ P{x}]

Here, the categorical definition of or is (T/T)/T and its type is < a, < a, a>> where a = << s, < e, t>>, t>.

        By promoting the type of " a maid or a cook" from << s, < e, t>>, t> to << s, << s, d>, t>>, t> (where d = << s, < e, t>>, t>), this treatment of disjunction allows one of the three readings of sentence (10) which cannot be predicted by the Montague-type disjunction. (Both treatments can predict the other two readings, i.e. the specific reading and the non-specific narrow scope or reading.)

(10) Mary is looking for a maid or a cook.

The reading in question is "Mary is looking for a maid or looking for a cook (but I don't know which)," where the object is non-specific. The derivation of this reading is given in R & P (1982).

        Although this seems, at first, another advantage of generalized conjunction, R & P (1982) find that it causes a problem. That is, it predicts that there are non-specific wide scope readings for phrases conjoined by and too. But while the sentence "Bill hopes that someone will hire a maid or a cook" has a non-specific wide scope reading, the sentence "Bill hopes that someone will hire a maid and a cook" has no reading equivalent to the non-specific reading of "Bill hopes that someone will hire a maid and hopes that someone will hire a cook." This is the first problem of this treatment of disjunction.

The second problem that R & P (1982) point out is that this treatment does not give one of the two readings for sentence (11):

(11) If Mary is swimming or dancing, then Sue is.

One reading which can be treated by generalized conjunction is that if Mary is engaged in one of the two activities (dancing or swimming), Sue is also doing one of the two activities. In this reading, Sue does not have to be doing the same thing as Mary. The translations of this reading is given in (11'):

(11') a. is swimming or dancing $\Longrightarrow$ $\lambda x [$ swim' (x) $\wedge$ dance'(x) $]$

b. If Mary is swimming or dancing, then Sue is $\Longrightarrow$
   $[$ swim'(m) $\vee$ dance'(m) $]$ --> $[$ swim'(s) $\vee$ dance'(s) $]$

The other reading, which I call the bound variable reading, is informally shown in (11"):

(11") $[$ swim'(m) --> swim'(s) $]$ $\wedge$ $[$ dance'(m) --> dance'(s) $]$

This reading cannot be obtained by generalized conjunction. Note that there is no disjunction in (11"). This reading says "If Mary is swimming, Sue is swimming, and if Mary is dancing, Sue is dancing." Thus, if Mary is doing one of these two things, Sue is doing the same thing.

1.2 Disjunctions introducing free variables

To solve the problems discussed above, R & P (1982) treat the disjunctions with the problematic readings as Heim (1982) and Kamp (1983) treat indefinites. Under Heim and Kamp's treatment, indefinites do not have quantificational force by themselves, but they introduce a free variable. For example, the intensional logic equivalent of their translation of "a maid" would be $\lambda P[$ maid'(x) $\wedge$ P{x} $]$. R & P (1982) thus let disjunctions introduce a single free variable. For instance, "a maid or a cook" translates to $\lambda P[$ P{x} $\wedge [$ maid'(x) $\vee$ cook'(x) $]]$. (Compare this with the last line of (9b), where x is bound by an existential quantifier.) However, it is not straightforward to get this translation from the translations of the two indefinite NPs (i.e. $\lambda P[$ maid'(x) $\wedge$ P{x} $]$ and $\lambda P[$ cook'(y) $\wedge$ P{y} $]$) by using generalized conjunction and Heim & Kamp's theory of indefinites.

(12) a. $\lambda P[P\{x\}$ $\wedge$ maid'(x)$]$ $\sqcup \lambda P[P\{y\}$ $\wedge$ cook'(y)$]$
   = $\lambda P[[P\{x\}$ $\wedge$ maid'(x)$]$ $\vee [P\{y\}$ $\wedge$ cook'(y)$]]$

b. $\lambda P[P\{x\}$ $\wedge [$maid'(x) $\vee$ cook'(x)$]]$

In (12), (a) is not equivalent to (b). For a sentence like "Mary has a maid or a cook", it does not make any difference which translation, (a) or (b), we choose. But for a sentence like "Mary had a dog or a cat and John kicked it," only the disjunction which introduces a single free variable is appropriate because it can have only one referential index. Thus, it seems that indefinites in disjunctions need a special requirement that they *may* introduce the same free variable, like R & P propose. However, this is problematic in view of Heim's "Novelty Condition" which says "An indefinite NP must not have the same referential index as any NP to its left." Under this condition, "a cat" should not have the same referential index as "a dog" in "a dog or a cat." Thus, we have to stipulate the following exception to the Novelty Condition: Indefinite NPs which constitute a disjunction can introduce the same free variable.[2]

---

[2]Mats Rooth (p.c.) pointed out to me that if we use a semantic version of the Novelty Condition, as in the File Change Semantics presented in Ch.3 of Heim (1982), the problem does not arise. For example, take a version of the File Change Semantics in Rooth (1987). There, the semantic value for any phrase is a relation between input assignment functions, output assignment functions, and in some cases individuals. Thus, $[[a\ dog_2]] = \{<g,x,g'>: dog'(x) \wedge g'= g^2_x\}$, $[[a\ cat_2]] = \{<g,x,g'>: cat'(x) \wedge g'= g^2_x\}$, $[[a\ dog_2\ or\ a\ cat_2]] = \{<g,x,g'>: dog'(x) \wedge g'= g^2_x\} \cup \{<g,x,g'>: cat'(x) \wedge g'= g^2_x\}$, and the Novelty Condition says $2 \notin Dom(g)$. Here, the disjunction of the two indefinites with the same index does not violate the Novelty Condition. (See also fn.28 on p.408 in Heim (1982).)

R & P (1982) do not provide any rule to predict the translations of various types of variable-introducing disjunction. One could give a separate rule for each type of phrase. However, this lacks generality and is hardly appealing especially when one syntactic category may have multiple types of translations. Thus in (13) I give a general type-shifting rule, which provides various types of phrases we need. (13) has two parts; the first part is for NP of type e. I separated out this from the rest in order to have type < e, t >, instead of type << s, e>, t >, as the lowest type of CN and IV. (This is just for simplicity 's sake.)

(13)
If α of category T has translation α' of type e, then it also has a translation of type << s, < e, t >>, t > that is as follows: λP[P{x} ∧x = α'], where P is variable of type < s, < e, t>>.

If α of category A has translation α' of type a, then it also has a translation of type << s, << s, a>, t>>, t> that is as follows: λζ[ζ{v} ∧v - ^ α'], where ζ is a variable of type < s, << s, a>, t>> and v is a variable of type < s, a>, and neither ζ nor v occurs free in α'.

For example, this predicts that: if "John" translates as j (type e), it also translates as λP[P{x} ∧x = j], where P is a variable of type < s,< e, t>> (abbriviated as b) and x is a variable of type e, and that: if "swim" translates as swim' (type < e, t>), it also translates as λP[P{P} ∧ P = ^ swim'], where P is a variable of type < s, << s, < e, t>>, t>> = < s, < b, t>> and P is as above. By using the above translation and rule (8) and by the assumption that the two indefinites in the disjunction can introduce the same free variable, a disjunction like "John or Bill" has the following translation:

λP[P{x} ∧x = j] ⊔ λP[P{x} ∧x = b]   (by (8))
= λP[[P{x} ∧x = j] ∨ [P{x} ∧x = b]]   (by (3c))
= λP[P{x} ∧[x = j ∨x = b]]

As for intransitive verbs, "swim or dance" (swim ==> λP[P{P} ∧P = ^swim'], dance ==> λP[P{P} ∧P = ^dance']) has a translation λP[P{P} ∧[P = ^swim' ∨P = ^dance']]. We can get the bound-variable reading of sentence (11) by using this translation. The semantics of this reading is given below:

(11''') (i) swim or dance ==> λP[P{P_1} ∧[P1 = ^swim' ∨P_1 = ^dance']]
    (ii) Sue is ==> λP[P{P_1}] (^λP[P{s}]) = P_1{s} [3]
    (iii) Mary is swimming or dancing ==> P_1{m}∧[P_1 = ^swim' ∨P_1 = ^dance']
    (iv) If Mary is swimming or dancing, Sue is ==>
        ∀P_1[[P_1{m} ∧[P_1 = ^swim' ∨P_1 = ^dance']] -> P_1{s}]

In (iv), following Heim, I assume that an invisible operator binds the free variables. (We can, of course, have an overt quantificational adverb here, as in "If Mary is swimming or dancing, Sue always is.") Intransitive verbs could be given a translation of a "simpler" type by adding the following rule:

If α, β are of category IV and their translations are α', β' of type < e, t>, then [α or β] of category IV translates to λx[P{x} ∧[P = ^ α' ∨P = ^ β']] of type < e, t>.

R & P (1982) in fact use a translation of this type for " swim or dance", yielding λx[P{x} ∧[P = ^ swim' ∨P = ^ dance']]. However, I think that my higher-type translation is well-motivated because it provides the same truth condition as that of R & P without postulating the ad hoc rule given above -- my translation follows from the type-shifting rule (13) and the general disjunction rule (8).

Now, to get the non-specific wide scope or reading for (10), we use a higher type translation for " a maid or a cook" by way of rule (13) and (8). In addition, we need a generalization of rule T 14 in PTQ, which I give in (14).

---

[3] The ellided verb has the translation λP[P{P_1}] .

(14) T 14

    If $\alpha \in D_{<< s, <A, t>>, t>}$, $\phi \in D_t$, and α, ϕ translate into α', ϕ' respectively,
    then $F_{10,n}(\alpha,\phi)$ translates into $\alpha'(^\wedge\lambda v_n \phi)$, where v is of type A.

Before presenting the semantic translation of this reading, however, I have to discuss one stipulation I have to add to my analysis. That is, all the free variables under the scope of an intension operator must be bound by an existential quatifier. Thus, in applying rule (13), the free variables in the original translation α', if any, must be bound existentially before α' is shifted to the higher-type translation. So, for example, the free variable x in $\lambda P[P\{x\} \wedge maid'(x)]$ will be bound by an existential quantifier before this NP is shifted to a higher-type NP. Although R & P (1982) do not discuss anything about this issue, I assume that they will also have to stipulate something like this in order to obtain the problematic reading of sentence (10). My stipulation may sound ad hoc, but it has certain similarlity to the first subrule of Existential Closure discussed by Heim, which says: Adjoin an existential quantifier to the nuclear scope of every operator. By "operators", she means quantifiers, negation, and temporal and modal operators. If we assume that this rule also applies in type-shifting, it seems reasonable to have an intension operator introduce an existential quantifier. Now, the translation of the non-specific wide scope or reading for (10) is given in (15).

(15)
1. a maid $\Longrightarrow$ $\lambda P[maid'(x) \wedge P\{x\}]$

      $\Longrightarrow$ $\lambda\Phi[\Phi\{P\} \wedge P = {}^\wedge\lambda P\exists x[maid'(x) \wedge P\{x\}]]$ (by (13))

    where P ia a variable of type $< s,< e, t>>$ (abbreviated as b) and Φ is a variable of type
    $< s,<< s,< b, t>>, t>>$. (Henceforth I abbreviate this as $\lambda\Phi[\Phi\{P\} \wedge P = {}^\wedge a\text{-maid'}]$.)
    (Similarly for "a cook".)
2. a maid or a cook (by (8)) $\Longrightarrow$ $\lambda\Phi[\Phi\{P\} \wedge [P = {}^\wedge a\text{-maid'} \vee P = {}^\wedge a\text{-cook'}]]$
3. Mary is looking for him$_1$ $\Longrightarrow$ look-for' $(P_1)(m)$ (The type of "look-for" is $<< s,< b, t>>, < e, t>>$.)
4. Mary is looking for a maid or a cook (by T14) $\Longrightarrow$
    $\lambda\Phi[\Phi\{P\} \wedge [P = {}^\wedge a\text{-maid'} \vee P = {}^\wedge a\text{-cook'}] ({}^\wedge\lambda P_1[\text{look-for'} (P_1)(m)])$

    $= {}^\wedge\lambda P_1[\text{look-for'} (P_1)(m)]\{P\} \wedge [P = {}^\wedge a\text{-maid'} \vee P = {}^\wedge a\text{-cook'}]$

    $= [\text{look-for'}(P)(m) \wedge [P = {}^\wedge a\text{-maid'} \vee P = {}^\wedge a\text{-cook'}]]$
5. By Existential Closure $\Longrightarrow$ $\exists P[\text{look-for'}(P)(m) \wedge [P = {}^\wedge a\text{-maid'} \vee P = {}^\wedge a\text{-cook'}]]$

    $= \text{look-for'}(^\wedge a\text{-maid})(m) \vee \text{look-for'}(^\wedge a\text{-cook})(m)$

In step 5, the second subrule of Existential Closure in Heim's indefinite analysis is used. In this theory of indefinites, it is assumed that complete logical forms correspond to texts, and a rule of construal called Text Formation attaches a sequence of sentences under a Text-node. In (15.5), the second subrule of Existential Closure adjoins an existential quantifier to this Text-node. Thus, the free variable P is bound. As you can see, the resulting translation expresses the intended meaning, i.e. Mary is looking for a maid (not a particular maid) or she is looking for a cook (not a specific cook). She is looking for one of the two, (but I do not know which.) In section 2, I will discuss cases in Japanese where NP disjunctions are better treated as introducing a single free variable. They will show that this treatment of NP disjunctions is not an ad hoc solution to problematic English sentences, but is essential to understand disjunctions in Japanese.

2. Disjunction In Japanese
2.1 Alternative questions and Yes/No questions
      It is a well-known fact that a sentence like (16) is ambiguous between an alternative question (AQ) and a yes/no question (YNQ) (cf. Karttunen 1977).

(16) Tell me whether John saw Mary or Susan.

The AQ reading would elicit an answer like "John saw Mary" or "John saw Susan", while under the YNQ reading, "Yes" or "No" would be an appropriate answer. In this paper, I adopt Karttunen's treatment of the semantics of questions. In his framework, he sets up an abstract question morpheme, which combines with a declarative sentence and forms a "proto-question." This proto-question is later fed to various types of question-forming rules, i.e. the alternative question rule, the yes/no question rule, and the WH-quantification rule. All types of question denote sets of propositions, which are of type $<< s, t>, t>$, and they combine with question embedding verbs like "tell", "know", and so on. Following Karttunen's framework, the semantics of AQ and YNQ can be represented as in (17a) and (17b) respectively. (Actually, Karttunen's AQ rule cannot give the AQ reading for sentence (16), as he notes in footnote 10. His AQ rule can only apply to alternative questions of the form "whether p or q" where p and q are sentences. Later, however, I will give a semantic rule for alternative questions which are not of the form "whether p or q.")

(17) a. { p: ∃ x [[x = m ∨ x =s] ∧ ˇp ∧ p = ^see'(x)(j)] }

   b. { p: ˇp ∧ p = ^[see'(m)(j) ∨ see'(s)(j)] ∨ p = ^[¬see'(m)(j) ∧ ¬see'(s)(j)] }

     In Japanese, however, the sentence syntactically equivalent to (16) is not ambiguous, but has only an YNQ reading.

(18) John-ga Mary ka Susan-o mita-ka oshiete kudasai.
      N   or   A saw-Q tell   please [4]

To express the AQ reading of (16), one can say as in (19).

(19) a. John-ga Mary-o mita-ka soretomo Susan-o mita-ka oshiete kudasai.
      N   A saw-Q or   A saw-Q tell   please
     "Tell me whether John saw Mary or whether he saw Susan."

   b. John-ga Mary ka Susan-no dochira-o mita-ka oshiete kudasai.
      N   or   of which-A saw-Q tell please
   ? "Tell me which of Mary or Susan John saw."

<u>Soretomo</u> is another form of <u>or</u> which is used for sentential disjunction, and I assume that the semantics of sentence (19a) can be derived by a rule analogous to Karttunen's AQ rule. What interests us in this paper is the second sentence where the disjoined NP is headed by WH-word <u>no-dochira</u> (which-of). The fact that sentences like (18), which have a plain disjoined NP within a <u>whether</u> (-ka) clause, have only the YNQ reading, while English sentences like (16) are ambiguous between AQ and YNQ suggests that disjunction in English should be treated in two different ways. If we assume that there is no transformational operation of disjunction reduction, the semantics of the AQ reading for sentences like (16) can be best understood by analogy to a Japanese example where there is no ambiguity between alternative questions and yes/no questions. (I will discuss this point in more detail after discussing Japanese examples.) I assume the following logical forms for YNQ and AQ in Japanese. (Don't be concerned with ∃ here; I'll come back to this later.)

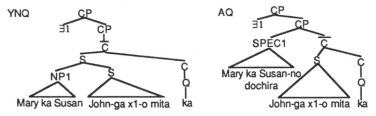

     Below, I will give the syntactic and semantic rules for alternative questions in Japanese, like (19b). (The semantics of sentence (18) can be obtained by analogy to Karttunen's YNQ rule.)

(20) Which-of-NP-disjunction (NP-disjunction-no dochira) Rule in Japanese:
   If [α ka β] ∈P_{NP}, then [[α ka β]-no dochira] ∈P_{WH}.
   If [α ka β] ∈P_{NP} translates to γ (by (8)), then [[α ka β]-no dochira] ∈P_{WH} also translates to γ. [5]

---

[4] N = nominative, A = accusative, Q = quantificational element

[5] In Japanese, NPs constituting disjunction headed by 'which-of' seem to be restricted to indefinites and definites, excluding quantified phrases. Thus, while [[John ka Mary]-no dochira] and [[kono hon ka ano hon]-no dochira] (this book or that book) are OK, [[takusan-no e ka (takusan-no) shashin]-no dochira] (many paintings or (many) pictures) is very strange.

By rules (13) and (8), [Mary ka Susan] $\in P_{NP}$, for example, translates to $\lambda P[P\{x\} \wedge [x = m \vee x = s]]$, and therefore [[Mary ka Susan]-no dochira] has the same translation although it is marked as a WH-phrase.

(21) Proto-question Rule:

If $\phi \in P_t$, then $[\phi\text{-ka}] \in P_Q$.

If $\phi \in P_t$ translates to ϕ', then $[\phi\text{-ka}] \in P_Q$ translates to $\lambda p[\check{} p \wedge p = {}^\wedge\phi']$.

(22) Alternative/WH-Question Rule:

If $\alpha \in P_{WH}$ and $\phi \in P_Q$ containing an occurrence of PRO_n and ϕ does not end with <u>dooka</u>, then $\gamma \in P_Q$.[6]

```
      /  \
    α    φ
```

If $\alpha \in P_{WH}$ translates to α' and $\phi \in P_Q$ translates to ϕ',
then $\gamma \in P_Q$ translates to $\lambda p[\alpha'({}^\wedge\lambda x_n[\phi'(p)])]$.

Rule (21) is analogous to the English Proto-Question Rule given in Karttunen(1977). In Japanese, however, there is an overt Q-morpheme <u>-ka</u> instead of an abstract one as in English. Rule (22), on the other hand, is analogous to the *WH-quantification Rule* given by Karttunen. In fact, I named the rule Alternative/WH-Question Rule because it can be used for WH-questions in general, e.g. John-ga dare-o mita-ka oshiete kudasai (= Tell me who John saw.)

Now, I give in (23) the Existential Closure rule which applies to logical forms. (23a) is for phrases which belong to P_t and (23b) for P_Q.

(23) Existential Closure Rule

a. If $\phi \in P_t$, and $\exists$ is an existential quantifier with selectional indices 1, ... , n, then $\gamma \in P_t$.

```
                           /  \
                     ∃ 1,...,n   φ
```

If $\phi \in P_t$ translates to ϕ', then $\gamma \in P_t$ translates to $\exists x_1, \ldots , x_n \phi'$.

b. If $\phi \in P_Q$, and $\exists$ is an existential quantifier with selectional indices 1, ... , n, then $\gamma \in P_Q$.

```
                           /  \
                     ∃ 1,...,n   φ
```

If $\phi \in P_Q$ translates to ϕ', then $\gamma \in P_Q$ translates to $\lambda p \exists x_1, \ldots , x_n \phi'(p)$, where p is a variable of type $< s, t >$.

The translation of sentence (19b) is given in (24).

(24) 1. Mary ka Susan   (by (13) & (8)) $\Longrightarrow \lambda P[P\{x\} \wedge [x = m \vee x = s]]$

2. Mary ka Susan-no dochira   (by (20)) $\Longrightarrow \lambda P[P\{x\} \wedge [x = m \vee x = s]]$
   or   of which

3. [[John-ga him_1 mita] ka]   (by (21)) $\Longrightarrow \lambda p[\check{} p \wedge p = {}^\wedge see'(x_1)(j)]$
   N   see   Q

4. [[Mary ka Susan-no dochira-o]$_n$ John-ga him_1 mita-ka]   (by (22))
   or   of which-A   saw-Q
   $\Longrightarrow \lambda p[[x = m \vee x = s] \wedge \check{} p \wedge p = {}^\wedge see'(x)(j)]$

5. By Existential Closure Rule (23b) $\Longrightarrow$
   $\lambda q \exists x [\lambda p[[x = m \vee x = s] \wedge \check{} p \wedge p = {}^\wedge see'(x)(j)]](q)$
   $= \lambda q \exists x [[x = m \vee x = s] \wedge \check{} q \wedge q = {}^\wedge see'(x)(j)]$

---

[6]There is a Japanese word "dooka" which is seemingly like "whether". So we can say "John-ga Mary ka Susan-o mita-ka <u>dooka</u> oshiete kudasai." However, it seems that "ka dooka" corresponds to English "whether or not," since in English "Tell me <u>whether or not</u> John saw Mary or Susan" has only an YNQ reading, not an AQ reading, and in Japanese the unambiguous AQ cannot combine with <u>dooka</u>: * John-ga Mary ka Susan-no dochira-o mita-ka dooka . . .

I treated α ka β as NP disjunction introducing a single free variable. This free variable will be bound by an existential quantifier which is introduced by a question-embedding intensional verb like "know", when the -ka clause is embedded to the verb by rule (25). This is important because, although in this case we could have used non-variable-introducing disjunction instead of variable-introducing dijunction, in other contexts we have to assume only variable-introducing disjunction. These are the contexts where the free variable seems to be quantified not by an existential quantifier but by a universal quantifier. I will discuss these cases in 2.2 and 2.3.

(25) Question Embedding rule (QE):

If $\delta \in P_{IV/Q}$ and $\phi \in P_Q$, then $\gamma \in P_{IV}$.

$$\begin{array}{c} / \setminus \\ \phi \quad \delta \end{array}$$

If $\delta \in P_{IV/Q}$ translates to δ' and $\phi \in P_Q$ to ϕ', then $\gamma \in P_{IV}$ translates to $\delta'(^\wedge\phi)$.[7]

What about a sentence like (26)? Can we get its correct semantics in exactly the same way as we did for sentence (19b)?

(26) John-ga inu   ka neko-no dochira-o katteiru-ka oshiete kudasai.
     N dog or cat-of   which-A   has-Q   tell   please
     (AQ reading of "Tell me whether John has a dog or a cat ")

(26') $\lambda p \exists x [[dog'(x) \vee cat'(x)] \wedge \ ^\sim p \wedge p = ^\wedge have'(x)(j)]$

The answer is "not quite." The translation given in (26') does not represent the intended reading of (26). Rather, it represents the semantics of a question "which dog or cat John has." We can imagine the following situation where this question is uttered: the speaker is looking at a certain set of dogs and cats in front of him whose names he knows, say, Fido, Felix and Fluffy, and he expects the listener to give him an answer like "John has Fido" or "John has Felix." When uttering sentence (26), however, the speaker does not expect the answer to identify a specific dog or cat. He is just expecting an answer like "He has a dog" or "He has a cat." In order to obtain the intended semantics of (26), then, what we should do is to shift the type of the NPs "a dog" and "a cat" by (13). The translation is given in (26").

(26")1. inu   ==> $\lambda P[dog'(x) \wedge P\{x\}]$

==> $\lambda \Phi[\Phi\{P\} \wedge P = ^\wedge\lambda P \exists x[dog'(x) \wedge P\{x\}]]$ (by (13))

where P ia a variable of type < s,< e, t>> (abbreviated as b) and Φ is a variable of type

< s,<< s,< b, t>>, t>>. (I abbreviate this as $\lambda \Phi[\Phi\{P\} \wedge P = ^\wedge a\text{-}dog']$.)
(Similarly for "neko".)

2. inu ka neko (by (8)) ==> $\lambda \Phi[\Phi\{P\} \wedge[P = ^\wedge a\text{-}dog' \vee P = ^\wedge a\text{-}cat']]$
   dog or cat

3. inu ka neko-no dochira (by (20)) ==> $\lambda \Phi[\Phi\{P\} \wedge[P = ^\wedge a\text{-}dog' \vee P = ^\wedge a\text{-}cat']]$
   dog or cat-of   which

4. [[John-ga him$_1$ katteiru] ka] (by (21)) ==> $\lambda p[^\sim p \wedge p = ^\wedge have'(P_1)(j)]$
   N   has   Q
   (The type of "have" is << s,< b, t>>, < e, t>>.)

5. [[inu ka neko-no dochira-o]$_1$ John-ga him$_1$ katteiru-ka] (by (22)) ==>

$\lambda p[[P = ^\wedge a\text{-}dog' \vee P = ^\wedge a\text{-}cat'] \wedge \ ^\sim p \wedge p = ^\wedge have'(P)(j)]$

6. By Existential Closure (23b) ==>

$\lambda p \exists P[[P = ^\wedge a\text{-}dog' \vee P = ^\wedge a\text{-}cat'] \wedge \ ^\sim p \wedge p = ^\wedge have'(P)(j)]$

Finally, what semantic rule can we assume for the AQ reading of sentence (16)? It seems that the NP disjunction in AQ should be syntactically treated as a WH-word although it does not have any overt WH morphology. Its semantics is like who or what except that the set denoted by the NP disjunction is more restricted than who or what: that is, while the semantics of who can be represented as $\lambda P[human'(x) \wedge P\{x\}]$, that of Mary or Susan is $\lambda P[P\{x\} \wedge [x = m \vee x = s]]$. It is worth noting that although the surface forms and the syntactic behavior are different between what and something and which girl and a girl, Karttunen's semantics for each pair is the same. In

---

[7]This rule is exactly analogous to Karttunen's QE rule.

Japanese, the WH-counterpart of Mary ka Susan is Mary ka Susan-no dochira, and their semantics is the same. The difference is that only the latter is used in alternative questions like (19b). In English, however, an NP disjunction can behave both like an ordinary NP and like a WH-phrase. Thus, sentences like "Tell me whether John saw Mary or Susan" or "Did John see Mary or Susan" are ambiguous between an AQ and a YNQ.

A possible logical form and semantic rules for alternative questions in English are given in (27), (28) and (29). ((28) and (29.1) are just like (21) and (22) for Japanese, respectively.)

(27)

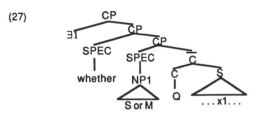

(28) Proto-Questin Rule:

    If $\phi \in P_t$, then $\gamma \in P_Q$, where Q is a question morpheme.
         / \
        Q ϕ

    If $\phi \in P_t$ translates to ϕ', then $\gamma \in P_Q$ translates to $\lambda p[\,^\smile p \land p = {}^\land \phi']$.

(29) AQ with NP-disjunction Rule:

1. If $\phi \in P_Q$ contains an occurrence of PRO_n and α is an NP disjunction, then $\gamma \in P_Q$.
                                      / \
                                     α ϕ

    If α translates to α' and $\phi \in P_Q$ translates to ϕ', then $\gamma \in P_Q$ translates to $\lambda p[\alpha'({}^\land \lambda x_n[\phi'(p)])]$.

2. If $\gamma \in P_Q$, then $\delta \in P_Q$.
           / \
    whether γ

    If $\gamma \in P_Q$ translates to γ', then $\delta \in P_Q$ also translates to γ'.

Whether in an AQ seems to be semantically vacuous, but it seems to be present because question embedding verbs subcategorize for a WH-clause. The semantics of the AQ reading of sentence (16) is given in (16').

(16')1. Mary or Susan (by (8)) ==> $\lambda P[P\{x\} \land [x = m \lor x = s]]$

    2. [Q [John saw him_1]] (by (28)) ==> $\lambda p[\,^\smile p \land p = {}^\land see'(x_1)(j)]$

    3. [whether [[Mary or Susan]$_1$ John saw him_1]] (by (29)) ==>

    $\lambda p[[x = m \lor x = s] \land {}^\smile p \land p = {}^\land see'(x)(j)]$

    4. By Existential Closure Rule (23b) ==> $\lambda p \exists x [[x = m \lor x = s] \land {}^\smile p \land p = {}^\land see'(x)(j)]$

2.2 Negation and Disjunction

In comparing the interaction of negation and NP disjunction in Japanese with that in English, we notice that the scope relation between negation and an existential quantifier in Japanese is the opposite from that in English (at least the prefered readings in English.) For example, sentense (30a) means that John likes neither, but (30b) can only mean that either John does not like a dog or he does not like a cat.

(30) a. John does not like a dog or a cat.
    b. John-wa inu ka neko-ga sukija-nai.
          N dog or cat-A   like-not

In (30a), not takes the widest scope while in (30b) the existential quantifier and the disjunction takes wide scope over nai. In fact, it seems that in Japanese quantifiers always take wide scope over nai. For example, consider the following sentences:

(31) a. ?John-wa takusan-no hon-o   mottei-nai.
        N   many   books-A have-not
    b. ?John-wa hotondo-no hon-o   mottei-nai.
        N   most   books-A have-not

If (31a) and (31b) are interpretable at all (these sentences are awkward because in ordinary speech, quantifiers "float" in Japanese as in "John-wa hon-o hotondo mottei-nai.") the sentences should be interpreted as the quantifier taking scope over nai.

      You might then ask how sentences like "John doesn't have a dog or a cat" (i.e. John has neither) or "John doesn't like Mary or Susan" (John likes neither) can be expressed in Japanese. Such sentences are expressed as follows:

(32) a. John-wa inu mo neko-mo kattei-nai.
        N dog or   cat-Q   have-not

    b. John-wa Mary mo Susan-mo sukija-nai.
        N   or   Q   like-not

In Japanese, mo has several uses, including equivalents of "even if" and "also". But I assume that the first mo is another form of or and the second mo is a quantificational element (Q-element) in Nishigauchi's terminology (1986). In his dissertaiton, he argues that WH-words in Japanese such as dare "who" and nani "what" do not have their own quantificational force, but that their quantificational force is determined by Q-elements which unselectively bind them, like mo, which corresponds to a universal quantifier, and ka, which corresponds to an existential quantifier. Thus, dare-mo means "everyone" and nani-ka means "something" in the following sentences.

(33) a. dare-mo-ga paatii-ni kita.   "Everyone came to the party."
        who-Q-N party-to came
    b. John-wa Mary-ni nani-ka-o okutta.   "John sent something to Mary."
        N   to what-Q-A sent

In a similar way, if we treat the NP disjunction inu mo neko or Mary mo Susan as an NP which contains a free variable (e.g. $\lambda P[[inu'(x) \vee neko'(x)] \wedge P\{x\}]$ by using rule (8), we can assume that the second mo is a Q-element which functions as a universal quantifier and takes scope over nai "not". The logical form and semantics of (32a), therefore, can be represented as follows:

(32a')

$\forall x \neg [\lambda P[[dog'(x) \vee cat'(x)] \wedge P\{x\}] (\lambda x [have'(x)(j)])]$

$= \forall x \neg [[dog'(x) \vee cat'(x)] \wedge have'(x)(j)]$

$= \forall x [\neg [dog'(x) \vee cat'(x)] \vee \neg have'(x)(j)]$

$= \forall x [[dog'(x) \vee cat'(x)] \rightarrow \neg have'(x)(j)]$

(32a') gives the correct reading for (32a) without violating the general scope relation between negation and a quantifier in Japanese.

      On the other hand, if we treat NP as Montague did and use generalized disjunction, we get $\lambda P \exists x [[inu'(x) \vee neko'(x)] \wedge P\{x\}]$ for the translation of inu mo neko. In this case, we should consider the second mo as a scope marker of some sort, which indicates that nai takes the widest scope. However, this not only violates the general scope relation between a quantifier and negation in Japanese, but also ignores the generalization we can make about mo as a Q-element, as we have seen in the case of WH-word + mo (and also see the next section). Thus, I argue that an analysis in terms of variable-introducing disjunction is necessary here.

2.3 Concessive Clauses

In this section, I will discuss yet another syntactic structure which includes disjunction: the concessive clause. Nishigauchi (1986) argues that no matter as in sentence (34) is an unselective binder with universal quantificational force which binds WH-phrases.

(34) No matter which book Mary buys, she (always) reads it.

(34), therefore, has the same semantics as the donkey sentence (35) does, which roughly represented as: ∀x [[Mary buys x & x is a book] -> she reads x].[8]

(35) If Mary buys a book, she (always) reads it.

Nishigauchi gives the following logical form for a concessive clause.

(36)

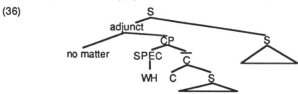

Although Nishigauchi says that no matter functions as an unselective binder, I assume that no matter is not an unselective binder but that there is an "invisible" universal quantifier in (34) as in the case of the bare conditinal; no matter probably functions like if. This is because (i) in sentences like "No matter whether . . . " no matter is not necessarily required presumably because whether can function like if, e.g. "Whether Mary buys a dog or a cat, I'll throw it away"; (ii) adverbs of quantification can play the role of unselective binders as in "No matter who comes in, I ususally kiss him" (= I kiss most people who come in.) A similar phenomenon can be obseved in sentences like (37), where the "invisible" operator is "overridden" by the adverb of quantification.

(37) If a person falls from the fifth floor, he or she will very rarely survive. (Heim 1982)

Thus, it seems more reasonable to treat no matter like if. In this way, we can keep the same tripartite structure for no matter sentences, too. That is, when we regard a sentence with quantification as having a tripartite structure consistig of an operator, a restrictor and the nuclear scope, as Heim does, no matter just belongs to the second part which restricts an invisible operator in the default case.

Now consider (38b), the Japanese counterpart of a concessive clause which corresponds to (38a):

(38) a. No matter whether Mary buys a dog or a cat, I will throw it away.
     b. Mary-ga inu ka neko-no dochira-o katte-mo, boku-wa sore-o suteru   tsumorida.
         N dog or cat-of which-A buys-Q   I-N it-A throw-away   will

It is interesting to note that (38a) cannot mean "No matter whether or not Mary buys a dog or a cat, . . . " Since ambiguous sentences like "Tell me whether Mary bought a dog or a cat" lose the AQ reading when whether is replaced by whether or not, it seems that there is an analogy between (38a) and an alternative question. Moreover, in (38b) the NP disjunction is headed by "-no dochira" (which of), which is used to express an alternative question in Japanese (see 2.1). If a plain NP disjunction is used instead, as in (39), it means "Even if Mary buys a dog or a cat, I'll throw it away."

---

[8]There are probably different presuppositions in the two sentences. For example, (34) implies that Mary reads even trashy books, but I have neglected these aspects here.

(39) has a presupposition like the following: I do not like any animals. If Mary buys a llama or some exotic pet, I will of course kick it out, but I will throw away even an ordinary pet like a dog or a cat.

(39) Mary-ga inu ka neko-o katte-mo, boku-wa sore-o   suteru   tsumorida.
     N dog or cat-A buys-Q   I-N   it-A   throw-away   will

Again, then, it is reasonable to say that an NP disjunction in English can behave like a WH-phrase syntactically. In Japanese, where there is no ambiguity between an ordinary NP disjunction and its WH-couterpart, the latter is used in the AQ and in the Japanese couterpart of the no matter sentence while in English an NP disjunction behaves like a WH-phrase in the AQ and the no matter sentence.

Now, what kind of logical form and semantic interpretation should we give to sentence (38b)? I think that mo in this sentence is a quantificational element (cf. 2.2) and occupies the head of COMP. Semantically, it triggers, in the default case, a universal quantifier which acts as an operator of the tripartite structure.[9] The universal quantifier functions unselectively, thus the donkey pronoun is possible. As I defined it in (20), the semantics of inu ka neko-no dochira (which of a dog or a cat) is the same as that of inu ka neko, which is derived by rule (8), i.e. $\lambda P[[dog'(x) \vee cat'(x)] \wedge P\{x\}]$. In an alternative question, the free variable in this NP is bound by an exsitential quantifier, but in a concessive clause, the free variable is bound by the universal quantifier introduced by mo. The syntactic and semantic rules for the concessive clause are given in (40), and the logical form and semantics of (38b) is given (41).

(40)
a. Proto Concessive Clause Rule:
   If $\phi \in P_t$, then $[\phi\text{-mo}] \in P_C$.[10]
   If $\phi \in P_t$ translates to ϕ', then $[\phi\text{-mo}] \in P_C$ translates to ϕ' also.

b. Concessive Clause Rule:
   If $\alpha \in P_{WH}$ and $\psi \in P_C$ containing an occurrence of PRO_n, then $\gamma \in P_C$.
                                                                        $\wedge$
                                                                    α ψ
   If $\alpha \in P_{WH}$ translates to α' and $\psi \in P_C$ translates to ψ', then $\gamma \in P_C$ translates to $\alpha'(^{\wedge}\lambda x_n \psi')$.[11]

c. Concessive-Matrix Rule:
   If $\gamma \in P_C$, $\delta \in P_t$, and Q is the universal quantifier with the selectional indices $1, \ldots, n$,
   then ζ $\in P_t$.
       $/$ $|$ $\backslash$
     $Q_{1...n}$ γ δ
   If $\gamma \in P_C$, $\delta \in P_t$ translate to γ' and δ' respectively, then ζ translates as:
   $\forall x_1, \ldots, x_n(\gamma' \rightarrow \delta')$.[12]

---

[9]We can say "dare-ga kite-mo boku-wa taitei au" (No matter who comes in, I'll usually meet him), which can mean "I meet most people who visit me." Here the adverb of quantificatin taitei "overrides" the universal quantifier.

[10]I introduced here a new category "C" (the concessve clause) of type t.

[11]This rule can be used recursively to handle a concessibe clause with more than one WH-phrase, like "dare-ga nani-o katte-mo . . . " (No matter who buys what . . .).

[12]We can modify this rule depending on what kind of quantifier Q is. For example, if Q is taitei (often), the translation should be $MOST x_1, \ldots, x_n \gamma' \delta'$. (MOST is a logical symbol with roughly the following interpretation: '$MOST u_1, \ldots, u_n \phi \psi$' is true with respect to an assignment g iff for most n-tuples $a_1, \ldots, a_n$ such that ϕ is true w.r.t. g', ψ is also true w.r.t. g', where g' is like g except that $g'(x_i) = a_i$ for $i = 1, \ldots, n$.

(41)a.

b. 1. [[Mary-ga him₁ katte] mo] (by (40a)) ==> $buy'(x_1)(m)$

2. [inu ka neko-no dochira] (by (20)) ==> $\lambda P[[dog'(x_1) \vee cat'(x_1)] \wedge P\{x_1\}]$

3. [[inu ka neko-no dochira-o]₁ Mary-ga him₁ katte-mo](by (40b)) ==>
   $[dog'(x_1) \vee cat'(x_1)] \wedge buy'(x_1)(m)$

4. boku-wa sore₁-o suteru tsumorida ==> $throw\text{-}away'(x_1)(i)$

5. By (40c) ==> $\forall x_1 [[[dog'(x_1) \vee cat'(x_1)] \wedge buy'(x_1)(m)] \rightarrow [throw\text{-}away'(x_1)(i)]]$

If we had used Montague-type NPs and generalized disjunction, we would have gotten the translation $\lambda P \exists x [[dog'(x) \vee cat'(x)] \wedge P\{x\}]$ for "a dog or a cat". But if we had used this translation for sentence (38b), we could not have obtained the donkey pronoun sore because there is no free variable for the universal quantifier to bind. When getting the semantics of alternative questions in 2.1, it was not necessary to use variable-introducing disjunction because in AQs the free variables were bound by an existential quantifier. But in concessive clauses, it is essential to use this kind of disjunction. Thus, as an uniform treatment of semantics of disjunction in Japanese, I argue for variable-introducing disjunction.

3. Summary

In this paper, I first discussed Partee and Rooth's papers (1982, 1983) and proposed a general type-shifting rule for phrases containig free variables. I also discussed the modification to Heim's Novelty condition in order to accomodate variable-introducing disjunction. The type-shifting rule and generalized conjunction along with this modification can provide variable-introducing disjuntions of different types, and we were able to obtain the non-specific wide scope or reading for the sentence "Mary is looking for a maid or a cook" and the bound-variable reading for the sentence "If Mary is swimming or dancing, Sue is," both of which were thought to be problematic for generalized conjunction. Then, I discussed disjunctions which appear in alternative questions, negation and concessive clauses in Japanese. I showed that treating NP disjunction as introducing a single free variable is essential to interpreting these sentences. Also, I have found that an NP disjunction is ambiguous in English while it is not in Japanese. In English, it sometimes functions like a WH-phrase. That is why a sentence like "Do you want coffee or tea" is unambiguously a YNQ to the Japanese, but it can be either an AQ or a YNQ in English. By looking at Japanese examples, I was able to give an appropriate rule to the AQ in English.

References

Barwise, Jon and Robin Cooper. 1981. "Generalized quantifiers and natural languages." *Linguistics and Philosophy* 4.2, 159-219.

Dowty, David R, Robert E. Wall and Stanley Peters. 1981. *Introduction to Montague Semantics*, D. Reidel Publishing Company.

Heim, Irene. 1982. *The Semantics of Definite and Indefinite Noun Phrases*, Doctoral dissertation, University of Massachusetts.

Kamp, Hans. 1981. "A theory of truth and semantic representation," in *Formal Methods in the Study of Language (Part I)*, 277-322, Mathematisch Centrum.

Karttunen, Lauri . 1977. "The Syntax and Semantics of Questions," *Linguistics and Philosophy* 1, 3-44.

Keenan, Edward, and Leonard Faltz. 1978. "Logical Types for Natural Language," *UCLA Occasional Papers in Linguistics* 3.

Kratzer, Angelika . 1986. "Conditionals," in Farley, A. M., Farley, P., McCullough, K. E., ed., *Papers from the Parasession Pragmatics and Grammatical Theory*, Chicago Linguistic Society.

Larson, Richard K. 1985. "On the Syntax of Disjuction Scope," *Natural Language and Linguistics Theory* 3, 217-264.

Nishigauchi, Taisuke.1986. *Quantification in Syntax*, Doctoral dissertation, University of Massachusetts.

Partee, Barbara and Mats Rooth. 1983. "Generalized conjunction and type ambiguity," in von Stechow, ed., *Meaning, Use, and Interpretation*, de Gruyter.

Partee, Barbara H. 1987. "Noun Phrase Interpretation and Type-Shifting Principles," in Groenendijk, J., de Jongh, D., and Stokhof, M., ed., *Studies in Discourse Representation Theory and the Theory of Generalized Quantifiers*, Foris, Dordrecht.

Rooth, Mats, and Barbara Partee. 1982. "Conjunction, Type Ambiguity and Wide Scope Or," in Flickenger, D., and Macken, M., and Wiegand, N., eds., *Proceedings of the First West Coast Conference on Formal Linguistics*, Stanford University.

Rooth, Mats. 1987. "Noun Phrase Interpretation in Montague Grammar, File Change Semantics, and Situation Semantics," in Gardenfors P., ed., *Generalized Quantifiers*, Reidel Publishing Company.

Minimal Disjointness
Joseph Aoun and Yen-hui Audrey Li
University of Southern California

In this work, we investigate the working of the concept of Minimality through its manifestation in the pronominal system of Mandarin Chinese. We argue that a unified account of Chinese referential and bound pronouns can be provided by assuming that the relation between pronouns and their binders is constrained by a disjointness principle incorporating a Minimality effect.

1. Locality requirements on pronouns

In Chinese, pronouns can either be coindexed with a name (referential pronoun) or bound by quantifiers (bound pronoun), as in (1) and (2) below:

(1) Zhang$_i$ shuo wo xihuan ta$_i$.   —— referential pronoun
            say I like him
    'Zhang said that I liked him.'

(2) Meigeren$_i$ dou shuo wo xihuan ta$_i$. —— bound pronoun
    everyone all say I like him
    'Everyone said that I liked him.'

In contrast to English, where referential pronouns and bound pronouns have very similar distribution, the parallelism between these two types of pronouns breaks down in Chinese. Whereas a referential pronoun can occur in the subject position of an embedded clause (as illustrated in (3)), a bound pronoun cannot occur in such a context (as in (4)):

(3) Zhang$_i$ shuo ta$_i$ de le jiang.
          say he get ASP prize
    'Zhang said that he got the prize.'

(4)*Meigeren$_i$ dou shuo ta$_i$ de le jiang.
    everyone all say he get ASP prize
    'Everyone said that he got the prize.'

The sentences (1-4) discussed so far show that referential pronouns can occur either in the subject or object position of the embedded clause and that bound pronouns occur only in the object position of the embedded clause. The fact that bound pronouns occur in the object but not subject position of the embedded clause might suggest that there is a subject/object asymmetry in the distribution of bound pronouns. However, this cannot be the case. A bound pronoun in the subject position of a more deeply embedded clause is possible, as illustrated in (5):

(5) Meigeren$_i$ dou yiwei ni shuo ta$_i$ de le jiang.
    everyone all think you say he get ASP prize
    'Everyone thinks that you said that he got the prize.'

The relevant facts discussed so far are schematically represented in (6):

(6)   CONTEXTS   RP   BP

    a. NP_i V $[_s$- NP_i V NP]   ✔   *
    b. NP_i V $[_s$- NP V NP_i]   ✔   ✔
    c. NP_i V $[_s$- NP V $[_s$- NP_i V NP]]   ✔   ✔

The fact that bound pronouns can occur in (6b-c) but not in (6a) suggests that
distance plays a role in the distribution of these bound pronouns. More
precisely, it is indicated in Huang (1982) that AGR does not exist in Chinese.
With this in mind, consider the paradigm in (6a-c). Let us discuss bound
pronouns first. Assuming that bound pronouns must be free in the minimal
domain of a subject, the opaque domain in which the bound pronoun must be free
is the matrix clause in (6a) since AGR is missing in Chinese. In this opaque
domain, the bound pronoun is not free; hence, the ungrammaticality of
representation (6a). In representation (6b) and (6c), on the other hand, the
bound pronoun is free in its opaque domain, the embedded clause which is the
minimal domain containing a subject. Representations (6b-c) thus are
grammatical.

Next we turn to referential pronouns. The grammaticality of
referential pronouns in (6a-c) suggests that the notion of SUBJECT is not
relevant for pronouns. Essentially, referential pronouns have to be free in
the minimal clause or NP in which they occur. This is the case for
referential pronouns in (6a-c). This analysis of referential and bound
pronouns can be extended to account for the behavior of resumptive pronouns.
Space limitations prevent us from discussing resumptive pronouns.

Before leaving the discussion of the paradigm (6), one further
clarification is necessary. We said so far that bound pronouns must be free
in the minimal clause or NP containing a SUBJECT and that referential pronouns
must be free in the minimal domain in which they occur. However, we did not
specify the type of disjointness requirements that each of these pronouns
obey. Along the lines of Aoun and Hornstein (1986), we would like to suggest
that the distinction between bound and referential pronouns may be understood
in light of the following considerations: bound pronouns must seek a c-
commanding antecedent. The antecedent is quantificational and at LF, after
the applicaton of Quantifier Raising (May 1977), will be in an A'-position.
Thus, bound pronouns seek an A'-binder. We would like to argue that bound
pronouns must be A'-free in the minimal domain containing a SUBJECT and that
referential pronouns must be free in the minimal clause or NP in which they
occur. Notice that the A'-disjointness requirement for referential pronouns
is trivially satisfied since they do not have an A'-binder. In brief, we are
suggesting that pronouns, whether bound or referential, obey the following
disjointness requirement:

(7) a. The A-disjointness Requirement
       A pronoun must be A-free in the least Complete Functional
       Complex (CFC) in which it occurs (see Chomsky 1986)

    b. The A'-disjointness Requirement
       A pronoun must be A'-free in the least CFC containing a
       SUBJECT and the pronoun

A confirmation of this analysis is provided by the behavior of anaphors
in Chinese. As discussed by Y.-H. Huang (1985), Tang (1987), Battisttela

(1987), Chinese has two types of anaphors: a short distance anaphor <u>ta-ziji</u> ´himself´ and a long distance anaphor <u>ziji</u> ´self´. Sentences in (8) illustrate their distribution:

(8) a. $Zhang_i$ hen xihuan $ziji_i$/$taziji_i$.
   ´Zhang likes self/himself.´

   b. $Zhang_i$ hen xihuan $ziji_i$/$taziji_i$ de mama.
      ´Zhang likes self/himself´s mother.´

   c. $Zhang_i$ shuo $ziji_i$/$taziji_i$ xihuan.
      ´Zhang said that self/himself liked (it).´

   d. $Zhang_i$ dui $ziji_i$/$taziji_i$ shuo ta xihuan.
      ´Zhang said to self/himself that she liked (it).´

   e. $Zhang_i$ renwei Mali xihuan $ziji_i$/*$taziji_i$.
      ´Zhang thinks that Mary likes self/himself.´

   f. $Zhang_i$ zhidao Mali renwei $ziji_i$/*$taziji_i$ xihuan.
      ´Zhang knows that Mary thinks that self/himself likes (it).´

Following Lebeaux (1983) and Chomsky (1986) who claim that anaphors are moved at LF, Battisttela (1987) suggests that anaphors raise at LF in Chinese. With this in mind, consider the sentences in (9) where the coindexing between the name, the long-distance anaphor and the pronoun is not acceptable:

(9) a. $Zhang_i$ zhidao *$ziji_i$ xihuan ta_i de nu pengyou.
      ´Zhang knows that self likes his girl friend.´

   b. $Zhang_i$ shuo *$ziji_i$ juede ta_i hen youqian.
      ´Zhang said that self felt he was rich.´

   c. $Zhang_i$ dui *$ziji_i$ shuo ta_i hen youqian.
      ´Zhang said to self that he was rich.´

The unacceptability of (9) is what we expect, given the A´-disjointness requirement on pronouns. After the anaphor <u>ziji</u> is raised to an A´-position at LF, (9c) would have the representation in (9´c):

(9´) c. $[_{S´1}$ $Zhang_i$ *$ziji_i$ x_i dui shuo $[_{S´2}$ ta_i hen youqian]].
      ´Zhang said to self that he was rich.´

In this representation, the domain where the pronoun in the subject position of the embedded clause must be A´-free is the matrix clause. This clause is the minimal clause containing a SUBJECT. Thus, the pronoun in (9´c) has to be A´-free in the matrix clause. However, it is A´-bound by the raised anaphor. Therefore, sentence (9c) is unacceptable because of the failure of the pronoun to meet the A´-disjointness requirement.

This analysis predicts that a pronoun can be bound by a long distance anaphor <u>ziji</u> in case a subject intervenes between the pronoun and the long distance anaphor. This prediction is fulfilled as illustrated in (10).

(10) a. [Zhangsan$_i$ dui ziji$_i$ shuo [$_@$Mali bu hui xihuan ta$_i$]]].
　　　　　　to self say 　Mary not will like him
　　'Zhangsan told self that Mary would not like him.'

　　b. [Zhangsan$_i$ dui ziji$_i$ shuo [$_@$Ma zhidao [ta$_i$ hen ben]]].
　　　　　　to self say 　Mary know 　he very stupid
　　'Zhangsan told himself that Mary knew that he was stupid.'

The domain where the pronoun must be A´-free is the clause @ in (10). Ziji is
outside the domain @, hence the acceptability of (10).

2. Minimal disjointness

We have indicated so far that pronouns in Chinese obey two disjointness
requirements. Next we would like to argue that the A´-disjointness requirement
must incorporate a minimality effect. Specifically, we would like to argue
that:

(11) A pronoun must be free from the most local A´-binder in the
smallest CFC containing the pronoun and a SUBJECT.

"the most local A´-binder" is defined as:
A is the most local A´-binder of B iff there is no C such that C
is an A´-binder and A c-commands C, C c-commands B.

To substantiate the proposal in (11), we start by noting that sentences such
as (4) improve when a modal occurs between the quantifier and the pronoun:

(12) Meigeren$_i$ dou shuo ta $_i$ hui de jiang.
　　everyone all say he will get prize
　　'Everyone said that he would get the prize.'

Not only would a modal improve the acceptability of a bound pronoun in (4),
but also wh-words such as shi-bu-shi 'whether', weishenme 'why', shei
'who', shenme 'what' in (13):

(13) a. Meigeren$_i$ dou xiang-zhidao shi-bu-shi ta$_i$ de le jiang.
　　　　everyone all want-know be-not-be he got prize
　　　　'Everyone wonders whether he got the prize.'

　　b. Meigeren$_i$ dou xiang-zhidao ta$_i$ weishenme de jiang.
　　　　everyone all want-know he why get prize
　　　　'Everyone wonders why he got the prize.'

　　c. Meigeren$_i$ dou xiang-zhidao ta$_i$ gen shei fen jiangpin.
　　　　everyone all want-know he with whom share prize
　　　　'Everyone wonders with whom he shared the prize.'

　　d. Meigeren$_i$ dou xiang-zhidao ta$_i$ de le shenme jiangpin.
　　　　everyone all want-know he got what prize
　　　　'Everyone wonders what prize he got.'

The contrast between the sentence in (4) on the one hand and (12-13) on the
other is not accounted for by the disjointness requirement formulated in (7).
We show below that this contrast and other similar contrasts can be accounted

for by incorporating the notion of minimality to the disjointness requiremen t, as in (11).

Note that what is common to the sentences in (12-13), in contrast to the unacceptable sentence (4), is that these sentences contain operators suchas modals and wh-words which are subject to Raising at LF. (Following Huang (1982), we assume that shi-bu-shi, a A-not-A question form, undergoes raising at LF). The LF representations of (12-13) will be (14-15):

(14) Meigeren$_i$ [x1$_i$ dou shuo [hui$_j$ [ta $_i$ x2$_j$ de jiang]]].
     'Everyone said that he would get the prize.'

(15) a. Meigeren$_i$ [x1$_i$ dou xiang-zhidao [shi-bu-shi$_j$ [x2$_j$ ta$_i$ dele jiang]]].
        'Everyone wonders whether he got the prize.'

     b. Meigeren$_i$ [x1$_i$ dou xiang-zhidao [weisheme$_j$ [ta$_i$ x2$_j$ de jiang]]].
        'Everyone wonders why he got the prize.'

     c. Meigeren$_i$ [x1$_i$ dou xiang-zhidao [shei$_j$ [ta$_i$ gen x2$_j$ fen jiangpin]]].
        'Everyone wonders with whom he shared the prize.'

     d. Meigeren$_i$ [x1$_i$ dou xiang-zhidao [shenme jiangpin$_j$ [ta$_i$ de le x2$_j$]]]
        'Everyone wonders what prize he got.'

If we compare the LF representations in (14-15), which are acceptable, with the LF representation in (9), which is unacceptable, we notice that the difference in acceptability may be traced back to the existence of an operator intervening between the QP and the bound pronoun: in (14-15), but not in (9), there is an operator intervening between the QP and the bound pronoun.

A confirmation of this observation is provided by the negation and negative polarity items. Sentences with negation and negative polarity items pattern with sentences with modals and questions words (12-13). The occurrence of negation and a negative polarity item in a higher clause improves the acceptability of a pronoun, as in (16) below:

(16) [Meigeren$_i$ dou mei gaosu renhe ren [ta$_i$ de le jiang]].
     'Everyone did not tell anyone that he got the prize.'

Assuming that the negative polarity item is raised at LF as suggested by Kurata (1986) or that negation is in an A'-position at LF, an A'-binder will intervene between the pronoun and the QP in (16).

We argued so far that in Chinese, pronouns obey an A'-disjointness requirement as well as an A-disjointness requirement. We furthermore suggested that the A'-disjointness requirement incorporates a minimality effect in (11): in case a distinct A'-binder intervenes between the pronoun and the quantificational antecedent, the pronoun can be bound to this quantificational antecedent. Of course, we expect the occurrence of a modal, negation or wh-word not to facilitate the bound pronoun interpretation in case the modal, negation, or wh-element does not intervene between a QP and its bound pronoun. This expectation can be tested in the contexts such as (18a-b) where the modal, negation, and wh-element do not intervene between the QP and the pronoun:

(18) a. modal/negation/wh-word...QP_i...pronoun$_i$
    b. QP_i...pronoun$_i$...modal/negation/wh-word

In other words, we should expect sentences of the context in (a–b) to be less acceptable than sentences of the context in (c) if the minimal disjointness requirement just discussed is correct.

    c. QP_i...modal/negation/wh-word...pronoun$_i$

Although the judgments become more subtle, a contrast is still found between sentences (19a–b) and (19c):

(19) a. *[Wo hui zhidao [meigeren$_i$ dou shuo [ta$_i$ de le jiang]]].
       ´I will know that everyone says that he got the prize.´

    b. *[Meigeren$_i$ dou shuo [ta$_i$ zhidao [wo hui de jiang]]].
       ´Everyone said that he knew that I would get the prize.´

    c. [Meigeren$_i$ dou shuo [ta$_i$ hui zhidao [wo de jiang]]].
       ´Everyone said that he would know that I got the prize.´

A bound pronoun interpretation is possible in (c) but less likely in (a–b). This contrast is predicted by the minimal disjointness requirement on pronouns: consider the LF representations of sentences in (19), as in (20) below:

(20) a. *[Wo hui$_j$ x1$_j$ zhidao [meigeren$_i$ x2$_i$ dou shuo [ta$_i$ dele jiang]]].
       I will   know   everyone   all say   he got prize

    b. [Meigeren$_i$ [x1$_i$ dou shuo [$_{s´1}$ ta$_i$ zhidao [$_{s´2}$ hui$_j$ [wo x2$_j$ de jiang]]]]]
       everyone   all say   he know   will I   get prize

    c. [Meigeren$_i$ [x1$_i$ dou shuo [$_{s´1}$ hui [$_{s1}$ ta$_i$ x2$_j$ zhidao [$_{s2}$ wo de jiang]]]]]
       everyone   all say   will   he know   I get prize

As mentioned, modals undergo raising at LF. In (a), the modal is raised within the matrix clause. In (b), the modal is not raised beyond its clause, the most embedded one, since modals only have scope over the clause in which they occur and cannot be raised beyond their clause. In (c), the modal is also adjoined to the S node of the clause in which it occurs. In these representations, the modal only comes to intervene between the pronoun and the coindexed QP in (20c). That is, the most local A´-binder for the bound pronoun is the raised QP in (a–b) but the modal is the most local A´-binder for the bound pronoun in (c). The pronoun is thus A´-free from the most local A´-binder in (c) but not (a–b). The contrast between (a–b) on the one hand and (c) on the other thus provides support for the proposal that pronouns obey a disjointness requirement sensitive to minimality.

    Negation and wh-words behave the same way as modals with respect to the contrast between (a–b) and (c) in (18):

(21) a.*[Shei zhidao [meigeren$_i$ dou shuo [ta$_i$ de le jiang]]]?
       ´Who knows that everyone said that he got the prize?´

b.*[Meigeren$_i$ dou shuo [ta$_i$ xiang-zhidao [shi-bu-shi wo de le jiang]]].
  ´Everyone said that he wondered whether I got the prize.´

c. [Meigeren$_i$ dou xiang-zhidao [shi-bu-shi ta$_i$ de le jiang]].
  ´Everyone wonders whether he got the prize.´

(22) a.*[Wo bu zhidao [meigeren$_i$ dou shuo [ta$_i$ de le jiang]]].
   ´I do not know that everyone said that he got the prize.´

b.*[Meigeren$_i$ dou shuo [ta$_i$ zhidao [wo mei de jiang]]].
  ´Everyone said that he knew that I did not get the prize.´

c. [Wo zhidao [meigeren$_i$ dou mei gaosu renhe ren [ta$_i$ de le jiang]].
  ´I know that everyone did not tell anyone that he got the prize.´

In (21a), shei is in the matrix clause. In (21b), the wh-word shi-bu-shi ´whether´ cannot be raised beyond the clause subcategorized by ´wonder´. In (21c), shi-bu-shi intervenes between the QP and the bound pronoun. The minimal disjointness requirement is satisfied in (c) but not in (a-b). The bound pronoun interpretation thus is more acceptable in (c) than in (a-b). Similarly, the negation or the raised negative polarity item intervenes between the QP and the bound pronoun in (22c) but not in (22a-b). The contrast between (a-b) on the one hand and (c) on the other in (21-22) provides further support for the claim that pronouns obey the minimal disjointness requirement.

We said so far that an A´-binder intervening between a pronoun and a quantificational element allows this pronoun to be bound by the quantificational element. Our analysis predicts that if a deeply embedded wh-word is raised at LF so as to intervene between a pronoun and an A´-antecedent, the pronoun can be bound by this quantificational antecedent. This prediction is born out, as shown by sentence (23c):

(23) a.*[Meigeren$_i$ dou zhidao [ta$_i$ caidao [shei de le jiang]]].
   ´Everyone knows that he guessed correctly who got prize.´

b. [Meigeren$_i$ dou zhidao [ta$_i$ gen shei fen jiangpin]].
  ´Everyone knows with whom he shared the prize.´

c. [Meigeren$_i$ dou shuo [ta$_i$ xiangxin [shei de le jiang ne]]]?
  ´Who did everyone say that he believed got the prize?´

Notice first that the contrast between (23a) and (23b) is not surprising. The wh-element shei intervenes between the QP and the pronoun at LF in (b) but not in (a), as shown in the LF representations of these two sentences:

(24) a.*[Meigeren$_i$ [x1$_i$ dou zhidao [$_{S´}$1ta$_i$ caidao [$_{S´}$2shei$_j$ [x2$_j$ dele jiang]]]]].
     everyone   all know   he guess   who   got prize

b. [Meigeren$_i$ [x1$_i$ dou zhidao [$_{S´}$1 shei$_j$ [ta$_i$ gen x2$_j$ fen jiangpin]]]].
   everyone   all know   this   he with   share prize

The fact that (23c) patterns with (23b) rather than (23a) is more surprising. This fact, however, is straightforwardly accounted for by our analysis. Note

that the wh-word shei in (c) has matrix scope; i.e., it must be raised from
its base position to the matrix COMP, leaving traces in the intermediate COMP
position:

(24) c. $[_{S'1}$ shei$_j$ $[_{S1}$ meigeren$_i$ $[_{S1}$ x1$_i$ dou shuo $[_{S'2}$x2$_j$ $[_{S2}$ ta$_i$
       who   everyone   all say
       xiangxin $[_{S'3}$x3$_j$ $[_{S3}$ x4$_j$ dele jiang ne]]]?
       believe   got prize Q-marker

Since intermediate traces in COMP independently can function as A'-binders,
the most local A'-binder for the pronoun in (c) is the intermediate trace of
shei in the COMP position of S'2, x2. The pronoun in this representation is
thus free from its most local A'-binder and sentence (23c) is acceptable.
Thus, the fact that (23c) patterns with (23b) rather than (23a) is directly
accouted for by incorporating the minimality requirement in the formulation of
the A'-disjointness requirement.

The previous discussion shows that the domain where modals, wh-
elements and negation can be raised interacts with the interpretation of
pronouns and that this interaction is accounted for by the minimal
disjointness requirement on pronouns. This leads us to expect that QPs
should behave the same as modals and wh-elements, since they are all
subject to raising at LF. The data with QPs, however, is less clear than
those with modals and wh-words. Speakers vary with respect to the
possibility of bound pronoun interpretation in the following instances:

(25) a. Meigeren$_i$ dou shuo ta$_i$ de le jiang.
      'Everyone said that he got the prize.'

    b. Meigeren$_i$ dou dui liangge ren shuo ta$_i$ de le jiang.
       'Everyone said to two people that he got the prize.'

    c. Meigeren$_i$ dou dui wo shuo ta$_i$ de le jiang.
      'Everyone said to me that he got the prize.'

Some speakers do not find distinction between the possibilities of bound
pronoun interpretation in these sentences; some find (b) to be better than (a)
and (c); still some others find (b) and (c) to be better than (a). To the
extent that there exist speakers who find (b) to be better than (a) and (c),
the contrast can be accounted for by assuming Quantifier Raising and the
Minimal disjointness requirement.

Before concluding, we would like to explore some of the consequences of
the analysis proposed in this work. Recall that as a consequence of the
raising of the anaphor ziji, the pronoun in sentences in (9) will be A'-bound
by the raised anaphor and thus fail to meet the A'-disjointness requirement.
Furthermore, we argued that the A'-disjointness requirement is sensitive to a
minimality effect. This leads us to expect that sentences in (9) would
improve in case an A'-binder intervenes between the anaphor and the pronoun.
This is indeed the case as illustrated in the sentences in (26), which
minimally contrast with (9), repeated for convenience.

(9) a. Zhang$_i$ zhidao *ziji$_i$ xihuan ta$_i$ de nu pengyou.
     'Zhang knows that self likes his girl friend.'

b. Zhang$_i$ shuo *ziji$_i$ juede ta$_i$ hen youqian.
'Zhang said that self felt he was rich.'

c. Zhang$_i$ dui *ziji$_i$ shuo ta$_i$ hen youqian.
'Zhang said to self that he was rich.'

(26) a. Zhang$_i$ zhidao ziji$_i$ hui xihuan ta$_i$de nu pengyou.
'Zhang knows that self will like his girl friend.'

b. Zhang$_i$ shuo ziji$_i$ juede ta$_i$ hui hen youqian.
'Zhang said that self felt he would be rich.'

c. Zhang$_i$ dui ziji$_i$ shuo ta$_i$ hui hen youqian.
'Zhang said to self that he would be rich.'

Another consequence of our analysis has to do with the raising of anaphors. Note that the account of (9) provides direct testing grounds for whether or not short-distance anaphors have to raise at LF. If short distance anaphors have to raise at LF like long distance anaphors, we would expect them to enter into A'-disjointness with pronouns. On the other hand, if short distance anaphors do not raise at LF, we would not expect such an A'-disjointness effect. It turns out that replacing the long-distance anaphor with the short-distance anaphor in (9) makes the sentences acceptable:

(27) a. Zhang$_i$ zhidao taziji$_i$ xihuan ta$_i$de nu pengyou.
'Zhang knows that himself likes his girl friend.'

b. Zhang$_i$ shuo taziji$_i$ juede ta$_i$ hen youqian.
'Zhang said that himself felt he was rich.'

c. Zhang$_i$ dui taziji$_i$ shuo ta$_i$ hen youqian.
'Zhang said to himself that he was rich.'

The contrast between the acceptability of (27) and the unacceptability of (9) clearly indicates that short distance anaphors, contrary to long distance anaphors, do not have to raise at LF.[1]

3. Conclusion

Summarizing, we argued in this paper for the existence of two types of disjointness requirements regulating the interpretation of pronominals: an A-disjointness requirement and an A'-disjointness requirement. We also argued that the A'-disjointness requirement incorporates a notion of minimality. In its opaque domain, the pronoun must be free from the first available A'-binder. This intervening A'-binder may be, for instance, a modal, a wh-word or a negation. The fact that minimality plays a role in the formulation of the disjointness condition is not surprising. Recently, anaphoric relations have also been shown to obey a very similar minimality effect. Along the lines of Chomsky (1986), it is possible to suggest that anaphors in Chinese must be bound by the first potential antecedent. Short distance anaphors, which we argued need not raise at LF, have to be bound by the first available antecedent in subject position, as illustrated in (28):

(28) a. Zhang, baba$_i$ xihuan taziji$_i$.
  'Zhang, father$_i$ likes himself$_i$.'

  b. *Zhang$_i$, baba xihuan taziji$_i$.
  'Zhang$_i$, father likes himself$_i$.'

  c. Zhang$_i$, gongzuo haile taziji$_i$.
  'Zhang$_i$, work hurt himself$_i$.'

As for long distance anaphors, we provided evidence that they have to raise at LF. Notice that as a consequence of the raising process, these anaphors satisfy the minimality requirement. After raising, they will be bound by the first available antecedent in subject position. To illustrate, consider sentence (29):

(29) [Zhang shuo [Mali renwei [ziji zui congming]]].
  'Zhang said Mary thought self is most clever.'

  a. [Zhang shuo [Mali ziji$_i$ renwei [x$_i$ zui congming]]].

  b. [Zhang ziji$_i$ shuo [Mali renwei [x$_i$ zui congming]]].

In case the anaphor <u>ziji</u> is raised to the minimal clause containing <u>Mali</u> as in (a), it will be bound by <u>Mali</u>. In case the anaphor is raised to the minimal clause containing <u>Zhang</u>, it will be bound by <u>Zhang</u>.

So far we illustrated the existence of a minimality requirement at work for the A'-disjointness requirement and for the binding of anaphors. It is well known that minimality does not affect A-disjointness. This is illustrated in the Chinese sentence in (30) where the pronoun <u>ta</u> has to be disjoint from both <u>Zhang</u> and <u>Mali</u>:

(30) Zhang dui Mali baoyuan ta.
    to   complain him
  'Zhang complained to Mary about him.'

One may wonder why minimality does not play a role for A-disjointness. We know since the work of H. Lasnik (1976, 1981) that coreferential pronouns do not look for an antecedent to be coindexed with. Bound pronouns, on the other hand, seek a c-commanding A'-antecedent. In our presentation, we suggested that the specific behavior of bound pronouns results from the tension between two requirements: a positive requirement to seek an A'-binder and a disjointness requirement. With this in mind, it is possible to surmise that only elements that seek an antecedent (i.e., anaphors and bound pronouns) obey a minimality effect.

Concluding, extraction processes and, as mentioned earlier, anaphoric relations have recently been shown to obey a very similar minimality effect. This effect prohibits a direct relation between an antecedent and its trace or an anaphor across some intervening element, be it a governor or a closer antecedent. The existence of this minimality effect has been used as evidence for partially or totally reducing anaphoric binding to government theory by assuming that anaphors raise at LF. In this work, we argued for the existence of a minimality effect constraining pronominal disjointness. To the extent that this effect cannot be traced back to LF extraction or government, we hope to have shown that the concept of minimality is to be viewed as a pervasive concept at work through distinct grammatical modules rather than an exclusive attribute of the government module.[2]

NOTES

[1]The facts discussed in (27) are compatible with the assumption that short distance anaphors optionally raise at LF.

[2]Rizzi (1987) argues that "minimality effects are exclusively triggered by potential governors of the different kinds: heads for head government, A and A'-specifiers for antecedent government in A and A'-chains respectively." (p.7) The minimality effect we have been assuming is naturally expressed in this relativized approach to minimality and may thus be viewed as providing indepedent support for it.

REFERENCES

Aoun, Joseph and Nobert Hornstein. 1986. Bound pronouns. ms. University of
    Southern California and University of Maryland.
Battistella, Edwin. 1987. Chinese reflexivization. ms. Unviersity of
    Alabama at Birmingham.
Chomsky, Noam. 1986. Knowledge of language. New York: Praeger.
Huang, C-T. James. 1982. Logical relations in Chinese and the theory of
    grammar. PhD dissertation, MIT.
Huang, Yun-hua. 1985. Reflexives in Chinese. Studies in English Literature
    and Linguistics 10, 163-188. National Taiwan Normal University.
Lasnik, Howard. 1976. Remarks on coreference. Linguistic Analysis, 2.1.
Lasnik, Howard. 1981. On two recent treatments of disjoint reference.
    Journal of Linguistic Research, 1.4.
Lebeaux, David. 1983. A distributional difference between reflexives and
    reciprocals. LI 14.4, 723-730.
Kurata, Kiyoshi. 1986. Asymetries in Japanese. ms. University of
    Massachusetts, Amherst.
May, Robert. 1977. The grammar of quantification. PhD dissertation, MIT.
Rizzi, Luigi. 1987. Relativized minimality. ms. Universite de Geneve.
Tang, C.-C. Jane. 1987. Chinese reflexives. to appear in NLLT.

Korean Assimilation

Young-mee Yu Cho

Stanford University

0. Anyone who attempts to describe assimilation phenomena in Korean will be immediately struck by the pervasive role that they play in the phonology of the language, as illustrated in (1).

(1) a. Dentals assimilate to labials, palatals, and velars.
   b. Labials and palatals assimilate to velars.
   c. The dental stop assimilates to the nasal /n/,
      the lateral /l/, and the fricative /s/.
   d. The dental nasal assimilates to the lateral /l/.

Though the processes themselves have been well documented in the literature(Martin 1951, 1982, Kim-Renaud 1973, C.-W. Kim 1973), not enough attention has been paid to the task of explaining why only certain types of assimilation are found in the language, and under what conditions such assimilatory processes take place. This paper is an attempt to answer these questions by showing how various seemingly unrelated rules can be collapsed into one single rule of spreading specified–and consequently marked– features to an adjacent unspecified segment. This simplification will be possible only if we assume Underspecification Theory(Kiparsky 1982, Archangeli 1984, Pylleyblank 1985) on the one hand and the theory of Feature Geometry(Mohanan 1983, Clements 1985, Sagey 1986) on the other.

In the first part of the paper, a detailed analysis of Korean Assimilation will be presented in which the conditions that govern the assimilation processes will be identified. The second part will attempt to verify and extend those conditions by looking at the other rules of the language such as Cluster Simplification and Neutralization.

1. If the redundant features are to be eliminated from the phonological representation and any other information concerning missing values in the feature matrix is to be supplied by rules, both language specific and universal, the first question one should ask is how to identify the maximally underspecified segments in a given language. In the vowel system, such processes as epenthesis and deletion enable one to identify the least specified vowel. Then the choice of the least marked vowel seems to be dependent on the phonological rules of a given language, even though there seem to be certain marking constraints: if available, a language tends to select a schwa or a high back vowel over the other vowels. Also it is not very likely that a language would have a round vowel as the least marked segment and it contains a rule of unrounding assimilation instead of often attested round assimilation.

In the consonant system, the coronal stop is considered the least marked segment universally(Kean 1975). Almost all of the languages have them in their consonant system(Maddieson 1984) and if a language has processes such as epenthesis and deletion, /t/ always functions as the least marked segment.(e.g.French epenthesis) Though the consonant epenthesis and deletion are not as readily available as the vowel epenthesis to help idenfity the least marked consonant in many languages, I argue that one should look for other processes, especially assimilation and neutralization to obtain evidence for the unmarked status of the coronal stop. As has been argued extensively in the framework of autosegmental theory, if we view assimilation as an instance of spreading certain sets of features, rather than as an instance of changing features already specified, assimilation provides crucial evidence for the feature specifications. (2) schematizes how assimilation is expressed in Autosegmental Theory.(Goldsmith 1981, Steriade 1982, Kiparsky 1982, Poser 1982)[1]

(2)
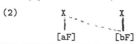

---

[1]There are two positions concerning how feature-changing assimilation is accomplished. Goldsmith and Steriade argue that you spread first, creating a contour, and then resolve the contour when it is impermissible. The other idea is that you delink the existing features and then spread, due to Kiparsky and Poser.

Within the theory of Underspecification, there is a stage in the derivation where only one type of assimilation is predicted, namely one-way assimilation from marked to unmarked features. This can be expressed in terms of rules which spread marked features to a slot where the features in question are not present, as in (3).

(3)

Before the specification of complement values, a representation like (3) is available for spreading to take place in a feature-filling fashion. For the Korean case, I argue that in order to state the asymmetrical behavior of the coronal stop we need to crucially rely on an underspecified matrix. If we assume a fully specified matrix, it is not clear why certain features (for example,[-cor], [+cont]) should spread rather than the opposite values of these features. We would need a separate stipulation of the markedness hierarchy to handle the one-way assimilations observed in many languages.

The role of neutralization in providing the information on the least marked consonant is less clear. However, it seems intuitively correct to assume that lexical neutralization is a process in which marked features are delinked so that a segment with certain specified features merges with a less marked segment. This is especially true in the framework of underspecification since unspecified features cannot be delinked until they are supplied by the rules. For example, both in Korean and Thai, laryngeal obstruents are neutralized to their corresponding plain obstruents in the coda position. If we assume that plain obstruents are not marked for laryngeal features, the neutralization is simply characterized as delinking the relevant laryngeal features, [+spread glottis] [+voice], etc. In language after language, we observe Neutralization of marked consonants such as voiced, aspirated, and glottalized consonants to the unmarked plain voiceless consonant but the voiceless consonant does not neutralize to a consonant with some laryngeal features.

(4)   [+spread glottis] ---> ∅/____]σ

On the other hand, an SPE formulation like (4) does not have the predictive power necessary in determining the directionality of change since in this framework changing [-spread glottis] to [+spread glottis] is no more costly or unnatural from the change of reverse direction.

1.1 Let us first introduce the consonant system of Korean.

(5) Korean Consonants

	labial	dental	palatal	velar	glottal
plain stops	p	t	c	k	
aspirate stops	ph	th	ch	kh	
tense stops	p'	t'	c'	k'	
plain continuants		s			h
tense		s'			
nasals	m	n		ŋ	
liquid		l			

It has been observed many times that /t/ is the least marked segment among Korean consonants. (6) lists some peculiar behavior of coronals, especially /t/, in addition to several assimilation processes mentioned in (1).

(6)   a. All coronal obstruents, regardless of their place and manner features are neutralized to /t/ in the coda position.

b. In cluster simplification, coronal obstruents are deleted regardless of their position.

c. In one type of Compound Tensification, coronals, but not labials and velars undergo tensification. (il-pun vs. il-tto)

d. Umlaut is a process in which vowels get fronted due to the following high front vowel. Umlaut takes place only when there is an intervening consonant, which should be other than a coronal obstruent. (api-->Epi, əti-->*eti) (C.-W. Kim 1973)

By assuming /t/ as the least marked consonant one can hope to account for the majority of asymmetrical processes observed in the language. Ultimately the choice of /t/ will be justified by the attainable generalizations in the statement of phonological rules. Given that /t/ needs to be maximally unspecified in the underlying representation, the following underspecification matrix arises. All the features of /t/ will be supplied by default rules. As a result, [+cor],[+ant],[-cont],[-son],[-constricted glottis], and [- spread glottis] will be unspecified while the opposite values of these features are specified in the underlying respresentation.

(7)   Underspecification of Korean consonants

	p	p*	ph	t	t*	th	s	s*	c	c*	ch	k	k*	kh	h	m	n	l	ŋ
[laryn]																			
c. g.		+			+			+		+			+						
s. g.			+			+					+			+	+				
[manner]																			
cont							+	+											
son																+	+	+	+
nas																	−		
[place]																			
cor	−	−	−						−	−	−		−		−				
back									+	+	+								
high								+	+	+	+	+	+						

2. Following the basic ideas of geometrical organization of features in Clements(1985) and Sagey(1986), we will assume that phonological features are grouped into class nodes, which are then organized hierachically so that their dependence and independence relationships are properly encoded. I will assume the following hierachy and its justification will be given mostly in the form of how such an organization captures the generalizatons in processes such as assimilation and neutralization.

(8)

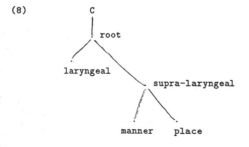

As will be demonstrated, some form of Feature Geometry is essential in describing assimilation processes since class nodes should be available as independent sites of assimilation. The fact that laryngeal, place and manner features each behave as functional units is an important argument for the tree strucutre.[2]

3. First of all we observe in Korean two kinds of assimilation processes, place assimilation and manner assimilation. If the two nodes in the hierarchy were not available as sites of assimilation, the fact that the place features and the manner features each behave as functional units would be left unexplained.

3.1 We observe in Korean that the dentals(/t/ and /n/) in exclusion to the lateral assimilate to the following consonant in place, as shown in (9). Also the palatal assimilates to the velar.

(9)   pat+ko-->pakko 'to receive'
        kotpalo-->koppalo 'straight'
        ket+co-->kecco 'to unwrap'
        hankan-->haŋkan 'the Han river'
        han+ben-->hamben 'once'

        nac+ko--->nakko'to be low'

(10) a.   ╷‑‑.   ╷   (place tier)
                  | ‑‑‑‑‑|
              [   ]   [(+high),(+back),-cor]

     b.   .‑‑.   .   (place tier)
                  | ‑‑‑‑‑.|
              [+high]   [+high, +back]

(10)a shows a formalization which expresses the fact that any specified features in the place tier spread to the unspecifed slot, i.e. to the dental.[3] (10)b is a rule that formalizes that the palatal which is less maked than the velar assimilates to the latter.

Another place assimilation is: labials assimilate to the following velar as in (11).

(11) kamki-->kaŋki
     epko-->ekko

(12)   .‑‑.   .   (place tier)
             | ‑‑‑‑‑‑.|
         [-cor]   [-cor, +high, +back]

Now let us consider why labials do not asssimilate to the palatal or vice versa. (13) is the configuration shown by the labial-palatal sequence.

(13)   .   .   (place tier)
              | |
          [-cor]   [+high]

The formulations introduced so far tell us two things: first the idea that velars are more marked than labials or palatals is right so that the features [+high], [+back] rather than [-high],[-back] need to be marked, as the choice of /t/ as the maximally unspecified segment

---

[2]The status of the manner node has not been fully confirmed in the literature. While there is no evidence in Korean that the feature [continuant] has to fall together with the other members of the set of features that comprise the manner tier, it is clear that such features as [sonorant], [nasal],and [lateral] form a unit phonologically. In the absence of evidence that there is a separate tier for [continuant], we have collapsed all of the features concerned with the degree and manner of constriction in one tier, following Clements(1985)

[3]We have used the feature system that utilizes [high] and [back] instead of [ant] because those features figure in the vowel system and there are a few rules that describe the interaction between vowels and consonants. However, the feature [ant] will do the same job in describing the consonant assimilation.

dictates us. Secondly, there is something quite similar about the three formulations in (10) and (12), that is, assimilation is best characterized as spreading of marked features to the less-specified(rather than unspecified) slot. [4]

Now let us consider why the lateral consonant does not participate in this sweeping assimilation process. We can invoke the principle of Structure Preservation to block the process.

(14) Structure Preservation
Lexical rules cannot mark features which are non-distinctive.
(Kiparsky 1983 1985, Borowsky 1986)

/l/ does not undergo assimilation even though the structural description for the rule is met because the rule of /l/ assimilating to places other than coronal will result in specifying non-distinctive features. This is because there is only one lateral in the lexicon, that is if it is a lateral, it has to be a coronal. No rule can insert the feature [-cor] into a feature matrix which contains the feature [+lateral]. On the other hand, stops, both oral and nasal, have corresponding stops which differ only in the place features.

With the constraint of SP we can have a very simple statement of place assimilation. That is, spread any feature in the configuration shown in (15) if the spreading does not create violation of the principle of SP.

(15)

F1   F2   F1 $\subseteq$ F2

(When a set of features F1 in the place node is a subset of
F2, a set of features which are specified in the place node
of the following segment.)

(15), together with SP accounts for all of the place assimilation which are observed in Korean.

3.2 In manner assimilation, we observe two processes. First, stops get nasalized before a nasal.

(16)a   kakmok-->kaŋmok 'wood'
        nap+nita--->namnita 'to sprout'
        kath+ni-->kanni 'to be the same'

   b   (manner tier)

   [ ]   [+son]

Secondly, /t/ undergoes manner assimilation in addition to nasalization. It also assimilates to the continuancy and laterality features of the following consonant.

(17) kutso--->kusso 'to harden'
     tikɨtliɨl-->tikɨlliɨl 'the letters t and l'

---

[4]This may be a parameter that each language selects. Korean allows assimilation if one segment is more marked than the other where 'more marked' will be later defined as a subset relation. Other languages do not allow non-coronal consonants to assimilate, in which case we may restrict the application of the rule to an empty slot. Or else we may introduce a different feature system in which labials and velars are dominated by two different sub-place nodes, labial and dorsal, as in Sagey (1986) and consequently do not have any features in common, perhaps other than [coronal], so that we can insure that there is no interaction between the two consonants.

(18)a.

```
    .  · · · · · · .        (manner tier)
    |            ·|
    [   ]       [+cont]
```

b.

```
    .  · · · ·  .(manner tier)
    |         ·|
    [   ]    [+son, -nas]
```

Again the question of why labials and velars do not undergo spirantization and lateralization can be solved if one resorts to the principle of SP. Labials and velars do not have continuant or lateral counterparts. A rule cannot assign such features as [+cont] and [+son, -nas] to non-dental consonants. Hence no manner assimilation of non-dentals.

Now, the simple principle (15) proposed to account for the place assimilation can be extended to the manner assimilation (maybe to any assimilation). (19) is a maximally simple statement of assimilation, where delinking is not required at all.

(19)

```
    . · · · · · · ·  .        (any node in the feature hierarchy)
    |             ·|
    [F1]         [F2]        F1≤F2
```

Before we leave this section, let us discuss one more assimilation, Lateralization. While all of the assimilation processes are cases of anticipatory assimilation: i.e. a segment assimilates to the following segment, Lateralization of the nasal is a mirror-image rule. Again we see our underspecification matrix provides a convincing case of spreading.

Now a word is in order as to why we select the features [+son] and [-nas], rather than the opposite values of these features. Korean has several rules which change /n/ to /l/ and vice versa. One of them is the assimilation shown in (20) a. Given our assumption that only specified features spread, the lateral should be more marked than the nasal. The other rule that is relevant in determining the feature makeup of the segments is shown in (20) b. The lateral gets neutralized to the nasal syllable-initially. Again the formulation of this fact is possible only if we assume that the lateral is more marked.

(20)
    a. wenlE-->wellE 'originally'
          kalnip-->kallip 'reed'
    b. /l/-->n/$____

(21)a.

```
    . · ·          .
    |     · · · ·  |
    [+son]   [+son, -nas]    manner-tier (mirror-image)
```

b.

```
    .
    |
    [+son]
    ‡
    [-nas]
```

We see that (21) was already mentioned in its more general form in (19) since the features of /n/ and /l/ are in a subset relation. [5]

(19) owes its simplicity and generality to two things: first is Underspecification which provides marked features, thus predicting the directionality of spread and the second is the functional independence of the class nodes the feature geometry predicts. Since assimilation is a rule that occurs in each node as long as its structural description is met, each node is

---

[5] The discussion so far has been limited to lexical assimilation and post-lexical assimilation with different constraints will be dealt with in a separate paper.

independent of the other nodes. For example, a rule of place assimilation does not care what is in laryngeal or manner tier, so that not only plain obstruents but sonorants or laryngeal obstruents trigger place assimilation.

3.3 It has been shown that the place and manner nodes are proven sites of assimilation, and thus the supralaryngeal node which consists of the place and manner nodes is also a node where (19) holds. Now the only remaining node is the laryngeal node. It appears at first sight that laryngeal features do not spread even though such spreading would meet the conditions in (19), as shown by the following data.

(22) kak+kho ---> kakkho, *kakhkho
     cap+hi--->ca phi , *caph hi   (Ch is one aspirated segment.)

First, the reason why /h/ does not trigger spread of [+spread glottis] can be ascribed to an independent rule that collapses the sequence of a plain(non-tense, non-aspirate) stop and /h/. I will assume /h/ to be specified for [+s. g.] in the laryngeal tier but to be empty in the supralarygeal node.[6] (23) expresses the coalesence.

(23)

Coalescence takes precedence over assimilation, and after Coalescence the structural description for assimilation no longer meets since there is only one segment.

Secondly, let us look at the case where a segment with laryngeal features other than /h/ follows a plain consonant. This is also a case where (19) predicts for the assimilation to occur since it has the following configuration.

(24) a.

[   ]   [+s.g./ +c.g.]   laryngeal node

                           supra-laryngeal node

                    F

   b. cak+pha-->cakpha (*cakhpha) 'destruction'
            > cakhpha ---> cakpha
         Assi   Neutr

There are three possible solutions to the problem of whether or not to assume laryngeal assimilation. First we can propose one solution in the following manner. The reason why spreading does not occur is ascribed to the independently needed Neutralization which changes any aspirated or tense obstruent into its corresponding plain obstruent in the coda-position. Laryngeal assimilation in fact occurs but its effect gets erased later due to Neutralization, as shown in (24)b.

However, there is a major problem with this option. Other assimilation rules clearly create linked structures to which coda-neutralization cannot apply, as shown in (25).

---

[6]The evidence can be found in the fact that /h/ is realized as /t/ after the application of neutralization of the laryngeal features. That is, the difference between /h/ and /t/ in their feature makeup is the presence and absence of [+s.g.].

(25) kat+so -->kasso-->*katso (By Coda Neutralization)
      kat+ci-->kacci-->*katci

Once we create a geminate /s/ by assimilation, the relevant coda neutralization that changes a continuant to a stop does not apply. If we assume laryngeal assimilation, we need to have the laryngeal neturalization apply in a fashion that does not observe the well-attested principle of Geminate Integrity. Why only the laryngeal neutralization behaves differently would remain a problem.

Second proposal goes as follows: there is no vacuous laryngeal assimilation. Our maximally simple rule of Assimilation of (19) should be revised so that the structural description of the rule should mention the place and manner nodes in order to exclude the laryngeal node. However, even this solution does not fare well in the presence of a particluarly problematic rule of Post-Obstruent Tensing, shown in (26).

(26) Tensification

$$\begin{matrix} C \\ [\text{-son}] \end{matrix} \longrightarrow [\text{c.g}]/\ \begin{matrix} C\_\_\_\_\_ \\ [\text{-son}] \end{matrix}$$

     kak+ca-->kakc'a 'individual'
     tɨt+ko--->tɨkko--->tɨkk'o 'hearing'
           Assi   Tens

In a sequence of two obstruents the second obstruent gets tensed. This is not only true of any two obstruents but also of a geminate created by Assimilation. This apparent violation of the Inalterability condition(Hayes 1986) can be avoided in two ways. One is to have a language-particular stipulation that Korean does not have a total geminate even in monomorphemic words and Assimilation never creates total geminates. If it is true, then there is no vacuous laryngeal assimilation and the language has only partial geminates of the form in (27).

(27)

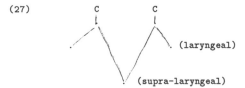

Due to the particular configuration of the geminate in the language, the rule of Post-Obstruent Tensification does not mention doubly-linked supra-laryngeal node. As a result, a rule can manipulate the laryngeal node without mentioning what is involved in the supra-laryngeal node.

The other way of solving the Inalterability problem(as well as to decide on whether or not to have vacuous laryngeal assimilation) is to resort to a phonetic implementation rule (again language-particular), which we will call the rule of Coda Unrelease. In Korean, the coda-consonant gets never released and it is impossible to realize an aspirated sound without releasing it because "aspiration is the acoustic consequence of exciting the vocal tract resonances.... during the release of the stop and the onset of the voicing."(Abramson 1971) Therefore aspiration is ruled out by the fact that the final stops are not released.[7]

---

[7]Thoughaspiration has clearly something to do with release, it is not clear whether tenseness has the same correlation with release. In view of the fact that many languages maintain voicing contrast in the absence of release, one can speculate that voicing does not depend on release. Korean cases do not involve voicing neutralizaiton and so it is easier to make a case for the phonetic implementation rule. Also in Thai, we observe the neutralization of the laryngeal features in the coda position and a phonetic rule of Unrelease. Further investigation is in order to determine whether realization of certain laryngeal features are closely related to the phonetic fact of release.

Also an electromyographic study (H. Park, et al 1982) of Korean final stops suggests that the neutralization of the tense consonant is not complete in that the electromyographic pattern for the tense consonant followed by the non-aspirated consonant resembled that for the initial tense stop. This study is particluarly relevant for the rule of Tensification in (26). Instead of having the rule insert the feature [+c.g.] to the second member of the clusters, now we can formulate the rule as inserting the feature to both of the clusters, as the study suggests. There are two major advantages with this last appoach. Once we assume the phonetic rule of Unrelease, no language particular prohibition against total geminates is called for and Assimilation can remain in its simple form of (19).

4. In this section we will see how Neutralization is stated when we assume Underspefication and Feature Geometry. (28) illustrates the relevant data.

```
(28)  Coda Neutralization
a. Continuants are neutralized to stops.
   kas --->kat   'a plant'
   noh-->not(as well as no) 'let go of'
b. palatals are neutralized to dentals.
   nac-->nat 'day'
   nach-->nat 'face'
c. any non-plain stops change to plain stops.
   pak'-->pak 'outside'
   aph-->ap 'front'
```

First, if we assume Neutralization of laryngeal features as part of Korean phonology, rather than relegating the burden to the phonetic implementation as discussed in the previous section, (28) c can be easily handled by a rule delinking all the features in the laryngeal tier. Whatever features there may be in the laryngeal tier, they will be delinked in the coda position. However, I have argued that a phonetic rule of Unrelease can better handle the phenomena.

Secondly, the data in (28) a can be obtained by delinking the continuant feature as shown in d. (28) b is the case in which the palatal /c/ gets neutralized to /t/. The rule that delinks the feature [+high] formalizes this fact. [8]

5. In this section, I will discuss what has been traditionally called Coda Simplification in Korean and argue that given our rule of Assimilation, no special rule is needed to account for the phenomenon of Coda Simplification. Instead, an extended application of Assimilation, paired with Syllable Mapping is enough to guarantee the surface realization of the coda consonant. Let us first look at the relevant data in (29).

---

[8] The neutralization of the palatal to the dental(or the alveolar) is not confined to Korean. There are such cases of centralization in Romance languages as well as in Malayalam. In Spanish the syllable final palatal nasal and lateral turn to central n and l(Mascaro 1987).

(29) Seoul/Kyungsang   Seoul   Kyungsang   Optional

      p(s)   (1)k   1(k)   1k
      1(s)   (1)p   1(p)   1p
      k(s)   (1)ph   1(ph)   1p
      n(c)
      1(th)
      1(h)
      n(h)

The above data represent the possible underlying clusters exhaustively. The first column
lists the cases in which the first consonant surfaces while in the second column the second
consonant gets realized in the Standard Korean. In Kyungsang dialect, it is always the
first consonant that surfaces(Whitman 1985) and in both dialects for some clusters both
members can be realized optionally, as shown in the last column. All past treatments have
assumed consonant cluster simplification rules. Some representative samples are shown in
(30).

(30)a. $[+cons] \longrightarrow 0 /$ $\left(\begin{matrix} [+cons] \underline{\quad\quad} \\ \left[+cor\right] \end{matrix} \right\} \atop \underline{\quad}\underline{\quad}[+cons] \right)$ $\begin{matrix} [+cons] \\ \# \end{matrix}$

                                                        B.G.Lee(1976)

     b. 1) $\begin{bmatrix} -cont \\ -cor \end{bmatrix} > [+lateral]$

         2) C1 >C2   S. Ahn(1985)

     c.   C   C   C   C   C
          /   /   -->   /   ⫫   -->   - -
        [bF]   [aF]   Neutr   [bF]   [aF]   WFC   [bF]

       J.Whitman(1985)

(30)a. and b attempt, without much success, to express the fact that coronal obstruents are
reduced whether they constitute the first or the second member of the cluster. These two
unrevealing rules make some ad hoc claims concerning the nature of the cluster reduction
and are not related to any other part of the phonology. For example, there is no reason why
non-coronal consonants should take precedence over coronal consonants and why the lateral
should behave differently from the other consonants.

   (30)c. is an autosegmental analysis in which Whitman tries to tie the phenomenon with
Neutralization and Syllabification in the language. Though his insight is right that those
clusters where the second member gets reduced are exactly those cases where the second
member undergoes Neutralization independently, a further stipulation is needed to ensure
that the features of the first segment link to the second.

   On the other hand, in our approach all we need to do is to revise Assimilation to the
effect that the target(the undergoer) has to be in the coda rather than having the leftward
spread as in (19). This parameter of syllable-controlledness is nothing new in the literature
of assimilation (as in Central Catalan(Mascaro 1987)). Now we revise Korean assimilation
as follows.

(31) Assimilation Revised---the target should be in the coda

              .   .   (any node)
              | |
             F1   F2   F1⊆ F2
            _|_
            coda   (mirror image)

With this much revision, we can account for the cluster facts with three independently needed rules, Neutralization, Assimilation and Syllabification. Neutralization and Assimilation are already introduced and now we would need the following rules for Syllabification.

```
(32) a. Syllabification Normal--one coda consonant (CVC)
         from right to left (Seoul)
         from left to right(Kyungsang)
     b. Syllabification Optional--two coda consonants
```

6. In sum, we have seen a case of assimilation where two parameters play a crucial role. The first is the distinction between marked (underlyingly specified) and unmarked (underlyingly unspecified)features, provided by Underspecification. Not all the assimilatory processes are feature-filling in the sense that there is only one operation: i.e. spread specified features to an underspecified slot. However, the Korean case can be handled as entirely feature-filling. The second parameter is structural. There is syllable-controlledness: i. e. the target should be in the coda.[9] In Korean, assimilation takes place only when the two parameters mentioned above are satisfied.

References

Abramson, Arthur (1971) ''Word Final Stops in Thai'' Haskins Laboratories.
Ahn, Sang-Cheol (1985) The Interplay of Phonology and Morphology
      Ph.D. Diss. Univ. of Illinois.
Archangeli, Diana (1984) Underspecification in Yawelmani Phonology and
      Morphology, Ph.D. Diss. MIT.
Borowsky, Toni (1986) Topics in the Lexical Phonology of English
      Ph. D. Diss. Univ. of Mass.
Clements, G. N. (1985) ''The Geometry of Phonological Features,'' in
      Ewen C. and J. Anderson, eds., Phonology Yearbook 2, Cambridge
      Univ. Press, Cambridge, pp. 225-52.
Goldsmith, John (1981) ''Subsegmentals in Spanish Phonology,'' in W.W.
      Cressey and D.J. Napoli,eds. Linguistic Studies in the Romance
      Languages 9. Georgetown Univ. Press, Washington, D.C.
Harris, James (1981) ''Spanish Spirantization as an Autosegmental
      Assimilation Rule.'' ms. MIT.
Hayes, Bruce (1986) ''Inalterability in CV Phonology,'' Language, 62:2
      pp. 321-52.
Kean, M.(1975) The Theory of Markedness in Generative Grammar
      Ph D. Diss. MIT.
Kim, C.-W.(1973) ''Gravity in Korean Phonology,'' Language Research
      9:2 pp. 274-81.
Kim-Renaud, Young-Key(1974) Korean Consonantal Phonolgy. Ph.D.Diss.
      Univ. of Hawaii.
Kiparsky, Paul (1982) ''From Cyclic Phonology to Lexical Phonology,'' in
      H. van der Hulst and N. Smith, eds. The Structure of Phonological
      Representations 1. Foris, Dordrecht. pp 131-76.
-------(1985) ''Some Consequences of Lexical Phonology,'' in Ewen, C. and
      J. Anderson, eds., Phonology Yearbook 2. pp83-136.
Martin, Samuel (1951) ''Korean Phonemics,'' Language 27. pp. 511-33.
------- (1982) ''Features, Markedness, and Order in Korean Phonology,''
      Linguistics in the Morning Calm. Hanshin, Seoul pp601-18.

---

[9] How languages may choose different parameters will be discussed in a separate paper. We may attempt to find phonetic explanations on why there should be such parameters as syllable-controlledness and left-to-right(regressive) directionality.

Mascaro, J.(1987) ''A Reduction and Spreading Theory of Voicing and
    Other Sound Effects.'' ms. Universitat Autonoma de Barcelona.
Mohanan, K.P. (1983) ''The Structure of the Melody.'' ms. MIT.
Park, Hea Suk, et al.(1982) ''An Electromyographic Study of Laryngeal
    Adjustments for the Korean Stops.'' Linguistics in the Morning
    Calm. Hanshin, Seoul.
Pullyblank, D. (1983) Tone in Lexical Phonology. Ph.D. Diss. MIT.
Sagey, E. (1986) The Representation of Features and Relations in
    Nonlinear Phonology. Ph. D. Diss. MIT.
Sohn, Hyang-Sook (1987) Underspecification in Korean Phonology.
    Ph. D. Diss. Univ. of Illinois.
Steriade, Donca (1982) Greek Prosodies and the Nature of Syllabification.
    Ph. D. Diss. MIT.
Whitman, John (1985) ''Korean Clusters'' ed. Kuno, S. Harvard Studies
    in Korean Linguistics pp. 280-90.

On Extraction from Adjuncts in VP

Peter Coopmans
University of Utrecht

0. Chomsky's (1986) proposal that extraction out of VP is possible only if an intermediate step is taken via adjunction to VP, as shown in (1), raises a number of questions with respect to standard adjunct island violations.

(1) ... α_i ... [$_{VP}$ t_i [$_{VP}$ ·· t_i ··]]

In this paper I will discuss a particular type of problem posed by sentential complements of factive verbs in Dutch that calls for a revision of the proposal to derive the adjunct island facts from a subjacency condition based on the notion of 'barrier'. I will show under which revisions of the barrier proposal this problem can be solved, and discuss the consequences of this solution for other cases of syntactic movement out of VP.[1]

1. Huang's (1982) <u>Condition on Extraction Domains</u>, given in (2), captures the fact that adjuncts are islands for syntactic movement because they fall outside the proper government domain of a verb.

(2) a phrase β cannot be extracted from a domain α if α is not properly governed

For this original formulation of the CED it is irrelevant whether the adjunct is a daughter of VP, IP or some other category. As a non-subcategorized constituent it will always be an island for syntactic extraction. Example (3a) shows the island property of a PP adjunct, (3b) the island characteristic of the subject NP, also not properly governed.

(3) a. *the concert [which [my brother slept [during t]]]
    b. *the man [who [[pictures of t] surprised Mary]]

For Chomsky's (1986) proposal to derive these CED effects from a condition forbidding movement across two barriers, it should make a difference where the adjunct is located structurally. If adjuncts are all generated as daughters of IP, they are structurally parallel to subjects and subjacency can be shown to be violated in the configuration in (4).

(4) ·· β_i ·· [$_{IP}$ ·· [$_\alpha$ ·· t_i ··]]

If α is a maximal projection, it will form a barrier because it is not θ-

---

[1] I am grateful to Marco Haverkort and Hans van de Koot, whose notes of Chomsky's (fall 1987) class lectures inspired me to develop the theoretical revision I will propose here.

governed and pass one on to IP as a result of the recursive definition of barrier formation (cf. Chomsky 1986: 14). Crossing two barriers in (4) results in a subjacency violation. For this account to work, two assumptions are needed. First, β must be totally divorced from IP; in other words, β is not allowed to adjoin to IP, and Chomsky stipulates that this holds universally for wh-phrases. Secondly, subject and adjuncts only behave uniformly with respect to (4) if the islandhood of α is not circumvented by intermediate adjunction to α. Adjunction to subjects is forbidden by the general prohibition against adjunction to arguments, but adjunction to adjuncts is freely allowed. The net effect of the latter is that it completely voids the adjunct island effects of the CED.

If adjuncts are daughters of VP, it is even less possible to derive the CED effects for subjects and adjuncts in a uniform way. In (5), the adjunct α will be the only barrier for the trace of α, because it is possible to adjoin β to VP, so that VP will not be a barrier for the trace.

(5) .. [$_{VP}$ β$_i$ [$_{VP}$ .. [$_α$ .. t$_i$ ..]]

Since it is simply impossible to get a total of two barriers for adjunct islands in VP, one cannot derive these CED effects from subjacency. If one also adjoins to α, it becomes even more problematic because one can then not even point to one barrier between β and its trace.

To maintain a uniform approach to subject and adjunct islands, I wish to argue that adjunction to VP should not provide the possibility of an extra escape hatch for wh-elements. Next to the explicit prohibition against adjunction of wh-phrases to IP, and the problems created by the possibility of adjunction to adjuncts, this seems to suggest that intermediate adjunction for syntactic movement should be prohibited altogether.

This conclusion is obviously too drastic in the light of many language-specific proposals which assume NP, CP or PP to adjoin to VP, for reasons of case, focus etc. and scope reasons for quantifiers at LF. However, what I will adopt as a starting point is that unless independently motivated for such reasons of case, focus etc., syntactic adjunction to a maximal projection is not an option just like that. A wh-element should go en route to COMP directly, not barred by VP as an intrinsic barrier.

2. Consider the Dutch fact in (6), discussed by Bennis (1986), among others.

(6) .. dat ik (het) betreur dat Jan dat gezegd heeft
       that I (it) regret that John that said has

The factive verb betreuren 'regret' can optionally take the element het 'it' in object position in construction with a postverbal sentence. When het is present, case is assigned to this nominal element to the left of the verb, and the postverbal sentence forms an A'-dependency with it through coindexation, as shown in (7).[2]

---

[2] The VPs in (7) and (8) are V'-categories in Bennis' account, but this is irrelevant for the argument to be developed here.

(7)

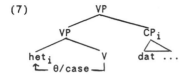

It is important to realize that het is not some dummy pronoun filling a
case-marked empty position. Bennis (1986) shows that all cases of dummy het
are instances of a relation between the referential expression het and a
coindexed constituent in an A'-position. In other words, (7) displays a
base-generated A'-dependency.
      The construction in (6) without het has most commonly been assumed to
follow from CP-postposing over V, leaving behind a case-marked trace
coindexed with the moved CP in an A'-position (cf. 8), where movement of the
object clause is enforced by something like Stowell's (1981) Case Resistance
Principle or other principles to that effect.

(8)

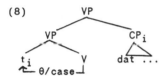

It is a well-known observation that the postverbal sentence becomes an
island for wh-extraction when het is present (9a). When het is absent, wat
is freely extractable (9b).

    (9) a. *Wat betreurde Marie het dat Jan gezegd had?
              what regretted Mary it that John said had
        b. Wat betreurde Marie dat Jan gezegd had?
              what regretted Mary that John said had

Since the structures in (7) and (8) are the same, regardless of whether they
are formed by base-generation or syntactic adjunction, the examples in (9)
should behave exactly the same with respect to extraction. In order to deal
with this difference, Bennis proposes that the version of (6) without het
has the base structure in (10), where the postverbal sentence is assumed to
fill an A-position.

    (10)

      The difference between (9a) and (9b) now follows if in (9a) extraction
has taken place from an adjunct island, while in (9b) from a regular
complement. For this to work, Bennis has to assume that CP does not need to
be linked to case for θ-visibility, against the standard view of Stowell
(1981), Chomsky (1981) and others. It cannot be argued that in (10) CP is
case-marked by the verb, because in Dutch case is always assigned on the
lefthand side of the verb. This view also goes against the idea that

thematic roles in Dutch are assigned to the left, as proposed by Koopman (1984).[3]

Given the problems noted in the previous section, Bennis' proposal to account for the ungrammaticality of (9a) as an adjunct island effect cannot be derived in the barriers framework straightaway. An attempt at making such an effect follow may show that the distinction between (9a) and (9b) need not be solved in terms of the distinction 'adjunct' versus 'complement' status of the postverbal CP. I take these problems to call for a revision of the notion 'barrier', treating the CP in (9a) as an opaque adjunct and the one in (9b) as a transparent adjunct. To derive the desired distinction between these adjuncts, it is necessary to make the following two assumptions:

(i) VP is not an intrinsic barrier
(ii) the distinction between a base-generated adjunct and a derived adjunct is visible in terms of categorial features, a distinction which can be shown to follow in part from a derivational view of the grammar.

To start with the second assumption, Chomsky (1987: class lectures) has suggested that it may be desirable to read off information from structures such as in (11a) whether they are base-generated or derived by adjunction.

(11) a. $[_{XP}$ NP $[_{XP}$ ...]]
b. $[_{NP}$ NP $[_{NP}$ ...]]

(11b), for example, could be interpreted as a small clause of the category NP, with a NP subject and predicate phrase headed by the category N. It could also be a NP category to which an internal NP has been adjoined. This has consequences for questions relating to predication etc. From a purely representional point of view, it is unclear which NP heads the small clause and thus whether one is a predicate of the other or vice versa.[4] A derivational approach might be able show whether adjunction has taken place by identifying the category to which an element has been adjoined as a base category. This can be achieved via the X'-theoretical primitives proposed by Muysken (1982). Muysken distinguishes the three categorial levels in (12)

---

[3] Bennis (1986) adopts the idea that θ-role assignment is non-directional, and takes the order of elements to follow from Case theory, which he does take to be directional. Since for him CPs do not have to be case-linked in order to be visible as θ-role bearers, he cannot resort to Stowell's (1981) Case Resistance to account for the obligatory rightmost position of a finite CP in Dutch. Instead, he invokes a nearly similar Unlike Category principle (cf. Hoekstra 1984) to derive the same effect. However, this principle is also taken to be directional, which makes the account essentially no different from one using case-linking and case-resistance to account for the order verb – finite clause.

[4] A relevant example is ..consider a man a fool, where either NP could be a predicate of the other NP subject, unless, of course, the rule of predication is stated in directional terms, as seems to be suggested by Manzini (1986).

with the features [± maximal] and [± projection].[5]

```
(12) head                [-projection; -maximal]
     projection          [+projection; -maximal]
     maximal projection  [+projection; +maximal]
```

Chomsky has suggested that with these features, the X'-schema can be stated as in (13), with the explicit condition that specifiers or complements of X (or adjuncts) be maximal projections [+p;-m]. Once features have been assigned, they cannot be changed in the course of the derivation.

(13) $[_X \ldots X \ldots]$, where $\ldots = [+p;+m]$

Assuming these X'-primitives allows one to distinguish the base generated version from the derived one in (11b). Base-generated adjunction will be represented as (14a) at D-structure and at S-structure. Derived adjunction will give (14b) at S-structure.[6]

(14) a. $[_{NP[+p;+m]}$ NP $[_{NP[+p;-m]} \ldots]]$ ($[_{N}max$ NP $[_{NP} \ldots]]$)

b. $[_{NP[+p;+m]}$ NP $[_{NP[+p;+m]} \ldots]]$ ($[_{N}max$ NP $[_{N}max \ldots]]$)

I will assume that XP is the projection in which all the arguments of a head X that have to be projected syntactically are projected. If it also turns out to be the maximal projections in Muysken's sense, it will be a X^{max}. The consequence of this adjustment clearly is that only XPs which are X^{max} can acquire barrier status. This will itself have little effect on the theoretical proposals of Chomsky (1986).

The preliminary conclusion in the previous section that <u>wh</u>-movement does not require intermediate adjunction to VP will follow if θ-government is sufficient to make VP transparent, so that VP will not be a barrier intrinsically. It can then only become a barrier by inheritance. The desired revisions of the definitions of Blocking Category (BC) and Barrier are given in (15) and (16) respectively, where <u>dominance</u> is interpreted as in May (1985). We will adopt Chomsky's definition of the bounding condition on syntactic movement as 1-subjacency in (17).

(15) τ (= X^{max}) is a BC for β iff τ is not θ-governed by a X[-p;-m] and τ dominates β

    - a category α is dominated by β only if it is dominated by every segment of β

---

[5] Muysken (1982) suggests that the fourth option of a category X [-projection; +maximal] may be used for non-projecting minor elements.

[6] Their simplified forms are given in brackets. I will keep using standard XP notation for maximal projection and only identify a maximal category as X^{max} if this turns out to make a relevant structural difference.

(16) τ is a barrier for β iff (i) or (ii):
    (i): τ immediately dominates δ, δ a BC for β;
    (ii): τ is a BC for β, τ $\neq$ I^{max}.

(17) β is 1-subjacent to α iff there are fewer than 2 barriers for β
that exclude α.

We can now account for the opaque adjunct in (9a) via the S-structure
in (18) and its transparent counterpart in (9b) via (19).

(18) V^{max} (19) V^{max}

     VP CP_i V^{max} CP_i

  NP_i V NP_i V

The V^{max} constituents in these structures cannot form barriers
intrinsically. In both (18) and (19) CP is in a non-argument position, not
θ-governed, and thus an intrinsic barrier. In (18) V^{max} will also become a
barrier by inheritance – since it immediately dominates the adjunct. This is
not the case in (19). CP will be a barrier, the only one, because V^{max} does
not dominate it – not every segment of V^{max} dominates CP. This is how we
obtain the difference in extraction in (9).
    Note that if this revision is correct, the prediction is that
extraction from a sentential complement in Dutch always passes one barrier.
This seems a welcome result, because it has often been noted that extraction
is generally much harder in Dutch than in English. So, for example,
violations of the wh-island condition are hardly ever marginal. This might
be related to the interference of this extra barrier.[7]

3. I will turn now to a discussion of some of the implications of this
revision for other islands facts. Belletti and Rizzi (1986) discuss PP-
extraction facts showing a subject-object asymmetry which they argue has to
follow from subjacency. In (20a) it is possible to have extraction of di cui
from a direct object, but not from a subject, regardless of whether the
subject is located under IP (as in 20b) or in VP (as in 20c).

(20) a.   Il ragazzo di cui amavi la sorella
           the boy of whom you loved the sister
      b.   *Il diplomatico di cui la segretaria ti ha telefonato
           the diplomat of whom the secretary called you
      c.   ??Il ragazzo di cui ti amava la sorella
           the boy of whom loved you the sister

Under the account sketched here, we can rephrase the structural descriptions
they propose as in (21):

_____

[7] This requires a more detailed view on whether a node which inherits
barrierhood is a stronger barrier if it is a BC (and perhaps a barrier)
itself. For some discussion, see footnote 8.

(21)

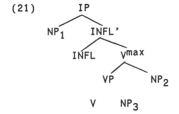

The object NP$_3$ is θ-governed, and hence will not induce any barriers (20a). Clearly, NP$_1$ is not θ-governed by a lexical head, and will thus be a barrier. Moreover, it will also make IP a barrier, hence a subjacency violation (20b). Similarly, NP$_2$ as a postverbal subject will not be θ-governed by a lexical head either, thus be a barrier and pass one on to V^{max} (20c).[8]

Sofar the account can deal with these conditions on syntactic movement in a fairly straightforward way. What is new is that the proposed revision makes certain specific predictions in conjunction with Belletti's (1988) view of the properties of unaccusative verbs. Belletti argues that the VP-internal case-marking of postverbal subjects of unaccusative verbs is one of inherent partitive case assigned by the verb itself. She observes that partitive case always selects an indefinite meaning for the NP marked as such, and that this is the reason why the definiteness effect is typically found with unaccusative verbs and similar passive constructions. This would be NP$_3$ in (21). Postverbal subjects of nonergative verbs get structural case directly from INFL. In (21) V^{max} will not be a barrier for that (government) relationship between INFL and NP$_2$.

However, ergative verbs clearly can also take definite subjects in postverbal position, as is shown in (22a).

(22) a. È arrivato Gianni
        arrived Gianni
     b. Ha parlato Gianni
        spoke Gianni

For this type Belletti assumes that Gianni has to be moved out to a position where it can be directly governed by INFL. Nominative case assignment to Gianni in (22a) will then be exactly parallel to that in (22b), where the subject follows an intransitive nonergative verb, or to the case marking of

---

[8] The reason why extraction such as in (20c) is usually considered slightly better than extraction from a preverbal subject (20b) may be related to the suggestion in the previous footnote that nodes which inherit barrierhood which are themselves non-θ-governed induce stronger subjacency violations. Finite IPs would be stronger barriers than VPs (which in our system can never be Blocking Categories) but also stronger than complement IPs (or small clauses) θ-governed by a selecting verb. This may also explain the weaker subjacency effects people tend to observe with extractions from subjects in small clauses and ECM complements (see also 35). If this line of reasoning is correct, one need not invoke the extra qualification of segments as weak barriers suggested by Belletti and Rizzi (1986).

<u>la sorella</u> in (20c).

Under our assumptions, the structure for (22a) will be as in (23), where <u>Gianni</u> is directly governed by INFL. What is more, it will not be dominated by V^{max}, and although it is not θ-governed, it will not induce enough barriers to violate subjacency in the case of PP-extraction.

(23)

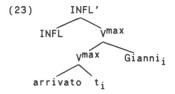

We thus predict that it should be possible to extract a PP from a definite postverbal subject of an ergative verb. Such cases should be much better than (20b) and (20c). This is confirmed by the judgements of native linguists: (24a) and (24b) contrast sharply with (20c) and also sound better than (24c).

(24) a. Questo è il directoro di cui è arrivata/ tornata la
         segretaria
         This is the director of whom is arrived/ returned the
         secretary

     b. Questo è il directoro di cui è stata arrestata appena la
         segretaria
         This is the director of whom was arrested just the
         secretary

     c. ??Questo è il directoro di cui ha telefonato la segretaria
         This is the director of whom has telephoned the secretary

This supports the idea that derived adjunction creates possibilities for extraction not available if the same position is base-generated. The suggested analysis allows us to distinguish between opaque and transparent subject NPs, analogous to the difference between opaque and transparent adjuncts in Dutch.

4. In this section I will discuss the consequences of this proposal for a similar extraction phenomenon in Dutch. This is the socalled 'wat-voor split', discussed by den Besten (1985), among many others. It is possible t subextract <u>wat</u> from an object NP, but not from a subject NP, as is shown by the examples in (25) and (26) respectively.

(25) a. [Wat voor boeken] heb jij gisteren <u>t</u> gelezen?
         What for books   have you yesterday read

     b. [Wat voor mensen] hebben <u>t</u> gisteren dat boek gelezen?
         What for people have   yesterday that book read

(26) a. Wat heb jij gisteren [<u>t</u> voor boeken] gelezen?
         What have you yesterday for books   read

     b. *Wat hebben [<u>t</u> voor mensen] gisteren dat boek gelezen?
         What have   for people yesterday that book read

Extraction from indirect objects is also problematic, though judgements sometimes vary with respect to such cases as in (27).

(27) a. Wat voor mensen heb jij t̲ zulke brieven gegeven?
         What for people have you such letters given
     b. ??Wat heb jij [t̲ voor mensen] zulke brieven gegeven?
         What have you for people such letters given

Again, subjects are opaque for subextraction because they are not θ-governed by a lexical head and will induce too many barriers, and most probably, indirect objects will too. As expected, direct objects are completely transparent. Den Besten has observed that in such examples as (28) wa̲t̲ can be extracted from a subject NP of a passive or an ergative verb, and has used this observation to argue that in these examples the subject remains in its underlying object position, with the dummy element e̲r̲ 'there' most likely occupying the subject position.

(28) a. Wat zijn er gisteren [t̲ voor brieven] geschreven?
        What are there yesterday for letters written
     b. Wat zijn er gisteren [t̲ voor mensen] naar huis gegaan?
        What are there yesterday for people to home   gone

     To draw the full analogy with Italian, observe that it is possible in Dutch to have an external argument in the VP (29a). The question is whether this one is an island for extraction or not. Hoekstra (1984:218) states that such NPs much less easily allow subextraction of wa̲t̲ (29c), but this view is not shared by all speakers.

(29) a. Er hebben gisteren enkele mensen mij hun boeken verkocht
         There have yesterday some people me their books sold
     b. Wat voor mensen hebben er gisteren jou hun boeken verkocht?
         What for people have there yesterday you their books sold
     c. ?*Wat hebben er gisteren voor mensen jou hun boeken verkocht?
         What have there yesterday for people you their books sold

It would be tempting to apply the Italian account to the Dutch case and to argue that both an internal argument subject as well as an external argument can occupy the same position in VP and that they nevertheless display different island effects for subextraction. Abstracting away from all kinds of intervening phrases, the choice would then come down to that between (30a) and (30b), where INFL would directly assign nominative case to the NP_1 position.

(30) a.   INFL'   b.   INFL'
         V^max   INFL   V^max   INFL
      NP_1   VP   NP_1   V^max
           NP   V   t   V

Since word order does not provide evidence to determine here the position of the NP from which wa̲t̲ is subextracted, we need to consider a different domain of data to determine the locality condition on subextraction.

Consider example (31b), which looks like a parasitic gap case.

(31) a. *Jan heeft [zonder e te bekijken] die boeken weggelegd
        John has without   to inspect those books away put
     b. Jan heeft die boeken [zonder e te bekijken] t weggelegd
        John has those books without to inspect   away put

Bennis and Hoekstra (1984) have argued that the possibility of a gap in the
zonder-adjunct clause in (31b) is provided by an A'-movement process that
optionally shifts the object die boeken to the VP-adjoined position, to the
left of the adjunct clause. Hence, the structure of (31b) is as in (32),
where e is the parasitic gap and t is the real gap.[9]

(32) Jan ... [$_{VP}$ die boeken$_i$ [$_{VP}$ [zonder ..e$_i$..] t$_i$ weggelegd]]

It seems possible to apply subextraction to this shifted object, though not
all speakers seem to be fully confident about its grammaticality.

(33) a. ?Wat heeft Jan [t voor boeken] zonder e te bekijken weggelegd?
        What has John   for books   without to inspect away put
     b. Wat voor boeken heeft Jan t zonder e te bekijken weggelegd?

It seems then that subextraction from an element in a non-θ-governed
position is not entirely felicitous, even if the position is a derived one.
If this conclusion is correct, it is not clear whether (31b) can be shown to
underlie such examples as (28), and the question arises then why the Italian
account is not fully applicable to the Dutch case. A possible answer could
be that this has to do with the fact that wat is a specifier, whose trace is
subject to a more specific well-formedness requirement than the trace of di
cui in (20). As a complement, the latter meets the ECP via θ-government, as
is carefully argued by Belletti and Rizzi (1986). It seems insufficient to
simply state, as is done by Koster (1987) for example, that as long as the
domain from which wat is extracted is θ-governed, the result will be
perfectly fine. This can be shown by the facts in (34).

(34) a. *Welk boek vroeg Jan [wanneer [hij t moest lezen]]]?
         Which book asked John when   he   should read
     b. **Wat vroeg Jan [wanneer [hij [t voor boek] moest lezen]]]?
         What asked John when   he   for book   should read

(34a) is a standard wh-island violation, pretty bad in Dutch. There is
no question that (34b) is even worse. Since the object from which wat has
been subextracted is itself properly governed, it must be that subextraction
is sensitive to a stricter notion than 1-subjacency. The most obvious
conclusion would be that the trace of the subextracted specifier has to be
antecedent-governed. This would explain why (34b) is worse than a standard
subjacency violation. However, if in order to be antecedent-governed a trace

---

[9] Huybregts and van Riemsdijk (1985) present an alternative account of
these facts, arguing that these are not the parasitic gap cases in the
'traditional' sense. What is relevant for the present argument, however, is
the assumption that the object has been preposed to an A'-position, which is
adopted under the Huybregts/van Riemsdijk account as well.

cannot be separated from its most local antedecent by even one barrier, the question arises why (33a) is not fully ungrammatical. This remains a problem under the barriers account if we wish to take antecedent goverment as the relevant notion for both (33a) and (34b).[10] I will leave this as a noted problem for further research on the transparency of derived non-argument positions.

5. In this section I will briefly discuss two theoretical problems involving the revision of 'barrier'. The system now suggests that extraction from small clause subjects should not be so good, because these subjects are not θ-governed by a head. Chomsky (1986) suggests at various places that the subject of a small clause or an ECM complement in English is as transparent for extraction as a regular object, but unfortunately he does not give the relevant examples. Kayne's (1983) examples in (35) show that Chomsky's view may be too lenient in this respect.

(35) a. *Which book do you believe the first chapter of to be full of lies?
     b. ?Which book do you believe the first chapter of?
     c. *A book that he found the first chapter of missing
     d. A book that he found the first chapter of yesterday

Similar facts in (36) have been noted for Italian by Longobardi (1985).

(36) a. *Maria con cui ritengo parlare del tutto inutile
        Maria with whom I believe talking completely pointless
     b. *Maria di cui considero dubitare inammissibile
        Maria of whom I consider doubting inadmissible

These suggest that subjects of clausal complements should not be treated on a par with objects selected by the verb. This allows us to use θ-government as the defining factor for BC-, and possibly barrier-, status of a X^{max}.[11]
    Chomsky (1986:33) also discusses such examples as in (37), which show a difference in extractability between arguments and adjuncts.

(37) a. It [$_{VP}$ is time [$_{CP}$ to visit Mary]]
     b. Who is it time to visit?
     c. *How is it time to fix the car?

If the CP in (37a) is truly a base-generated adjunct, the account sketched here would induce too many barriers, incorrectly predicting (37b) to be

---

[10] This suggests that a locality condition closely resembling antecedent goverment is violated in (34b) because of the intervening wh-element in COMP, but not in (33a), where the antecedent is found in the first available A'-position. This can be made to follow straightfowardly under some version of relativized minimality as proposed by Rizzi (1987) or principle A of Generalized Binding as adopted by Aoun, Hornstein, Lightfoot and Weinberg (1987).

[11] But recall footnotes (7) and (8) for a possible qualification concerning strength of barrierhood.

ungrammatical. There may, however, be a different analysis for these examples. Sentences such as <u>Time to visit Mary, I don't have</u> suggest that the noun plus the CP form one constituent, in which case it might be possible to treat the CP as the complement of the noun <u>time</u>. If this is correct, the facts in (37) would be no different from those in (38). For the latter Chomsky (1986:43) has suggested that minimality may be the source of the ungrammaticality of the adjunct extraction in (38b).

(38) a. Which book did John announce [a plan [to read t]]?
     b. *How did John announce [a plan [to fix the car t]]?

If such noun-complement structures can be motivated for the examples in (37), suggested independently by the possibility of constituent preposing, our account would make the same predictions for (37) and (38).

6. If one wishes to derive standard adjunct and subject island effects uniformly within a theory à la <u>Barriers</u>, a revision is needed to exclude unwanted transparency of adjuncts in VP. I have argued here that this result can be achieved by treating VP as intrinsically transparent, so that intermediate adjunction does not become an option for <u>wh</u>-movement to COMP, and by allowing the grammar to distinguish between base-generated and derived adjunction. This not only allows one to account for certain well-known adjunct island facts in Dutch, but has some desirable consequences for a distinction between opaque and transparent VP-internal subjects in Italian and Dutch.

References

Aoun, Joseph, Norbert Hornstein, David Lightfoot and Amy Weinberg. 1987. Two types of locality. LI. 18.537-577.
Belletti, Adriana. 1988. The case of unaccusatives. LI. 19.1-34.
Belletti, Adriana and Luigi Rizzi. 1986. Psych-verbs and Th-theory. to appear in NLLT.
Bennis, Hans. 1986. Gaps and dummies. Dordrecht: Foris Publications.
Bennis, Hans and Teun Hoekstra (1984) Gaps and parasitic gaps. TLR. 4.29-87
Besten, Hans den. 1985. The ergative hypothesis and free word order in Dutch and German. Studies in German grammar, ed. by Jindrich Toman, 23-64. Dordrecht: Foris Publications.
Chomsky, Noam. (1981) Lectures on government and binding. Dordrecht: Foris Publications.
Chomsky, Noam. 1986. Barriers. Cambridge, MA: MIT Press.
Hoekstra, Teun. 1984. Transitivity. Dordrecht: Foris Publications.
Huang, James. 1982. Logical relations in Chinese and the theory of grammar. Doctoral dissertation, MIT.
Huybregts, Riny and Henk van Riemsdijk (1985) Parasitic gaps and ATB. NELS 15.169-187.
Kayne, Richard. 1983. Connectedness. LI. 14.223-249.
Koopman, Hilda. 1984. The syntax of verbs. Dordrecht: Foris Publications.
Koster, Jan. 1987. Domains and dynasties: The radical autonomy of syntax. Dordrecht: Foris Publications.
Longobardi, Giuseppe. 1985. The theoretical status of the adjunct condition ms. Scuola Normale Superiore, Pisa.

Manzini, Maria Rita. 1986. Phrase structure and extractions. Abstract GLOW
      Newsletter 16.
May, Robert. 1985. Logical form. Cambridge, MA: MIT Press.
Muysken, Pieter. 1982. Parametrizing the notion 'head'. Journal of
      Linguistic Research. 2.57-75.
Rizzi, Luigi. 1987. Relativized minimality. ms. Univ. of Geneva.
Stowell, Tim. 1981. Origins of phrase structure. Doctoral dissertation,
      MIT.

EMPTY CONSONANTS AND DIRECT PROSODY[1]

Megan Crowhurst
University of Arizona

1.0 Introduction

A topic which has received considerable attention in recent work is the status of the skeletal tier in phonological representations. Proponents of the skeletal tier, such as Clements and Keyser (1983) and Levin (1985), argue that phonemic melodies dock into a level of structure composed of X (or C,V) slots where the consonantal and vocalic properties of labelled segments are taken to follow from syllable position and feature composition. Under this view, only skeletal slots and not phonemic melodies are subject to rules of syllabification. Thus, (1a) but not (1b) is a possible syllabic representation for the string blackstrap molasses[2]. Recent prosodic theories (Hyman, 1985; McCarthy and Prince (MP), 1986, 1987; Hayes, 1987) have eliminated the skeleton, claiming that its function is absorbed by prosodic units and principles of association. In such theories, phonemic melodies link to prosodic templates consisting of moras (or weight units) on a distinct tier immediately dominated by syllable nodes, that is, prosody is DIRECT[3]. An example appears in (1b) where blackstrap molasses is syllabified with melody units linking either to moras

---

[1] Grateful acknowledgements go to the faculty and graduate students in the University of Arizona's Linguistics Department, who have made varied contributions to this paper. In particular, Diana Archangeli has offered valuable assistance in every stage of its development.

[2] Arguments for the moraic tier are presented by the authors cited above. For a representation which includes both skeletal and moraic tiers, though differently positioned, see Hock (1986). I do not address the issue of higher syllabic structure in this paper. Presumably, at least onsets must be abstractly represented to account for phenomena in which several prevocalic consonants behave as a unit.

[3] I will refer to any theory with this property by the general term DIRECT PROSODY.

or directly to syllable nodes[4]. Each syllable
optionally includes an onset and/or coda, subject to
language particular constraints on syllable
structure. Moras are represented in (1b) by m.

(1)(a)

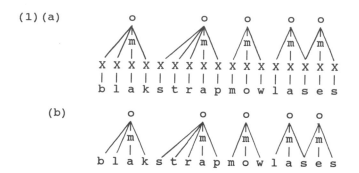

(b)

A problem with the direct prosody representation
(1b) is the following. Since the only level of
structure intervening between melody and syllable
nodes is moraic, there is no mechanism for
independently representing peripheral elements such
as onsets and nonmoraic coda segments. Such elements
are therefore predicted to be optional and should
have no phonological status unless present on the
surface. I present data from Southern Paiute (Uto-
Aztecan) and Seri (Hokan) in which empty consonant
effects are observed in exactly these nonmoraic
positions. I argue that these empty consonant
effects are not convincingly explained unless a
skeleton is assumed[5]. In other words, I argue
against (1b) in favour of (1a) in which an X tier
intervenes between the melody and moraic tier[6].

---

[4] To avoid creating confusion by referring to a
number of similar theories, I will use the prosodic
model proposed by McCarthy & Prince (1986, 1987).

[5] I assume the theory of underspecification of
Archangeli and Pulleyblank (1987) in which all underspecified segments receive default feature values and
are phonologically realised at the surface level. On
this view, empty segments cannot be radically
underspecified phonemes, since such segments must
eventually be realised.

[6] For arguments supporting an X tier, see Levin
(1985). The function of Levin's "Rime" is
implemented by moras in the skeletal representations

The paper is organised as follows. I first outline the prosodic theory developed in McCarthy and Prince (1986, 1987). I then present the facts of Seri and S. Paiute, and compare the skeletal and direct prosody accounts in section 3. Finally, in section 4, I isolate the properties of the test case which crucially decides for a skeletal analysis. From this, I conclude that a skeletal tier, in addition to a moraic tier, is essential in phonological representations.

2.0 Direct Prosody

The prosodic framework of McCarthy and Prince (1986) was proposed to provide a constrained account of reduplication which expresses the prosodic nature of reduplicative affixes and of domains of affixation. Of importance to this paper are claims which direct prosody makes about general processes of syllabification and the implications of these claims for data lending itself to an "empty X" analysis (cf. Clements and Keyser, 1983).

McCarthy and Prince (1987) encode the fundamentals of their model in several principles which function as wellformedness conditions on prosodisation. The principles of central importance to the present discussion are MORAFICATION and MORA SYLLABIFICATION. Morafication (2) ensures that the first mora links to a vocalic segment, the second, if present, to either a v^7 or a c (in languages with only light syllables, syllable nodes expand as only one mora).

(2) Morafication.

$$_{\sigma}[m \cdots \qquad m\ m]_{\sigma}$$
$$\mid \qquad\qquad\quad \mid$$
$$v \qquad\qquad\quad \{v,c\}$$

Mora Syllabification (3) expands syllable nodes as at least one and at most two moras (thus, only the moraic level intervenes between melodies and syllable nodes in direct prosody).

---

in this paper.

7 v and c refer to vocalic and consonantal melodies respectively.

(3)   Mora Syllabification.

      o --> m (m)

An additional principle, the SATISFACTION CONDITION,
requires that moraic templates be maximally filled.
Thus, if a language permits moraic consonants, then
an unassociated mora may be filled by a c. Where
moraic consonants are prohibited, an unassociated
mora is filled by spreading a (previously linked) v
to the second mora. Nonmoraic consonants link
directly to the syllable node as onsets and codas,
subject to language particular constraints.

    Applying (2) and (3) to underlying melody
strings produces configurations such as those in (4).
The hypothetical string <u>gadlan</u> syllabifies as (4a) if
the language allows moraic consonants, and as (4b) if
consonants are nonmoraic. In languages permitting
(4a), both vv and vc are heavy (e.g. Mokilese). In
languages with structures like (4b) (e.g. S. Paiute)
vv is heavy and vc is light. Where moraic consonants
are permitted, coda consonants in excess of one
attach directly to the syllable node as part of the
coda, as in (4c). In this case, vv and vc are heavy,
and extra coda consonants do not contribute to
syllable weight.

To reiterate a previous point, direct prosody
makes two predictions which are important in the
ensuing discussion. Onsets never occupy moras[8].
Second, peripheral elements, including both onsets
and nonmoraic coda segments, are always optional, and
can appear only when some nonmoraic pre- or
postvocalic consonant is available to link directly
to a syllable node.

_____

[8]   More specifically, onset consonants never
occupy moras by themselves. Hyman (1985) and Hayes
(1987) associate prevocalic consonants to a mora (or
weight unit) only when it already contains a vowel.

3.0   The Data

3.1 Seri

Marlett and Stemberger (1983) argue for the
existence of empty consonants (empty Xs) in Seri on
the basis of vowel deletion processes occurring in a
variety of contexts.   Consider the forms in (5) where
a c-initial base appears with the neutral and distal
prefixes.   Note that the distal prefix yo- surfaces
with a short vowel.

(5)	base		neutral	distal
(a)	-meke	'be lukewarm'	t-meke	yo-meke
(b)	-pi:	'taste'	i-t-pi:	i-yo-pi:
(c)	-pokt	'be full'	t-pokt	yo-pokt

(6) shows that when the v-final distal prefix is
followed by a stem beginning with /a/ or /e/, the
stem final v does not appear, and the /o/ of the
prefix is long[9].

(6)	base		neutral	distal
(a)	-ap	'sew (basket)'	i-t-ap	i-yo:-p
(b)	-ataX	'go'	t-ataX	yo:-taX
(c)	-eme	'be used up'	t-eme	yo:-me

These facts are accounted for by a rule of SHORT
LOW VOWEL DELETION (7)[10] which deletes a stem initial
short low vowel /a,e/ when it is preceded by a v-
final prefix.   After deletion, the prefix final v is
lengthened in compensation.

(7)   Short Low Vowel Deletion.

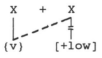

$$X \quad + \quad X$$

{v}   [+low]

---

[10]   Marlett and Stemberger's rules have been
simplified to reflect only information relevant to
the central points under discussion.

A small number of Seri verbs are exceptional to Short Low Vowel Deletion even though they apparently begin with a short /a/ or /e/[11]. The relevant cases are given in (10).

(8)   (Marlett and Stemberger's (5))
       <u>base</u>   <u>distal</u>
  (a) -amWx   'be brilliant   yo-amWx/*yo:-mWx
  (b) -enx   'play stringed   i-yo-enx/*i-yo:-nx
             instrument'

In the distal forms in (8), stem initial /a,e/ is present and /o/ is not lengthened. In other words, these stems behave like the consonant initial bases in (5).

Marlett and Stemberger account for the exceptional behaviour of the stems in (8) by positing a stem initial empty consonant. I will represent these forms abstractly as in (9), with an initial unassociated X slot.

(9)   X X X X X (=8a)   X X X X (=8b)
           | | | | | | |
           a m W x   e n x

(10a) and (10b) contain derivations for (6a) (/i-yo-ap/ --> [iyo:p]) and (8a) (/yo-amWx/ --> [yoamWx]) under this skeletal analysis.

(10)(a)

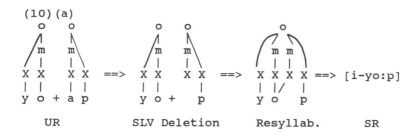

    UR   SLV Deletion   Resyllab.   SR

---

[11] All the exceptional forms in this section belong to a class of 21 verbs, all apparently v initial, which behave consistently in phonological processes as though they begin with a consonant.

(b)

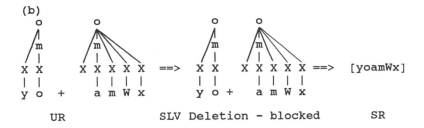

	UR		SLV Deletion - blocked		SR

The context for Short Low Vowel Deletion is satisfied
in (10a). Once /a/ is deleted, /o/ lengthens because
an empty mora is available to be filled. However, if
we assume that Short Low Vowel Deletion requires
adjacency on the skeletal tier in order to apply,
then the rule is blocked in (10b) by the unassociated
X. /o/ is prevented from spreading to the empty X
position since vowels are moraic and X has no mora[12].

As a second example, consider the form in (11)
where a v-initial stem appears with the irrealis
prefix si-. Here, the regular process of Short Low
Vowel Deletion has applied to delete /a/ and lengthen
/i/.

(11) <u>base</u>   <u>irrealis</u>
     (a) -ap   'sew (basket)'   i-si:-p

(12) shows that when si- precedes c-initial stems,
prefix final /i/ is not present.

(12) <u>base</u>   <u>distal</u>   <u>irrealis</u>
     (a) -ka: 'look for'   i-yo-ka: i-s-ka:
     (b) -meke 'be lukewarm' yo-meke   s-meke

The presence and absence of /i/ in these
contexts is accounted for by the rule of I-DELETION
in (13) which deletes a prefix final /i/ when the
following root is c-initial. If a prefix containing
an /i/ targeted by the rule concatenates with a v-
initial stem, deletion does not apply.

---

12 Alternatively, it might be the case that
lengthening is triggered by Short Low Vowel Deletion
and does not occur unless the rule has applied.

(13) I-Deletion.

      Once again, (14) shows that certain v-initial
forms do not behave as expected, but permit instead
the application of I-Deletion even though these verbs
appear not to begin with a consonant. Crucially,
Short Low Vowel Deletion does not apply to these
forms.

(14)   (Marlett and Stemberger's (15))
            base   irrealis
      (a)   -aX   'be hard'   ss-aX
      (b)   -enx   'play stringed instrument'   i-ss-enx

Once again, the behaviour of the exceptional forms in
(14) can be explained if they begin with an empty X
position which satisfies the structural description
of I-Deletion. Notice also that after I-Deletion has
applied, the prefix /s/ is geminated in the irrealis
forms in (14), but not in (12). If I-Deletion
deletes not only the vowel but also its skeletal
position (unlike Short Low Vowel Deletion, which
deletes only the features associated with the
position) then gemination is the result of spreading
/s/ to fill the empty stem initial X position in the
exceptional forms.

      I have shown that a skeletal analysis
satisfactorily accounts for empty onset effects in
Seri. A direct prosody analysis, however, encounters
a serious problem. Direct prosody representations
for the forms in (6a) and (6c), which behave
unexceptionally with respect to Short Low Vowel
Deletion and I-Deletion, are given in (15a). These
forms are represented as v-initial. The
representations in (15a) correctly predict that Short
Low Vowel Deletion, which requires an initial short
low vowel, applies to (6a) and (6c), and that I-
Deletion, which requires an initial consonant, does
not. Consider now the direct prosody representations
for the exceptional stems in (8), given in (15b).

(15)(a) Regular forms   (b) Exceptional forms
        (=6a, 6c)   (=8a, 8b)

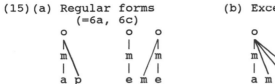
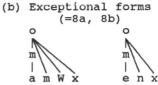

Since prevocalic consonants are nonmoraic and no
higher syllabic structure is represented, no
mechanism exists under direct prosody to abstractly
represent an onset where needed in the exceptional
cases in (15b). The configurations in (15a) and
(15b) are thus identical in relevant respects.
Hence, direct prosody does not predict that the
exceptional forms in (15b) will behave differently
from the regular forms in (15a).

3.2 Southern Paiute

     In S. Paiute, apparently v-final morphemes have
the property of inducing differing assimilation
effects in the initial c of a following morpheme when
the two are concatenated. In the forms in (16) the
initial c of the second morpheme is spirantised by a
process of intervocalic lenition. In (17), the
initial c of the second morpheme is geminated. (18)
contains pairs with semantically related first
morphemes.

(16)
  (a) nammɨ + qwavinu- --> nammɨXwavinu- 'to camp
                                          overnight first'
  (b) ma   + patcɨ'a --> mavatcɨ'aih   'to
                                          fasten, fastens'
  (c) qammi + tɨ'mappi --> qammirɨ'mappi 'roasted
                                          jackrabbit.'

(17)
  (a) ii   + pɨanɨ   --> iippɨanɨ   'my old
                                          relative'
  (b) ii   + tɨqqa   --> iittɨhqaih   'eats
                                          beforehand'
  (c) qUhtca + qa   --> qUhtcaqqa   'to be grey'

  (d) tOhtsi + tɨ'mappi --> tOhtsittɨmwɑppi 'roasted
                                          bread'

(18)
  (a) ivi   + ku   --> iviɣu   'when
                                          drinking'

```
(b)  ivi    + pakai    --> ivippaɣai      'to drink
                                          while walking'
(c)  aŋqa   + qa       --> aŋqaɣa         'to be red'

(d)  aŋqa   + qannI    --> aŋqaqqannI     'red house'
```

In a skeletal account, the geminating cases can be explained by the presence of an empty X at the end of the first morpheme. As illustrated in (19a) (=17a) gemination is effected by wholly assimilating the empty skeletal position to the features of the following c. In the spirantising cases, represented in (19b) (=18c), there is no morpheme final empty X and the feature [+continuant] spreads from the final v to the following morpheme initial c. Once again assuming that rules of assimilation require skeletal adjacency, the presence of the unassociated X slot in the geminating forms blocks [+continuant] spread. After gemination, [+continuant] spread would be prevented by geminate blockage. Thus, spirantisation and gemination are mutually exclusive.

(19)(a)

Direct prosody representations of the processes illustrated in (19) are given in (20). The nearest equivalent to an empty skeletal position in a direct prosody analysis is an unassociated mora. Thus, as illustrated in (20a), the geminating forms above could be abstractly represented with an empty mora at the end of the first morpheme. Gemination would then result from multiply associating the following morpheme initial c with both the empty mora and the initial syllble of the second morpheme. Spirantisation under direct prosody, illustrated in (20b), proceeds as in a skeletal analysis.

(20)(a)

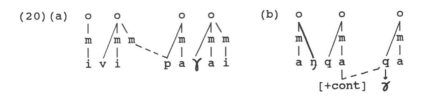

If consonants in S. Paiute are permitted to occupy moras, however, the direct prosody analysis encounters two problems. First, such a solution requires the licensing of trimoraic syllables in cases such as (21), where a geminate-inducing morpheme ends in a long, tautosyllabic v. This requirement violates the ceiling of two moras per syllable imposed by McCarthy and Prince's principle of Mora Syllabification in (3).[13]

(21)

The second difficulty is that stress in S. Paiute is moraic, falling on alternate moras. The forms in (16), (17), and (18) illustrate that consonants do not count as moras for stress; stress is marked on every second vowel[14]. Therefore, an empty c cannot be represented as in (20a), (21) with an empty mora.

These problems can be amended by positing the representation in (22) for the geminating cases, in which no empty mora is present. In this case, gemination results from multiply associating a single c with distinct syllable nodes.

(22)(a)   (b)

However, this solution raises a different problem. The representations in (22a) and (22b) (=20b) are the same in relevant respects, and thus provide identical input to geminating and spirantising rules,

---

[13] Hayes (1987) argues that trimoraic syllables in Estonian and nonstandard dialects of German are motivated by three-way length distinctions. However, no such argument is available for S. Paiute.

[14] Chomsky and Halle (1968:345)

predicting the unattested *anɢaχχa, with a geminate spirant. The only remaining solution is to propose a lexical diacritic such as [+root node spread] for the geminating cases, at considerable cost to the grammar. Thus, direct prosody yields the wrong results for S. Paiute since it cannot satisfactorily account for empty consonant effects in the coda, where coda consonants have been shown to be nonmoraic.

4.0   Properties of the Test Case and Conclusion

In the foregoing, I have argued that a skeletal account, but not a direct prosody analysis, can explain empty consonant effects in Seri and S. Paiute. In section 3 I showed that apparently v initial stems in Seri which behave as though they are c initial can be accounted for in a skeletal analysis by positing an empty X before the initial vowel. Direct prosody cannot account for these effects since prevocalic consonants (i.e. onsets) cannot occupy a mora. Furthermore, I showed that empty codas in S. Paiute can be accounted for with an empty X position in a skeletal analysis. These effects are unexplained in a direct prosody account: an empty mora analysis is not available because S. Paiute consonants are nonmoraic for stress.

Although empty consonant data is a potentially fruitful testing ground for deciding between a skeletal and direct prosody analysis, not all such cases aid in making the distinction. The crucial property of such decisive test cases is that a nonmoraic position, either an onset or a coda, where consonants may not occupy moras, is involved. Crucially, the Seri empty consonant is in onset position and is intervocalic. Thus, the phenomenon cannot be explained by dually associating a preceding consonant as both coda and onset. In S. Paiute, the important factors are that the empty consonant is in coda position, yet consonantal codas cannot be moraic: unless an empty position can be abstractly represented in certain cases, forms are indistinguishable despite the fact that they provide input to different rules of assimilation. It is for these reasons that I conclude that a skeletal tier is essential in phonological representations.

References.

Archangeli, D. and D. Pulleyblank. 1987. The Content and Structure of Phonological Representations. U of Az/USC ms.

Chomsky, N. and M. Halle. 1968. The Sound Pattern of English. NY: Harper & Row.

Clements, G.N. and S.J. Keyser. 1983. CV Phonology. Cambridge: MIT Press.

Hayes, B. 1987. 'Compensatory Lengthening in Moraic Phonology'. UCLA ms.

Hock, H. 1986. 'Compensatory Lengthening: In Defense of the Concept "Mora"'. Folia Linguistica 20, 431-460.

Hyman, L. 1985. A Theory of Phonological Weight. Dordrecht: Foris.

Levin, J. 1985. A Metrical Theory of Syllabicity. MIT dissertation.

Marlett, S. and J.P. Stemberger. 1983. 'Empty Consonants in Seri'. LI 14.4.

McCarthy, J. and A. Prince. 1986. 'Prosodic Morphology'. UMass/Brandeis ms.

--------. 1987. 'Quantitative Transfer in Reduplicative and Templatic Morphology'. UMass/Brandeis ms.

Prince, A. 1987. 'Categories and Operations in Prosodic Morphology' (in collaboration with J. McCarthy). Colloquium presentation, University of Arizona, October 1987.

Sapir, E. 1930. Southern Paiute, A Shoshonean Language (Proceedings of the American Academy of Arts and Sciences, Vol. 65, No. 1).

The Syntax of Wh-in-Situ

Robert Fiengo, CUNY
C.-T. James Huang, Cornell University
Howard Lasnik, University of Connecticut
Tanya Reinhart, University of Tel Aviv

1. Island Violations and the Pied-Piping Hypothesis

It is by now well known that wh's-in-situ fail to exhibit the full range of island effects that characterize syntactic *wh*-movement. This is illustrated by the contrasts below:

(1)	a.	*What do you remember where we bought t?
	b.	Who remembers where we bought what?
(2)	a.	*Who do you like books that criticize t?
	b.	Who likes books that criticize who
(3)	a.	*Who do you think that pictures of t are on sale?
	b.	Who thinks that pictures of who are on sale?
(4)	a.	*Who did you get jealous because I spoke to t?
	b.	Who got jealous because I spoke to who?
(5)	a.	*What color hair did you meet [students with t]?
	b.	Who met [students with what color hair]?

The (a) sentences illustrate the effects, under overt *wh*-movement, of the Wh Island Condition, the CNPC, the Subject Condition, and the Adjunct Condition. In the corresponding multiple questions in (b), a wh-in-situ occurring in an island can be construed with a wh-phrase in the matrix COMP outside the island. A similar contrast also obtains with respect to the Coordinate Structure Constraint:

(6)	a.	*Who did you see John and t?
	b.	?Who saw John and who?

Under the LF movement hypothesis, these contrasts led Huang (1982) to conclude that the bounding conditions, subsumed under Subjacency and the Condition on Extraction domain (CED), apply only to syntactic instances of Move α, but do not affect movement in LF, though the ECP does apply at LF (in addition to S-Structure) ruling out examples like those starred below:

(7)	a.	Why did you buy what?
	b.	*What did you buy why?
(8)	a.	Who bought what?
	b.	*What did who buy?
(9)	a.	*Who left why?
	b.	*Why did who leave?

The irrelevance of the bounding conditions in LF is further evidenced by the grammaticality of Chinese singular questions akin to the (a) sentences in (1)-(6).

(10) ni   xiang-zhidao [shei mai-le shenme]?
     you wonder   who bought what
     '*What do you wonder who bought?'

(11) ni   zui   xihuan [piping shei de   shu]?
     you most like   criticize who REL book
     '*Who do you like books that criticize?'

(12) ni   renwei [shei de hua   zui   piaoliang]?
     you think   who 's picture most pretty
     '*Who do you think that pictures of are most pretty?'

(13) ni   [yinwei wo shuo-le shenme] er   bu gaoxing?
     you because I said   what   then not happy
     '*What are you unhappy because I said?'

The general nature of the absence of island effects in LF is further evidenced by the fact that LF movement may cross more than one island. Thus, in contrast to the doubly ungrammatical (14a) and (15a), the sentences (14b), (14b), and (16)-(17)   are   well-formed:

(14)   a.**Who do you remember where we bought books that
                criticize t?
     b.   Who remembers where we bought books that cricitize
              who?
(15) a.   **Who do you remember where pictures of t are on sale?
     b.   Who remembers where pictures of who are on sale?
(16) [Zhangsan nain [shei xie   de   shu]] zui heshi?
      Zhangsan read   who write REL book most appropriate
      '*That Zhangsan read the books that who wrote is the most
appropriate?'
      (Who is the x such that it is most appropriate for Zhangsan to read
      the books that x wrote?)

(17) ni   zui   tongqing [bei [shei xie   de   shu] piping   de   ren]?
     you most pity   by who write REL book criticize REL person
     'You sympathize most with persons that are criticized by books
     that who wrote?
     (Who is the x such that you sympathize most with the persons
     who are criticized by the books that x wrote?)

However, the conclusion, though not implausible, raises the question of what makes the syntactic and LF components different in this way. The hypothesis remains a stipulation as long as it is not related to other, independently established properties of LF. Note that this problem is not solved under the D-linking hypothesis of Pesetsky (1987), nor by the analysis suggested in the previous section, since the wh's-in-situ that may occur in islands are clearly not limited to those that are D-linked, but may be N°'s that are analyzed above as pronominal clitics that do not undergo QR.

    A solution to this problem was proposed in Choe (1987), Nishigauchi (1985), Pesetsky (1987), and Longobardi (1987).   In cases where a non-D-linked wh-phrase appears to violate Subjacency or the CED, the theory proposed, that the relevant LF movement pied-pipes the entire island in which the wh-phrase occurs, but does not move it out of the island. A piece of very interesting evidence comes from the fact that, in Japanese and Korean, a question with a wh-phrase in a complex NP is often not given an answer that specifies the value of the wh-word alone, but requires one that at least repeats the other material in the island. This requirement also obtains in Chinese. Thus, the Chinese question (18) can have (19a) and (19b) as possible answers, but not (19c):

(18)   ni   xihuan [shei xie   de shu]?
       you   like   who write REL book
       '*You like the book that who wrote?'

(19) a.   wo xihuan [Zhangsan xie   de shu].
           I   like   Zhangsan write REL book
           'I like the book that Zhangsan wrote.'

      b.   Zhangsan xie de (shu).
           'The book (or the one) that Zhangsan wrote.'

      c.   ??Zhangsan.

The requirement of (19b) as a minimal answer seems to indicate that (18) is a question concerning the identity of the book (in terms of the identity of its author), but not a question that directly concerns the identity of the author alone. That is, it seems that the relevant "wh-phrase" to undergo movement in LF is the entire complex NP that contains *shei*, and not *shei* alone. A mechanism of feature percolation is proposed in Nishigauchi (1985) (cf. Longobardi (1987)) to execute this idea, whereby the entire island in (18) is treated as having the feature [+wh] which matches the [+wh] feature of the COMP to which it moves. Since the wh-word *shei* is not moved out of the island, no violation of Subjacency actually happens, despite appearances to the contrary. According to the pied-piping hypothesis, then, both syntactic movement and movement in LF obey island constraints. The problem concerning the supposed Syntax-LF asymmetry disappears, a strict correspondence between the two components is established, and the existence of syntactic movement in LF receives further support.

2.   Problems with the Pied-Piping Hypothesis

Attractive as it appears, however, the pied-piping hypothesis raises important problems that seem to cast serious doubt on its correctness as a key to the Syntax-LF asymmetry. In the first place, as Huang (1982) had already pointed out (in discussing it as a straw man then), the pied-piping hypothesis runs counter to superiority facts. To see this, first note that the following contrasts are quite clear and systematic:

(20) a.   *Where did [people from t] buy what?
      b.   What did [people from where] buy t?
(21) a.   *Who did [pictures of t] please who?
      b.   Who did [pictures of who] please t?

The ill-formedness of the (a) sentences shows that overt movement out of a subject is blocked (by the CED). The (b) sentences, on the other hand, show that movement from the same position in LF does not show CED effects. In order to maintain CED (or Subjacency) as a valid condition in LF, the pied-piping hypothesis claims that movement to COMP actually involves the entire subjects *pictures of who* and *people from where* . Making this move does not help, however, because the LF structures resulting from such movement should be the same as those of (22), but the latter are, of course, ill-formed.

(22) a.   *What did who buy?
      b.   *Who did what please?

Similarly, the contrast between (23) and (24) with respect to the Adjunct Condition cannot be attributed to an LF movement that pied-pipes the entire adjunct island in (24), given the ill-formedness of (25):

(23)   *Who did you get angry because I spoke to t?
(24)   Who got angry because I spoke to who?
(25)   *Who got angry why?

A similar conclusion can be reached in Italian, as Rizzi has remarked to us in personal communication.   In Italian, a wh-in-situ is disallowed in the preverbal subject position of an adjunct clause (26a), but not if it is properly contained in a subject in such a position (26b):

(26) a.   *Questo e' successo mentre chi parlava alla stampa?
            'This happened while who was speaking to the press?'

      b.   ??Questo e' successo mentre l'avvocato di chi parlava alla
stampa?
            'This happened while the lawyer of whom was speaking to
            the press?'

Although the marginal status of (26b) might be taken to be an effect of CED, there is independent evidence that this is not the case. The following contrast shows that if a wh -in-situ is not in final position, the structure is somewhat deviant:

(27) a.   Gianni e' stato arrestato mentre andava a Milano con chi?
            'Gianni was arrested while he was going to Milan with
who?'

      b.   ??Gianni e' stato arrestato mentre andava con chi a
Milano?
            ??'Gianni was arrested while he was going with whom to
Milan?'

A CED explanation of the marginality (27b) of course would not distinguish it from (27a). This contrast may be explained by the fact that the wh-in-situ must be focal, and the natural focus position in Italian is the sentence final position. If so, the marginality of (26b) can be explained on a par with (27b), without invoking CED.

    Further indication of the lack of CED effects is given by the fact that overt extraction from the postverbal subject of a non-ergative verb is disallowed, but the corresponding wh-in-situ is possible:

(28) a.   *Di chi parlava [l'avvocato t]?

'Of whom spoke the lawyer?'

b.   Questo e' successo mentre parlava l'avvocato di chi?
'This happened while was speaking the lawyer of whom?'

The idea of pied-piping would not help in these cases to avoid the conclusion that CED does not hold in LF. Consider (26a, b) and (28b): if the phrase *the lawyer of whom* is pied-piped alone, CED is still violated when the phrase is extracted from the adverbial clause; if it was possible to simply pied-pipe the whole adverbial clause into the main COMP, with no further movement needed, there would be no explanation of the ill-formed (26a). Finally, if the phrase *the lawyer of whom* could be moved to the COMP of the adverbial clause and then the adverbial clause could be moved to the main COMP, we would have no way to distinguish (26a) and (26b): either both would violate ECP, or neither would.

A second type of problem that argues against the pied-piping hypothesis has to do with the fact that it does not appear to be applicable to the whole range of island violations observed in LF. If the requirement of repeating all the material in an entire island in an elliptical answer is taken to be symptomatic of pied-piping, then the impossibility of using such an elliptical answer suggests that no pied-piping takes place. Now, contrary to those cases where a *wh*-word is contained in a relative clause (or as a possessive NP), the most natural elliptical answer to a question whose *wh*-word occurs in a sentential subject or adverbial clause is one which spells out the value of the *wh*-word alone:

(29)   [shei kan zheben shu] zui   heshi?
who read this   book most appropriate
'*That who read this book is most appropriate?'

    a.   *Zhangsan kan zheben shu.
'That Zhangsan read this book.'

    b.   Zhangsan.

(30)   zhejian shi [gen shei lai-bu-lai]   zui you guanxi?
this   this with who come-or-not most have relation
'This thing is most related to whether who will not or not?'

    a.   *gen Lisi lai bu lai.
'With whether or not Lisi will not.

    b.   Lisi.

If pied-piping is not involved in these sentences, then it is not clear how CED can be maintained in LF. What we can conclude from this is that although certain facts about elliptical answers indicate that pied-piping may occur with some questions, this strategy does not provide a real answer to island violations.[1]

---

[1] It has been noted (first by Kayne, we believe) that a question like *Whose mother did you see?* may take *John's* but not *John* as a minimal answer. Though this correlates with the pied-piping of *whose mother* in the question, the correlation is not complete, since *Whose mother's friend did you see?* takes *John's* as a possible answer. This shows that one cannot depend too much on

A third consideration that casts doubt on the pied piping hypothesis is that certain scope facts require a *wh*-word in an island to occur, at the LF level, outside of the island. This is at variance with the pied-piping hypothesis, which attempts to preserve island conditions in LF by the assumption that the *wh*-word never leaves the island. Consider first the sentence below:

(3 1)   Who did everybody see a picture of t?

This sentence contains three quantificational noun phrases whose scope order, under a natural reading, may be *who > everybody > a picture of t* (Who is the person x such that everybody saw one picture or another of x?). Since the *wh*- and the existential quantifier are separated in scope order by the universal, they do not occur as a constituent at LF. A similar situation arises in (32), where the scope order may be *who > most people > every picture of t*:

(32)   Who did most people like every picture of t?

The significance of these facts will be obvious when we consider the following Chinese sentences:

(33)   meige ren dou mai-le [yiben [shei xie   de] shu]?
       every man all bought one   who write REL book
       'Everybody bought a book that who wrote?'

(3 4) daduoshude ren dou mai-le [[shei xie   de] meiben shu]?
       most   man all bought who write REL every   book
       'Most people bought every book that who wrote?'

The only significant difference between the Chinese sentences and their English counterparts is that here a wh-in-situ, *shei*, occurs within a relative clause headed by a QNP. The range of possible scope interpretations is identical to that of the corresponding sentences. Thus (33) has the interpretation "Who is the person x such that everybody bought one book or another that x wrote?", an interpretation according to which 'who' occurs in a position at LF separated from 'a book that x wrote', with 'everybody' intervening between them. This fact is inconsistent with the fundamental claim of the pied-piping hypothesis.

An additional problem posed by sentences like (33)-(34) is what an operator like *every book that who wrote* is supposed to mean. The pied-piping hypothesis implies that it is a wh-operator which would be existential in nature (Karttunen (1977)), but it is also clear that the entire NP is a universal quantifier. A standard view about such a phrase is, of course, that we have two independent QNPs here, a [+wh] existential quantifier, and a universal quantifier. Furthermore, since the [+wh] quantifeir must take clausal scope, it must have scope over the universal which dominates it. In other words, such phrases are standard cases of "inversely-linked quantification" of the type discussed in May (1977).[2]

possible elliptical answers to argue about the existence (or non-existence, for that matter) of pied-piping.

[2] In this connection, note that *wh*-phrases with *how many* also pose a similar problem. In sentences like the following:
       (i)   How many students has every professor taught t?

We have seen several empirical problems with the pied piping hypothesis. There is also a fundamental problem of a more theoretical sort. Any assumption of LF pied-piping inevitably leads to the question of its relationship to syntactic pied-piping. Although there exists a fairly wide range of possibilities for pied-piping in syntax, the possibilities vary considerably by construction. Appostive relatives seem freest in allowing large amounts of material to be pied-piped. At the opposite extreme are embedded questions, which allow very little pied-piping. The restrictions on pied-piping in embedded questions are illustrated below:

(35) a. I wonder who Bill spoke to.
b. ?I wonder to whom Bill spoke.
c. I wonder whose mother Bill spoke to.
d. I wonder whose friend's mother Bill spoke to.
e. *I wonder pictures of whom Bill saw.
f. *I wonder Mary and whom Bill saw.
g. *I wonder the books that who wrote Bill bought.
h. I wonder which man Bill saw.

It seems that only specifiers may trigger pied-piping in these cases (see Lasnik (1987) for more details). In particular, except for those constructions that fall under Ross's Left Branch Condition, pied-piping of an entire island is strictly disallowed in both embedded and direct questions. Even in appositives, pied-piping of the sort shown in (35f) and (35g) is impossible:

(36) a. *John, Mary and whom came yesterday, ...
b. *John, the books that who wrote sold very well, ...

The LF pied-piping hypothesis must assume that LF pied-piping of a [+wh] phrase into COMP is radically different syntactic pied-piping. But unless there

(ii) How many students does every professor believe he has taught? the NP *how many students* actually contains two operators: a [+wh] operator ranging over numbers (e.g., 1, ..., n), and a [-wh] existential quantifier ranging over individual students. That the two operators should be distinguished is motivated by the fact that they may have distinct scope properties. The [+wh] operator may have wider scope than the subject *every professor*, while at the same time the [-wh] existential quantifier may have narrower scope than the latter. So, if "95" is the answer to (i), the interrogator may most naturally understand every professor to have each taught 95 students, but not necessarily the same 95 students that another professor has taught. In the case of (ii), it is even possible for the [-wh] existential quantifier to have only the embedded, *de dicto*, scope reading, so that every professor believes that there are 95 students that he has taught. It is interesting to note that in the latter situation the [-wh] existential quantifier occurs in a position c-commanding a syntactic domain larger than its semantic scope. In a system that takes scope to be defined by c-command, this provides evidence for the existence of a lowering operation of the sort considered in May (1977). The LF representation of (ii) might be something like (iii):
(iii) (For which x: x a number) (For every y: y a professor) (y believes that
(for x-many z: z a student) (y has taught z)).

is a principled reason for this radical difference, the problem concerning the (partial) Syntax/LF asymmetry is simply reassigned: it is not presence or absence of Subjacency or CED, but rather, absence or presence of unconstrained pied piping. The asymmetry remains.

3. An Alternative

Having argued against pied-piping as an explanation for the Syntax/LF asymmetry, we wish to indicate our agreement with its prononents that the strategy to derive the asymmetry from something else is both methodologically sound and theoretically desirable. Although pied-piping does not seem to be the correct answer, something else might allow one to achieve that goal. We will now show that there are, in fact, independent properties of grammar that explain this asymmetry.

Chomsky (1986), citing Torrego (1985), notes that a phrase that is moved to (SPEC of) COMP does not constitute a barrier for movement of an element contained in that phrase. In the following Spanish example, *del que* 'by whom' has been extracted from the NP *que libros del que* 'what books by whom' which had been moved into the lower COMP:

(37)   este es el autor [del que]$_i$ no sabemos [$_{CP}$ [que libros t$_i$] leer].

       'This is the author [by whom]$_i$ we know [$_{CP}$[what books t$_i$] to read].

This poses a problem for the CED, since extraction of *del que* has taken from a phrase in COMP which is, under normal assumptions, not properly governed. Similarly, although extraction from within a subject is impossible (as predicted by the CED), this impossibility is overcome once the subject is itself moved to COMP.   This is shown by the contrast shown below:

(38)   *esta es la autora [de la que]$_i$ [$_{IP}$ [varias traduciones t$_i$] han ganado premios internacionales].
       'This is the author by whom several translations have won international awards.'

(39)   [de que autora]$_i$ no sabes [$_{CP}$ [que traducciones t$_i$] han ganado premios internacionales].
       'By what author don't you know what translations have won international awards?'

A similar contrast is also observable in English:

(40)   a.   *Who do you think that [$_{IP}$[pictures of t] are on sale]?
     b.   ?Who do you wonder [[which pictures of t][are on sale]

To account for these exceptions to CED, Chomsky (1986) stipulates, under the *Barriers* system, that if A theta-governs B, then A also L-marks the Specifier of B. In the example (40b), *wonder* theta-governs CP, so the phrase *which pictures of t* is characterized as being L-marked, and therefore not a Blocking Category (BC) nor a barrier for movement. The SPEC of CP therefore does not exhibit CED effects. (The subject *pictures of t* in (39) is not L-marked, since it is the SPEC of IP which is not theta-governed. The matrix verb *wonder* theta-governs CP in both (40a-b), not IP.)

The CED effects seem to be weakened in more than the SPEC of CP position. Lasnik and Saito (forthcoming) have observed that the following sentence is better than (40a):

(41)   ?Who do you suggest that pictures of t I should buy?

Compare also:

(42)   a.   *Vowel harmony, I think that articles about t have been published.
       b.   ?Vowel harmony, I think that articles about t, you should read carefully.

These sentences show that a topicalized phrase does not block extraction as much as a subject does. This fact suggests that Chomsky's stipulation in terms of SPEC L-marking is not general enough. What is significant about these sentences is that the phrases that do not block extraction are phrases in A'-positions. Regardless of how it might be derived in a more principled way, we might propose the following as a generalization (cf. Lasnik and Saito, forthcoming):[3]

(43)   α is a barrier only if it is not an A'-binder.

There is, in fact, already something available in Chomsky's system to achieve the effect of (44), as Wayne Harbert has independently pointed out to us. A vital assumption in Chomsky's (1986) framework is the following condition on adjunction operations (p. 6):

(45)   Adjunction is possible only to a maximal projection that is a nonargument.

This condition limits, in the basic cases, adjunction sites to the two categories IP and VP. The condition is needed to block certain unwanted but potentially possible successive-cyclic adjunctions that would otherwise render the entire system vacuous. Chomsky further reasons that (44) may be derived from considerations of Theta Theory (p. 16). Regardless of its origin, suffice it to say that (44) also admits topicalized phrases and phrases in COMP (both being nonarguments) as possible adjunction sites.

Chomsky's theory of adjunction is related to another property of the *Barriers* framework: the "segment theory of domination" originally proposed by May (1985):

---

[3] A question arises about the status of subjects that are topicalized. In particular, one may wonder why the sentence *Who do you think that pictures of t are on sale?* cannot be saved by first (vacuously) topicalizing the subject *pictures of who* to its immediately dominating IP. The answer is that, whatever its explanation, it seems that vacuous topicalization should be blocked anyway, given the ungrammaticality of *John, came yesterday. On the other hand, non-vacuous topicalization of the subject does help to overcome Subject Condition effects, thus strengthening the generalization (44): *??Who do you think that many pictures of t, Mary believes are on sale?* (This sentence is taken from Lasnik and Saito, forthcoming.) (For some explication of the non-vacuous movement hypothesis, see Chomsky (1986) and Bowers (1987).)

(4 5) α dominates β iff every segment of α dominates β.

This definition of "dominates" has consequences for adjunction structures only. In a non-adjunction structure, a node contains exactly one segment. But an adjunction structure like . . . [α β [α ...]] . . . is said to have a single node α consisting of two segments, but does not contain two nodes of the type α. In this structure, β is not dominated by α (nor excluded by the latter). This, together with the theory of barriers, which refers to an element included (dominated) by a category and another element excluded by it, makes it possible to extract something from a barrier by successive adjunction. That is, by first adjoining β to α before further moving it out, one can cross a node by crossing "half" of it at a time. A phrase that is a possible adjunction site thus is not a barrier for movement. More specifically, sentence (40b) may be more thoroughly represented as follows:

(4 6) Who$_i$ do you wonder [$_{CP}$ [$_{NP}$ t$_i$ [$_{NP}$which pictures of t$_i$]] [$_{IP}$ are on sale]]?

First, the subject *which pictures of who* is moved into the embedded COMP; since it is now a non-argument, it becomes a possible adjunction site, by (44). This allows *who* to be adjoined to it and then moved into the higher COMP, without crossing a whole barrier node at any time. The relative acceptability of (40b) thus follows. In the rest of this section we will exploit this aspect of the *Barriers* framework and the facts represented by generalization (43), and show that the problem of Syntax/LF asymmetry can be accounted for, under an appropriate semantics of quantification and syntax of scope.

Consider first the following sentence, which poses a problem for Subjacency (more specifically CED) under the system developed in May (1977):

(4 7) Pictures of everybody are on sale.

(47) allows the QNP *everybody* to have scope over the entire sentence, meaning that for each person x, pictures of x are on sale. The LF representation of (47), given below, together with the application of QR that derives it, violates the CED:

(4 8) [$_S$ Everybody$_i$ [$_S$ [$_{NP}$ pictures of t$_i$] are on sale]].

Under the *Barriers* system, nothing we have discussed up to now solves the problem, either. This is because the NP *pictures of t* occurs in subject position and is therefore not a possible adjunction site, but the sentence does not exhibit Subject Condition effects. The key to the problem, we propose, is that in the sentence (47), not only may QR affect *everybody* ; it can also affect the containing NP *pictures of everybody*: that is, both of them may be considered QNPs. The NP *everybody* is of course quantificational, ranging over individuals, say {John, Bill, Mary}. But *pictures of everybody* can likewise be considered a QNP ranging, in this case, over {John's pictures, Bill's pictures, Mary's pictures}. At least nothing seems to prevent such a construal, nor the application of QR adjoining *pictures of everybody* to IP in (47), resulting in (49):

(4 9) [$_{IP}$ [$_{NP}$ pictures of everybody] [$_{IP}$ t are on sale]].

This will enable the smaller QNP *everybody* to be adjoined, under QR, first to *pictures of everybody*, then to the higher IP, with neither steps of adjunction crossing any barrier at all. The fact that scope interpretation of *everybody* does not show CED effects thus follows without any stipulation that restricts CED from applying in LF. The well-formedness of the following sentences follows in the same way:

(50) Who did pictures of who please?

The NP *pictures of who*, though not itself a [+wh] operator that directly moves into a [+wh] COMP (given the strict conditions on pied-piping noted above), can nevertheless be analyzed as a [-wh] QNP (ranging over, again, {John's pictures, Bill's pictures, Mary's pictures}) that falls under the domain of QR. IP-adjunction of this QNP will then enable the wh-in-situ to be adjoined to it and then moved into the COMP.

Under our proposal, the contrast between the (50) and the ill-formed *Who did pictures of t please you?* follows from the fact that *pictures of who* in (50) can be IP-adjoined at LF but not at S-Structure. This in turn follows from the fact that QR (as an instance of IP-adjunction) is a rule of LF, not of Syntax. This also follows from a stipulation made in Chomsky (1986) that allows VP-adjunction but disallows IP-adjunction of wh-phrases, though we suspect that there may be a way to derive this as a theorem. More generally, we may assume that IP-adjunction in LF is equivalent to QR, which affects any expression that is quantificational in nature. On the other hand, if IP-adjunction happens in the Syntax, it is identified as a case of topicalization. That the subject *pictures of t* in *Who did pictures of t please you?* cannot have been IP-adjoined in Syntax presumably follows from the general impossibility of vacuous subject topicalization (*John, came, cf. footnote 3). In addition, certain restrictions exist which prevent "weak" NPs (Barwise and Cooper (1981)) that are in focus from being topicalized. Thus, while strong NPs like *every picture, most people,* and *that book* are topicalizable, weak NPs like *wh*-phrases are not:

(51) ?I believe that every picture, he has seen.
(52) ?I hope that most of the books, you will like.
(53) *Who said that which pictures, you took?
(54) *Who thinks that what, you will buy?

It is also well known that embedded topicalization structures are relatively marked (cf. Emonds (1976); also Hooper and Thompson (1973)). All these combine to reduce the possibilities of S-Structure IP-adjunction, and explain why *apparent* violations of island constraints are much more widespread in LF than in Syntax.

Let us turn now to examples pertaining to other island constraints. Consider the contrast shown in (55) (=(5)) and (56):

(55) a. *What color hair did you meet [many students with t]?
     b. Who met [many students with what color hair]?
(56) a. *Which table did you buy [the books on t]?
     b. Who bought [the books on which table]?

Each of the (a) sentences is ruled out by CED, since a *wh*-phrase has been extracted out of an adjunct modifier of the object NP, crossing two barriers (the adjunct PP node and the object NP node which inherits barrierhood from it). The grammaticality of the (b) sentences follows in the following way. In (56b), for example, the object NP *books on which table* may be IP-adjoined under QR. This creates a non-argument position that enables the PP *on which table* to be adjoined to it. In turn, the NP *which table* may be adjoined to this PP, and then moved into COMP:

(57)

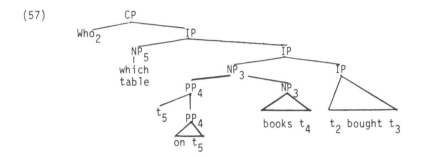

In postulating that PP_4 may undergo adjunction, we consider it a quantificational expression ranging over some appropriate PP meanings, e.g., {on this table, on that table, on the long table, etc.}. Similarly, in the case of a *wh* word occurring in an adjunct clause, as in *Who got angry because I talked to who?*, the entire *because*-clause may be IP-adjoined, as it ranges over, say, {because I talked to Mary, because I talked to Jane, etc.}. In the case of Wh Island violations, as in *Who remembers where we bought what*, the entire embedded clause may be adjoined to the matrix IP, as a quantificational expression ranging over interrogative propositions, {where we bought the book, where we bought the pencil, etc.}. Each time an island is IP-adjoined, it ceases to be an island for extraction. All other apparent island violations may be similarly accounted for, as well as the superiority violation represented by cases like *What did which man buy?*. In this last case, the NP *which man* may first be IP-adjoined as a QNP ranging over individual men. Then the determiner *which* can be taken as a wh-operator that ranges over Specifier meanings, e.g. {this, that, my, John's, etc.}. This determiner may be first adjoined to the QNP *which man* and then moved into COMP. The LF structure of *What did which man buy* is:[4]

---

[4] By taking the relevant wh-operator to be *which* rather than *which man*, we may give one the impression that we are subscribing to a theory of unrestrictive quantification of a type assumed in standard logic. But this is not the case. We still take *which* to be a restrictive quantifier that ranges over determiner meanings, i.e., "for which x, x a determiner meaning". This view is entirely consistent with the view of taking NPs as generalized quantifiers (cf. Barwise and Cooper (1981)). It is free from Higginbotham's (19??) criticism of Karttunen's *which bachelor is a man* as involving unrestrictive quantification.

(58) [CP [Which$_2$ what$_3$] did [IP [t$_2$ man]$_4$ [IP t$_4$ buy t$_3$]]].

We thus derive the Syntax/LF asymmetry with respect to Subjacency and CED from (a) the theory of adjunction within the *Barriers* framework, and (b) the existence of QR in LF vs. its absence in Syntax. The idea that certain constructions properly containing QNPs may be construed as QNPs themselves that are subject to QR may have some resemblance to the idea of pied-piping, but the two must be clearly distinguished. Pied-piping under *wh*-movement is severely limited to cases where *wh*-phrases occur as specifiers of NPs, presumably under a general principle governing featrure percolation in Syntax. On the other hand, the scope of QR is semantically defined, and it may affect any constituent that may be semantically construed as being quantificational. If our account is right, it enables us to maintain a strict correspondence hypothesis between Syntax and Logical Form, thereby providing very strong arguments for the existence of the latter as a level of syntactic representation. In addition, given the important role that QR plays in it, this account also lends further support to the existence of QR as a syntactic process of adjunction.

4. ECP Effects

A question that arises from this account of the LF/Syntax asymmetry is whether it preserves ECP effects in LF, preventing long-distance movement of an adjunct or subject whose trace needs to be antecedent-governed. We have assumed, following Huang (1982) and Lasnik and Saito (1984), that the following facts fall under the ECP:

(59) *Who did what please t?
(60) *Who remembers where we bought why?

These sentences can be ruled out in the following way. According to our current assumption, a *wh*-phrase in situ may first undergo QR before moving into COMP, then movement of *what* into COMP in (59) does not cross any barrier:

(61) [CP [what$_3$ who$_2$] did [IP t$_3$ [IP t$_3$ please t$_2$]]]?

The initial trace t$_3$ is antecedent-governed by the intermediate trace adjoined to IP. However, the intermediate trace is also subject to the ECP, as argued in Lasnik and Saito (1984). We can then rule out (61) on the basis of the fact that the intermediate trace is not antecedent-governed, given the COMP-indexing mechanism first proposed by Aoun, Hornstein and Sportiche (1981). Similarly for a sentence like *What did you buy why?*. Both subject and adjunct superiority effects thus continue to fall under the ECP, as before.

Turning to (60), the proposed account does not block the extraction of *why* from the embedded Wh island. This is because the entire island may be adjoined to the matrix IP, and ceases to be a barrier for the extraction of *why* into the matrix COMP. This situation is no different from what happens with complement wh-phrases in situ:

(62) Who remembers where we bought what?

Our account still allows us to distinguish between (60) and (62), however, along with other superiority facts. In the LF structure of (60), there is one intermediate trace of *why* that cannot be antecedent-governed, in particular the trace that it leaves behind when it moves into the matrix COMP (thereby doubly filling the latter). In the case of (62), the movement and adjunction of *what* does not need to leave an intermediate trace, since the initial trace is already lexically governed in accordance with the ECP, as reasoned in Lasnik and Saito (1984).

But this account is clearly insufficient to rule out singular questions in Chinese-Japanese where the relevant question phrase is an adjunct located in an island. For example, (63) is ungrammatical, and (64) cannot be interpreted as a direct question that seeks a value for *why*:

(63) *ni   xihuan [[Lisi weishenme piping   de]   shu]?
       you like   Lisi why   criticize REL book
       '*You like [books [that Lisi criticized why]]?

(64) ni   xiang-zhidao [shei weishenme bu lai]?
      you wonder   who why   not come
      'Who$_2$ do you wonder [why$_3$ [t$_2$ will not come t$_3$]]?

Not: 'Why do you wonder [who will not come t]?'

Take the intended but unavailable reading of (64) for example. Adjunction of the embedded clause *shei weishenme bu lai* to the matrix IP would void the barrierhood of the embedded question, enabling *weishenme* to move into the matrix COMP as much as it does *shei*. Furthermore, since the matrix COMP is empty at S-Structure, the intermediate trace left by *weishenme* must be antecedent-governed. This must be the case, or the following sentence would be wrongly predicted to be uninterpretatble as a direct *why*-question:

(65) ni   renwei [Zhangsan weishenme mei   lai]?
      you think   Zhangsan why   not come
      'Why do you think [Zhangsan didn't come t]?'

Note that the derivation of the LF-structures of (63)-(64) from their S-Structures in Chinese-Japanese is very much on a par with the derivation of S-Structures from D-Structures for corresponding sentences in English:

(66) *Why$_2$ did you wonder [what I bought t$_2$]?
(67) *How$_2$ did you read [the book that John wrote t$_2$]?

As Lasnik and Saito (1984) and Chomsky (1986) show, the crucial offending trace in these structures is the (last) intermediate trace left behind when *why* or *how* gets out of a given island, not the one immediately before it enters the matrix COMP. That is, in the representation (68) for (66), the offending trace is t'$_2$, not the VP-adjoined t"$_2$.

(68) [$_{CP}$ why$_2$ did you [$_{VP}$ t"$_2$ [$_{VP}$ wonder [$_{CP}$ what t'$_2$ I bought t$_2$]]]]

Since we have assumed that the adjunction of an island voids the latter's barrierhood, the ECP effects of sentences like (63)-(64) in Chinese-Japanese cannot be derived.

One solution to this dilemma, we would like to suggest, is to adopt an idea of May (1985), who argues that in an adjunction structure, the top segment of the node consisting of n segments is an absolute barrier to government. (At the same time, we continue to assume with Chomsky that only complete categories (nodes with all segments included) constitute barriers for Subjacency and CED--which is reminiscent of May's (1977) suggestion that Chomsky-adjoined nodes don't count as bounding nodes.)   This requires a reformulation of "government". Chomsky discusses two definitions of government, one in terms of domination and one in terms of "exclusion", with respect to the adjunction structure (69), and considers whether α is a possible governor for β, but simply assumes that α is possible governee for δ.

(69) $\ldots \delta \ldots [_\gamma \ldots \alpha \ldots [_\gamma \ldots \beta \ldots]\,]$

What we need is a definition that excludes α as a possible governee:

(70) α governs β iff α m-commands β and for every γ, γ a barrier, if γ does not exclude β then γ does not exclude α.

The immediate result of (70) is that only those categories that are lexically governed (or theta-governed) can undergo successive-cyclic adjunction, but those whose traces need to be antecedent-governed cannot. Since adjunct traces require antecedent-government, all intermediate traces left by successive movement or adjunction are required. An intermediate trace left at an adjunction site, however, cannot be antecedent governed because the node-segment that dominates it blocks government from outside. As an example, consider again (64). Recall that the only way to void the barrierhood of the Wh Island is for the embedded clause to be adjoined to the matrix IP and for the wide scope wh-phrase to adjoin to this embedded clause before moving into the matrix COMP. The LF-structure for the Chinese sentence (64) under the why-question reading would look like (71):

(71) $[_{CP}$ why$_2$ $[_{IP}$ $[_{CP}$ t"$_2$ $[_{CP}$ who t$_2$ will not come$]]_3$ $[_{IP}$ y o u wonder t$_3]]]$

But in this structure the intermediate trace (t"$_2$) of why is not antecedent governed. The unavailability of a reading represented by (71) thus follows as a consequence of the ECP. (The lack of such effects with lexically-governed wh-phrases follows, again, from the fact that their successive adjunction need not leave a trace behind.)

The definition (70) is motivated not only by ECP effects in LF, but is also needed to block overt adjunct extraction from A'-phrases. Recall that sentences like (40b) are quite acceptable:

(40b)   ?Who$_2$ do you wonder [[which pictures of t$_2$][are on sale]]?

Extraction of an adjunct from an A'-phrase in COMP is completely ill-formed, however:

(72) *[On which table]$_2$ do you wonder [[which books t$_2$] [I will buy]]?

The distinction between (40b) and (72) does not follow from Chomsky's system (since successive adjunction of *on which table* would cross no barrier), but is an immediate result of the definition (70).[5]

5. Some Consequences

The redefinition of government suggested in (70) will have wide reaching consequences which we cannot address in full. Here we briefly discuss two of them.
The first is that there is no successive VP-adjunction, at least in cases where adjuncts are moved. As Chomsky notes, successive VP-adjunction of adjuncts is necessary to allow their (apparent) long-distance extraction, as evidenced by sentences like (73):

(73) How$_2$ do you think [t'$_2$ [John fixed the car t$_2$]?

Under the assumption that VP is not L-marked, it is by definition a Blocking Category and a Barrier. If VP adjunction cannot take place, the matrix VP would block antecedent-government of t'$_2$ by how$_2$, and (73) would be incorrectly ruled out by the ECP. Our proposed account, if correct, will force us to abandon this account of (73). An idea is to simply assume that VP is not a BC (nor a barrier) because it is L-marked. Chomsky points out that VP must be theta-governed (by I), since VP-movement across a Wh Island produces only weak Subjacency effects:

(74) Fix the car, I wonder whether he will t.

It is possible that the trace of VP is actually L-marked (or lexically governed), and not just theta-governed, and that actually L-marking is required (when antecedent-government does not obtain), not the weaker theta-government. If so, the requirement of do-support when the I^0 is non-lexical immediately falls out under the ECP:

---

[5] The complete ungrammaticality of the following sentence also suggests the presence of a CED effect:
(i)   *Which table do you wonder which books on t I will buy?
Under the assumption that the A'-phrase *which books on which table* is not a barrier, extraction of *which table* would cross only one barrier, the adjunct PP *on which table*. This is not a satisfactory result since (i) is at least as bad as any 2-subjacent or longer extraction. Perhaps the A'-phrase *which books on which table*, though not an inherent barrier, is a barrier by inheritance. To achieve this, we need to prevent adjunction of *which table* to this A'-phrase, and employ Chomsky's definition of government for cases that involve barriers by inheritance. On the other hand, this may be seen as evidence that CED should not be subsumed under Subjacency as Chomsky as suggested. Crossing one CED island seems sufficient to produce bad enough results, though "pure" 1-subjacent effects seem quite weak (e.g., crossing one Wh island, or crossing noun phrase complements). See text below for more discussion.

(75) Fix the car, I wonder whether he *(did) t.

To execute the idea that VP is L-marked, we might hypothesize that I^o is lexical. (Since it does not theta-govern the subject, the subject is still a BC.) In a finite clause, if the IP contains an auxiliary, the inflected Aux is lexical and it L-marks the VP. If there is no auxiliary, V raises into I to support the non-lexical I^o and lexicalizes the latter. (The V-trace is antecedent-governed, the VP being now L-marked by the inflected V, as reasoned by Chomsky.) In a gerundive or participial clause, V raises into INFL to support -*ing*, and in an infinitive *to* is a lexical I^o (it is sufficient to lexically govern a VP trace). In all cases, then, VPs are L-marked. (If VP-movement takes place, do support (instead of V-raising) is obligatory. V-raising bleeds the process of VP-movement, because a moved VP would contain a V-trace not bound or governed by its antecedent.)

A problem with this view noted by Chomsky is how one can rule out non-local movement of an (uninflected) V from VP into C^o.

(74) *[CP What$_2$ [C' eat$_3$ [IP you will [VP t$_3$ t$_2$]]]]?

The problem is that the trace of the verb, t$_3$, is not separated from its antecedent by any barrier, if VP is L-marked. If VP is not L-marked, then both VP and IP will be barriers, and (74) is ruled out by the ECP, as desired. However, (74) can be ruled out by ECP if we adopt the Minimality Condition. If VP is not L-marked, then the INFL *will* is a closer governor of t$_3$, and under the MC the I' is a barrier even though it is not a maximal projection nor a BC. Unlike Chomsky, who assumes that the I^o is not a closer governor that satisfies the Minimality Condition, we may assume that it does satisfy the MC as a governor of the trace t$_3$, though not its proper governor. (We might say that ECP requires either L-marking (not just theta-government) or antecedent government. The INFL *will* in (74) governs VP and its subject, as well as the trace t$_3$. But it properly governs only the VP (by L-marking it, as a lexical category that theta-governs VP). Since it does not theta-govern the trace t$_3$, it does not L-mark it; and since it also does not antecedent-govern the trace, the trace is not properly governed.)

If the idea of analyzing VP as being L-marked can be worked out successfully, this in fact will simplify matters considerably. Note that unlike successive COMP-movement and IP-adjunction, which have considerable overt, independent evidence, the evidence for successive VP-adjunction seems to be completely theory-internal (at least in English), and one may wonder why there is no similar overt evidence for successive VP-adjunction. Especially if IP-adjunction is excluded under *wh*-movement, there is even more reason to ask why VP-adjunction should be allowed. These questions do not arise, of course, once VP is analyzed as being L-marked.

Another consequence of our proposal is that the theory of government and the theory of movement can only be partially unified under a theory of barriers, but the unification is not complete. Only a full category, one that dominates all of its segments, is a barrier for movement, but the top segment of a barrier alone blocks government. There is something suggesting that this might not be a bad result. Recall that the theory of barriers ties together the two conditions Subjacency and CED. But it seems that Subjacency effects are weaker than CED effects, even when they involve the same number of barriers crossed. For example, Wh islands and noun phrase complement constructions permit extraction of the following kind to some degree:

(75) ?This is the book which I wonder who wrote.
(76) ?This is the book that John made the claim that he wrote.

However, it seems that crossing a single barrier in a CED violation seems to produce much worse results:

(77) *Which table do you wonder which books on t John will buy?

Recall that since *which books on t* is in an A'-position, it is a possible adjunction site. Thus the extraction of *which table* need only cross one barrier, the PP containing *on t*, but the result is clearly worse than (75)-(76).

Chomsky (1986) also notes that the Minimality Condition is relevant to the definition of a barrier to government, but not of a barrier for movement. Like (70), this also has the effect of further restricting movement of non-L-marked elements.

Our discussion of these consequences is obviously incomplete, though the issue is clear. If these turn out to be desirable consequences, then the account for the Syntax/LF asymmetry proposed above will receive considerable support. The existence of LF will be further supported, also, as a result of the possibility of maintaining a strict correspondence hypothesis between Syntax and LF. If these turn out to be undesirable consequences, it seems we must hold on to the weaker correspondence and allow the two components of grammar to be different with respect to the theory of bounding.

References

Aoun, Hornstein, and Sportiche. 1981. Some Aspects of Wide Scope Quantification. JLR 1.
Barwise and Cooper. l98l. Generalized Quantifiers and Natural Language. L & P 4.2.
Bowers. 1987. Extended x-bar theory, the ECP, and the Left Branch Condition. WCFL 6, Arizona.
Choe. 1987. LF Movement and Pied Piping LI l8.2.
Chomsky. 1986. Barriers. MIT Press.
Emonds. 1976. A Transformational Approach to English Syntax. Academic Press.
Huang. 1982. Logical Relations in Chinese and the Theory of Grammar. MIT diss.
Kartunnen. 1977. Syntax and Semantics of Questions. L & P 1.
Lasnik and Saito. 1984. On the Nature of Proper Government. LI 15.2.
Lasnik and Saito. Move @ . (forthcoming).
Longobardi. l987. In defense of the Correspondence Hypothesis. In Huang and May, Logical Structure and Linguistic Structure. Reidel.
May. 1977. The Grammar of Quantification. MIT diss.
May. 1985. Logical Form. MIT Press.
Nishigauchi. 1985. Japanese LF: In Defense of Subjacency. Kobe mimeo.
Pesetsky. 1987. wh-in-situ: Movement and Unselective Binding. In The Representation of Indefiniteness, Reuland and ter Meulen, eds. MIT Press
Hooper and Thompson. 1973. On the applicability of Root Transformations. LI 4.4.
Torrego. 1985. On Empty Categories in Nominals. UMass Boston mimeo.

The above work was supported by NSF Grant #BNS - 8519578 (Robert May, Principal Investigator.)

Passives, Verb Raising, and the Affectedness Condition

Nobuko Hasegawa
University of Massachusetts, Amherst

1. Introduction

One of the main issues on the passive construction is how to capture the relationship between actives and passives, in particular, how to capture it by maintaining the working hypotheses such as those in (1).

(1) a. D-Structure is a pure representation of argument structure.
   b. The linking of thematic roles to grammatical relations is unique.

(Pesetsky (1987))

In what follows, I will argue that passives are the same as actives except that they involve a passive morpheme; thus, these hypotheses are trivially satisfied.

The second issue is how to account for passives in different languages without losing generality. I will take up below passives in English, German/Dutch, and Japanese and argue that differences in these languages follow mainly from the parameterization of a categorical feature on passive morphemes; [+N] for English and German/Dutch and [-N] for Japanese.

It is often said that passives exhibit the characteristics in (2), which certainly hold in English.

(2) a. A passive morpheme is attached to an 'unmarked' (active) verb.
   b. The 'unmarked' (active) verb is a transitive verb.
   c. [NP,S] does not receive a θ-role.
   d. [NP,VP] does not receive Case within VP.
   e. An active object shows up as a passive subject.

Obviously, not all of these characteristics are shared by passives of other languages. For example, in German/Dutch, as (3) shows, pure intransitives (intransitives with a subject (external) θ-role) can be passivized.

(3) a. Es wurde getanzt.   (German)
   b. Ir wordt gedanst.   (Dutch)
      it was   danced
      'There was dancing.'

And in Japanese, only the so-called pure passive (4b) exhibits the characteristics of the English passive, but the passive morpheme -(r)are can attach to any type of predicate in adversity passives (5) and in honorific passives (6).[1] Furthermore, no change in argument structure or in Case assignment is observed in honorific passives (6). Thus, what seems strictly observed across languages is only (2a), the existence of a passive morpheme.

(4) a. Sensei-ga   kodomo-o   sikat-ta.   (active)
      teacher-nom.   child-acc   scold-past
      'The teacher scolded the child.'

    b. Kodomo-ga sensei-ni   sikar-<u>are</u>-ta.   (pure passive)
       child-nom teacher-by scold-pass.-past
       'The child was scolded by the teacher.'

(5) (Adversity Passive)
    a. John-ga   sensei-ni   kodomo-o sikar-<u>are</u>-ta.   (tr.)
       -nom teacher-by child-acc scold-pass.-past
       'John was affected by the teacher's scolding (his) child.'

    b. John-ga   ame-ni   hur-<u>are</u>-ta.   (intr.)
       -nom.   rain-dat. fall-pass.-past
       'John suffered from rain's falling.'

(6) (Honorific Passive)
    a. Sensei-ga   kodomo-o sikar-<u>are</u>-ta.   (tr.)
       teacher-nom child-acc   scold-hon.-past
       'The teacher scolded (honorific) the child.'

    b. Sensei-ga   tat-are-ta.   (pure intr.)
       -nom.   stand-pass.-past
       'The teacher stood up (hon.)'

    c. Sensei-ga   kaze-de   taor(e)-(r)are-ta.   (ergative intr.)
       -nom cold-with collapse-pass.-past
       'The teacher came down (hon.) with a cold'

    The claim I would like to advance is that whatever process the passive construction may involve, it is derived from the basic property (2a), the presence of the passive morpheme that attaches to an 'unmarked' or 'base' verb. Recent proposals on passives, such as Borer (1984), Jaeggli (1986), Roberts (1985), etc., in fact, all suggest this direction. One way to express this generalization, while maintaining the working hypotheses in (1) in a straightforward fashion is to consider the active sentence to be a complement of a passive morpheme. Such an analysis has, in fact, been presented in Japanese syntax.[2] Details aside, deep structures such as (7) have been presented for three types of passives.[3]

(7) a. [(kodomo) [$_S$ sensei kodomo sikar] (r)are-ta] (for (4b))
    b. [John [$_S$ sensei kodomo sikar] (r)are-ta]   (for (5a))
    c. [(sensei) [$_S$ sensei kodomo sikar] (r)are-ta] (for (6a))

Although I do not subscribe to the exact details of these previous analyses, the conception behind them is appealing: i.e., the working hypotheses in (1) are observed without any extra stipulation. As the deep structures in (7) now stand, however, various technical problems arise, since the embedded sentence is obviously 'defective' and it is more like a verb plus all of its arguments (cf. N. Hasegawa (1980)). What -(r)are really subcategorizes for is not a sentence (IP or CP) but rather a VP in the sense of Fukui (1986), Kitagawa (1986), Kuroda (1986), Sportiche (1986), etc., who advocate that a VP is a category in which a thematic complex is completed; i.e., a subject (external) argument is generated under VP along with internal arguments. In such a framework, an active sentence ordinarily involves the raising of the subject of VP to SPEC of IP, so that the subject receives structural Case (nominative), which is shown in (8).

(8) a. John killed Mary.
    b. [$_{IP}$ e [INFL [$_{VP}$ John kill Mary]]]
    c. [$_{IP}$ John$_i$ [INFL [$_{VP}$ t_i kill Mary]]]

2. A Verb Raising Analysis of the Passive

Given the assumption that a VP is thematically complete, the passive can now be characterized as (9).

(9) a. The passive predicate selects a VP as its complement.
    b. The passive predicate requires the Verb-Incorporation, Verb Raising (VR), an instance of Head-to-Head movement (=Move e).[4]

Then, the passive sentence (10a) has the D-Structure (10b).[5]

(10) a. Mary was killed by John.
     b. [$_{IP}$ e [$_{I'}$ was [$_{VP1}$ e [$_V$ -en] [$_{VP2}$ John kill Mary]]]]

Note that VP1 in (10b) is identical to the VP in (8a), the active sentence; thus, the Hypotheses in (1) are straightforwardly maintained. Now, VR applies to kill, moving it to the higher predicate -en, giving rise to (11).

(11) [$_{IP}$ e [$_{I'}$ was [$_{VP1}$ e [$_V$ kill$_i$-en] [$_{VP2}$ John t_i Mary]]]]

This movement satisfies the Head Movement Constraint of Travis (1984).[6]

(12) the Head Movement Constraint
     Movement of Head is restricted to the head that subcategorizes it.
                    (Cf. Travis (1984), Chomsky (1986))

The verb in VP2 moved away, so that its object no longer receives Case from it. Consequently, it must move to the position where structural Case is available, namely the SPEC of IP. Mary moves first to the SPEC of VP1: the subject position of -en, which is θ′ but not a Case-marked position, and then to the SPEC of IP.

(13) [$_{IP}$ Mary$_j$ [$_{I'}$ was [$_{VP1}$ t_j [$_V$ kill$_i$-en] [$_{VP2}$ John t_i t_j]]]]
                                                              (by)

In this way, the passive properties (2d) and (2e) naturally follow without altering the Case-assigning property or argument structure of a verb. Then, the problem here is how a subject θ-role is represented in passives. In my analysis, a subject θ-role is assumed to be given to the SPEC of VP at D-Structure for both actives and passives. At S-Structure, it shows up in the SPEC of IP in actives, and in passives, I would like to argue, it appears in the form of by phrase. That is, by is inserted in the environment (13) by a general convention. I assume the following system that rules the θ-role assignment and Case realization of arguments.[7]

(14) **The θ-Marking Convention:**
  a. θ-Marking: *A* θ-marks *B* if *B* is dominated by *A*'s projection (*B* is m-commanded by *A*) and is sister to *A* or to *A*'s projection.
  b. Direct Argument (DA): an NP that is θ-marked by V⁰.
  c. Indirect Argument (IA): an NP that is θ-marked through some other θ-role assigner, such as P (including, to, for, by, etc), which transmits a θ-role of V⁰ to the NP. This P can be null at D-Structure, but may be spelled out later if it meets (15) below.

(15) **The Case Assignment Convention:**
    A θ-role assigner (P) for an IA assigns Case to it (and is spelled out as P) if there is no other way for an IA to receive structural Case.

What is particularly relevant here is that the subject NP is an IA, being indirectly θ-marked by an (empty) P, which will not be spelled out, unless it also functions as a Case-assigner. Let us assume that the Case-assignment by an (empty) P is an option in the last resort. In ordinary cases, a subject NP is raised to the SPEC of IP. When this position is unavailable, a P, θ-assigner, for the subject is spelled out; as by, if the θ-role involved is Agent. In passives, the SPEC of IP is taken up by an object NP (DA), which does not have any other means to receive Case, since its governing verb has moved away. Consequently, the subject NP cannot move up there and the last-resort option, the spell-out of by, is called for to assign Case to it.

3. Parameters
3.1 the Passive Predicate: [+N] vs. [-N]
    This VR analysis, in principle, makes the occurrence of the passive predicate general. Any VP, regardless of types of verbs, must be able to be a complement of the passive predicate, which in fact is the case in Japanese as discussed in Section 1. Then, the questions that immediately arise are those in (16).

(16) a. Why is the English passive predicate -en combined only with transitive verbs?
   b. Why can the German/Dutch passive predicate be combined with either transitives or pure-intransitives; but not with ergative-intransitives or seem-type verbs? Or why does the German passive involve only the predicates that assign a subject θ-role?
                                                        (cf. Jaeggli (1986))
   c. Why can the Japanese passive predicate -(r)are be combined with any type of verb?

    Answers to these questions lie in the differences in categorical features of passive predicates. I consider the Japanese passive predicate -(r)are as [-N] (and [+V], namely a verb) because it behaves just like a verb in many respects. The passive predicate in English and German/ Dutch, on the other hand, is more like an adjective and is [+N]. The basic parameter of the passive construction is (17).

(17) Parameter on passive predicates
A passive predicate is either [+N] or [-N]
  a. [+N] : English, German/Dutch
  b. [-N] : Japanese

Let us first discuss [+N] passive predicates--English and German/Dutch cases. One thing that naturally follows from this [+N] feature is that it is to be Case-marked. This is basically the same as the recent claims by Borer (1984), Jaeggli (1986), and Roberts (1985) that -en absorbs Case. The obligatory Case-assignment on a passive [+N] predicate immediately provides an answer to the question (16a). The only way for the passive predicate to receive Case is from the verb that has just been raised by VR; hence, the raised predicate must be transitive. If VR does not apply or the raised predicate does not assign Case to the passive predicate, the structure must be ruled out because -en cannot receive Case.

As for (16b), I would like to assume, following Jaeggli's proposal, that the Case-marking property of verbs can be parameterized so that pure-intransitives in German can assign Case, while those in English cannot. We may say that if a verb assigns Objective Case at all, it must at least select a subject argument. I.e., the selection of a subject argument is a necessary condition for a verb's Case assigning property. Languages may be parameterized as to whether it is a sufficient condition for Case assignment. In German/Dutch, it is; while it is insufficient in English. The presence of an object in addition to a subject argument is required for a verb in English to assume the Case assigning property. I propose the parameter (18).[8]

(18) Parameter on Verb's Case Assigning Property
  a. Necessary condition on Case assigning property (universal)
      = presence of a subject θ-role.
  b. Auxiliary condition (language particular)
      = presence of an object θ-role (Direct Argument)
      [+] : English
      [-] : German/Dutch

This parameter, which I assume is independent of passives, explains why sentences like 'it was danced' are allowed in German/Dutch, but not in English. I.e., In German/Dutch, the passive morpheme can be Case-marked by the verb, dance, which was raised from the lower VP. Furthermore, this explains why even in German/Dutch ergative-intransitives or the seem type of predicate cannot be passivized.

(19) a. *Es wird gewachsen
        it is   grown

    b. *Es wird geschienen dass [$_S$ . . .]
        it is   seemed   that   (Roberts (1985))

    c. *In dit weeshuis wordt er door de kinderen erg snel gegroeid.
        in this orphanage is   it by the children very fast grown
                                                  (Jaeggli (1986:593))

These predicates do not have a subject θ-role and they cannot assign Case to the passive predicate.

3.2. Japanese

Let us now consider the last question (16c). The answer to it lies in the parameter (17): the Japanese passive predicate -(r)are is [-N]. The natural assumption that follows from it is that -(r)are does not require Case and it does not have to be combined with a predicate that assigns Case. Hence, any type of verb can be passivized; not only transitives but also intransitives of both pure and ergative types are expected to be passivized. Thus, we obtain (20), to which VR applies, deriving (21).

(20) a. transitive

$[_{IP}$ e $[_{VP}$ e $[_{VP}$ sensei   kodomo sikar] (r)are] ta]
              teacher child   scold pass. past

  b. intransitive (pure)

$[_{IP}$ e $[_{VP}$ e $[_{VP}$ sensei   tat] (r)are] ta]
              teacher stand pass. past

  c. intransitive (ergative)

$[_{IP}$ e $[_{VP}$ e $[_{VP}$ sensei kaze-de   taor(e)] (r)are] ta]
              teacher cold-with collapse pass. past

(21) a. $[_{IP}$ e $[_{VP}$ e $[_{VP}$ sensei   kodomo t_i] sikar$_i$-(r)are] ta]
   b. $[_{IP}$ e $[_{VP}$ e $[_{VP}$ sensei t_i] tat$_i$-(r)are] ta]
   c. $[_{IP}$ e $[_{VP}$ e $[_{VP}$ sensei   kaze-de t_i] taor(e)$_i$-(r)are] ta]

In (21a), since the verb sikar 'scold' has moved away to the higher predicate -(r)are by VR, the object kodomo 'child' must move to the position where it receives Case, namely the SPEC of IP. The VP subject, sensei 'teacher' is Case-marked by an empty P that is spelled out as ni-(yotte). The outcome is (22a); exactly the same derivation as the English passive (13). In (21b) and (21c), where intransitives occur, there is no object that requires Case. Hence, the subject can move to the Case marked position, the SPEC of IP; suppressing the last-resort option of spelling-out of an empty P.[9]

(22) a. $[_{IP}$ kodomo$_j$-GA $[_{VP}$ t_j $[_{VP}$ sensei-ni(yotte) t_j t_i] sikar$_i$-
                                     (r)are] ta]
    a'. Kodomo-ga sensei-ni(yotte) sikar-are-ta. (Pure) (=(4b))
    'The child was scolded by the teacher.'

   b. $[_{IP}$ sensei$_j$-GA $[_{VP}$ t_j $[_{VP}$ t_j t_i] tat$_i$-(r)are] ta]
    b'. Sensei-ga tat-are-ta   (Honorific) (=(6b))
    'The teacher stood up (hon.)'

   c. $[_{IP}$ sensei$_j$-GA $[_{VP}$ t_j $[_{VP}$ t_j kaze-de t_i] taor(e)$_i$-(r)are] ta]
    c'. Sensei-ga kaze-de taor(e)-(r)are-ta   (Honorific) (=(6c))
    'The teacher came down (hon.) with a cold.'

This gives rise to a pure passive in (22a) and honorific passives in (22b) and (22c). Although we have just seen the cases where VR applies in Syntax (i.e., before or at S-Structure), without Case requirement on

-(r)are, VR does not even have to apply in Syntax, as long as
morphological verb incorporation takes place in PF.

If VR does not apply in Syntax, the embedded transitive verb in
(20a) governs its object and assigns the objective Case (O) to it, making
the SPEC of IP available for a VP subject to move to. This gives rise to the
S-Structures in (23) instead of those in (22).[10]

(23) a. [$_{IP}$ sensei$_i$-GA [$_{VP}$ t$_i$ [$_{VP}$ t$_i$ kodomo-O sikar] (r)are] ta]
    a'. Sensei-ga kodomo-o sikar-are-ta.   (Honorific) (=(6a))
    'The teacher scolded (hon.) the child.'

    b. [$_{IP}$ sensei$_i$-GA [$_{VP}$ t$_i$ [$_{VP}$ t$_i$ tat] (r)are] ta]
    b'. Sensei-ga tat-are-ta   (Honorific) (=(6b))
    'The teacher stood up (hon.)'

    c. [$_{IP}$ sensei$_i$-GA [$_{VP}$ t$_i$ [$_{VP}$ t$_i$ kaze-de taor(e)] (r)are] ta]
    c'. Sensei-ga kaze-de taor(e)-(r)are-ta   (Honorific) (=(6c))
    'The teacher came down (hon.) with a cold.'

Thus, the existence of pure and honorific passives in Japanese naturally
follow from the feature [-N] on the passive predicate -(r)are.

We still have not accounted for adversity passives (cf. (5)). Here, I
would like to employ another assumption that [-N] passive predicates can
be either intransitive (without a subject θ-role) as has been assumed so
far for passive predicates in general or transitive (with a subject θ-role).
In view of the presence of various transitive/intransitive pairs in
language, it is not surprising to find a similar pair with respect to the
passive predicate, -(r)are, since it is a verb after all. Then, along with
the D-Structures in (20), those in (24) must be possible, where the SPEC of
the VP whose head is -(r)are is occupied by a subject argument, John.[11]

(24) a. [$_{IP}$ e [$_{VP}$ John [$_{VP}$ sensei   kodomo sikar] (r)are] ta]
                teacher   child   scold pass. past

    b. [$_{IP}$ e [$_{VP}$ John [$_{VP}$ sensei tat]   (r)are] ta]
                teacher stand-up pass.   past

When an embedded verb is intransitive, (24b), it does not matter whether
VR applies in syntax or PF. There is no object that requires Case in the
complement VP. The only operation involved in such a case is to raise the
subject of -(r)are to the SPEC of IP. This is shown in (25b) and (26b)
below.[12]

When a transitive is embedded as in (24a), where VR applies affects
grammaticality. If VR applies in Syntax, a complement verb moves to the
higher predicate -(r)are, leaving the object NP Caseless. Unlike the case
of intransitive -(r)are in (20), this object NP cannot move anywhere,
because the SPEC of the higher VP is occupied by a θ-role bearing item. It
cannot move directly to the SPEC of IP either, for the same reason the
lower subject in (24b) cannot; namely, it is too far away (cf. fn. 11).
Thus, if VR applies to (24a) in Syntax, the sentence is ruled out by Case
Theory. If VR applies in PF as in (26a), on the other hand, the object of
the transitive verb in the lowest VP can receive Case from its governing

verb, and the subject of $-(r)are$, John, moves to the SPEC of IP, receiving *GA*, and the subject of the lower VP receives *NI* (cf. fn. 12).[13]

(25) S-Structures (VR in Syntax)
  a. *$[_{IP}$ John$_j$-*GA* $[_{VP}$ t_j $[_{VP}$ sensei-*NI*   kodomo t_i] sikar$_i$-
                                   [no Case] $(r)are$] ta]

  b. $[_{IP}$ John$_j$-*GA* $[_{VP}$ t_j $[_{VP}$ sensei-*NI* t_i] tat$_i$-$(r)are$] ta]
  b´. John-ga sensei-ni tat-$(r)are$-ta.   (Adversity)
     'John was affected by the teacher's standing up.'

(26) S-Structures (VR in PF)
  a. $[_{IP}$ John$_i$-*GA* $[_{VP}$ t_i $[_{VP}$ sensei-*NI* kodomo-*O* sikar] $(r)are$] ta]
  a´. John-ga sensei-ni kodomo-o sikar-are-ta. (Adversity)   (=(5a))
     'John was affected by the teacher's scolding (his) child.'

  b. $[_{IP}$ John$_i$-*GA* $[_{VP}$ t_i $[_{VP}$ sensei-*NI* tat] $(r)are$] ta]
  b´. John-ga sensei-ni tat-$(r)are$-ta.   (Adversity)
     'John was affected by the teacher's standing up.'

In short, we obtain the paradigm in (27) and (28) in Japanese.

(27) Intransitive $-(r)are$ (without a subject θ-role)
     VR in Syntax   Transitive in VP --- Pure Passive
                      Intransitive in VP --- Honorific Passive
     VR in PF   Transitive in VP --- Honorific Passive
                      Intransitive in VP --- Honorific Passive

(28) Transitive $-(r)are$ (with a subject θ-role)
     VR in Syntax   Transitive in VP --- *(no Case on object)
                      Intransitive in VP --- Adversity Passive
     VR in PF   Transitive in VP --- Adversity Passive
                      Intransitive in VP --- Adversity Passive

     Where VP applies has bearings on the selection of a governing category for an item inside the lowest VP. Let us consider the S-Structures in (29): English passive (29a), pure passive (29b) (in which VR has applied), and adversity passive (29c) (in which VR has not applied).

(29) a. $[_{IP}$ Mary$_j$ $[_{I'}$ was $[_{VP1}$ t_j $[_V$ kill$_i$-en] $[_{VP2}$ (by) John t_i t_j]]]]
    b. $[_{IP}$ kodomo$_j$-*GA* $[_{VP1}$ t_j $[_{VP2}$ sensei-ni(yotte) t_j t_i]
                                     sikar$_i$-$(r)are$] ta]
    c. $[_{IP}$ John$_i$-*GA* $[_{VP1}$ t_i $[_{VP2}$ sensei-*NI* kodomo-*O* sikar] $(r)are$] ta]

The question here is whether the lowest VP (=VP2) counts as the governing category (GC) for the NP trace in object position, t_j in (29a) and (29b). If so, it must be bound by John in (29a) and by sensei in (29b); which is obviously not the case. Thus, what we want as GC for t_j is the higher VP (=VP1)(or IP). We can obtain this result naturally, if we assume that the GC for α is the minimal complete functional complex that contains (the entire chain of) the governor, the subject, and α. Since the governor for t_j has moved away from VP2, this VP cannot be the GC in (29a) and (29b).

Hence, the GC is a higher VP (VP1) (or IP). If VR does not apply, as in (29c), on the other hand, the GC for the object of the lowest VP is that VP, since it is a complete functional complex (involving, the governor, the subject, and itself). This difference is responsible for the well-known fact about the Japanese reflexive zibun. Namely, zibun in pure passives cannot be bound by the 'former' or 'logical' subject, but by the 'new' subject or the 'former' object. In contrast, zibun in adversity passives can be bound by both 'subjects'. The contrast often cited is (30) vs. (31).

(30)a. John-ga Mary-ni(yotte) zibun-no heya-de sikar-are-ta.
      -nom   -by   self -'s room-in scold-pass.-past
    'John$_i$ was scolded by Mary$_j$ in self$_{i/*j}$'s room.'

b.[$_{IP}$ John$_j$-ga [$_{VP1}$ t$_j$ [$_{VP2}$ Mary-ni(yotte) zibun-no heya-de t$_j$ t$_i$]
                                        sikar$_i$-(r)are-ta]]]

(31)a. John-ga Mary-ni zibun-no heya-de sigoto=s-are-ta.
      -nom   -by self -'s room-in work -pass.-past
    'John$_i$ was affected by Mary$_j$'s working in self$_{i/j}$'s room.'

h [$_{IP}$ John$_j$-ga [$_{VP1}$ t$_j$ [$_{VP2}$ Mary-ni zibun-no heya-de sigoto=s]
                                       (r)are-ta]]]

In (30), pure passive, zibun is bound only by John, while in (31), adversity passive, it is ambiguous between John and Mary. In (30), as shown in (29b) the GC is either VP1 or IP. In (31a), on the other hand, VR has not applied yet, and its GC is the lower VP, VP2. Since zibun is to be bound by the subject of the GC or any subject higher than that, either John or Mary can be an antecedent for zibun in (31). In (30), on the other hand, John is the only subject qualified to be a binder.[14]

3.3. Agent Phrase: Implicit Argument

    In this VR analysis of passives, the property (2c); i.e., a subject argument is not present, cannot be considered as a real characteristic. As argued in Section 2 above, a subject argument is present at D-Structure even in passives, which is realized as an agent phrase at S-Structure. Then, the question to ask is how come an agent phrase (subject argument) can be null in passives, if the Projection Principle is to be met. A proper answer to this question will automatically account for the contrast often cited between passives and middles with respect to the presence or absence of an 'implicit' argument as a controller of a purpose clause or a subject-oriented adverb shown in (32).

(32) a. The book was sold to make money.
      b. *The book sold to make money.

      c. The ship was sunk deliberately.
      d. *The ship sank deliberately.

Since I assume that a subject argument is present even in passives, its non-presence in (32a/c) must be due to the presence of an empty category (EC) there. What kind of EC can it be then? This position, the SPEC of VP, is a position governed by a higher predicate; namely, the passive predicate or the verb just moved by VR (or both), and PRO should not be allowed.[15] For the reasons rather apparent (cf. Jaeggli (1986)), neither NP-trace (anaphor) nor variable is possible there (in English). Contrary to Jaeggli's (1986) claim, however, pro is to be possible as long as it meets the condition on the occurrence of pro; namely, (33).

(33) A non-anaphoric pronominal EC is allowed if it is locally governed and identified by a [+N] feature complex, such as AGR.

In ordinary pro-drop languages, this condition is met between an IP-subject and INFL. Now in the passive construction, if a VP-subject is in fact occupied by pro, it must be identified by its governor, which is a passive predicate in this case. I have already argued that passive predicates may be [+N], at least in English and German/Dutch; and thus, it is natural for it to be equipped with a feature complex. This is the same line of conception as Roberts (1985), who considers the passive -en as a clitic. We can set up a parameter as to what kind of feature complex [+N] passive predicates can assume. A parameter I would like to suggest is (34), which I draw on Jaeggli's (1986) insightful discussion.

(34) Parameter on a feature complex of [+N] passive predicates
   a. It agrees with what is expressed in an Agent phrase.
                                             (e.g. Kota and Papauan)
   b. It has a fixed 'arbitrary' or 'impersonal' complex; hence, the presence of an overt agent phrase is disallowed (e.g. Polish)
   c. It is virtually unspecified and gets along with any type of agent phrase, though the default is 'arbitrary' or 'impersonal'.

English and German/Dutch are obviously of the third type. The overt presence of an agent phrase overrides the 'impersonal' or 'arbitrary' feature of a feature complex of passive predicates; however, if pro shows up in the SPEC of VP, it can be properly identified as 'impersonal' or 'arbitrary' by its governor, a passive predicate.
   When a passive predicate is [-N], which I have just argued to be the case in Japanese, it cannot serve as identifier. Then, such a language exhibits either one of the following: (i) it cannot have a pro agent (with arbitrary or impersonal reading) but requires the presence of a lexical agent phrase; (ii) it has an independently motivated system of allowing an EC that serves as 'implicit argument'. Japanese falls in the second type. I argued elsewhere (N. Hasegawa (1984/85)), following Huang (1985), that Japanese allows an EC in a governed position, which is a variable bound by an empty operator.[16]
   The above describes the basic system of my VR analysis of passives, which is summarized in the 'flow-chart' in the appendix below.

4. The Affectedness Condition

   Within the framework that assumes (1b), it is often considered that passives and middles are quite similar in that they both involve the movement of an object NP to subject position.

(35) a. The book was sold (by John).   (passive)
     b. The book sells well.   (middle)

In my analysis, however, this similarity between passives and middles is rather accidental. Middles involve a verb whose lexical specification has been altered in Lexicon: they do not select a subject θ-role and, thus, they do not assign the objective Case (observing the Burzio's generalization), which triggers the movement of an object to a subject position.

(36)a. The book sells well.
   b. $[_{IP}$ e INFL $[_{VP}$ (e) sell the book well $]$ $]$ —>
   c. $[_{IP}$ the book$_i$ INFL $[_{VP}$ (e) sell t_i well $]$ $]$

On the other hand, NP-Movement is forced in passives due to the prior movement of the verb (VR), this is recapitulated in (37).

(37)a. The book was sold (by John).
   b. $[_{IP}$ e $[_{I'}$ was $[_{VP}$ e -en $[_{VP}$ (John) sell the book $]$ $]$ $]$ $]$ --VR-->
   c. $[_{IP}$ e $[_{I'}$ was $[_{VP}$ e $[_V$ sell$_i$-en$]$ $[_{VP}$ (John) t_i the book $]$ $]$ $]$ $]$]->
   d. $[_{IP}$ the book$_j$ $[_{I'}$ was $[_{VP}$ t_j $[_V$ sell$_i$-en$]$ $[_{VP}$ (by John) t_i t_j $]$ $]$ $]$ $]$

Thus, the ways NP-movement has come about are different, though both constructions involve the movement of the object NP to the SPEC of IP for Case reason. Given this difference, it is rather natural to seek an account for the noted contrast between middles and passives with respect to unaffected arguments (cf. Anderson (1977), Jaeggli (1986), Pesetsky (1987), Roberts (1985), etc.) The fact is that if an object argument is 'unaffected', it cannot appear as a subject of middles (and also of nominal passives), but it can be a subject of sentential passives. This is shown in (38)-(40). The (c) examples are OK, because the object is of 'affected' type.

(38) passive
   a. The movie has been enjoyed (by everyone).
   b. This fact is known (to everyone).
   [c. The town was destroyed (by the army)]

(39) middle
   a. *The movie enjoys easily.
   b. *The fact knows easily.
   [c. The town destroyed easily.]

(40) nominal passive
   a. *The movie's enjoyment (by everyone)   (a´. enjoyment of the movie)
   b. *this fact's knowledge   (b´. knowledge of this fact)
   [c. the town's destruction (by the army)   (c´. destruction of the town)]

There may be various ways to approach this contrast and different formulations of the Affectedness Condition have been proposed recently (e.g., Jaeggli (1986), Roberts (1985), Pesetsky (1987)). Here, I would like to propose yet another version of this condition that makes use of structural and derivational differences between passives on the one hand and middles and nominal passives on the other. The difference is that in passives, (the head of) the θ-marker does not govern the chain of the moved NP at S-Structure but it does in middles and nominal passives, because they are not subject to VR. My version of the Affectedness Condition is (41).

(41) the Affectedness Condition
When B is an 'unaffected' argument of A :
If A θ-marks B and governs the chain of B , then A Case-marks B .

Let us take the (a) sentences in (38) - (40) as examples to illustrate how (41) works. The head, enjoy or enjoyment, θ-marks its 'unaffected' object argument, the movie. Thus, as long as enjoy or enjoyment governs the chain of its object, it must Case-mark the object. Obviously, this requirement is not met in middles; a middle verb does not assign objective Case; hence (39) must be ruled out. Similarly in nominal passives, the noun enjoyment governs the trace of the movie, though the movie receives Case by 's not from the noun itself. Hence, (40) must also be out. In the passive case (38), on the other hand, since the verb moves away from the original site by VR, it no longer governs the chain of its object. Hence, (41) is not applicable and the object is allowed to receive Case from AGR in INFL. The intuition behind (41) is that an unaffected argument must be closely tied up with its θ-role assigner in order for it to be identified as its argument, as long as the θ-role assigner is there (somewhat relating to the visibility condition). But such an association becomes meaningless if the θ-role assigner itself moves away. This is certainly a stipulation at this stage but at least it works without employing too many elaborate assumptions.

5. Conclusion

I consider the following four points advantageous to my VR analysis of passives over previous analyses, though it owes much to the insights and generalizations presented in previous works, in particular, Borer (1984), Jaeggli (1986), Roberts (1985), and Fukui (1986).

(i) The difference between passives and actives is minimal in my analysis. The working hypotheses in (1) are observed in a straight-forward way.

(ii) By parameterizing a categorical feature on passive predicates, either [+N] vs. [−N], a wide range of passive phenomena in various languages are captured, which include German/Dutch impersonal passives, Japanese adversity and honorific passives.

(iii) In previous analyses, where the entire passive predicate (of English) is taken as [+N], there is not a principled explanation for why it cannot assign of to its object. I.e., why sentences like 'It was killed of Mary' is ungrammatical (cf. Marantz (1984), Roberts (1985)). In my analysis, such a question does not even arise, though the same [+N] feature is given to the passive predicate. Mary is the object of kill not of the [+N] passive predicate. Thus, Mary is not in a position that -en θ-marks or governs; i.e., it is simply not the right environment for the of-Insertion.

(vi) The difference between passives on the one hand and middles and nominal passives on the other can easily be captured, which is manifested in a rather simple statement of the Affectedness Condition (41).

Appendix

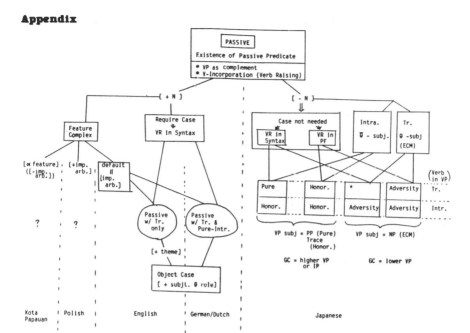

Notes

* I would like to thank Hajime Hoji, Yoshihisa Kitagawa, David Pesetsky, Hiroaki Tada, Koichi Takezawa, and Edwin Williams for discussions, criticisms, and suggestions. All errors are mine.

1 -(R)are cannot attach to potential verbs, such as deki 'can do', wakar 'understand', and all the derived potential forms (e.g. yom-e 'can read', tabe-rare or tabe-re 'can eat'). Note that one of the potential morphemes, rare, is identical to the passive morpheme. This complementary distribution of potential and passive morphemes may suggests that they are different manifestations of the same morpheme, though I will not deal with potentials in this paper.

2 Also for English passives by K. Hasegawa (1968).

3 For example, -(r)are- in (4b), pure passive, has been analyzed as a predicate taking a complement sentence (cf. Kuroda (1965), Howard and Niyekawa-Howard (1976), Inoue (1976), etc.) as in (7a), and (7b) has widely been assumed for adversity passives, and finally, honorific passives are analyzed something like (7c) by Ostler (1980).

4 I consider that (9b) is required for morphological reasons. In other words, VR may take place in PF, as long as morphological incorporation can be performed there. However, in English and German/Dutch, but not in Japanese, as I will argue below, VR must take place in syntax for Case reasons.

5 Though the category V is given to the passive predicate -en, which may very well be A. I will argue later that -en is at least [+N] (and [+V]?), which suggests it is an adjective.

6 As Chomsky (1986) argues, the Head Movement Constraint may be derived from the ECP. I.e., the violation of this constraint gives rise to the structure that the moved head cannot antecedent govern its trace.

7 Details must be worked out carefully, which is beyond the scope of this paper. See Emonds (1986) for relevant discussion.

8 Another way to express this parameter is whether Burzio's generalization (i) holds with the parentheses, with an object, open (in English) or closed (in German/Dutch).
   (i) Burzio's Generalization
       A verb (with an object) assigns objective Case, iff it assigns a subject θ-role.
       With the parentheses open : English
       With the parentheses closed : German/Dutch
Note that the Case assigning property of pure-intransitives in German/Dutch is not exercised in ordinary 'active' sentences. Since if it is, it results in a θ-Criterion violation (too many Case-marked NPs without θ-roles).

9 I assume the following Case system for Japanese. The accusative O is given to a Direct Argument (in the sense of (14)) and GA to an item governed by TENSE; and NI to an Indirect Argument (as the spell-out of a null proposition (θ-role assigner for IA)). See N. Hasegawa (1984/85), Takezawa (1987) for relevant discussion on GA and NI marking. See Saito (1982) for a different view.

10 (23b) and (23c) are identical to (22b) and (22c) in phonological strings.

11 Due to the space limitation, only one example is provided as a representative of intransitive verbs; i.e, (24b). Though a pure intransitive is used there, a relevant verb can also be ergative, since -(r)are does not require Case.

12 Note that the VP-subject of the lower VP cannot move to the SPEC of IP, because it is too far; a violation of the ECP. The lower subject may be able to receive Case either (i) from the θ-transmitter (a null-P), just like the case of the agent of the pure passive (22); or (ii) from the passive predicate -(r)are (an exceptional Case marking by a higher predicate). (ii) is expected from Burzio's generalization (cf. fn. 8), since this -(r)are selects a subject θ-role. For reasons not clear to me, the exceptional Case is realized as NI in Japanese, which holds true also in Causatives. I would like assume (ii) here, considering (i) as the last-resort option. (ii) is preferred empirically as well: there are systematic differences between the agent phrase of direct passives and the NI-phrase of adversity passives; the former being more like PP, while the latter being more like NP (cf. Quantifier Float facts in Harada (1976), Miyagawa (1988), Ueda (1986), etc.) See fn. 14 below.

13 As in the case of 'intransitive' version of the passive morpheme, (25b) and (26b) are identical in phonological strings.

14 Another difference here is that the subject of VP2 in (30) is in PP, whereas the one in (31) is an NP, exceptionally Case-marked by the higher -(r)are (cf. fn. 11). Thus, John as well as Mary c-commands (hence, binds) zibun in (31), while Mary in (30), being inside PP, does not c-command (hence, cannot bind) zibun.

15 Cf. Fukui (1986), who advocates a system in which a VP-subject is ungoverned and PRO is allowed there, which functions as controller for a purpose clause and a subject-oriented adverb in sentences such as those in (32).

16 Hoji (1985) argues that Japanese does not observe a condition on pro such as (33) and freely allows pro in any governed position. My analysis of the passive is independent of the controversy over whether pro is allowed in Japanese. It can get along with Hoji's analysis: i.e., although -(r)are is [-N], pro can occupy a VP-subject position, since its occurrence is free in his system.

References
Anderson, Mona. 1977. Transformations in Noun Phrases. ms., University of Connecticut, Storrs.
Borer, Hagit. 1984. The Projection Principle and Rules of Morphology. NELS. 14. 16-33.
Chomsky, Noam. 1986. Barriers. Cambridge: MIT Press.
Emonds, Joseph. 1985. A Unified Theory of Syntactic Categories. Dordrecht: Foris.
Fukui, Naoki. 1986. A Theory of Category Projection and Its Applications. Doctoral dissertation, MIT.
Harada, Shin-Ichi. 1976. Quantifier Float as a Relational Rule. Metropolitan Linguistics. 1. 44-49.
Hasegawa, Kinsuke. 1968. The Passive Construction in English. Lg. 44. 230-243.
Hasegawa, Nobuko. 1980. The VP Constituent in Japanese. Linguistic Analysis. 6. 115-130.
Hasegawa, Nobuko. 1984/85. On the so-called 'Zero Pronouns' in Japanese. The Linguistic Review. 4. 289-341.
Hoji, Hajime. 1985. Logical Form Constraints and Configurational Structures in Japanese. Doctoral dissertation, University of Washington.
Howard, Irwin, and Agnes Niyekawa-Howard. 1976. Passivization. Syntax and Semantics. vol. 5. Japanese Generative Grammar, ed. by Masayoshi Shibatani. New York: Academic Press.
Huang, C.-T. James. 1984. On the Distribution and Reference of Empty Pronouns. LI. 15. 531-574.
Inoue, Kazuko. 1976. Henkei Bunpoo to Nihongo. Tokyo: Taishukan.
Jaeggli, Osvaldo. 1986. Passive. LI. 17. 587-622.
Kitagawa, Yoshihisa. 1986. Subjects in Japanese and English. Doctoral dissertation, University of Massachusetts, Amherst.
Kuroda, S.-Yuki. 1965. Generative Grammatical Studies in the Japanese Language. Doctoral dissertation, MIT.
Kuroda, S.-Yuki. 1986. Whether we Agree or not: Rough Ideas about the Comparative Syntax of English and Japanese. ms., University of California, San Diego.
Marantz, Alec. 1984. On the Nature of Grammatical Relations. Cambridge: MIT Press.
Miyagawa, Shigeru. 1988. Numeral Quantifiers in Japanese. Proceedings of Eastern State Conference on Linguistics, Ohio State University.
Ostler, Nicholas. 1980. A Non-Transformational Account of Japanese Case-Marking and Inflexion. MIT Working Papers in Linguistics. 2. 63-91.
Pesetsky, David. 1987. The Lexicon and Lexical Decomposition: Experiencer Predicates. a paper presented at the International Congress of Linguistics, East Berlin.
Roberts, Ian. 1985. The Representation of Implicit and Dethematized Subjects. Doctoral dissertation, University of Southern California.
Saito, Mamoru. 1982. Case Marking in Japanese: a Preliminary Study. ms., MIT.
Sportiche, Dominique. 1987. A Theory of Floating Quantifiers. NELS. 17. 581-592.
Takezawa, Koichi. 1987. A Configurational Approach to Case-Marking in Japanese. Doctoral dissertation, University of Washington.
Travis, Lisa. 1984. Parameters and Effects of Word Order Variation. Doctoral dissertation, MIT.
Ueda, Masanobu. 1986. On Quantifier Float in Japanese. University of Massachusetts Occasional Papers in Linguistics vol. 11: Oriental Linguistics. 263-309.

Finite Control in Modern Persian
Peggy Hashemipour
University of California, San Diego

1. Introduction. Based on Binding Principle A which requires that anaphors be bound by a c-commanding antecedent within a certain domain, an analysis of control phenomena has been proposed where the controlled position is filled by PRO, an anaphoric empty category which must be A-bound by a nominal in the superordinate clause. In general, most accounts consider data from languages which select infinitival complements. As a result, PRO is not governed (or Case-marked) from within the embedded clause, and thus its binding domain is the root S, thereby satisfying Binding Principle A. However, this paper examines a construction found in Modern Persian, which differs notably from previously studied languages. In Persian control, the embedded clause is finite instead of nonfinite, as shown in (1-4) below.

(1) *häsän$_i$ säiy=kärd [ke e$_{i/*j}$ qäza-ro bo-xor-e]*
     Hasan$_i$ tried   [that e$_{i/*j}$ food-AC SJ-eat-3S]
     'Hasan$_i$ tried [e$_{i/*j}$ to eat the food].'

(2) *häsän$_i$ be räis-eš$_j$ qol=dad [ke e$_{i/*j/*k}$ un kar-o änjam=be-de]*
     Hasan$_i$ to boss-3S$_j$ promised [that e$_{i/*j/*k}$ that work-AC perform=SJ-give]
     'Hasan$_i$ promised his boss$_j$ [e$_{i/*j/*k}$ to do the work].'

(3) *pune$_i$ häsän-ro$_j$ vadar=kärd [ke e$_{*i/j/*k}$ qäza-ro bo-xor-e]*
     Pune$_i$ Hasan-AC$_j$ compelled [that e$_{*i/j/*k}$ food-AC SJ-eat-3S]
     'Pune$_i$ compelled Hasan$_j$ [e$_{*i/j/*k}$ to eat the food].'

(4) *mo'ällem$_i$ äz reza$_j$ täqaza=kärd [ke e$_{*i/j/*k}$ zud bi-ad mädrese]*
     teacher$_i$ from Reza$_j$ requested [that e$_{*i/j/*k}$ soon SJ-come:3S school]
     'The teacher requested that Reza come to school early.'

We will see that the Persian phenomena fall into the general schema of control, such that when the embedded [NP,IP] (subject) is null, coreference with a matrix nominal is obligatory. That is, in (1-4) the empty subject cannot freely refer to any other NP, as indicated by the indices. The lexical properties of the control predicate determine with which matrix nominal the embedded [NP,IP] corefers. For example, in (1-2) the null subject is bound by the matrix subject, and in (3-4) by the matrix complement.

This paper will examine the characteristics of the construction in (1-4). To begin, I will show that these data are control phenomena. However, the fact that the embedded clause in Persian control is finite instead of nonfinite is problematic for standard approaches to control. I will present evidence that the models of control proposed in Manzini 1983 and Bouchard 1984 fail to give adequate accounts. In addition, language particular facts indicate that models which assume that the controlled element is an empty pronominal (Huang 1987, Borer 1987) are also insufficient. Finally, I will adopt and extend the nonovert operator analysis of control given in Clark 1985. I will argue that this approach offers several insights into the structure of finite control as compared to nonfinite control. First, the presence of the complementizer *ke* in (1-4) and the lack of *that-t* effects in Persian WH-movement are treated as the same phenomenon. Next, the differences of the two kinds of control result from the parametric setting of two elements of grammar: Case assignment and the ability of AGR to play a role in the control relation.

2. General Characteristics of Control. In addition to being the classic type of predicates associated with control, such as *try, want, promise, allow*, and other verbs not listed in (1–4), these sentences display other traditional characteristics of control phenomena. First, there are both obligatory and nonobligatory control predicates in Persian. The verbs *säiy=kärdän* 'try' in (1) and *vadar=kärdän* 'compel' in (3) are obligatory control verbs. They only allow complement clauses with empty subjects; lexical subjects, as shown in sentences (5) and (6), are not permissible.

(5) **häsän säiy=kärd [ke bäcce qäza-ro bo-xor-e]*
Hasan tried [that child food-AC SJ-eat-3S]
*Hasan tried [the child to eat the food].

(6) **pune häsän-ro vadar=kärd [ke bäcce qäza-ro bo-xor-e]*
Pune Hasan-AC compelled [that child food-AC SJ-eat-3S]
*Pune compelled Hasan [the child eat the food].

That is, in addition to the required bound reading between the embedded subject and some matrix nominal, the embedded [NP,IP] must be null.

Moreover, the obligatory control verbs *säiy=kärdän* 'try' and *vadar=kärdän* 'compel' adhere to the four properties of control proposed in Koster 1984. First, the embedded subjects in (1) and (3) are obligatorily linked to a matrix antecedent. Second, the matrix antecedents in (1) and (3) c-command the empty subjects. Third, the antecedent of the controlled element must be unique. That is, the empty subject in (3) cannot be bound by both *Pune* and *Hasan*. Finally, the domain of the bound relationship of matrix antecedent and the embedded subject is the root S.

In contrast, the verbs *qol=dadän* 'promise' (2) and *täqaza=kärdän* 'request' (4) are nonobligatory control predicates. The embedded subject position may be filled with a lexical NP, or with a pronoun that may refer to a matrix antecedent. The following sets of sentences are the full paradigm of overt, pronominal, and null subjects for the verbs *qol=dadän* (7) and *täqaza=kärdän* (8). In the (c) sentences, when the embedded subject is empty, it only refers to the matrix controller.

(7)
a. *häsän$_i$ be räis-eš$_j$ qol=dad [ke äli$_k$ un kar-o änjam=be-de]*
Hasan$_i$ to boss-3S$_j$ promised [that Ali$_k$ that work-AC perform=SJ-give:3S]
'Hasan$_i$ promised his boss$_j$ [that Ali$_k$ would do the work].'

b. *häsän$_i$ be räis-eš$_j$ qol=dad [ke un$_{i/j/k}$ un kar-o änjam=be-de]*
Hasan$_i$ to boss-3S$_j$ promised [that he$_{i/j/k}$ that work-AC perform=SJ-give:3S]
'Hasan$_i$ promised his boss$_j$ [that he$_{i/j/k}$ would do the work].'

c. *häsän$_i$ be räis-eš$_j$ qol=dad [ke e$_{i/*j/*k}$ un kar-o änjam=be-de]*
Hasan$_i$ to boss-3S$_j$ promised [that e$_{i/*j/*k}$ that work-AC perform=SJ-give]
'Hasan$_i$ promised his boss$_j$ [e$_{i/*j/*k}$ to do the work].'

(8)
a. *mo'ällem$_i$ äz madär$_j$ täqaza=kärd [ke reza$_k$ zud bi-ad bi-ad mädrese]*
teacher$_i$ from mother$_j$ request=did:3S [that Reza$_k$ soon SJ-come:3S school]
'The teacher requested from the mother that Reza$_k$ come to school early.'

b. *mo'ällem$_i$ äz madär$_j$ täqaza=kärd*
   teacher$_i$ from mother$_j$ request=did:3S
   [*ke un$_{*i/j/k}$ zud bi-ad mädrese]*
   [that s/he$_{*i/j/k}$ soon SJ-come:3S school]
   'The teacher requested from the mother that s/he come to school early.'

c. *mo'ällem$_i$ äz madär$_j$ täqaza=kärd [ke e$_{*i/j/*k}$ zud bi-ad mädrese]*
   teacher$_i$ from mother$_j$ request=did:3S [that e$_{*i/j/*k}$ soon SJ-come:3S school]
   'The teacher requested from the mother that she come to school early.'

Another characteristic of Persian control is that it is local. The controlled subject in the deeply embedded clauses in (9-10) must be identified
with some NP in the most immediate superordinate clause. In (9), the only
readings possible are where the empty element refers to *Ali*, the subject of
the immediately superordinate clause. Sentence (10) is illicit since the reflexive anaphor, the embedded subject, and, by transitivity, the embedded verb
agreement do not match the subject of the most immediate superordinate
clause. Sentence (11) is the only possible alternative, where the matrix subject controls the intermediate subject, which in turn controls the most deeply
embedded null subject.

(9) *moin$_i$ mi-dun-e ke äli$_j$ mi-xad e$_{*i/j}$ be-re*
    Moin$_i$ CN-know-3S that Ali$_j$ CN-want:3S e$_{*i/j}$ SJ go
    'Moin$_i$ knows that Ali$_j$ wants e$_{*i/j}$ to leave.'

(10) **moin$_i$ mi-xad ke säiy=kon-äm [e$_i$ xod-eš-o eslah=kon-e]*
     Moin$_i$ CN-wants that try=SJ:do-1S [e$_i$ RFL-3S-AC shave=SJ:do-3S]
     *'Moin wants me to try to shave himself.'

(11) *moin$_i$ mi-xad ke e$_j$ säiy=kon-äm ke e$_i$ xod-äm-o eslah=kon-äm*
     Moin$_i$ CN-want:3S that e$_j$ try=SJ:do-1S that e$_i$ RFL-1S-AC shave=SJ:do-1S
     'Moin$_i$ wanted me$_j$ to try PRO$_{*i/j}$ to shave myself.'

From these sentences, we conclude that there is a control relation between the embedded null subject and a nominal in a local domain. However, the
fact remains that the embedded verb appears in the subjunctive mood, which is
indicated by the prefix *be-*, the present stem of the verb, and the appropriate
agreement suffixes. Crucially, it is not in its infinitive form as in English.
Apart from the verb morphology, there is additional evidence that the embedded verbs are finite in (1-4). First, embedded subjunctive verbs as occur with
other matrix predicates, in which case an overt embedded subject may be used
as shown in sentences (12-15).

(12) *häsän mi-tärs-e [ke pune be-re]*
     Hasan CN-fear-3S [that Pune SJ-go:3S]
     'Hasan is afraid that Pune is leaving.'

(13) *häsän fekr=mi-kon-e [ke pune qäza-ro dorost=kon-e]*
     Hasan think=CN-do-3S [that Pune food-AC fix=SJ:do-3S]
     'Hasan thinks that Pune will fix the food.'

(14) *häsän omid=var-e [ke pune bi-ad]*
     Hasan hope-3S [that Pune SJ-come:3S]
     'Hasan hopes that Pune will come.'

(15) *momken-e [ke pune qäza-ro dorost=kon-e]*
    possible-is [that Pune food-AC fix=SJ:do-3S]
    'It is possible that Pune will fix the food.'

According to the Visibility Condition, the embedded subjects in (12-15) must be Case-marked in order to receive a Theta-role. Yet, the matrix verb does not Case-mark them, since Case assignment under VP in Persian is right-to-left. Moreover, if the embedded subject were Case-marked by the matrix V, then it would bear the overt objective marker *-ra*, which marks proper names and specific nominals. As shown in (16-19), marking the embedded subject with *-ra* renders the sentences ungrammatical.

(16) **hasän mi-tärs-e [(ke) pune-ra be-re]*
    Hasan CN-fear-3S [(that) Pune-AC SJ-go:3S]
    'Hasan is afraid that Pune is leaving.'

(17) **hasän fekr=mi-kon-e [(ke) pune-ra qäza-ro dorost=kon-e]*
    Hasan think=CN-do-3S [(that) Pune-AC food-AC fix=SJ:do-3S]
    'Hasan thinks that Pune will fix the food.'

(18) **hasän omid=var-e [(ke) pune-ra bi-ad]*
    Hasan   hope-3S [(that) Pune-AC SJ-come:3S]
    'Hasan hopes that Pune will come.'

(19) * *momken-e [(ke) pune-ra qäza-ro dorost=kon-e]*
    possible-is [(that) Pune-AC food-AC fix=SJ:do-3S]
    'It is possible that Pune will fix the food.'

A second piece of evidence which indicates that the embedded verb is finite is that the embedded clause is a binding domain for an anaphor. As commonly assumed, when INFL is finite, it governs the [NP,IP]. If it is nonfinite, the governing category of the subject is the matrix S, so long as it is the minimal maximal category containing the element, an accessible SUBJECT, and a governor, i.e. the matrix V. When INFL is nonfinite, the embedded [NP,IP] could be filled with an anaphor which is A-bound by some matrix nominal. Consider now sentences (20-21) where the formal Persian reflexive pronoun *xod* occurs in the [NP,IP] of an embedded subjunctive clause, and its antecedent *Ali* is the matrix subject.

(20) **äli fekr=mi-kon-e ke xod xošhal be-še*
    Ali think=CN-do-3S that RFL happy SJ-become:3S
    *'Ali thinks that himself will be happy.'

(21) **äli ejaze=dad ke xod xošhal   be-še*
    Ali allowed that RFL happy SJ-become:3S
    'Ali allowed himself to be happy.'

As such, the complement clause in (20-21) must be the governing category of the anaphor, since it is the minimal maximal clause containing the element, its governor (INFL), and an accessible SUBJECT (AGR). Thus, the ungrammaticality of these sentences results from trying to bind the anaphor outside of its governing category, the embedded clause. Given that (1-4) are control structures, let us consider some possible analyses of the Persian data, keeping in mind that the embedded clause is the governing category of the controlled element, and that the embedded [NP,IP] is a Case position.

3. Analyses of Control with PRO. The Persian data are problematic for the standard idea that the controlled empty category (PRO) must not occur in a Case position (cf. Chomsky 1981, Manzini 1983, Bouchard 1984, among others). Some further conclusions are based on this claim. For example, the reason that only subjects are controlled under these types of predicates is that the [NP,IP] of an infinitival clause is the only Caseless position. Moreover, control phenomena, in part, motivated the formulation of the Case Filter. That is, the reason that a lexical NP cannot appear in the embedded [NP,IP] in (22b) below is that it is not Case-marked.

(22) a. John tried [PRO to leave]

    b. *John tried [Mary to leave]

Next, the Persian data are a problem for the formulation of control domain. Bouchard 1984 proposed that propositions embedded under control predicates are lexically marked to undergo S'-Deletion, thereby allowing the matrix V to govern the embedded [NP,IP]. Therefore, the governing category of the controlled element is the root S. However, we have seen that in Persian the embedded INFL(AGR) governs the controlled position. As such, the Bouchard 1984 analysis is troublesome if we assume that government of an element A is unique, i.e., A should have at most one governor.

Manzini 1983 offers an alternative solution to the definition of the control domain, since she claims that the controlled [NP,IP] must be bound in its DOMAIN-GOVERNING CATEGORY (23), which is dependent on the notion C-DOMAIN (24).

(23) DOMAIN-GOVERNING CATEGORY
    B is a domain-governing category for A iff
        a. B is a governing category for the c-domain of A, and
        b. B contains a subject accessible to A

(24) C-DOMAIN
    B is the c-domain for A iff
    B is the minimal maximal category dominating A

According to (24), the c-domain of the embedded [NP,IP] in (1-4) is the embedded IP. (23) and (24) predict a difference in control according to whether the c-domain of an element has a governing category or not. What is crucial is whether the embedded clause has a COMP or not. An embedded clause without a COMP has a domain-governing category, the matrix S, since it is the minimal maximal category containing the c-domain and an accessible subject. As a result, obligatory coreference between the controlled subject and a matrix nominal must obtain. However, embedded clauses with a COMP, i.e. those dominated by both CP and IP, do not have a domain-governing category, since the first maximal category dominating the c-domain is the embedded CP. Yet this category does not have an accessible subject. Hence Manzini 1983 predicts that empty category in [NP,IP] should freely refer. That is, it can refer to a matrix nominal as in (25), or it can have arbitrary reference as in (26).

(25) John asked [how PRO to behave himself].

(26) John asked [how PRO to behave oneself].

However, as shown in sentences (1-4), free reference is not possible in Persian even when there is an embedded COMP. Rather obligatory coreference is required. As such, the controlled subject is bound outside of its governing category and domain-governing category.

4. Analyses of Control with an Empty Pronominal. Recently, another type of analysis of control has been proposed which claims that the controlled element is an empty pronominal. Huang 1987 is such an account which sets out to jointly characterize the distribution of the empty category in control structures and the null subject in subjectless sentences by a Generalized Control Rule. Under this approach, either an NP or AGR can be a controller. As such, the null subject found in control structures and that of subjectless sentences are variants of an empty pronominal.

However, this claim is not borne out in Persian, which is also a null subject language. According to Huang, the empty third person singular subjects in (27-29) are controlled within their control domain by the AGR.

(27) *pro ba moin molaqat=kärd*
pro with Moin meet=did:3S
'He met with Moin.'

(28) *moin$_i$ goft [ke pro$_{i/j}$ färda zud mi-ad]*
Moin$_i$ said [that *pro$_{i/j}$* tomorrow soon CN-come:3S]
'Moin$_i$ said [that he$_{i/j}$ would come early tomorrow].'

(29) *moin$_i$ omidvar-e [ke pro$_{i/j}$ ketab-o bära äli bi-är-e]*
Moin$_i$ hope-3S [that *pro$_{i/j}$* book-AC for Ali SJ-bring-3S]
'Moin$_i$ hopes [that he$_{i/j}$ is bringing the book for Ali].'

Even though the empty pronominals are identified by the embedded AGR in (28-29), they freely refer outside the embedded clause, as predicted by Binding Principle B. While this appears to be correct for these sentences, a problem arises once we consider null subjects embedded under Persian control predicates, as in (30-32) and also (1-4).

(30)

a. *äli$_i$ be nasser$_j$ sefareš=kärd [ke pro$_{*i/j/*k}$ ba moin molaqat=kon-e]*
Ali$_i$ to Nasser$_j$ recommended [that *pro$_{*i/j/*k}$* with Moin meet=SJ:do-3S]
'Ali$_i$ recommended to Nasser$_j$ that he$_{*i/j/*k}$ meet with Moin.'

b. *äli$_i$ be nasser$_j$ sefareš=kärd [ke un$_{i/j/k}$ ba moin molaqat=kon-e]*
Ali$_i$ to Nasser$_j$ recommended [that *he$_{i/j/k}$* with Moin meet=SJ:do-3S]
'Ali$_i$ recommended to Nasser$_j$ that he$_{i/j/k}$ meet with Moin.'

(31)

a. *moin$_i$ äz nasser$_j$ täqaza=kärd [ke pro$_{*i/j/*k}$ färda zud bi-ad]*
Moin$_i$ from Nasser$_j$ requested [that *pro$_{*i/j/*k}$* tomorrow soon SJ-come]
'Moin$_i$ requested from Nasser$_j$ that he$_{*i/j/*k}$ come early tomorrow.'

b. *moin$_i$ äz nasser$_j$ täqaza=kärd [ke un$_{i/j/k}$ färda zud bi-ad]*
Moin$_i$ from Nasser$_j$ requested [that *he$_{i/j/k}$* tomorrow soon SJ-come]
'Moin$_i$ requested from Nasser$_j$ that he$_{i/j/k}$ come early tomorrow.'

(32)

a. *moin$_i$ be nasser$_j$ pišnähad=kärd*
   Moin$_i$ to Nasser$_j$ suggested:3S
       [ke   pro$_{*i/j/*k}$ ketab-o bära äli bi-är-e]
       [that pro$_{*i/j/*k}$ book-AC for Ali SJ-bring-3S]
   'Moin$_i$ suggested to Nasser$_j$ that he$_{*i/j/*k}$ bring the book for Ali.'

b. *moin$_i$ be nasser$_j$ pišnähad=kärd*
   Moin$_i$ to Nasser$_j$ suggested:3S
       [ke   un$_{i/j/k}$ ketab-o bära äli bi-är-e]
       [that he$_{i/j/k}$ book-AC for Ali SJ-bring-3S]
   'Moin$_i$ suggested to Nasser$_j$ that he$_{i/j/k}$ bring the book for Ali.'

According to the Generalized Control analysis, the control domain of the embedded subject in (30-32) is the embedded clause. Since the empty pronominal is controlled by AGR, we would expect the null subject to freely refer outside of the embedded clause. However, as shown in sentences (30-32), as well as in (1-4), free reference is impossible. Only an overt pronoun in the embedded subject position can freely refer.

One case of obligatory *pro*-drop and its interaction with nonobligatory control further substantiate this fact, as shown in (33-34). In nonemphatic sentences, *pro*-drop is required with first or second person subjects.

(33) *pro ba moin molaqat=kärd-äm*
    pro with Moin   meet=did-1S
    'I met with Moin.'

(34) *moin omidvar-e [ke pro ketab-o bära äli bi-är-i]*
    Moin hopes [that *pro* book-AC for Ali SJ-bring-2S]
    'Moin hopes [that you are bringing the book for Ali].'

However, the conditions on obligatory *pro*-drop seem to change once a first or second person subject is embedded under a control verb. In (35) and (36), first person and second person subjects have been embedded under nonobligatory control predicates. Even though the embedded AGR appears to fully identify the null subjects, sentences (35) and (36) are ungrammatical.

(35) **äli be nasser sefareš=kärd [ke e ba moin molaqat=kon-äm]*
    Ali to Nasser recommended [that *e* with Moin meet-3J.do-1S]
    'Ali recommended to Nasser that I meet with Moin.'

(36) **moin be nasser pišnähad=kärd [ke e ketab-o bära äli bi-är-i]*
    Moin to Nasser suggested [that *e* book-AC for Ali SJ-bring-2S]
    'Moin suggested to Nasser that you bring the book for Ali.'

The only possible alternatives are (37) and (38), where an overt pronoun occurs in the embedded [NP,IP].

(37) *äli be nasser sefareš=kärd [ke män ba moin molaqat=kon-äm]*
    Ali to Nasser recommended [that I with Moin meet=SJ:do-1S]
    'Ali recommended to Nasser that I meet with Moin.'

(38) *moin be nasser piŝnähad=kärd [ke to ketab-o bära äli bi-är-i]*
Moin to Nasser suggested:3S [that you book-AC for Ali SJ-bring-2S]
'Moin suggested to Nasser that you bring the book for Ali.'

The ungrammaticality of sentences (35) and (36) results from the fact that the embedded subject is empty, but does not refer to the selected matrix controller. From sentences (27-38), we conclude that *pro*-drop and control in Persian are two distinct processes. Combining the two results in an otherwise unnecessary stipulation as to why obligatory *pro*-drop of first and second person must not occur when the requirements on control are met.

Huang (p.c.) has suggested that modifying the Generalized Control Rule so that an NP and AGR must simultaneously control the null pronominal can account for Persian finite control in (1-4) and sentences (30-32,35,36). This alteration has some unfavorable consequences, however. It must be constrained so that it is applicable only to finite control. Apart from labeling Persian control (as well as that of Dogrib, Rumanian, and other languages exhibiting the same properties) as highly marked, it also results in a dissimilar treatment of nonfinite and finite control.

The Borer 1987 model of control given is similar to Huang's Generalized Control in that it also proposes that the empty subject in control structures and the empty subject of *pro*-drop are one and the same. However, her account of the distribution of the pronominal across the two constructions is different. Borer 1987 claims that the INFL in these distinct structures may differ in the specification of four features: [I-Subj], [Ident], [Nom], and [Anaph].[1] The feature [I-Subj] refers to the ability of INFL to select an I-subject.[1] [Ident] indicates whether or not rich inflection obtains. [Nom] denotes the ability of an INFL to assign Nominative Case. Finally, an INFL(AGR) is [+Anaph] if it lacks inherent features, and therefore, requires a binder. Anaphoric AGR must be bound by some referential element in order for it to I-identify its subject. INFL(AGR) embedded under control predicates is [+Anaph]. Borer asserts that the binding of AGR by some matrix NP is only possible when INFL moves to the embedded COMP position, as shown in (39). Otherwise, anaphoric AGR would not satisfy Binding Principle A, as required.

(39) NP_i ... $[_{CP} [_{C'}$ INFL(AGR)$_i [_{IP}$ $pro [_{I'}$... t_i ...

Certain questions about the Borer analysis arise once we consider the feature specification of the INFL embedded under nonobligatory control predicates. From the sentences in (4) and (8), we saw that *täqaza=kärdän* 'request', as well as with other verbs of the same type allow the alternation of lexical subject, overt pronominal, and null subject. The paradigm is repeated below.

(40)
a. *mo'ällem$_i$ äz madär$_j$ täqaza=kärd [ke reza$_k$ zud bi-ad mädrese]*
teacher$_i$ from mother$_j$ requested:3S [that Reza$_k$ soon SJ-come:3S school]
'The teacher requested from the mother that Reza come to school early.'

---

1. Briefly, an I-subject is identified and coindexed with INFL. For further discussion of I-identification and I-subject, I refer the reader to Borer 1986.

b. *mo'ällem$_i$ äz madär$_j$ täqaza=kärd*
   teacher$_i$ from mother$_j$ requested:3S
      [ke un$_{*i/j/k}$ zud bi-ad mädrese]
      [that s/he$_{*i/j/k}$ soon SJ-come:3S school]
   'The teacher requested from the mother that s/he come to school early.'

c. *mo'ällem$_i$ äz madär$_j$ täqaza=kärd*
   teacher$_i$ from mother$_j$ request=did:3S
      [ke e$_{*i/j/*k}$ zud bi-ad mädrese]
      [that e$_{*i/j/*k}$ soon SJ-come:3S school]
   'The teacher requested from the mother that she come to school early.'

Moreover, another set of sentences is possible, where the matrix complement does not occur. In that case, the embedded subject may be a null subject which freely refers, an overt pronoun, which also freely refers, or a lexical NP.

(41)

a. *mo'ällem$_i$ täqaza=kärd [ke reza$_k$ zud bi-ad mädrese]*
   teacher$_i$ requested:3S [that Reza$_k$ soon SJ-come:3S school]
   'The teacher requested that Reza come to school early.'

b. *mo'ällem$_i$ täqaza=kärd [ke un$_{i/j}$ zud bi-ad mädrese]*
   teacher$_i$ requested:3S [that s/he$_{i/j}$ soon SJ-come:3S school]
   'The teacher requested that s/he come to school early.'

c. *mo'ällem$_i$ täqaza=kärd [ke e$_{i/j}$ zud bi-ad mädrese]*
   teacher$_i$ requested:3S [that e$_{i/j}$ soon SJ-come:3S school]
   'The teacher requested that s/he come to school early.'

All of the sentences in (40–41) have a [+I-Subj] INFL(AGR), since an I-subject is selected in every case. Moreover, AGR is [+Nom] since the embedded [NP,IP] is assigned Nominative Case. However, the specification of the features [Anaph] and [Ident] is complex. Certainly when the sentence entails control as in (40c), the embedded AGR is [+Anaph], and it is [-Anaph] for the remaining sentences in (40) and (41) since a lexical NP or overt pronominal may fill the embedded [NP,IP]. The specification of the feature [Ident] would seem straightforward since all the embedded verbs in (40–41) are morphologically identical, and therefore appear to be [+Ident] across the board. However, in Borer's system it is not so simple. When AGR is controlled, as in (40c), it is [-Ident], since by itself it cannot identify an embedded null subject. The case of noncontrol with a matrix complement (40a and b) is also [-Ident], since it does not permit *pro*-drop. Only sentences (41a-c) have a [+Ident] embedded AGR, because *pro*-drop is freely allowed.

As such, nonobligatory control predicates in Persian could select propositions with three distinct feature matrices of AGR given in (42).

(42) Control   Non-control   Non-control
      with a matrix with no matrix
      complement   complement

$$
\begin{bmatrix} \text{+I-subj} \\ \text{+Nom} \\ \text{+Anaph} \\ \text{-Ident} \end{bmatrix}
\begin{bmatrix} \text{+I-subj} \\ \text{+Nom} \\ \text{-Anaph} \\ \text{-Ident} \end{bmatrix}
\begin{bmatrix} \text{+I-subj} \\ \text{+Nom} \\ \text{-Anaph} \\ \text{+Ident} \end{bmatrix}
$$

       (40c)   (40a-b)   (41a-c)

Yet, the morphology of the embedded verbs with the distinct feature matrices is identical. In addition, the selection of a feature should be empirically motivated by structural factors in the matrix clause, since it is the control predicate which subcategorizes for a particular feature. While the setting [-Anaph, +Ident] is structurally motivated, i.e., there is no nominal in (41a-c) which could serve as a matrix antecedent of the embedded AGR, the other specifications have no structural basis. The constituency of the matrix clauses in (40a-c) is the same. Moreover, Borer (1987) asserts that AGR, and not the null pronominal, is controlled. As a result, it is odd to propose that when the [NP,IP] is empty, then the embedded INFL(AGR) is [+Anaph, -Ident]. Also, there is no means of predicting the setting of [Anaph], [Ident] via redundancy rules. Although, it holds that if AGR is [+Anaph], then it is [-Ident], the opposite is not true, i.e. *[-Anaph]-->[+Ident]. Therefore, while Borer 1987 offers insight into the role that AGR may bear in control, we reject this analysis on the basis of an empirically weak account of nonobligatory control in Persian.

5. A Nonovert Operator Analysis of Control. Where previous accounts of control regard the Persian data as problematic, the model of control proposed in Clark 1985 does not. Under this approach, the formal representation of control is as in (43), where a nonovert operator in the SPEC(C) A'-binds a variable in the embedded controlled position.

(43) ...NP_i...$[_{CP}$ Op_i $[_{IP}$...x_i...$]$

The operator is identified via a predication process with a matrix nominal. As required by Principle A of A'-Binding, the variable is bound within its governing category, the embedded CP. That is, the operator is coindexed with and c-commands the variable from an A'-position. Comparing the English sentence in (44) and the Persian sentence in (45), we see that in the nonovert operator analysis, the opaque domains of finite and nonfinite control are defined in the same terms. That is, there is no reference to governing category or domain-governing category, which, as we saw earlier, caused problems in our attempt to generalize a domain for both types of control.

(44) $John_i$ tried $[_{CP}$ Op_i $[_{IP}$ e_i to sleep].

(45) $häsän_i$ $säiy=kärd$ $[_{CP}$ Op_i ke $[_{IP}$ e_i $qäza$-ro bo-xor-e]
      $Hasan_i$ tried $[_{CP}$ Op_i that $[_{IP}$ e_i food-AC SJ-eat-3S]
      'Hasan$_i$ tried $[_{CP}$ Op_i $[_{IP}$ e_i to eat the food].'

The anaphoric properties of the controlled subject in (44-45) are represented by the fact that the variable, an A'-anaphor, must bound by the null operator. In turn, the local characteristic of control is denoted by the requirement that the domain of the predication process be the root S. That is, the NP from which the operator receives its reference must be in the immediately superordinate clause.

Moreover, in the nonovert operator model, the fact that control constructions must have a proposition with a null subject is indicated via the selectional restrictions of the matrix predicate. For example, obligatory control verbs such as English *try* and Persian *saiy=kardan* 'try' s-select a CP which contains a operator. This selection is parallel to the manner that the English verb *wonder* selects a [+WH] CP. However, the level at which such selectional restrictions are met differs in English and Persian. As argued in Clark 1985, selectional restrictions in English are satisfied at S-structure, since there is syntactic WH-movement. However, in Persian WH-elements remain in situ at S-structure, indicating that there is LF WH-movement. From this we conclude that selectional restrictions, such as those of matrix control predicates, must also be met at LF.

The nonovert operator model presents a question which generally remains untouched in other analyses: what accounts for the appearance of the complementizer *ke* in Persian control and the obligatory absence of the complementizer *that* in the English construction? One reason why English does not permit the complementizer is that its presence would obstruct the A'-binding of the variable by the operator in (44). However, this does not seem to be the case in Persian. Several provisions of Government and Binding theory explain why the complementizer *ke* in (1–4) and (45) does not count as a potential A'-binder nor block the A'-binding of the variable by the operator. First, in general complementizers are nonreferential, and variables, as A'-anaphors, by definition must pick up their reference from inherently referential elements. Only the elements in the SPEC(C) are potentially referential.

Many languages which have **that-t* effects exhibit what Chomsky (1986) and Rizzi (1986) call Specifier-HEAD agreement where the specifier of C and the complementizer must share the same features. For example, the Spec(C) and C in English are specified for the feature [WH]. Since the complementizer *that* is [−WH], Specifier-HEAD agreement will not obtain so long as a [+WH] element is in the Specifier position, and the complementizer is in C. The English system is relatively simple compared to other languages such as Irish, which according to Chung and McCloskey 1987 has an elaborate complementizer complex. Irish has a series of complementizers which may bear a variety of features such as [Past], [Negative], [Relative Clause], and [Interrogative].

Compared to English and Irish, the Persian complementizer system is the least complex. Certain language particular facts indicate that Specifier-HEAD agreement between the Spec(C) and the Persian complementizer *ke* is vacuous, since the complementizer is not specified for the feature [WH]. This is shown in sentences (46–51), where in (46–47) *ke* may occur in clauses where at the LF the Spec(C) will be filled with a [+WH] element. It may appear in a complement clause where the Spec(C) is empty as in (48–49). Finally, as seen in (50) and (51), the complementizer *ke* may be preceded by adjunct phrases which bear the feature [−WH]. In short, *ke* can agree with any element in the Spec(C).

(46) *madär ne-mi-dunest ke pesär-eš ci xorde bud*
   mother NEG-CN-knew that son-3S what eaten AUX:3S
   'The mother wondered what her son had eaten.'

(47) *doktor porsid ke ki qåza-ra xorde bud*
doctor asked that who food-AC eaten AUX:3S
'The doctor asked who had eaten the food.'

(48) *moin fekr=mi-kon-e (ke) pesär-eš qåšäng baš-e*
Moin think-3S (that) son-his beautiful SJ:be-3S
'Moin thinks (that) his son will be beautiful.'

(49) *moin dust=dar-e (ke) bäcce-š be-xab-e*
Moin like-3S (that) child-his SJ-sleep-3S
'Moin likes for his child to sleep.'

(50) *mi-tärs-äm mäbada (ke) färamuš=kon-e*
CN-fear-1S lest (that) forget=SJ:do-3S
'I am afraid that he may forget.'

(51) *här cänd (ke) moin märiz-e väli qåza-ro dorost=mi-kon-e*
even=if (that) Moin sick-is but food-AC fix=CN-do-3S
'Moin will fix the food even if he is sick.'

Therefore, the absence of *that-t* effects in Persian WH-movement and control is a result of the lack of feature specification of the complementizer *ke*.

One of the crucial differences in Clark's analysis of control involves his claim that the matrix control predicate Case-marks the embedded nonovert operator.[2] However, it is precisely this proposal that is instrumental in explaining the difference between nonfinite control and finite control. The A'-chain of obligatory control structures in English is given in (52), where the nonovert operator is in a Case position, but the embedded variable is not.

(52) ... V ... [Op_i [e_i ...
              [+Case] [-Case]

In addition, control A'-chains in Clark's account adhere to a wellformedness condition, given in (53), which requires that an A'-chain have only one Case-marked position.

(53) *[e] where e is a nonovert operator
     COMP [+Case]
     [+Case]

---

2. Clark's (1987) claim that control predicates in English assign Case is controversial since some theoretical assumptions regarding Case assignment are based on the fact that lexical subjects cannot occur in the clauses embedded such verbs, as in *John tried [Mary to leave]*. The ungrammaticality was assumed to result from the lack of Case. Under Clark's, model the illicitness of this sentence results from some intrinsic properties of control, and not from the lack of Case. First, the embedded proposition in this sentence does not pertain to the matrix controller John, as required by the predication process. Second, the selectional restrictions of the verb *try* are not met, since the embedded subject Mary has moved to the Spec(C) in order to receive Case. The English verb *try* only selects CPs with null operators.

As such, either the operator or the variable may be Case-marked, but not both. Because of A'-chains without any Case-position, the Visibility Condition cannot be used instead of the wellformedness condition in (53). The Visibility Condition places Case assignment as a requirement for Theta-assignment in A-chains. While not all A'-chains must obey the Visibility Condition, the A'-chains in obligatory control do adhere to the condition. In particular, the A'-chains in sentences (1-4) have a unique Theta-role and a unique Case-position.

The fact that A'-chains embedded under control predicates must adhere to the Visibility Condition explains, in part, the difference of nonfinite control in English, and finite control in Persian. The A'-chains of (1-4) must have a Case-position, so that they may receive a Theta-role. However, unlike English control verbs, those in Persian do not assign Case to the nonovert operator; Case assignment under VP is right-to-left. Case-marked complements appear preverbally. Examples are given in (47) and (51). As seen in sentences (1-4), sentential complements occur post-verbally, and as a result, the matrix V does not assign Case to their heads and specifiers. As such, the nonovert operator in Persian control is not Case-marked. In order for the Visibility Condition to be met, the embedded variable must be Case-marked by its governor, the embedded INFL, as indicated in the A'-chain in (54).

(54) ... V ... [Op$_i$ [e$_i$ ...
            [-Case] [+Case]

Another difference between nonfinite and finite control concerns how to account for the fact that only subjects are controlled in clauses embedded under control predicates. Consider the structure in (52) again. In English, since the operator is Case-marked by the matrix predicate, the variable must not be Case-marked. The only non-Case position for the variable is the subject of an infinitive.

However, this explanation will not work for finite control, since the variable must occur in a Case position, of which there are many. In finite control, the fact that only subjects are controlled under these predicates results from the independently motivated requirement that the embedded AGR must be coindexed with its subject. For the predication process to be satisfied, the indices of the embedded AGR, the variable, the nonovert operator, and the matrix controller must match. That is, the indices should refer to the same NP, as shown in the structural configuration in (55). Evidence of this is given in sentence (56) where, even though by standard.procedure, the AGR and the embedded subject are coindexed, the embedded indices do not match that of the selected controller. As mentioned earlier, the only possible alternative for sentence (56) is for the overt pronoun *to* 'you' to appear in the embedded subject position.

(55) [$_{IP}$ ... NP$_j$ ... [$_{CP}$ Op$_j$ [$_{IP}$ [e$_j$] [$_{I'}$ I +AGR$_j$

(56) *doktor be madär$_i$ pišnähad=kärd
      doctor to mother$_i$ suggested:3S
              [Op$_{i/j}$ [ke e$_j$ en däva-ra här šäb bo-xor-i$_j$
              [Op$_{i/j}$ [that e$_j$ this drug-AC each night SJ-eat-2S$_j$
          'The doctor suggested to Mother$_i$ [Op$_{i/j}$ [that
            you$_j$ should take$_j$ this medicine every night.'

Therefore, the fact only subjects are controlled is due to two independent principles: AGR and its subject must be coindexed when rich inflection obtains; all indices must be identical in a predication process. Contrasting finite control with nonfinite control, we see that the A'-chain of finite control contains a Case-assigner, whereas the one of nonfinite control does not. Moreover, the structure in (55) explains why objects are not controlled under Persian control predicates: they do not bear a coindexation relation with their Case-assigners.

6. Conclusion. In this paper, I have set forth an analysis of Persian finite control that captures its inherent similarity with nonfinite control. I have shown that independently motivated principles of the grammar account for the properties of Persian control. First, control in Persian permits the presence of the complementizer *ke*. However, its appearance is due to its apparent lack of features, which do not have an effect on Specifier-HEAD agreement. As a result, the complementizer does not alter the A'-binding of the variable by the operator. Second, since the A'-chain of control must meet the Visibility Condition, there must be at most one Case position in the chain. Unlike the English null operator, the one in Persian is not assigned Case, and therefore, the variable in the embedded [NP,IP] must have Case. Next, the fact that the embedded AGR must be coindexed with the embedded [NP,IP] for independent reasons explains why only subjects are controlled in these constructions. To conclude, I have argued that the nonovert operator model of control is well motivated given the uniformity of the accounts of finite and nonfinite control, as well its insights into the overall differences of the two types.

References

Borer, Hagit. 1986. I-Subjects. LI.17.375-416.

Borer, Hagit. 1987. Anaphoric AGR. to appear in O. Jaeggli and K. Safir (eds.) Dordrecht: Reidel Inc.

Bouchard, Denis. 1984. On the Content of Empty Categories. Dordrecht: Foris Press.

Chomsky, Noam. 1981. Lectures on Government and Binding. Dordrecht: Foris Press.

Chomsky, Noam. 1986. Barriers. Cambridge: MIT Press.

Chung, Sandra and James McCloskey. 1987. Government, Barriers, and Small Clauses in Modern Irish. LI.18.173-238.

Clark, Robin. 1985. Boundaries and the Treatment of Control Theory. Doctoral dissertation, University of California, Los Angeles.

Huang, C. T. James. 1987. Towards a Generalized Theory of Control. unpublished manuscript.

Koster, Jan. 1984. On Binding and Control. LI.15.417-459.

Manzini, Maria Rita. 1983. On Control and Control Theory. LI.14.421-448.

Rizzi, Luigi. 1986. Relativized Minimality. unpublished manuscript.

A UNIFIED APPROACH TO COPULAR SENTENCES[*]

Lorie Heggie

University of Southern California

1. Introduction

Sentences such as (1) and (2) are generally assumed to be "equative" because they contain what appears to be a referential NP on each side of the copula.

    (1) John is the teacher.
    (2) The teacher is John.

The existence of identity statements involving deixis such as *That man is John* suggest that equative sentences do exist; however, the goal of this paper will be to demonstrate that the sentences in (1) and (2) can be more accurately characterized as involving the presence of a subject and a predicate, rather than being equative. This approach not only accounts for many of the properties of the sentences in (1) and (2), but also readily extends to provide an account for the relation between clefting and pseudoclefting.

Two possible structures for (1) are illustrated in (3) and (4).

    (3) [[John] [is] [the teacher]]
    (4) [[John$_i$] [is [$_{NP}$ t$_i$ [$_{NP}$ the teacher]]]]

The structure in (3) illustrates the hypothesis argued for by Williams (1984) that equative sentences involve no hierarchical structure; both NPs are equally selected and Case-marked by the copula. The second structure, in (4), illustrates an analysis proposed by Stowell (1978) and Couquaux (1979) that the copula is a raising verb when it involves predication. As a raising verb, the copula is assumed to assign neither theta-roles nor Case. It simply has the property of selecting a predication structure, which I assume to be an adjoined small clause, following Stowell (1984). The structure in (4) will be argued to be the correct structure for *John is the teacher*, where *the teacher* is a predicate which assigns an external theta-role to *John*, which then raises in order to get Case.

There are three possibilities for the structure corresponding to sentences like *The teacher is John* in (2).

    (5) [[the teacher] [is] [John]]
    (6) [[the teacher$_i$] [is [$_{NP}$ t$_i$ [$_{NP}$ John]]]]

The first option, in (5), illustrates Williams' hypothesis that these sentences involve a flat configuration which may permute freely. The

* I am grateful to Osvaldo Jaeggli and Mürvet Enç for many helpful discussions. All remaining errors are mine.

129

structure in (6) illustrates a second possibility where *John* is now
the predicate of *the teacher.* Both of these options are problematic.
The first, in (5), ignores the evidence for hierarchy in these
structures, and the second option would force the rigid
designator *John* to be a predicate, which cannot be the case as names
almost never behave like predicates.[1] Alternatively, the configuration in (6) might serve as a possible structure for an equative
sentence where *be* would assign Case to *John*, as suggested in Safir
(1985). The NP *John* should then behave as an argument of the copula,
which is not the case. The structure which I will argue for is that in
(7), where the predicate *the teacher* has raised into Comp and forced
Subject-AUX inversion.

(7) $[_{COMP}$ the teacher$_i$ $[is_k]$ $]$ $[$ $[John_j]$ $[_{INFL}$ t_k $[_{NP}$ t_j $[_{NP}$ t_i $]$ $]$ $]$ $]$ $]$

On this view, the inverted forms of sentences such as *John is the
teacher* involve a kind of syntactic focus which requires movement at
S-structure. This movement does not, however, trigger a Principle C
violation of the Binding Theory because *the teacher* is a predicate. I
adopt here the Predicate Principle proposed in Safir (1987).

(8) The Predicate Principle (Safir, 1987)
A potential referring expression is a predicate or else free.
I will begin my argument by presenting evidence that the postcopular
position is not inherently a position of reference. Next, I will
demonstrate that definite descriptors in the precopular position do
not in fact behave as definite, referential elements. Thirdly, I will
provide evidence for the predicate being in Comp. All of these data
are problematic for any approach which attempts to maintain a "flat"
configuration for these copular sentences or treats both NPs as
arguments. Moreover, the analysis being advocated here can be
extended to the analysis of specificational pseudoclefts.

2. Evidence for the Predicate Position
The first piece of evidence comes from the behavior of
pronominal clitics in copular sentences in French. As illustrated in
(9), clitics can correspond to an argument position.

(9) Je la/le vois.
I her/him-see
'I see her/him.'
There is also a second type of clitic which corresponds to a predicate.
This clitic is illustrated in (10b) where le stands for the predicate
très douée 'very talented', which appears in (10a).

---

[1] See Rapoport (1987) for these exceptions.

(10) a. Christine sera très douée.
'Christine will be very talented.'
b. Christine le/*la sera.
'Christine it/it(FEM)-is'

There is no agreement in predicate clitics; there is only the one form, le. When a clitic is inserted into a copular sentence in French, we find that the clitic may correspond to the definite NP of a sentence like (1), but it cannot correspond to the proper name in postverbal position after inversion of the NPs, a fact first noticed by Ruwet (1975).

(11) a. Monsieur Ducros l'est, mon docteur
'Mr. Ducros   it-is, my doctor'
b.*Mon docteur l'est, Monsieur Ducros.
'My doctor it-is, Mr. Ducros'

Specifically, the predicate clitic may correspond to *mon docteur* 'my doctor' in (11a), but not to *Monsieur Ducros* 'Mr. Ducros' in (11b). These data suggest that only predicate clitics may appear in these sentences; only *mon docteur* may correspond to a clitic, but not *Monsieur Ducros*. Proper names, however, should normally be capable of licensing a referential pronominal clitic. To test further whether or not this is possible, consider the sentences in (12).

(12) a. Jean et Marie sont les parents de Christine.
'John and Mary are the parents of Christine'
b.*Jean et Marie les sont.
'John and Mary them-are'
c. Jean et Marie le sont.
'John and Mary it-are'

The plural subject necessarily disambiguates the form of the clitic in (12b), revealing that only a predicate clitic may surface, as in (12c). It is impossible for the postcopular proper name to license a referential clitic.

These data suggest that the postcopular position of sentences as in (1) is not a position of referentiality. Otherwise, a referential clitic would be allowed. In addition, for inverted sentences as in (2), the postcopular proper name does not take on the properties of a predicate to license a predicate clitic, as shown in (11b).

3. Predicates Remain Predicates

The following data demonstrate that definite descriptors in pre-copular position do not correspond to arguments, nor do they introduce a discourse referent. First, consider the sentence in (13), which illustrates the behavior of intensive reflexives.

(13) The/*an organizer of our group himself will have to do it.

As illustrated in (13), intensive reflexives can only adjoin to definite arguments. When we test the behavior of the intensive reflexive *himself* in copular sentences, its distribution is unexpected.

(14) a. John himself is the organizer of our group.
    b. John is the organizer of our group himself.
    c.*The organizer of our group himself is John.
    d. The organizer of our group is John himself.

As shown in (14a) and (14d), *himself* may adjoin to *John*, or it may extrapose (e.g., *John left himself*), as in (14b). However, it cannot adjoin to the definite NP *the organizer of the group* in (14c) or in (14b). The fact that *himself* may never adjoin to a predicate is even clearer in (15b) because of the difference in gender.

(15) a. With a dress and wig on, John himself is the strangest looking woman.
    b.*With a dress and wig on, John is the strangest looking woman$_i$ herself$_i$.

We are thus led to the conclusion that although the definite NP in (14c) is in what appears to be a subject position, it is not an argument. I conclude that it must therefore be a predicate.

Now consider the sentences in (16) and (17).

(16) a. [Son meilleur ami d'enfance]$_i$ adore les enfants. Il$_i$ est marrant.
    b. [His best friend from childhood]$_i$ loves children. He$_i$'s neat.

(17) a.*Son meilleur ami$_i$ est maintenant Jean-Jacques, mais il y a trois ans il$_i$ était Michel.   (Kayne, 1972)
    b.*His best friend$_i$ is now Jean-Jacques, but three years ago he$_i$ was Michel.

As illustrated in (16), subjects such as *his best friend* can normally introduce a discourse referent which can be referred back to later in the discourse. However, when this same NP is found in precopular position as in (17), it cannot introduce a discourse referent. As with the definite NP in (14), *his best friend* appears to be referential, but does not in fact possess the properties of a referential NP.

    A third piece of evidence that definite NPs in postcopular position are indeed predicates comes from their behavior in control structures, first observed in Ruwet (1975). The sentence in (18) illustrates the fact that as an argument, *our teacher* does not encounter any problems controlling an embedded PRO.

(18) Our teacher tried [PRO to teach us calculus]

In (19), however, this is not the case.

(19) a. John tried [PRO to be our teacher]
    b.*Our teacher tried [PRO to be John]

With the NP *John*, control obtains; with the NP *our teacher*, it does not. These facts cannot be explained by earlier analyses. On the present analysis however, the reason for this difference in behavior can be explained in terms of the Extended Null Operator Generalization (ENOG), discussed in Heggie (1987).

    (20) The Extended Null Operator Generalization (Heggie, 1987)

            An empty category at D-structure (PRO, *pro*, and null operator) must constitute a minimally satisfied theta-grid.

Essentially, empty categories which are base-generated at D-structure do not assign any theta-roles; they cannot select any arguments or complements. They must therefore substitute for a constituent whose theta-grid is complete, i.e., there are no theta-roles which must be assigned from the position occupied by the empty element. This generalization thus predicts that PRO, pro and null operators can never be base-generated in the position of a predicate.

    Returning to the examples in (19), in (19a), PRO is generated in the subject position of the embedded clause in the configuration [PRO [our teacher]], where it receives a theta-role from *our teacher*, and raises to an ungoverned position. In (19b), on the other hand, PRO has been base-generated in a predicate position as in [John [PRO]], leaving *John* without a theta-role. The sentence in (19b) thus violates the Theta Criterion. In addition, John does not receive Case.

4. Fronted Predicates as Elements in Comp

    Having established that in sentences such as *John is the teacher*, *John* is a subject and *the teacher*, a predicate, the question arises as to what the structure must be for the inverse counterpart *The teacher is John* I will argue that the predicate moves into Comp, triggering SUBJ-AUX inversion, as in (7).

    The first argument comes from the distribution of *only*. As shown in (21a), *only* may modify an element in a A-position. However, it cannot modify an element which has moved to Comp at S-structure, as (21b) indicates.

    (21) a. John saw only the teacher
          b.*Only what/who did John see?

Consider now the following sentences:

    (22) a. Only John is the teacher.
          b. John is only the teacher.
          c.*Only the teacher is John.
          d. The teacher is only John.

When we test the behavior of *only* with copular sentences, as in (22), we find that *only* may modify *John* in either pre- or post- copular position as in (22a) and (22d); however, *the teacher* may be modified by *only* only in its postverbal position. The sentence in (22c) thus suggests that *the teacher* is in a structural position which is not available for *only* to modify, that is, Comp.[2]

The next two sets of data come from clefting phenomena, the structure of which can be found in (23).

(23) $[_{IP}$ it be $[_{CP}$ XP$_i$ $[_{CP}$ OP$_i$+that $[_{IP}$ ....t_i............ $]$

Following essentially the insights of Chomsky (1977), Barss (1984) and Stowell (1984), I assume that the cleft position is base-generated as the subject of a small clause headed by CP. A null operator is generated in the predicate CP and raises at S-structure to the Spec of Comp to form an A'-chain with the cleft position as the head. The chain then transmits theta-roles and Case to the cleft position as the Comp position is coindexed with it via predication. This mechanism thus allows for the felicitous identification of the null operator.

Turning to the examples in (24) and (25), the facts are the following: a subject in precopular position like *John Smith* may be clefted, as in (24b), but all other possibilities for clefting do not obtain.

(24) a. John Smith is my doctor.
　　 b. It's John Smith that is my doctor.
　　 c.*It's my doctor that John Smith is.
(25) a. My doctor is John Smith.
　　 b.*It's my doctor that is John Smith.
　　 c.*It's John Smith that my doctor is.

To understand why there is such a restriction on the clefting of these sentences, consider their D-structure.

(24b') It is $[_{CP}$John$_i$ $[_{CP}$[OP$_i$+that] t_i is $[_{NP}t_i$ $[_{NP}$my doctor]]]]

(24c')*It is $[_{CP}$my doctor$_i$ $[_{CP}$[OP$_i$+that] John$_i$ is $[_{NP}t_i$ $[_{NP}t_i]]]]$

(25b')*It is $[_{CP}$my doctor$_i$ $[_{CP}$[OP$_i$+that-is$_k$] John$_i$ t_k $[_{NP}t_i$ $[_{NP}t_i]]]]$

(25c')*It is $[_{CP}$John$_i$ $[_{CP}$[OP$_i$+that-my doctor$_i$-is$_k$] t_i t_k $[_{NP}t_i$ $[_{NP}t_i]]]]$

As can be seen in (24b'), an A'-chain is formed from the embedded subject position, where *John* receives a theta-role from *my doctor*.

---

[2] One could imagine a context in which (24)c would be possible if several people uniquely identified as "the teacher", "the butcher", "the father", etc. are claiming to be John and the statement is made that only the teacher is John. This context is only an apparent counterexample, however, as in this case, the sentence must have an equative reading.

In (24c'), however, the null operator moves from a predicate position, *my doctor*, thus violating the ENOG cited earlier in (20) and leaving the subject *John* without a theta-role. In (25b') there is a similar configuration. The null operator moves from a predicate position, leaving its subject without a theta-role, as predicted by ENOG. The last case, (25c'), violates the Doubly-Filled Comp Filter since not only the null operator, but also the predicate *my doctor* has moved into Comp.[3] These facts are not predicted if these sentences are hypothesized to involve a flat configuration.[4]

The second set of clefting phenomena comes from data first discussed in Ruwet (1975). It involves the nature of the complementizer in cleft sentences in French. Following the formulation in Pesetsky (1982) of an earlier insight of Kayne's, French has a rule where *que* 'that' changes to *qui* 'who' when it is needed to properly govern a subject trace, as in (26).

(26) $[_{CP} \text{wh}_i/t_i \text{ que }] \dashrightarrow [_{CP} \text{qui}_i] / \underline{\quad\quad} [_{IP}... [t_i, +\text{Nom}]...]$

Keeping this in mind, consider the sentences in (27), where the predicate has been clefted.

(27) C'est verts, et non bleus, que/*qui les yeux de Christine sont.

'It's green, and not blue, that Christine's eyes are.'

Note that the complementizer cannot be *qui*, but only *que*, demonstrating that there is no subject trace that needs to be governed. Turning now to (28), we find that when what has been argued to be the predicate in copular sentences, that is, the definite postverbal NP, is clefted, again only *que* may be found.

(28) a. C'est le meilleur ami d'Arlette (et non de Jeannette) que Jean est.

'It's the best friend of Arlette (and not of Jeannette) that John is.'

b. *C'est le meilleur ami d'Arlette (et non de Jeannette) qui est Jean.

The sentence in (28b) indicates that *le meilleur ami d'Arlette* 'the best friend of Arlette' is not related to a subject position. This interpretation of these data is confirmed by the fact that the clefting of a subject allows for a grammatical sentence only if *que* has been changed to *qui*, as illustrated in (29a) and (29b).

---

[3] The ungrammaticality of this sentence may also be characterized as a violation of the Wh-Island Constraint as there has been movement of an element to Comp which creates a chain to a position not included in Comp.

[4] The fact that these sentences may be embedded as in *I thought that the teacher was John* suggests that the fronting mechanism active in these sentences may optionally adjoin to IP, and that Subject-AUX inversion must follow from some inherent property of the copula yet to be explained.

(29) a.*C'est Jean (non Claude) qu' est le meilleur ami
d'Arlette.
b. C'est Jean (non Claude) qui est le meilleur ami
d'Arlette.
'It's John (not Claude) that is the best friend of Arlette.'
Thus, we have more evidence for an approach where copular sentences
with definite NPs involve predication. Clearly, these sentences
involve a hierarchical structure, as evidenced, for example, by the
appearance of island effects in English cleft sentences.

5. Crosslinguistic Evidence

The last piece of data which I would like to present before
exploring pseudoclefts involves Ilonggo, a language spoken in the
Philippines and discussed in Schachter (1973). Ilonggo provides
overt, morphological evidence for an analysis of the copula which
allows for the focussing of the predicate in copular sentences.
Consider first the sentences in (30).

(30) a. Nag-dala   ang-babayi   sang-bata
AGT-bring TOP-woman OBJ-child
'The woman brought a child.'
b. Nag-dala   ang-babayi   sa-bata
AGT-bring TOP-woman OBJ-child
'The woman brought the child.'
c.*Nag-dala   ang-babayi   ang-bata
AGT-bring TOP-woman TOP-child
'The woman brought the child.'

The sentence in (30a) illustrates a simple, declarative sentence with
focus on *babayi* 'woman'. This focus serves in this case to
render *babayi* definite. The sentence in (30b) demonstrates that to
make the object definite, one must change the object morpheme to *sa*
'the', and not, as in (30c), to another topic marker. The requirement
that there be only a single occurrence of the topic marker per clause
holds of all sentences, except when the verb is the copula.

(31) a. Babayi ang-maestra
woman TOP-teacher
'The teacher is a woman.'
b. Ang-babayi ang-maestra
TOP-woman TOP-teacher
'The teacher is the woman.'

As demonstrated in (31), a predication as in (31a) only requires a
single topic marker on the subject *babayi* 'teacher'. To make the
second NP definite, a second topic marker is used, creating a doubly-
focussed structure. A similar phenomenon is shown in (32) with a

cleft sentence where the clause predicated of *babayi* carries a topic marker.

> (32) Ang-babayi ang nag-dala sang-bata
> TOP-woman TOP AGT-bring OBJ-child
> 'It's the woman that brought a child.'

Thus Ilonggo provides crosslinguistic evidence for the ability of the copula to allow a predicate to be focussed, parallel to the fronting analysis I have argued for for *The teacher is John* in (2).

To summarize, I have shown that sentences such as *John is the teacher*, which have been assumed to be equative, in fact exhibit a number of properties which suggest that they are predicate structures and that the inverse sentence *The teacher is John* is related to the former sentence in that it is derived by movement of the predicate *the teacher* into Comp, thereby triggering SUBJ-AUX inversion. We have considered evidence from the behavior of clitics in French, intensive reflexives, coreference, control, the behavior of *only*, cleft sentences in English, and complementizer choices in French cleft sentences. Going one step further now, I will demonstrate that on this analysis not only do we explain the preceding data, but we also have the key to understanding the relationship between cleft and pseudocleft sentences.

6. Deriving Specificational Pseudoclefts

Turning now to (33), we start with the cleft sentence *It's Bill's tie that Mary hates*:

> (33) a. It's Bill's tie that Mary hates.
> b. $[_{IP}$ it $[$ be $[_{CP}$ Bill's tie$_i$ $[_{CP}$ QP$_i$+that $[_{IP}$ Mary hates t_i $]]]]]$

As in (23), I assume that *be* has selected a CP-small clause which passes Case and a theta-role to its subject by the movement of a null operator into Comp. The claim that cleft sentences may only base-generate a null operator is motivated by two sets of data. First, it is necessary to distinguish a *wh*-question such as *How sick is John* from *It's sick that John is*, which is ungrammatical as a syntactic cleft. Second, as argued for extensively in Rochemont (1986) and Delahunty (1982) (for different reasons), the appearance of *wh*-elements in the complementizer of cleft sentences is an extremely limited phenomenon, and appears to occur only when the clefted element is nominal, purely on an analogy with relative clauses. Thus, in standard English, we would not allow *It's Bill's tie what Mary hates* precisely because *what* is not a relative pronoun.

Returning to pseudoclefts, I propose that pseudoclefts are the overt operator counterpart to clefts. Whereas clefts contain null operators and are thus bound by the properties of null operators, pseudoclefts contain overt *wh*-operators, allowing them a much greater degree of freedom. For example, as captured by ENOG, predicates can never be clefted. Hence, the ungrammaticality of *It's sick that John is*. However, since pseudoclefts involve an overt operator, which can assign theta-roles, the pseudocleft counterpart *What John is is sick* is grammatical.

Turning to (34) and (35), we have the derivation of first what has been called an inverse pseudocleft and the next step, which is a specificational pseudocleft.

(34) a. Bill's tie is what Mary hates.
b. $[_{IP}$ Bill's tie$_i$ [be $[_{CP}$ t$_i$ $[_{CP}$ what$_i$ $[_{IP}$ Mary hates t$_i$]]]]]

(35) a. What Mary hates is Bill's tie.
b. $[_{CP}$ $[_{CP}$ What$_i$ Mary hates t$_i$]$_i$ is$_k$ $[_{IP}$ Bill's tie$_i$ [t$_k$ $[_{CP}$ t$_i$ $[_{CP}$ t$_i$]]]]]

In (34), *what* is base-generated and moved to the Spec of Comp. It gains an index from the predication structure and transmits its theta-role to *Bill's tie*. It does not, however, transmit Case as it itself requires Case in order not to violate the Case Filter. This forces *Bill's tie* to raise to subject position in order to get Case. Thus, this sentence is the structural equivalent to *John is the teacher*. In (35), the predicate *what Mary hates* raises to Comp and triggers SUBJ-AUX inversion, parallel to the sentence *The teacher is John*.

The claim that specificational pseudoclefts involve inversion of a predicated structure is not new. Williams (1983) argues that specificational pseudoclefts involve a late stylistic inversion rule. We now turn to the evidence for deriving specificational pseudoclefts from clefts.

6.1 The "Free Relative" as a Predicate

The first piece of evidence which argues that the "free relative" in pseudoclefts is indeed a predicate comes from a fact noted in Williams (1983) that predicates under the copula cannot be universally quantified, as shown in (36a), unless the universal quantifies over properties, as in (36b).

(36) a.*John is every teacher.
b. John is everything I want to be.
Consider now the pseudocleft sentences in (37).

(37) a.*Bill's tie is whatever Mary hates.
b.*Whatever Mary hates is Bill's tie.

As predicted, it is impossible to quantify the *wh*-element in these sentences. It is, however, possible to find a free relative in postcopular position.

(38) a. John is whatever he was three years ago.
b.*Whatever he was three years ago was John.
c. Whatever he was three years ago is/*was
what John is now.

The sentence in (38a) demonstrates that *whatever* may in fact quantify over a property, but, as shown in (38b), (38a) must be a simple predication; it cannot involve an A'-chain as the fronting of the free relative renders it ungrammatical. The sentence in (38c) confirms this analysis as it is possible to equate two free relatives; however, this sentence must be a predication with an NP head and not a CP head because it violates tense harmony, a known property of specificational pseudoclefts (Higgins, 1973). Thus, we can conclude that the "free relative" in pseudoclefts has the property of disallowing quantifiers, a property known to be true of predicates under the copula.

A second piece of evidence comes again from clefting.

(39) a. It's [Bill's tie] that ___ is [what Mary hates].
b.*It's [what Mary hates] that [Bill's tie] is ___.
c.*It's [what Mary hates] that ___ is [Bill's tie].
d.*It's [Bill's tie] that [what Mary hates] is ___.

The clefting of pseudocleft sentences parallels exactly the behavior observed earlier with sentences such as *John is the teacher* and *the teacher is John*, suggesting that these sentences also involve inversion to Comp position of a predicate.[5]

6.2 APs as Subjects

Having argued that the "free relative" in pseudoclefts is in fact a predicate, I will also argue that an AP such as in *[AP important to himself] is what John is* in pseudoclefts behaves as a subject, drawing from data first observed by Higgins (1973). The first piece of evidence comes from the behavior of comparatives.

(40) a. [What John is] is more [important to him] than
[what Bill is] is.
b.*[What John is] is more [important to himself] than
[what Bill is] is.

In (40), the phrase *important to himself*, which unambiguously denotes a specificational interpretation and thus should be a subject, cannot enter into a comparative whereas *important to him*, which is

---

5 See Williams (1983) for further arguments that the "free relative" in pseudoclefts is a predicate.

unambiguously a predicate, can. The type of comparative in (40) is limited to predicates, which *important to himself* is not.

A second piece of evidence for the subjecthood of *important to himself* involves extraction out of the AP (from Higgins, 1973).

(41) a. [What John is] is [proud of that book].
      b.*This is the book that [what John is] is [proud of _].
      c. [What John is] seems to be [important to that woman].
      d. That's the woman who [what John is] seems to be [important to _].

As illustrated in (41), extraction is impossible out of the AP in (41b), but not out of the AP in (41d). This is predicted if *important to himself* is a subject. The structure of (41b) would be that of (25c').

6.3 Further Predictions

A number of further predictions are made concerning specificational pseudoclefts if they involve the movement of a predicate to Comp. First, they will not be able to be controlled, directly parallel to the sentence in (19b), a hypothesis borne out in (42b).

(42) a. [What(ever) John rode] tried [PRO to jump that fence].
      b.*[What John rode] tried [PRO$_i$ to be [a beautiful Hanoverian] t$_i$].

Secondly, any kind of movement which requires some element to move past the focussed predicate should be ungrammatical, assuming that the predicate is already in the Spec of Comp position. This prediction is borne out in data first observed by Higgins (1973) for Wh-questions, in (43), for exclamatory expressions, as in (44), and in Yes-No questions in (45).

(43). a. [How important to him] is [what Tom is]?
       b.*[How important to himself] is [what Tom is]?
(44). a. [How important to him] [what Tom is] is!
       b.*[How important to himself] [what Tom is] is!
(45) a. Is [what Tom is] [important to him]?
      b.*Is [what Tom is] [important to himself]?
      c. Is [important to himself] [what Tom is]?

As expected, in (45c), because *important to himself* is the subject, a yes-no question may be formed parallel to *Is John the teacher.*

The last set of data which I would like to consider is one involving pronominal coreference. The basic difference in the behavior of pronominal coreference between declarative sentences and specificational pseudoclefts is given in (46).

(46) a. [What(ever) he$_i$ saw in the mirror] horrified Tom$_i$.
      b.*[What he$_i$ saw in the mirror] was [Tom$_i$].

As shown in (46a), normally a pronoun embedded in a free relative may corefer with a name that follows. This is however not the case with specificational pseudoclefts, as (46b) illustrates. Whereas this behavior of specificational pseudoclefts may have been a mystery in the past, on the analysis that I have argued for, the coreference behavior shown in (46b) is predicted; the pronouns retain the same coreference possiblities as their base has.

(47) a. John$_i$ smashed his$_i$ car.
   b. It's [his$_i$ car] [that John$_i$ smashed].
   c. [His$_i$ car] is [what John$_i$ smashed].
   d. [What John$_i$ smashed] was [his$_i$ car].

(48) a.*He$_i$ smashed John$_i$'s car.
   b.*It's [John$_i$'s car] [that he$_i$ smashed].
   c.*[John$_i$'s car] is [what he$_i$ smashed].
   d.*[What he$_i$ smashed] was [John$_i$'s car].

As illustrated in (47) and (48), the A'-chain preserves the coreference relations of the base sentence. Thus, (47) and (48) provide more evidence that the approach being advocated here is correct.

7. Conclusion

I have argued that many sentences which have been regarded as being equative and involving either a flat configuration or a Case assigning feature from the copula are in fact predicate sentences that allow for the fronting of the predicate into Comp. This claim, however, cannot take into account the sentences in (49) and (50), where what I have claimed to be a predicate is in fact behaving perfectly as a subject in the [NP,IP] position for a Yes-No question (cf. (49)) and a raising context (cf. (50)).

(49) Is the teacher John?

(50) The teacher seems to be John.

We have not, however, ruled out the existence of equative sentences; they in fact exist for cases such as *He's John*. The prediction then is that sentences such as (49) and (50) must be equative, that is, *the teacher* must pick out a unique referent from the discourse, rather than refer to any individual with the property of being a teacher. That this is the correct approach to these sentences is suggested by the impossibility of raising for the precopular constituents in the specificational pseudoclefts in (51), which can only refer to a property and not a person.

(51) a.*What John is seems to be a fool.
   b.*What John is seems to be proud of himself.

REFERENCES

Barss, Andrew. 1984. "Chain Binding". Manuscript, MIT

Chomsky, Noam. 1977. "On Wh-Movement." In Culicover et al, (eds.), Formal Syntax, 71-132.

Couquaux, Daniel. 1979. "Sur la syntaxe des phrases predicatives en français." Linguisticae Investigationes III:2, 245-284.

Delahunty, Gerald. 1982. Topics in the Syntax and Semantics of English Cleft Sentences, Indiana University Linguistics Club, Bloomington, Indiana, 47445.

Heggie, Lorie. 1987. "The Range of Null Operators: Evidence from Clefting." Manuscript, University of Southern California.

Higgins, Roger. 1973. On the Nature of Pseudoclefts, Doctoral Dissertation, MIT.

Pesetsky, David. 1982. "Complementizer-Trace Phenomena and the Nominative Island Condition." The Linguistic Review 1, 297-343.

Rapoport, Tova. 1987. Copular, Nominal, and Small Clauses: A Study of Israeli Hebrew, Doctoral Dissertation, MIT.

Rochemont, Michael. 1986. Focus in Generative Grammar, Philadelphia: John Benjamins Publishing Company.

Ruwet, Nicolas. 1975. "Les Phrases Copulatives en Français." Recherches Linguistiques 3, 143-191.

Safir, Ken. 1985. Syntactic Chains, Cambridge: Cambridge University Press.

_____. 1987. "What Explains the Definiteness Effect?." In E. Reuland and A. ter Meulen (eds.), The Representation of (In)definiteness. Cambridge: MIT Press, pp. 71-97.

Stowell, Tim. 1978. "What Was There Before There Was There." Chicago Linguistics Society 14, 458-471.

_____. 1984. "Subjects Across Categories." The Linguistic Review 2, 272-285.

_____. 1985. "Null Operators and their Antecedents." Proceedings of NELS XVI, 476-493.

Williams, Edwin. 1983. "Semantic vs. Syntactic Categories." Linguistics and Philosophy 6, 423-446.

_____. 1984. "There-Insertion." Linguistic Inquiry 15:1, 131-153.

Affricates are not Contour Segments
José Ignacio Hualde
University of Southern California

1. Contour Segments and Edge Effects

In Sagey (1986), a distinction is established between two types of segments involving multiple articulations, depending on whether or not these articulations are phonologically ordered. CONTOUR SEGMENTS which possess ordered articulations are thus distinguished from COMPLEX SEGMENTS, whose articulations are unordered. Phonological ordering is made to follow from the presence of incompatible features in a·segment. If a segment bears the features [+f] and [-f] these two features will have to be ordered and we will have a contour segment. The class of contour segments would then include affricates, prenasalized stops, short diphthongs and segments bearing contour tones .

The prediction is made that contour segments will show EDGE EFFECTS. That is, the contour segment in (1) will be considered a [+f] segment for phonological processes whose trigger or target is to its left; but will be considered a [-f] segment for rules involving its right side:

(1)   X
          / \
        [+f] [-f]

Sagey argues that affricates do in fact behave in the manner predicted by their consideration as contour segments. We will have shown that affricates are correctly characterized as contour segments if they are treated as [-cont] by rules involving their left side and as [+cont] for rules whose conditioning environment is on their right side. That is, if affricates are indeed contour segments with the structure in (2) they should undergo rules of the types exemplified in (3a) and (3b) and not be affected by rules such

143

as (3c) or (3d):

(2)   X
           / \
     [-cont][+cont]

(3) a. [-cont] ---> Z / Y ___
    b. [+cont] ---> Z / ___ Y

    c. [-cont] ---> Z / ___ Y
    d. [+cont] ---> Z/ Y ___

There are two ways in which affricates may fail to show edge effects, thus falsifying the predictions made by the proposed structure. First, an affricate will not show edge effects if it triggers or undergoes a rule for which the relevant context is on the wrong side; for instance, if an affricate is affected by rule (3c) or (3d). I will refer to these cases as instances of overapplication of a rule to affricates. Second, an affricate may fail to show edge effects by not being affected by a rule sensitive to the [cont] value present on the relevant side of the affricate. This would be the case if a rule like (3a) affected stops but not affricates or a rule like (3b) affected fricatives but not affricates. These cases will be referred to as underapplication of rules to affricates.

I will show that instances of both overapplication and underapplication of rules to affricates do exists and that a single language, Basque, does indeed present counterevidence of the two kinds mentioned: overapplication and underapplication of rules to affricates. To the extent that the existence of edge effects constitutes the most solid evidence for proposing a contour configuration for affricates, the contour segment hypothesis for affricates is undermined.I will then conclude that affricates are not contour segments. I will also show that the Basque data are inconsistent with the treatment of affricates as a type of stop characterized by some additional feature such as [+delayed release]. The final conclusion will then be that affricates are complex segments bearing both plus and minus continuant specifications. These features are only ordered in the phonetic component and in a totally predictible manner : [-cont], [+cont].

I will first examine instances of underapplication.

2. Underapplication of rules to affricates

Sagey (1986; 93-4), citing Kenstowicz and Kisseberth (1979) and Wonderly (1951), shows that Zoque has a rule of type (3a) which, as predicted by the contour segment hypothesis, treats affricates as [-cont] segments. The rule of Zoque voices a [-cont] segment after a nasal, (4). It affects stops and affricates, which under the contour segment hypothesis are [-cont] from their left side, examples are shown in (5a). Fricatives are not affected by the rule. As shown in (5b), in nasal-fricative sequences, either no rule applies or the nasal is deleted:

(4) Zoque Non-continuant Voicing:
[-cont] ---> [+voice] / [+nasal] _____

(5)a. /min-tam/   [mindamʌ]   'come! (pl.)'
       /pʌn-kʌsi/   [pʌngʌsi]   'on a man'
       /pʌn-čʌki/   [pʌnǰʌki]   'figure of a man'
       /N-pama/   [mbama]   'my clothing'
       /N-tatah/   [ndatah]   'my father'
       /N-čoʔngoya/   [nǰoŋgoya]   'my rabbit'
       /N-kayu/   [ŋgayu]   'my horse'

    b.   [winsaʔu]   'he received'
                       [woʔmsoŋ]   'quail'
       /N-sʌk/   [sʌk]   'my beans'
       /N-šapun/   [šapun]   'my soap'

The behavior of Zoque affricates with respect to rule (4)

is totally consistent with the representation proposed in (2). It is in fact the only possible behavior consistent with this representation. I will show now that Basque possesses two rules also of the type in (3a), like Zoque Noncontinuant Voicing, but which excludes affricates, in a manner inconsistent with the contour segment hypothesis.

One of these two rules in Basque is actually rather similar to the rule in Zoque. This is a rule that voices stops after a nasal or lateral. The rule is given a linear formulation in (6):

(6) Basque Stop Voicing
    [-cont] ---> [+voice] / [-cont, +son] _____

Basque Stop Voicing is a lexical rule, whose domain of application includes verbal inflectional morphology and some nominal morphological strata. As the examples in (7) show, stop initial suffixes undergo the rule, but affricate initial suffixes do not. For each suffix examples with vowel-final stems are also given to show the underlying forms of the suffixes:

(7)a. Verbal inflection:
    perfective
    /neka-tu/   [nekatu]   'get tired'
    /ar-tu/   [artu]   'take'
    /afal-tu/   [afaldu]   'have dinner'
    /lan-tu/   [landu]   'labor'
    /ken-tu/   [kendu]   'take away'
    future
    /neka-tu-ko/   [nekatuko]   'get tired'
    /egin-ko/   [eɣiŋgo]   'do, make'
    /eśan-ko/   [eśaŋgo]   'say'
    /il-ko/   [ilˈɣo]   'die, kill'

    imperfective
    /neka-tsen/   [nekatsen]   'get tired'

/ar-tsen/	[artsen]	'take'
/afal-tsen/	[afaltsen]	'have dinner' *[afaldzen]
/lan-tsen/	[lantsen]	'labor' *[landzen]
/ken-tsen/	[kentsen]	'take away' *[kendzen]

b. Nominal inflection

/baɕo-tik/	[baɕotik]	'from the forest'
/lerin-tik/	[lerindik]	' from Lerin'
/non-tik/	[nondik]	'from where'
/uɕurbil-tik/	[uɕurβildik]	'from Usurbil'

/baɕo-ko/	[baɕoko]	'of the forest'
/lerin-ko/	[leriŋgo]	' of Lerin'
/non-ko/	[noŋgo]	' of where'
/orain-ko/	[orayŋgo]	' of now'
/uɕurbil-ko/	[uɕurβilɣo]	' of Usurbil'
/bein-ko/	[beyŋgo]	' of once'

/baɕo-tsat/	[baɕotsat]	' for a forest' *[basodzat]
/bein-tsat/	[beyntsat] *[beyndzat]	' at least (lit. 'for once')
/uɕurbil-tsat/	[uɕurβiltsat] *[uɕurβildzat]	'for Usurbil'
/martin-tsat/	[martintsat] *[martindzat]	' for Martin '

As for nasal or lateral plus fricative sequences, the distinction between fricatives and affricates is neutralized in this position, in favor of the affricate:

(8) /mendi-sale/ [mendisale]   ' mountaineer'
    /aɾan-sale/ [aɾantsale]   ' fisherman'

An explanation for the fact that affricates are not voiced by rule (6) that can be suggested is that a voiced affricate [dz] is not part of the inventory of most Basque dialects. There are however (Biscayan) Basque dialects that have this voiced affricate, in words such as those in (9):

(9) [dzaŋga]   'immersion'
     [dzirdzartak]   'beams'
     [dzartako]   'blow'

In these dialects affricates also fail to voice in the context of rule (6). That this hypothetical explanation is not along the right lines is clearly shown by the next set of facts to be immediately discussed.

There is a second rule of the type in (3a) that shows underapplication to affricates. In a number of Basque dialects noncontinuant coronal segments are palatalized after a high front vowel or glide. A linear formulation of the rule is given in (10):

(10) Coronal Non-continuant Palatalization
     [-cont, +cor] ---> [+high] / [+high, -back] ____

The examples given in (11) are from the Markina dialect (Rollo, 1925). As the examples show, the rule applies to /t/ (as well as to /l/ and /n/) (11a), but not to the continuant coronal /s/, (11b). The affricate /ts/ is also unaffected, (11c):

(11)a. /itaun/   [it'aun]   'question'
       /ituři/   [it'uři]   'fountain'
       /irudi-tu/   [irudit'u]   'imagine' (perf.)
       /amai-tu/   [amayt'u]   'finish' (perf.)
       /mendi-tik/   [mendit'ik]   'from the mountain'
       /mutil-a/   [mutiʎe]   'the boy' (abs.)
       /neska-tila/   [neskatiʎa]   'girl'
       /ipin-i/   [ipiñi]   'put' (perf.)
       /min-es/   [miñes]   'with pain'
    b. /gison/   [gison]   'man'
       /bisi/   [bisi]   'live' (perf.)
       /isen/   [isen]   'name'
       /lisun/   [lisun]   'mould, rust'
       /nois-ean/   [noysien]   'at times'

c. /itsar̄-i/   [itsar̄i]   'awake (perf.)'
/itsul-i/   [itsuli]   'fall (perf.)'
/lits-a-ke/   [litsake]   '(he) would be'
/amai-tse-a/ [amaytsie] 'the ending' (abs.)
/alai-tsu/   [alaytsu]   'happy'
/mendi-tsat/ [menditsat] 'for the mountain' (prol.)

It must be pointed out that both the palatal fricative [š] and the palatal affricate [tš] do occur in this and all Basque dialects . Examples from the Markina dialect are given in (12):

(12)   /mendi-a/ [mendiše] 'the mountain' (abs.)
       [perišak] 'the holidays' (abs.)
       [ušetu] 'drive away' (perf.)
       [itšaso] 'sea'
       [itšaropen] 'hope'
       [etše] 'house'
       [kutša] 'box'

As in the case of the Voicing rule seen above, affricates fail again to show edge effects, against the predictions of the contour hypothesis. The representation of affricates as contour segments predicts that if a rule of progressive palatalization affects /t/ after /i/, it should also affect /ts/ in the same environment. The fact is, however that affricates do not undergo the rule in this case.

An example of underapplication to affricates of a rule of type (3b) is provided by KiNande, a Bantu language of Eastern Zaire. In this language, /s/ is palatalized before a high front vowel or glide; but /ts/ is not affected in this context:[1]

(13) KiNande Palatalization
a. /s/ --> [š] / ___[+high, -back]
    but not /ts/ --> *[tš]

---

[1] I want to thank Mutaka Ngessimo for the KiNande data and Larry Hyman for bringing the KiNande facts to my attention.

b. [ešyombene] 'goats'
   [eβišimi] 'bugs (spec.)'
   [ešiseke] 'reeds'
c. [eβitsihya] 'to sneeze'
   [eritsikya] 'to cause to lose'
   [eritsirya] 'to make promise not to do s.t.'

We will now examine instances of overapplication. That is, cases where rules of types (3c) or (3d) do affect affricates, against the predictions made by the hypothesis of the contour configuration of these segments.

3. Overapplication of rules to affricates

The conception of affricates as contour segments makes the prediction that rules of the types in (3c) and (3d) should not affect affricates, since the appropriate [cont] value would not be adjacent to the conditioning environment of the rule. A rule that confirms this prediction is Aspiration in Nahuatl. In this language, stops are aspirated when adjacent to a syllable boundary :

(14) Nahuatl Aspiration:
[-cont] ---> [+spread] / ___]$_\sigma$

The contour hypothesis predicts that affricates will not undergo Aspiration, since it is their [+cont] feature that would be adjacent to the conditioning environment. This prediction is indeed confirmed by the data. The rule applies to stops, but not to affricates and fricatives (cf. Archangeli and Pulleyblank (1987) who credit Budway (1986) for the data. Similar data are offered by Sagey (1986; 95) from Sierra Popoluca):

(15)a. [ʔihkopʰki]   'he blinked'
     [petʰkoh]   'type of tree'
     [po:kʰʎiʔ]   'smoke'
   b. [ʔosto:ʎ]   'hole, cave'
     [wicʎiʔ]   'thorn'

[ʎa:ŋkocʎiʔ]   'tooth'

The nonapplication to affricates of the Aspiration rule in Nahuatl is the expected situation consistent with the contour hypothesis.

There also exist, however, rules of the same type, (3c), that apply to affricates, against the predictions of the contour hypothesis. A case that is totally parallel to the Aspiration rule just seen, but where both stops and affricates are affected by the rule is found in Turkish. In this language stops are devoiced syllable-finally (Archangeli & Pulleyblank, 1987):

(16) Turkish Devoicing:
[-cont, -son] ---> [-voice]/ ___σ]

As the examples in (17) show (from Archangeli &Pulleyblank, who cite Clements & Keyser, 1983), the rule applies to stops and, against the predictions made, to affricates. Fricatives are not affected:[2]

(17)

	nominative	plural	possessed	
a.	ip	ipler	ipi	'rope'
	sebep	sebepler	sebebi	'reason'
	bit	bitler	biti	'louse'
	kanat	kanatlar	kanadı	'wing'
b.	kıč	kıčlar	kıčı	'rump'
	pabuč	pabučlar	pabuǰu	'slipper'
	*pabuǰ	*pabuǰlar		
c.	kısım	kısımlar	kısmı	'part'
	čezir	čezirler	čezri	'root
	deniz	denizler	denizi	'see'

_____

[2] Fricatives are actually said to be partially devoiced. But this partial (phonetic) devoicing is in contrast with the complete devoicing of affricates and stops. I thank Ellen Kaisse for the observation.

Under the contour hypothesis the affricates in (17b) should not undergo the devoicing rule, since their [-cont] specification is not adjacent to the conditioning environment, the syllable boundary:

(18)   X
        r   o
             / \
        [-cont] [+cont]]$_\sigma$

The fact that affricates do in fact undergo this rule, argues against their representation as contour segments.

Basque also presents a case of overapplication of a rule of type (3c) to affricates. In Basque, a deletion rule simplifies sequences of two stops by deleting the first stop in the sequence. This rule applies obligatorily to word internal stop sequences and also across certain word boundaries in rapid speech. Examples are given in (19) (most examples from Salaburu, 1984):

(19)			
/bat	paratu/	[baparatu]	'put one'
/bat	traban/	[batraban]	'one stuck'
/bat	kurri/	[bakurri]	'run one'
/guk	pistu/	[gupistu]	'we light'
/guk	kendu/	[gukendu]	'we take away'
/bat+naka/		[banaka]	'one by one'
/bat+batean/		[bapatean]	'at once'

The cluster simplification rule also affects affricate-stop sequences. In this context, affricates do not delete, but become fricatives. That is, they lose their noncontinuancy:

(20)			
/its+tegi/	[isteγi]	'dictionary'
/its+keta/	[isketa]	'conversation'
/arits+ki/	[ariski]	'oak wood'
/arits+mendi/	[arismendi]	'oak mountain'

/ots+tu/   [ostu]   'become cold'
                                                    (perf.)

Fricatives are not affected by this rule, and fricative-stop sequences are frequently found both morpheme-internally and across morphemes:

(21) /eśka/   [eśka]   'ask for'
     /daśta/   [daśta]   'taste'
     /begi+s+ta/ [beɣista]   'survey'

In Hualde (1987), I argued that this process is consistent with a representation of affricates as contour segments, even though affricates do not show the predicted   edge effects for the purposes of the rule.I proposed to account for these facts by means of a delinking rule, which in a sequence of two adjacent segments where the first segment is characterized by the features [-cont, -son] and the second segment also bears the feature [-cont], delinks the supralaryngeal node dominating [-cont] in the first segment. This rule will delink all supralaryngeal features of a stop, but will leave all the features of a fricative if the input is an affricate, if the representations in (22) are adopted:

(22)stop-stop sequence   affricate-stop sequence

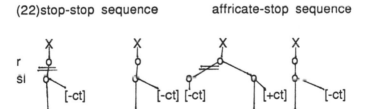

Archangeli & Pulleyblank (1987) argue that instances of overapplication of rules to affricates, such as the Basque Deletion Rule or the Turkish Devoicing Rule seen above, are not incompatible with a representation of affricates as contour segments. They suggest that the different behavior of affricates with respect to the Nahuatl Aspiration rule on the one hand, and with respect to the Turkish Devoicing Rule and the Basque Stop Deletion Rule, on the other hand, follows from the MAXIMAL/MINIMAL PARAMETER for determining adjacency. Nahuatl Aspiration is a minimal scansion rule, which requires feature-adjacency, whereas the Turkish and Basque rules are maximal scansion rules, requiring adjacency only at the skeletal slot level for their application. In this analysis, instances of overapplication of rules to affricates are no longer evidence against the contour segment hypothesis. But neither do they constitute evidence in favor of this hypothesis. The contour configuration of affricates is simply assumed a priori in Archangeli and Pulleyblank (1987) and Hualde (1987). Since, on the other hand, the instances of rule underapplication to affricates remain unexplained by the contour segment hypothesis, I will propose to abandon the representation of affricates as contour segments.

4. The Stop Hypothesis

What then are the alternatives to the representation of affricates as contour segments? An obvious alternative is to go back to the SPE (Chomsky and Halle, 1968) conception of affricates as a type of stop characterized by the feature [+delayed release].

The disadvantage of using the feature [+del rel] is that it obscures the fact that affricates sometimes are not treated as stops because they share, in part, the nature of the sibilant fricatives. Such a case is the Markina Basque Palatalization Rule. Recall that in this Basque dialect /l/, /n/, and /t/ are palatalized, but both /s/ and /ts/ are excluded from palatalization. If we characterize the input of the rule as [-cont, -del rel], we are missing the point that the nonpalatalizability of /ts/ is related in a clear sense to the nonpalatalization of /s/. That is, /ts/ is not excluded for being an affricate, but because it participates in some sense of the nature of /s/. This common behavior of /s/ and /ts/ could be captured by attributing to both segments a feature such as [+strident]. In this and all other cases, where affricates fail to be affected by rules affecting stops (Basque Voicing, Nahuatl Aspiration), we could then assume that the input of the rule must be characterized as [-cont, -strid]. If the input is simply characterized as [-cont], on the other hand, both stops and affricates will undergo the rule. This would be the case with Zoque Voicing and Turkish Devoicing.

A problem that remains in this approach is the Basque Stop Deletion Rule. As argued in Hualde (1987), if affricates are characterized as [-cont, +del rel] it is not possible to account for the process by means of a single simple rule. We need two rules applying in the same environment: a rule deleting stops, excluding affricate segments, and another rule changing affricate segments into fricatives. Exactly the same situation obtains if we use the feature [strident]:

(23) a. [-cont, -son, -strid] ---> 0 /____ [-cont]
      b. [+strid] ---> [+cont]/ ____ [-cont]

Yet, both rules in (23) account for what arguably is a single process, namely, the suppresion of an oral occlusion before a second occlusion. The consideration of affricates as a type of stop would force us to make use of two separate rules to account for one single process of cluster simplification.

In what follows, I will argue that the most adequate representation of affricates is one that retains from the Contour Segment Hypothesis the characterization of affricates as both [-cont] and [+cont] segments, but which does not assume the necessary phonological ordering of these features, given the absence of edge effects in a number of processes examined above.

Phonetically, the stop and fricative parts of an affricate are clearly ordered; but this ordering of features can take place at a late stage, since the order is predictably [-cont] [+cont].

5. The Complex Segment Hypothesis

Under the hypothesis that affricates are complex segments with phonologically unordered contradictory specifications for the feature continuant the account of the Basque Stop Deletion process given in (22) (cf. Hualde, 1987) can be maintained virtually unchanged as a node delinking rule.

The question is if there is any way to predict when a rule affecting stops will apply or fail to apply to affricates. We saw that the position of the conditioning environment is not what determines the different results, since edge effects are not observed universally. It seems that we must stipulate the existence of a parameter whose setting will determine whether a rule taking segments characterized as [a cont] as input will also apply to [αcont]/[-α cont] segments. Let us then assume such a parameter, with two settings "exclusively [αf]" if segments which are both [αf] and [-αf] will not undergo the rule and "inclusively [α f]" if [αf]/[-αf] segments are allowed to undergo the process . The setting will have to be specified for each rule. If this parameter is set as "inclusively", a rule affecting [α cont] segments will also affect segments characterized as both [αcont] and [-αcont], that is affricates. If the setting is "exclusively", on the other hand, the specification [a cont] of the input will exclude affricates.

The Nahuatl   Aspiration rule which affects only syllable final stops but not affricates, will specify that input segments must bear exclusively a [-cont]   specification. Turkish Devoicing, which affects both syllable-final stops and affricates, will indicate only that the   input segments must inclusively bear the feature [-cont]. The same difference in parameter setting obtains between Basque Voicing, which affects only stops after nasals or laterals, and Zoque Voicing which affects both stops and affricates after nasals. Basque Voicing is formulated as taking exclusively [-cont] inputs; Zoque Voicing as accepting inclusively [-cont] inputs. Markina Basque Palatalization has also an exclusively [-cont] setting, and, therefore, excludes affricates from the set of possible inputs. Finally, for KiNande Palatalization the input must be exclusively [+cont].

References

Archangeli, Diana and Douglas Pulleyblank. 1986. The Content and Structure of Phonological Representations. Cambridge, Mass: MIT Press (in press).

Archangeli, Diana and Douglas Pulleublank. 1987. Maximal and Minimal Rules: Effects of Tier Scansion. Proceedings of NELS 17. Cambridge, Mass: MIT.

Budway, K. 1986. Geminates and the Applicability Constraint in Huasteca Nahuatl. Presented at Lasso, Tempe, Arizona.

Chomsky, Noam and Morris Halle. 1968. The Sound Pattern of English. New York: Harper and Row.

Clements, George N. and Samuel Keyser. 1983. CV Phonology: A Generative Theory of the Syllable. Cambridge, Mass: MIT Press.

Hualde, José I. 1987. On Basque Affricates. Proceedings of WCCFL 6. 77-89.

Kenstowicz, Michael and Charles Kisseberth. 1979. Generative Phonology. New York: Academic Press.

Rollo, William. 1925. The Basque Dialect of Marquina. Amsterdam: H. J. Paris.

Sagey, Elizabeth. 1986. The Representation of Features and Relations in Nonlinear Phonology. Doctoral dissertation, MIT.

Salaburu Etxeberria, Pello. 1984. Arau fonologikoak: hizkuntz teoria eta Baztango euskalkia, II. Bilbao: Univ. País Vasco.

Wonderly, Williams. 1951. Zoque: Phonemics and Morphology. Reprinted from IJAL 17, 18.

Liberation and Inversion in GPSG
Thomas E. Hukari
University of Victoria
Robert D. Levine
University of British Columbia

0. Introduction. We offer an alternative to the syntactic account of English inversion found in Gazdar Klein, Pullum and Sag, 1985. Ours is set in a somewhat different theoretical context in which a liberation convention rather than a metarule is employed. As will become evident below, the theoretical framework differs in other respects as well, following suggestions found in Zwicky (1986). In particular, general immediate dominance rules do not directly project to trees, rather, they induce instantiated immediate dominance rules. This is similar in some respects to earlier work in GPSG (cf, Gazdar and Pullum, 1981) insofar as we employ general rules to induce more fully specified rules.[1]

Indices appear in the feature composition of categories in our instantiated immediate dominance rules and we show in conclusion that these, in conjunction with the feature instantiation principles, can be used to drive semantic translation, offering an improvement over the semantics of control outlined in Hukari and Levine (in press).

1. Subject-Auxiliary Inversion in GPSG. Inverted interrogative clauses in English are a familiar phenomenon. Note that some verbs are sensitive to inversion, showing unique distributional properties in inversion constructions (and see also Hudson, 1977).

(1) Aren't I fun to talk to?/*I aren't fun to talk to.
(2) Ought I (%to) speak to Sandy?/I ought *(to) speak to Sandy.[2]
(3) Need I (%to) see Kim?/I need *(to) see Kim.
(4) Dare I (%to) eat a peach?/No one dared (to) eat a peach.

This gives justification for the use of a feature [+Inversion] as in Gazdar, Pullum and Sag (1982) and in GKPS.

A number of analyses of inversion are logically possible in GPSG, and we explore these possiblilites here. Tree (6) represents the analysis in Gazdar, Klein, Pullum and Sag, 1985, Generalized Phrase Structure Grammar--hereafter, GKPS. The control system in GKPS fails to account for subject-verb agreement in the inverted construction. In (5), NP_2 controls VP_3 and the CAP says that the agreement feature (AGR) in VP_3 must then agree with NP_2.[3] This agreement specification is passed down to V_4 as a Head feature (and to AP_5 by the CAP). But in (6), an inverted structure, the control formalism does not identify NP_2 as the controller of either V_4 or AP_5, so the AGReement specifications are just wishful thinking (cf, Hukari and Levine, in press).

---

[1]Jacobson (1987) clearly is thinking along similar lines in footnote 22 when she suggests that the slash termination metarule (reformulated to contain variables) operates on instantiated (ID) rules.

[2]Grammaticality judgments of forms marked with the percentage sign vary. The authors find them ungrammatical.

[3]The indices have no ontological status in the context of GKPS, but they will enter the analysis below. See Gazdar, Pullum, Klein, Carpenter, Hukari and Levine (in press) for a reconstruction of indices in a feature system along the lines of GKPS.

(5) Uninverted Structure

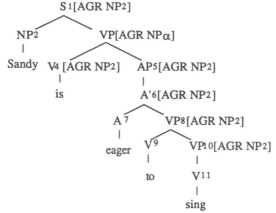

(6) SAI Metarule, GKPS (1985).

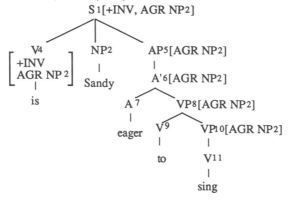

Tree (6) is derived via a a metarule in the GKPS analysis:

(7) <u>Subject-Auxiliary Inversion, GKPS (1985)</u>
 a. SAI Metarule: VP[+AUX] → W ⟹ S[+INV] → W, NP
 b. Basic ID rule: VP[+AUX] → H[42], XP[+PRD]
 c. Derived ID rule: S[+AUX, +INV] → H[42], NP, XP[+PRD]
 d. Phrase Structure Rule (i.e., Local Tree) Projecting from (c):

Control Agreement Principle is inapplicable

S[+AUX, +INV, AGR NP$_\alpha$] → V[42,+AUX, +INV, <u>AGR NP$_\alpha$</u>] + <u>NP</u>$_\alpha$ + AP[+PRD, <u>AGR NP$_\alpha$</u>]

Control Agreement Principle is inapplicable

The derived Immediate Dominance (ID) rule (7c) licensing the top of (6) is induced
by their Subject Auxiliary Inversion Metarule, derived from the VP rule (7b)--con-
verting VP into an S and adding a subject.

Alternative approaches are problematic as well. (8) approximates the small clause analysis in Gazdar, Pullum and Sag (1982).

(8) Small Clause.

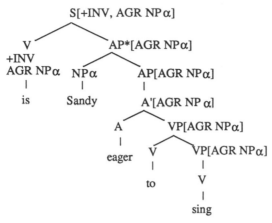

Their analysis does not, in fact, allow for AP or NP clauses and hence offers no analysis for the inversion of copula <u>be</u> in construction with predicate AP or NP-- unlike the metarule in (9a).

(9) <u>Small Clauses</u> (cf, Gazdar, Pullum and Sag, 1982).
   a. A Metarule: VP[+AUX] → W, XP[-SUBJ] ⇒ VP[+INV] → W, XP[+SUBJ]
   b. Basic ID rule: VP[+AUX] → H[42], XP[+PRD]
   c. Derived ID rule: S[+AUX, +INV] → H[42], XP[+PRD, +SUBJ]
   d. Phrase Structure Rule (i.e., Local Tree) Projecting from (c):

Control Agreement Principle is inapplicable

S[+AUX, +INV, <u>AGR NP_α</u>] → V[42,+AUX, +INV, <u>AGR NP_α</u>] + AP*[+PRD, <u>AGR NP_α</u>]

Control Agreement Principle is inapplicable

But even if the analysis can be extended in this fashion, the feature instantiation principles will not cause the agreement specification in AP* (or NP*) to extend upward to S and (via the Head Feature Convention) down to the auxiliary verb, as indicated in (9d).

     An extraction analysis--represented in (11)--while a formal possibility, faces the fact that multiple extractions generally are not possible in English, and it would be necessary to posit multiple extraction in (10).

(10) [s <u>Who</u> [s/NP <u>is</u> [s/V/NP Sandy [VP/V/NP V/V eager to talk to NP/NP]]]]?

(11) Extraction.

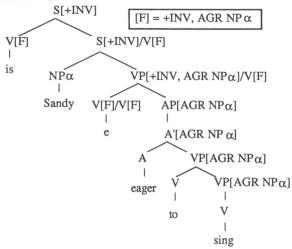

There is still another possibility that comes to mind in the context of tree (6), based on the disjunctive definition of the notion 'controller' in GKPS, where NP complements to certain head Vs are stipulatively identified as controllers of sister infinitival complements (e.g., *persuade* constructions). Thus one could identify the type of [+AUX, +INV] verbs as <NP, < VP, S >>-for those subcategorized for VP complements--while their [+AUX, -INV] counterparts would be normal <VP, VP> in type, and attempt to construct a definition of control along the lines of clause ii in the GKPS definition of controller. But this approach will not work out in a manner parallel to the *persuade/expect* case, because even if one can ensure that the subject is the controller of the complement VP in inverted structures, the problem is the same as that already noted in connection with the small clause approach: the AGR value will not percolate to the S mother to subsequently come to rest on the inverted [+AUX] head. What is necessary, rather, is first some guarantee that S contains an AGR value, and second some way to make the subject the controller of the inverted [+AUX] head itself--for example, by making the type of inverted auxiliaries <NP, <VP, S>> and allowing NP sisters of such lexical heads to be controllers of those heads. The first point is rather dubious, since it is difficult to argue that a root S should be treated as a predicative category. Even if this were granted, however, the second point seems to lead to an extremely infelicitous semantics: the types of [+INV] and [-INV] auxiliaries would now differ significantly in a way which has absolutely nothing to do with the difference between interrogative and declarative semantics, following, for example, Karttunen's (1977) account. To eliminate this completely syntax-motivated complication, the translation for α[+INV] will need to be $\lambda\mathscr{P}[\lambda v_{VP}[(\alpha[-INV])'(v_{VP}(\mathscr{P}))]]$--an expression which makes explicit the undesirably coincidental nature of the relationship between the semantics of the two kinds of auxiliary. If we wish to avoid such distortions--which strike one as merely the converse case of the distortion of syntax to serve the purposes of semantic interpretation, a practice condemned in, e. g., Cooper (1983)--then this line of attack on the problem must be rejected as well.

2. Liberation. Following Levine (1987, ms) we consider here an interesting alternative to a metarule approach--liberation, based on ideas of Arnold Zwicky

(1985, 1986). Liberation is a generalization of the metarule idea, but in place of individual rule-to-rule mapping schemas, we employ a general convention which says, in effect, replaces a daughter category in a rule with categories which would, otherwise, be its daughters. Our approach more closely follows the spirit of Zwicky (1985) and works roughly as in (12).

(12) Liberation. Given a set of pairs of categories L and two ID rules (a) and (b)
   a. $C_0 \rightarrow C_1, ..., C_i, ...C_m$
   b. $C'_0 \rightarrow C'_1, ..., C'_i, ...C'_n$, where $C'_0 = C_i$, $<C_0, C_i> \in L$, then the liberation principle says there is an ID rule (c)
   c. $C_0 \rightarrow C_1, ..., C_{i-1}, C_{i+1},...C_m , C'_1, ..., C'_i, ...C'_n$.

That is, C_i is eliminated and C_0 inherits the daughters of C_i. See the appendix for a more formal treatment.
   The general form of the grammar will be as in (13).

(13) Form of the Grammar.
$$\text{Set of Immediate Dominance Rules}$$
$$\downarrow$$
$$\text{Feature Instantiation}$$
$$\text{Principles \& Indexing}$$
$$\downarrow$$
$$\text{Set of Instantiated Immediate Dominance Rules}$$
$$\downarrow$$
$$\text{Liberation}$$
$$\downarrow$$
$$\text{Liberation Set of Immediate Dominance Rules}$$
$$\downarrow$$
$$\text{Linear Precedence Rules}$$
$$\downarrow$$
$$\text{Set of Phrase Structure Rules}$$

Note that we are working with rule sets. A relatively straightforward relationship can be established between rule sets and (nonlocal) trees if we assume an indexing convention, as in (14).

(14) Indexing. Each category in the set of instantiated ID rules is assigned an index so that for each nonterminal category which is introduced as a daughter in an ID rule in the set, an identical category appears as a mother in some other ID rule (and, otherwise, no two categories in the set bear the same index).

Consider how this might work for VSO languages--as outlined in (15)--under the assumption that a verb and its complements form a grammatical constituent, VP, in such languages--despite the apparently flat tree (branching) structure. <S, VP> will be in the set of liberation categories, and we take liberation to be obligatory here.

(15) VSO Languages. <S, VP> $\in L$ and liberation is obligatory.
   a. Basic ID rules
   i. S $\rightarrow$ XP, H[-SUBJ]
   ii. VP $\rightarrow$ H, NP
   b. Set of instantiated ID rules licensing a (nonlocal) tree obey the feature instantiation principles.

i. $S_1 \rightarrow \underline{NP_2}, VP_3[AGR:\ NP_2]$

$\quad\quad \underline{\lfloor\quad\quad\quad\quad\quad\quad\quad\rfloor}$

Control Agreement Principle

ii. $VP_3[\underline{AGR:\ NP_2}] \rightarrow [Verb, \underline{AGR:\ NP_2}]_4, NP_5$

$\quad\quad\quad \underline{\lfloor\quad\quad\quad\quad\quad\quad\quad\quad\quad\rfloor}$

Head Feature Convention

$\cdots$

c. Liberation Set of ID rules preserve agreement marking from (b).

i-ii. $S_1 \rightarrow NP_2, [Verb, AGR:\ NP_2]_4, NP_5$

$\cdots$

d. Phrase Structure rules/Local Trees. Linear Precedence Rule: $V < NP$

i-ii. $S_1 \rightarrow [Verb, AGR:\ NP_2]_4 + NP_2 + NP_5$

$\cdots$

Returning to the notion that liberation is a generalization of the metarule idea, we note certain differences between the two. If metarules are interpreted as, in effect, subcategorization redundancy rules--which they are in GKPS (1985)--then there is a particularly clear empirical difference between the two approaches: in the GKPS framework, metarules, by their very nature, affect only lexically headed ID rules, whereas in a liberation framework such a restriction will only obtain in a more or less coincidental fashion in individual languages, and in the general case will involve liberation of daughters in non-lexically headed rules as well. A second difference pertains to the description of free word order--as opposed to free con-stituent order--languages: for the latter, the absence of any Linear Precedence statements suffices, but in the case of the former, a large network of metarules, all 'conspiring' to mingle the daughters of phrasal constituents, seems unavoidable, whereas all that the liberation framework entails is a lack of any restrictions on the set of categories liberable with respect to each other. Other phenomena, such as extraposition from NP and head extraction with respect to complements, both found in English, are also difficult to account for using metarules--restricted to lexically-headed ID rules--but are easily expressible through the liberation metaprinciple (see Levine (1987, ms) for discussion). In general, discontinuous constituency phenomena seem to constitute a strong empirical basis for adopting the liberation framework in one of its varieties.

3. English Inversion by Liberation. Turning to English inversion, let's assume that <S[+INV], VP> is in the set of liberation categories in English, and liberation is obligatory, as in (16).

(16) <S[+INV], VP> $\in$ *L* and liberation is obligatory.

As in GKPS (1985), [+INV] is a marked specification and the default formalism guarantees only root clauses are [+INV]. Consider first a set of basic ID rules.

(17). Basic ID rule set for tree (6).
a. $S \rightarrow NP, H[-SUBJ]$
b. $VP[+AUX] \rightarrow H[7], XP[+PRED]$
c. $AP \rightarrow H1$
d. $A1 \rightarrow H[\#], VP[INF]$
e. $VP[INF,+AUX] \rightarrow H[12], VP[BSE]$
f. $VP \rightarrow H[1]$

Now imagine a fully instantiated rule set--that is, one in which all the ID rules bear all feature information in the tree--as in below where category has been assigned an index in such a way that each category on the right side of a rule corresponds to a category on the left side of another, as in the indexing convention.[4]

(18) Instantiated ID rule set for tree (6).
  a. $S_1[+INV, +Q] \rightarrow NP_2$, $VP_3[+INV, +Q, AGR: NP_2]$
  b. $VP_3[+INV, +Q, AGR: NP_2] \rightarrow$ [is, +INV, +Q]$_4$, $AP_5[AGR: NP_2]$
  c. $AP_5[AGR: NP_2] \rightarrow A^1_6[AGR: NP_2]$
  d. $A^1_6[AGR: NP_2] \rightarrow$ [eager]$_7$, $VP_8[INF, AGR: NP_2]$
  e. $VP_8[INF, +AUX, AGR: NP_2] \rightarrow$ [to]$_9$, $VP_{10}[BSE, AGR: NP_2]$
  f. $VP_{10}[BSE, AGR: NP_2] \rightarrow$ [please]$_{11}$

Note that we want the the agreement value in VP_3 to be passed down through the ID rules to VP_{10}.
    Suppose that the feature instantiation principles are reformulated to operate on such sets of fully instantiated ID rules, so the AGR value in VP_3 is passed down to VP_{10} by the CAP. This captures an interesting property of feature instantiation principles in GKPS: they never appeal to linear order. If, in fact, feature percolation principles operate over ID rules this then follows from the architecture of the theory--since ID rules say nothing about linear order.
    But if the control principles, which regulate the transmission of [AGR NP_2] above, operate over a set of instantiated ID rules , then this information will be preserved under liberation, as in the following where the boldface elements are eliminated by liberation.

(19) Liberation
a. $S^1[+INV, +Q] \rightarrow NP_2$, **$VP_3[+INV, +Q, AGR: NP_2]$**
b. $VP_3[+INV, +Q, AGR: NP_2] \rightarrow$ [is, +INV, +Q]$_4$, $AP_5[AGR: NP_2]$
aLb. $S_1[+INV, +Q] \rightarrow NP_2$, [is, +INV, +Q]$_4$, $AP_5[AGR: NP_2]$

So feature percolation in (6) is accounted for by the **instantiated** ID rules in (18) regulated by the feature instantiation principles, while the liberated rule set (20) licenses the actual branching in the tree.

(20) Liberation ID rule set for (6).
aLb. $S_1[+INV, +Q] \rightarrow NP_2$, [is, +INV, +Q]$_4$, $AP_5[AGR: NP_2]$
c. $AP_5[AGR: NP_2] \rightarrow A^1_6[AGR: NP_2]$
d. $A^1_6[AGR: NP_2] \rightarrow$ [eager]$_7$, $VP_8[INF, AGR: NP_2]$
e. $VP_8[INF, +AUX, AGR: NP_2] \rightarrow$ [to]$_9$, $VP_{10}[BSE, AGR: NP_2]$
f. $VP_{10}[BSE, AGR: NP_2] \rightarrow$ [please]$_{11}$

The local trees or--equivalently--phrase structure rules as in (22) are admitted once linear precedence is taken into account.

(21) Linear Precedence Rules (GKPS, 1985)
  a. [SUBCAT] < ¬[SUBCAT]
  b. [+N] < P2 < V2

(22) Phrase Structure Rules for (6).
aLb. $S_1[+INV, +Q] \rightarrow NP_2 +$ [is, +INV, +Q]$_4$, $AP_5[AGR: NP_2]$
c. $AP_5[AGR: NP_2] \rightarrow A^1_6[AGR: NP_2]$

---

[4]We assume a reconstruction of indices along the lines of Gazdar, Pullum, Klein, Carpenter, Hukari and Levine (forthcoming).

d. $A1_6[AGR: NP_2] \rightarrow [eager]_7 + VP_8[INF, AGR: NP_2]$
e. $VP_8[INF, +AUX, AGR: NP_2] \rightarrow [to]_9 + VP_{10}[BSE, AGR: NP_2]$
f. $VP_{10}[BSE, AGR: NP_2] \rightarrow [please]_{11}$

This approach seems to offer promise as an account of inversion on two grounds. First, it offers an explanation for subject-verb agreement in inverted structures without introducing additional complexity in the agreement formalism. Second, in providing an account of the percolation of AGR, it sets up the semantics in an approach similar to the one outlined in Hukari and Levine (1987, in press), where the control-semantics is driven by the syntax. We turn very briefly to control semantics below.

4. Control Semantics. Some reflection should make it obvious that the semantics can be driven off the set of ID rules which licenses the nonlocal tree. Specifically, the preliberation set of fully instantiated ID rules contains the relevant information, under the assumption that lexical items are included. Note that each category in this set of instantiated ID rules contains an index--and corresponding to each nonterminal daughter category in any ID rule there is an identical mother category in some other ID rule (i.e., nonterminals are "rewritten"). Given the uniqueness of these indices, constructing the semantics of control from the syntactic AGReement feature is a relatively straightforward exercise.

So the semantics of (5)--the uninverted clause--should be derivable from a set of instantiated immediate dominance rules virtually identical to those in (20)-- without +INV and +Q. This is also true of (6) as roughly outlined below--where VP_3 counts for semantic translation since it is in the set of instantiated ID rules even though it is not in the branching structure of (6).[5]

(23)
    a. $S_1[+INV, +Q] \rightarrow NP_2, VP_3[+INV, +Q, AGR: NP_2]$
      $\Rightarrow VP_3[+INV, +Q, AGR: NP_2]'(NP_2')$
    b. $VP_3[+INV, +Q, AGR: NP_2] \rightarrow [is, +INV, +Q]_4, AP_5[AGR: NP_2]$
      $\Rightarrow \lambda\mathscr{P}[[is, +INV, +Q]_4'(AP_5[AGR: NP_2]'(^\mathscr{P}))]$

Then the problem of the semantics of control in inverted structures reduces simply to the semantics of control since, as in the syntax of control, a type-driven semantic translation operates on the set of preliberation instantiated ID rules.

For the sake of completeness we include a translation schema for control. This type-driven translation is similar in some respects to the semantics for UDCs in GKPS, except that semantic translation operates over the set of instantiated, preliberation ID rules licensing a tree rather than the tree representation itself.

Consider a general schema for ID rules as below where subscripts are for reference in the schema, and not to be taken as indices.

(24) Semantic Schema for Control. Given (Instantiated) ID rules of the form
    $C_0 \rightarrow C_1, ..., C_i[AGR], ..., C_n$

Then we translate AGR as follows, where C_0 is not S and C_i is a predicative category.

(25)
    i. If $C_0(AGR) = C_i(AGR)$, then

---

[5]We leave aside matters particular to the semantics of interrogatives, which will involve the translation of Q in S.

a. $C_0[AGR\ \alpha] \Rightarrow EXT_{SUB}\ (\lambda v_\alpha[C_0'(v_\alpha)])$ iff C_H, the head of C_0, $\in ME_a$, where $a = <...,<t(\alpha), S>...>$ (e.g., $<S, <NP, S>>$, the type of **try'**);
b. otherwise, $C\ [AGR\ \alpha] \Rightarrow \lambda v_\alpha[C_0']$ (e.g.,$<S, S>$, the type of **seem', to'**);
ii. if $C_j(INDEX) = C_i(AGR)(INDEX)$, $\tau(C_j) = \alpha$, and $\tau(C_H) = <S, <NP,$ $VP>>$ (e.g. **persuade'**), then $C_0 \Rightarrow \lambda\mathscr{P}[EXT_{OBJ}\ (\lambda v_\alpha[FR(C'_1,...,C'_{j-1}, C'_{j+1}, ...,C'_n, v_\alpha)](C'_j)(\mathscr{P})]$;
iii. a. $C_i[AGR\ \alpha] \Rightarrow C_i'(v_\alpha)$ in either (i) or (ii) above;
b. $EXT_{SUB} = \lambda v_{VP}[\lambda\mathscr{P}[\mathscr{P}\{^\wedge\lambda x[v_{VP}(^\wedge\lambda PP(x))]\}]]$, and
c. $EXT_{OBJ} = \lambda v_{<\alpha,\ VP>}\lambda\mathscr{P}_1\lambda\mathscr{P}_2[\mathscr{P}_1\{^\wedge\lambda x[v_{<\alpha,\ VP>}(^\wedge\lambda PP(x))(\mathscr{P}_2)]\}]$.

Clause (ia) handles subject EQUI cases (e.g. try), (ib) takes care of subject-raising (e.g. seem) while (ii) is for object-control (e.g. persuade).[6]

This schema is a considerable improvement over Hukari and Levine (forthcoming), which must access the workings of the syntactic Control Agreement principle. Given the conditions on coindexing of categories in the set of preliberation ID rules noted above and the workings of the Control Agreement Principle, we can assume that indexal identity is never accidental. So, for example, if the agreement values in a VP mother and a predicative daughter are the same (e.g. $C_0(AGR) = C_i(AGR)$)--and this includes identity of indices--this must be due to the workings of the CAP.

The type-assignments assumed here are different from those in GKPS or Montague's PTQ (Montague, 1973); so we assume, for example, that **try'** has a propositional argument, not a property argument. A very simple illustration of semantic interpretation can be provided for

(26) Kim tries to leave.

We utilize the following ID rules from GKPS;

(27)
a. $S \rightarrow XP, H[-SUBJ]$
b. $VP \rightarrow H[15], VP[INF,+NORM]$
c. $VP[INF, +AUX] \rightarrow H[12], VP[BSE]$
d. $VP \rightarrow H[1]$

In order to conform to the indexing requirement, all the categories mentioned when the rules are instantiated will have to bear indices, and conformity with the feature instantiation principles of the grammar will then be checked. The relevant set of instantiated ID rules will then something like the following:

(28)
a. $S_1 \rightarrow NP[*]_2, VP_3[AGR\ NP[*]_2]$
b. $VP_3[AGR\ NP[*]_2] \rightarrow V[15, AGR\ NP[*]_2]_4, VP[INF, +NORM, +AUX, AGR\ NP[*]_2]_3]_5$
c. $VP[INF, +NORM, +AUX, AGR\ NP[*]_2]_5 \rightarrow V[12, AGR\ NP[*]_2]_6, VP[BSE, AGR\ NP[*]_2]_7$
d. $VP[BSE, AGR\ NP[*]_2]_7 \rightarrow V[1, BSE, AGR\ NP[*]_2]_8$

---

[6]we assume that believe (as a "raising" verb) semantically takes a proposition and that the general translation schema permits NP' and VP' to combine by functional application forming a proposition which, in turn, combines with V', so $VP \rightarrow$ [believe], NP, VP $\Rightarrow$ believe'(VP'(NP')).

The only feature instantiation principles relevant here are those which drive the appropriate features down the head path and enforce feature matching between controllers and the AGR feature of controllees. The rule set in (28) is equivalent to a tree under the assumption that categories with identical indices are not just type- but token-identical objects in syntactic representation. The interpretation mapping will start at the 'bottom' of this pseudo-tree--rule iv.--and work its way up, just as in the GKPS system; but here we are dealing with a non-branching object without linear orderings. It is an interesting fact--here captured as a theorem of the revised formalism--that linear ordering plays no role at all in the GKPS semantics.

(29)
a. $[_{VP}$ **leave** $] \Rightarrow \lambda\mathcal{P}_1[\text{leave}'(\mathcal{P}_1)]$
b. $[_{VP}$ **to leave** $] \Rightarrow \lambda\mathcal{P}_2[\lambda\mathcal{P}_1[\text{to}' \ (\text{leave}'(\mathcal{P}_1))](\mathcal{P}_2)]$
  $\rightarrow \lambda\mathcal{P}_2[\text{to}' \ (\text{leave}'(\mathcal{P}_2)]$
c. $[_{VP}$ **tries to leave** $] \Rightarrow$
  $\text{EXT}_{\text{SUB}} \ (\lambda\mathcal{P}_3[\text{tries}'(^\wedge\mathcal{P}_2[\text{to}' \ (\text{leave}'(\mathcal{P}_2)))](\mathcal{P}_3))(\mathcal{P}_3])$
  $\rightarrow \lambda v_{VP}[\lambda\mathcal{P}[\mathcal{P}\{^\wedge\lambda x[v_{VP}(^\wedge\lambda PP(x))]\}]](\lambda\mathcal{P}_3[\text{tries}' \ (\text{to}' \ (\text{leave}'(\mathcal{P}_3)))(\mathcal{P}_3)]$
  $\rightarrow \lambda\mathcal{P}[\mathcal{P}\{^\wedge\lambda x \ [(\lambda\mathcal{P}_3[\text{tries}' \ (^\wedge\text{to}' \ (\text{leave}'(\mathcal{P}_3)))(\mathcal{P}_3)](^\wedge\lambda PP(x))]\}]]$
  $\rightarrow \lambda\mathcal{P}[\mathcal{P}\{^\wedge\lambda x \ [\text{tries}' \ (^\wedge\text{to}' \ (\text{leave}'(^\wedge\lambda PP(x))))(^\wedge\lambda PP(x))\}]]$
d. $[_S$ **Kim tries to leave** $]$
  $\rightarrow \lambda\mathcal{P}[\mathcal{P}\{^\wedge\lambda x \ [\text{tries}' \ (^\wedge\text{to}' \ (\text{leave}'(^\wedge\lambda PP(x))))(^\wedge\lambda PP(x))\}](k^*)$
  $\rightarrow k^*\{^\wedge\lambda x \ [\text{tries}' \ (^\wedge\text{to}' \ (\text{leave}'(^\wedge\lambda PP(x))))(^\wedge\lambda PP(x))\}\}$
  $\rightarrow \lambda x \ [\text{tries}' \ (^\wedge\text{to}' \ (\text{leave}'(^\wedge\lambda PP(x))))(^\wedge\lambda PP(x))\}](k)$
  $\rightarrow \text{tries}' \ (^\wedge\text{to}' \ (\text{leave}'(^\wedge\lambda PP(k))))(^\wedge\lambda PP(k))\}]$

Appendix

We offer here a formal definition of liberation. Let Σ be a set of instantiated ID rules--where each category is appropriately indexed so that the set of ID rules is equivalent to a tree in which no ordering relation is imposed on sisters. The indexing condition on the ID rules in Σ is roughly as described above. We first turn to some preliminary definitions before inductively defining liberation-sets of ID rules derived from Σ by liberation

<u>Definition 1, L_{obl}</u>. The relation L_{obl} is a set of ordered pairs of categories. Intuitively, this is the set of category-pairs $<C, C'>$ for which C' obligatorily gives up its daughters to C.

<u>Definition 2, L_{opt}</u>. The relation L_{opt} is a set of ordered pairs of categories distinct from L_{obl} (i.e., $L_{obl} \cap L_{opt} = \emptyset$). Intuitively, it is the set of category-pairs for which liberation is optional.

<u>Definition 3, L</u>. L is $\wp(L_{obl} \cup L_{opt})$.

L (i.e., L', L'') at any inductive level in Definition 5 below is a set of liberation pairs of categories such that $L_{obl} \subseteq L \in L$, that is, L contains all the obligatory liberation pairs and possibly some of the optional ones. Note that there is no unique L at any inductive level. Rather, we have a family of possibilities drawn from the set L .

<u>Definition 4</u>. $\Sigma = \text{LIB}^0(\Sigma, L^0)$ (where we arbitrarily take $L^0 = L_{obl}$).

<u>Definition 5</u>. If a pair of ID rules r_j and $r_k \in \text{LIB}^{i-1}(\Sigma, L)$ satisfies conditions (a)-(e) below
a. $r_j = C_o \rightarrow C_1, \ldots, C_{m-1}, C_m, C_{m+1}, \ldots, C_n,$

b. $r_k = D_0 \rightarrow D_1, \ldots, D_n$,

c. C_0 and C_m extend, respectively C and C', $<C, C'> \in L'$,

d. $C_m = D_0$, and

e. there is no rule r", r" $\in$ LIB$^{i-1}(\Sigma, L)$ such that r" satisfies (b) above, r_k satisfies (a) and (c)-(d) are true (that is, r_j and r_k are bottom-most in any relevant 'chain'),then the liberation of r_j and r_k replaces them as in (f)-(h):

f. (LIB$^{i-1}(\Sigma, L)$-$\{r_j, r_k\}) \subseteq$ LIB$^i(\Sigma, L')$,

g. $C_0 \rightarrow C_1, \ldots, C_{m-1}, D_1, \ldots, D_n, C_{m+1}, \ldots, C_n \in$ LIB$^i(\Sigma, L')$,

h. nothing else is in LIB$^i(\Sigma, L')$.

Note that a level LIB$^i(\Sigma, L')$ is not defined if conditions (a)-(e) cannot be satisfied. This is not to say there is no LIB$^i(\Sigma, L)$ for some other L in L. In fact, at each inductive level we have a collection of alternatives: $\{$LIB$^i(\Sigma, Lx) \mid Lx \in L\}$.

Definition 6. LIBERATION(Σ, L). LIB$^m(\Sigma, L) \in$ LIBERATION(Σ, L) if and only if, for some L $\in L$, no two rules r_j and r_k in LIB$^m(\Sigma, L)$ satisfy Definition 5 above, m = i-1.

LIB$^n(\Sigma, L_{obl})$ is in LIBERATION(Σ, L) for some integer n in the case where each inductive level, following definition 5, is formed using only L_{obl}. This can usefully be thought of as the case where all liberation pairs are obligatory (i.e., $L = L_{obl}$). Since Σ is finite and liberation is a replacement operation, replacing two ID rules in LIB$^{i-1}(\Sigma, L_{obl})$ with a new rule (somewhat analogous to the functional composition of the two), the cardinality of LIB$^i(\Sigma, L_{obl})$ will be one less at each level. Eventually either the set, call it LIB$^n(\Sigma, L_{obl})$, is reduced to a singleton (containing one ID rule)-- if all category pairs are in L_{obl}--or it is reduced to rules where L_{obl} in Definition 5 no longer pertains. In either case, LIB$^n(\Sigma, L_{obl})$ yields no further levels and therefore it is in LIBERATION(Σ, L), which is now a singleton.

Clearly LIBERATION($\Sigma, L_{obl}) \subseteq$ LIBERATION(Σ, L) when optional liberation pairs are introduced. We leave as a question for further investigation the cardinality of LIBERATION(Σ, L). Could this, for example, exceed the cardinality of the set of levels LIB$^i(\Sigma, L_{obl})$, $0 \le i \le n$, if we made all optional pairs obligatory instead?

Clause (e) may be mystifying. It prevents the formation of useless ID rules by forcing liberation to take place only on the bottommost pair of ID rules in the case of a chain of rules where liberation could otherwise take place all along the chain, as in the following set of ID rules, where <A, B>, <B, C>, and <C, D> are in L_{obl}. Assume for simplicity's sake that L_{opt} is empty.

LIB$^0(\Sigma, L) = \Sigma$:

A $\rightarrow$ B, a

B $\rightarrow$ C, b

C $\rightarrow$ D, c

D $\rightarrow$ e, d

Ignoring clause (e), any adjacent pair of rules would be candidates for liberation, but only the last two also satisfy (e) and at the next level the set of ID rules will be as follows.

LIB$^1(\Sigma, L)$:

A $\rightarrow$ B, a

B $\rightarrow$ C, b

C $\rightarrow$ e, d, c

The last rule is the liberation of the last two ID rules in $LIB^0(\Sigma, L)$ above, which are now eliminated. The next level can be formed with the bottom two rules undergoing liberation, since no other pair of rules will satisfy clause (e), thus yielding

$LIB^2(\Sigma, L)$:
A → B, a
B → e, d, c, b

Finally, the last rule is eliminated by liberation and $LIB^3(\Sigma, L)$ is $LIB^n(\Sigma, L)$:

$LIB^3(\Sigma, L)$:
A → e, d, c, b, a.

Acknowledgements

This project was supported in part by a Faculty Research Grant, University of Victoria (Hukari), and by a Canada Research Fellowship (Levine). We thank conference participants for their questions and comments--in particular, Mark Johnson, Lauri Karttunen, and Carl Pollard.We also thank Robert Carpenter, Geoffrey Pullum and Arnold Zwicky for their help.

References

Cooper, R. 1983. Quantification and syntactic theory. Dordrecht: Reidel.

Gazdar, G., E. Klein, G. Pullum, and I. Sag. 1985. Generalized phrase structure grammar. Cambridge, Mass.: Harvard University Press.

Gazdar, G., G. Pullum, and I. Sag. 1982. Auxiliaries and related phenomena in a restrictive theory of grammar. Language 58.591-638.

Gazdar, Gerald, and Geoffrey Pullum. 1981. Subcategorization, constituent order and the notion 'head', in M. moortgat, H.v.d. Hulst and T. Hoekstra (3ds), The scope of lexical rules. Dordrecht: Foris, 107-123.

Gazdar, Gerald, Geoffrey Pullum, Ewan Klein, Robert Carpenter, Thomas Hukari, and Robert Levine. In press. Category structures. Computational Linguistics.

Hudson, Richard A. 1977. The power of morphological rules. Lingua, 42, 72-89.

Hukari, Thomas and Robert Levine. In press. Generalized phrase structure grammar: a review monograph. Linguistic Analysis.

Levine, Robert. 1987. Head extraction and direct liberation. Ms., University of British Columbia.

Montague, Richard. 1973. The proper treatment of quantification in ordinary English. In J. Hintikka, J. Moravcsik and P. Suppes (eds), Approaches to natural Language: Proceedings of the 1970 Stanford Workshop on Grammar and Semantics. Dordrecht: D. Reidel Publishing Co., 221-242.

Jacobson, Pauline. 1987. Review of Generalized Phrase Structure Grammar. Linguistics and Philosophy 10.389-486.

Karttunen, Lauri. 1977. Syntax and semantics of questions. Linguistics and Philosophy, 1, 3-44.

Zwicky, Arnold. 1985. Free word order in GPSG. Paper presented at the Linguistic Society of America summer meetings, Georgetown University.

Zwicky, Arnold. 1986. Concatenation and liberation. In A. Farley, P. Farley and K.-E. McCullough (eds), Papers from the 22nd regional meeting of the Chicago Linguistic Society, 65-74.

LF-Binding of Anaphors*

Fusa Katada

University of Southern California

0. Introduction

The idea that anaphors raise at LF (Lebeaux 1983, Chomsky 1986a, and Pica 1987), accounts for a specific syntactic role of antecedents, known as subject-orientation. Subject-orientation alone, however, does not serve as sufficient evidence for the raising of anaphors; it is only a necessary consequence if anaphors raise. This paper substantiates the raising analysis and argues in favor of the LF-binding of anaphors. I will provide independent evidence for the raising of anaphors and give a sufficient reason for it.

1. Long-Distance vs. Local Subject-Orientation

It is well known that anaphoric elements either obey or do not obey locality conditions. Japanese posseses both types of anaphors. As illustrated in (1a) below, zibun (self) behaves like a long-distance anaphor (Akatsuka 1976; Inoue 1976; Kuno 1973; Kuroda 1965; and others) in that it does not obey the Specified Subject Condition (SSC). Zibun-zisin (self-self) (Kurata 1986) and mizukara (self) (Kitagawa 1986), on the other hand, are local anaphors[1]; i.e. they obey the SSC. (1a, b) furthermore show that both types of reflexives are subject-oriented[2]; i.e. the non-subject Bill is not a possible antecedent for either reflexive.

(1)a. John$_i$-ga Bill$_j$-ni [Mike$_k$-ga zibun$_{i/*j/k}$ -o
      SB   IO   SB   zibun-zisin?$_{*i/*j/k}$ DO
     semeta to] itta.   mizukara*$_{i/*j/k}$
     blamed that told   'John told Bill that Mike blamed zibun.'

   b. John$_i$-ga Bill$_j$-ni zibun$_{i/*j}$ -no koto-o hanashita.
        SB   IO zibun-zisin$_{i/*j}$ DO matter-DO told
                mizukara$_{i/*j}$
    'John told Bill self's matter.'

(2) indicates that neither reflexive obeys the Nominative Island Condition (NIC); yet subject-orientation is strictly obeyed:

(2) John$_i$-ga [Bill$_j$-ga Mike$_k$-ni [zibun$_{i/j/*k}$ -ga
    SB   SB   IO   zibun-zisin?$_{*i/j/*k}$ SB
    tensaida to] itta to] omotteiru.   mizukara?$_{*i/j/*k}$
    genius   that told that think
    'John thinks that Bill told Mike that self is a genius.'

This fact shows that locality and subject-orientation are two separate issues; the long-distance vs. local anaphor classification and the presence vs. absence of subject-orientation are not implicationally related.

The absence of NIC effects may be reducible to the absence of AGR in Japanese, along the line of Huang (1982). This language specific property, however, does not explain the contrast displayed by zibun and zibun-zisin/mizukara with respect to the SSC. In other words, the binding theory applying at S-structure (e.g. Chomsky 1981) cannot explain why only zibun, and not zibun-zisin or mizukara, can violate Principle (A). Similarly, a theory that refers to the notion of `thematic structure´ as a domain defining property (e.g. Giorgi 1984) cannot distinguish long-distance vs. local domains for the two types of reflexives found in a single language.

2. The LF-Representation of Anaphors

I claim that the contrast displayed by zibun and zibun-zisin/mizukara (long-distance vs. local subject-orienation) is reducible to LF-raising of anaphors and the Empty Category Principle (ECP). Central to this claim is the proposal in (3), which consists of two parts:

(3)a. Zibun, but not zibun-zisin or mizukara, is an operator.
   b. Operators undergo LF-movement.
      (Hereafter, I will use the diacritic feature notation [+top]
      to denote an operator-property.)

(3a) is a stipulation at this moment, however, shortly I will propose an account of what type of expression may count as an operator. Furthermore, in section 4, I derive the conclusion that zibun is an operator, from independent evidence related to its behavior at LF. (3b) provides for a unified treatment of operators. That is, due to (3a), zibun, but not zibun-zisin or mizukara, undergoes LF-raising, just as other well known operators do, such as quantifier phrases and WH-phrases (May 1977; 1985). After all, (3a and b) serve as a sufficient reason for why some anaphors raise.

To explain how (3) accounts for long-distance vs. local subject orientation, I propose another characteristic difference that underlies the two types of anaphors. This difference may be characterized as `lexical vs. non-lexical´ anaphors[3]. That is, zibun is a lexical anaphor that is found in the structure (4a), while zibun-zisin and mizukara are non-lexical anaphors that are found in the phrasal structure characterized in (4b) and (4c)[4], respectively:

(4)   a. NP   b. NP1   c. NP1   d.   NP1
          | /   \ | /   \
          N´   SPEC   N´   (PP)   SPEC   N´
          | | | /   \ | |
          N   NP2   N   NP2   P   NP2   N
          | | | | | | |
         zibun   zibun zisin   mizu   kara   zibun-no hahaoya
         [+op]   [+op]   [+op]   [+op] GN (mother)

In (4b), zibun is in the specifier of NP1. This structure looks like the structure of zibun-no hahaoya (self´s mother) in (4d), with one difference: in (4b), the genitive marker no is suppressed[5], and this makes the specifier position not lexically governed. Here, I am assuming that in Japanese, case markers are

lexical governers (Saito 1985), and that head government is not
relevant to proper government in Japanese.

Long-Distance Raising: The bare form zibun in (4a) undergoes
raising due to its [+op] property. The raising mechanism follows
the general theory of movement (Chomsky 1986b). Assuming that the
bare form zibun functions as an NP, a maximal projection, the
raising of zibun proceeds via adjunction. Zibun can adjoin to any
Xmax that is not an argument. Therefore, possible adjunction
sites will be VP and PP. As long as the trace left by the raising
of zibun is lexically governed, free extraction of zibun is
possible under the following assumption:
(5) there is no cyclic movement at LF, and subjacency can be
    violated. (Huang 1982; Saito and Lasnik 1984)

Moreover, free extraction of zibun applies to the position
[NP,S]. This follows, given that case markers in Japanese are
lexical governers. Or else, one may claim that [NP,S] in Japanese
is lexically governed by V (Chomsky 1984, UCSD lecture), which in
turn views the Japanese S as a projection of V, not INFL (Kitagawa
1986; Kuroda 1986). In any case, the fact that zibun-binding
displays no NIC effects is consistent with other movement rules in
Japanese such as WH-movement (Saito 1985), which does not obey the
NIC. (6) characterizes the requisite LF-representation of zibun,
which shows that its VP-adjunction can be done in an unlimited
domain:
(6)   ... NP-ga ... [VP zibun [VP ... [CP* ... t ...]]]
      where CP* stands for zero or more occurences of clauses.

In (6), the trace is lexically governed, and the subject NP
locally c-commands (or governs) zibun. Non-subject NPs generally
occur VP internally in positions which do not c-command the raised
zibun. This asymmetric c-command relation displayed by subjects
and objects explains why zibun exhibits multiply ambiguous
subject-orientation and cannot be bound by non-subjects.

Local Raising: Zibun-zisin, on the other hand, is a non-
lexical anaphor. I propose that, in (4b), it is NP2, and not NP1,
that plays a role in coindexation. Nevertheless, the head zisin
bears the same index as zibun through SPEC-head agreement, and the
index percolates up from the head to NP1. I also propose that,
unlike properties designated by an index, the operator-property
[+op] is not an agreement feature; thus SPEC-head agreement does
not transfer the property [+op] from SPEC of NP zibun to the head
zisin. Accordingly [+op] is not available for percolation to NP1,
and NP1 itself does not bear the property [+op]. As a
consequence, nothing forces NP1 to raise; what raises is thus not
the entire NP1 (zibun-zisin), but rather NP2 (zibun) in the
specifier position. Since this specifier position is not
lexically governed, due to the lack of the genitive case marker
no, the trace of zibun must be antecedent-governed in order to
satisfy the ECP. This requirement makes the raising of zibun out
of zibun-zisin always local. The requisite LF-representation of
zibun-zisin is thus as follows:
(7) NP-ga [VP1 [CP NP-ga [VP2 zibun [VP2 [NP [SPEC t] zisin] ...

In (7), the trace is not lexically governed, however, it is antecedent-governed by zibun, which is locally adjoined to VP2. In this structure, VP2 is not a barrier since it does not exclude the adjoined zibun. VP2, however, becomes a barrier and blocks antecedent government if zibun crosses VP2 and adjoins to the higher VP1. In other words, the extraction of zibun out of zibun-zisin is always clause bound. Suppose zibun-zisin appears in the position [NP,S] of the embedded CP. As long as this CP is L-marked, it is not a barrier, and zibun can raise to a higher VP. This will explain why zibun-zisin displays no NIC effects. In short, local subject-orientation displayed by zibun-zisin is reducible to local-raising of the specifier of NP. (As for mizukara, see Katada (in preparation).)

In general, my analysis proposes the following:

(8) Subject-orientation (whether long-distance or local) is a property of anaphoric expressions that involve LF-raising.

Non-Operator Anaphors: My analysis implies the existence of non-operator ansphors. Such anaphors do not raise at all. I propose that kare-zisin (he-self) counts as such an example. Kare-zisin has a structure identical to that of zibun-zisin:

(9) [NP1 [SPEC NP2 kare] [N zisin]]
                    [-op]

I propose that kare is not an operator, and thus kare-zisin involves no-movement at all. This predicts that kare-zisin is interpreted from its position in situ. As a consequence, kare-zisin is not necessarily subject-oriented. This prediction is borne out perfectly. As noted in Nakamura (1986), kare-zisin in (10) is capable of referring to a non-subject, as well as subject, of the appropriate person, number, and gender (kare is 3rd person, singular, and male):

(10)a. John$_i$-ga Bill$_j$-ni kare-zisin$_{i/j}$-no koto-o hanashita.
          SB   IO   he-self   GN matter-DO told
       `John told Bill about kare-zisin. ´

   b. Mary$_i$-ga Bill$_j$-ni kare-zisin*$_{i/j}$-no koto-o hanasita.
          SB   IO   he-self   GN matter-DO told
       `Mary told Bill about kare-zisin. ´

   c. John$_i$-ga boku$_j$-ni kare-zisin$_{i/*j}$-no koto-o hanasita.
          SB I   IO   GN matter-DO told
       `John told me about kare-zisin. ´

Natural Class of Operator Anaphors: A characteristic difference between operator anaphors and non-operator anaphors can be seen in (11), where the lexical properties of kare and zibun are compared:

(11) | [kare] | [zibun] |
      | --------------- | ------- |
      | 3rd person | ? |
      | singular | ? |
      | male | ? |
      | -anaphoric | ? |
      | +pronominal | ? |
      | --------------- | ------- |
      | [-op] | [+op] |

(?´s stand for underspecified values.)

Kare has fixed feature values of [person, number, gender, anaphoric, pronominal], as we saw in (12). In other words, kare has its own inherent semantic contents. The question marks underneath zibun, on the other hand, indicate that the relevant feature values of zibun are underspecified in the lexicon; these feature values of zibun are determined syntactically by binding theory. In other words, zibun lacks inherent semantic content, and in this sense, it is very close to a null element. Basically, these types of expressions bear operator properties and raise at LF. In general, morphologically simplex anaphors that allow long-distance binding share common properties with zibun; they are subject-oriented and the relevant feature values are underspecified in the lexicon. In my terms, such expressions are referred to as OPERATOR ANAPHORS. The following anaphors are candidates for such examples; sig in Danish, ziji in Chinese, and caki in Korean, among others.

3. The Absence vs. Presence of Connectivity Effects

In the previous section, I have distinguished between operator and non-operator anaphors. Zibun is an instance of an operator anaphor, while zibun-zisin or mizukara is not. In this section, I demonstrate the difference between the two types of anaphors as manifested in binding phenomena drawn from scrambling facts. I assume, following Saito (1985), that scrambling is an S-structure adjunction, which implies that scrambled elements are in A´-positions. First, observe in (12) how scrambling of the three reflexives affects their coreference possibilities:

(12)a. John$_i$-ga   zibun?$_i$ -o semeta.
            SB   zibun-zisin$_i$ DO blamed
                   mizukara$_i$ `John blamed self.´
   b. zibun???$_i$ -o John$_i$-ga t$_i$ semeta.
      zibun-zisin$_i$ DO   SB   blamed
      mizukara$_i$ `Self, John blamed.´

In (12b), the object reflexives are scrambled to sentence initial position. This operation does not seem to affect the coreference possibility of zibun-zisin and mizukara; thus they allow `backward´ reflexivization. However, the scrambling of zibun reduces the grammaticality of the intended interpretation.

While this contrast is clear to many speakers of Japanese, including myself, some speakers find the scrambled zibun to also allow backward reflexivization. However, even to these speakers, the following contrast in (13a and b) is quite clear:

(13)a. Dareka$_i$-ga   zibun?$_i$ -o semeta.
       someone SB   zibun-zisin$_i$ DO blamed
                    mizukara$_i$ `Someone blamed self.´

   b. zibun?*$_i$ -o dareka$_i$-ga t$_i$ semeta.
      zibun-zisin$_i$ DO someone SB   blamed
      mizukara$_i$ `Self, someone blamed.´

There seems to be a slight contrast already in the interpretation of the reflexives before scrambling. I marked this contrast by

placing one (?) on zibun. Yet, the point remains that there is a
marked contrast in the interpretation of zibun before and after
scrambling. This is not the case for zibun-zisin or mizukara.
This contrast becomes clearer when the reflexives are locally
scrambled. That is, as discussed in section 1, zibun in (14a)
below displays multiple subject-orientation, whereas zibun-zisin
and mizukara display local subject-orientation only:

(14)a. John$_i$-ga Bill$_j$-ni [Mike$_k$-ga   zibun$_i$/*$_j$/$_k$ -o
       SB   IO   SB   zibun-zisin?*$_i$/*$_j$/$_k$ DO
                                      mizukara*$_i$/*$_j$/$_k$

       semeta to] itta.
       blamed that told   `John told Bill that Mike blamed self.´

However,   as   (14b) below shows, scrambling changes these
coreference possibilities.   In (14b), the locally scrambled zibun
most naturally refers to a higher subject John, but not a lower
subject Mike.   The locally scrambled zibun-zisin and mizukara can
now refer to either a higher subject John or a lower subject Mike:

(14)b. John$_i$-ga Bill$_j$-ni [zibun$_i$/*$_j$/?*$_k$ -o [Mike$_k$-ga t
       SB   IO   zibun-zisin$_i$/*$_j$/$_k$ DO
                            mizukara$_i$/*$_j$/$_k$

       semeta to] itta.
       blamed that told   `John told Bill that self, Mike blamed.´

In general, we have (15):
(15) Scrambled zibun-zisin and mizukara allow backward
     reflexivization; scrambled zibun does not.

     The fact that scrambling changes the possibility of the
binding of zibun-zisin and mizukara is independently observed in
Kurata (1986) and Kitagawa (1986), respectively. Their attention,
however, was focused on the fact that the local reflexives, zibun-
zisin and mizukara, can now be bound by the matrix subject. The
behavior of scrambled zibun was not brought into their discussion.
My interest in this paper greatly differs from theirs in that my
immediate concern lies in the contrast displayed by zibun on the
one hand and zibun-zisin/mizukara on the other with respect to
backward reflexivization described in (15).
     The cases in (12) - (14), where zibun-zisin and mizukara
allow backward reflexivization, are instances of `connectivity´,
in the sense of Akmajian (1970) and Higgins (1973).   In such
cases, the preposed elements are not c-commanded by their
antecedent at S-structure, however, the c-command requirement is
satisfied if the preposed elements act as if they were in the
original position. Let us restate (15) in terms of connectivity:

(16) Scrambled zibun-zisin and mizukara exhibit connectivity
     effects; the bare form zibun does not.

     The presence vs. absence of connectivity is also observed
expression internally. As noted in Muraki (1979), zibun displays
connectivity if it is embedded in a scrambled phrase. Observe
(17):

(17)a. John$_i$-ga [zibun$_i$ -no hahaoya]-o semeta.
          zibun-zisin$_i$ GN mother   DO blamed
          mizukara$_i$ `John blamed self´s mother. ´

   b. [Zibun$_i$ -no hahaoya]$_j$-o [John$_i$-ga t$_j$ semeta.]
      Zibun-zisin$_i$ GN mother DO   SB   blamed
      Mizukara$_i$ `Self´s mother, John blamed t. ´

In (17b), zibun in the specifier of NP equally allows backward reflexivization. I thus formulate another generalization:

(18) Zibun embedded in a scrambled phrase exhibits connectivity; the scrambled bare form zibun does not.

     Accounting for connectivity effects, two major proposals are available in the literature. The first proposal may be referred to as Reconstruction. Under this proposal, the moved element is reconstructed into its trace left by scrambling; consequently binding theory treats (17a and b) on a par. Since Reconstruction has to be an LF-phenomenon, this proposal argues in favor of LF-binding. The second proposal is known as Chain Binding (Barss 1986). Chain Binding achieves the same effect as that of Reconstruction but at S-structure. If the notion of `chain´ is applied to (17b), the trace t is in the same chain as that of the phrase containing the reflexive, and it is locally c-commanded by John; accordingly, backward reflexivization is allowed.
     Notice, however, that the Japanese data persistently challenges both Reconstruction and Chain Binding. The crucial facts are the contrasts described in (16) and (18). Neither Reconstruction nor Chain Binding has anything to say about these contrasts. Why should it be the case that the bare form zibun exhibits no connectivity effects?

     Since the different behavior of the scrambled bare form zibun with respect to connectivity cannot be read off from S-structure, it must be associated with its unique behavior at LF. The only possible way to account for (16) and (18) is to stipulate:

(19) Zibun-zisin, mizukara, and zibun-no hahaoya undergo reconstruction, but the bare form zibun does not.

     I claim that the stipulation (19) is derivable from the central proposal I made in the previous section, repeated below:
(20)a. Zibun is an operator.
    b. Zibun-zisin or mizukara as a whole is not.

In order to explain how (19) is attributive to (20), I propose the following assumption, which applies to operators in general:

(21)a. Operators can and must remain in A´-positions at LF.
    b. Non-operators in A´-positions must undergo reconstruction.

     In support of the assumption (21), observe the following, in which the object phrase containing the reflexive is marked by mo, a quantificational element (QE):

(22)a. John$_i$-ga [zibun$_i$ -no hahaoya]-mo semeta.
       zibun-zisin$_i$ GN mother   QE blamed
       mizukara$_i$ `John blamed self's mother, also.´

    b. [*Zibun$_i$ -no hahaoya]$_j$-mo [John$_i$-ga t$_j$ semeta.]
     *Zibun-zisin$_i$ GN mother   QE   SB   blamed
     *Mizukara$_i$ `Self's mother also, John blamed t.´

The contrast in (22a and b) indicates that none of the reflexives
exhibit connectivity if the scrambled phrase is a mo-marked
object[8]. This fact is clearly contrastive with (17). (17) and
(22) are identical with only one difference; whether the scrambled
object zibun-no hahaoya (self's mother) is o-marked or mo-marked.
Under the assumption (21), the contrast between (17b) and (22b)
comes as no surprise, since the particle mo quantifies the
preceding NP. Since the scrambled mo-marked object is now an
operator, it does not reconstruct; consequently the reflexives in
(22b) do not display the connectivity.
    Under the assumption (21), the scrambled bare form zibun
remains in an A´-position, due to its being an operator. On the
other hand, zibun-zisin or mizukara as a whole are not operators,
thus they undergo reconstruction. The two types of reflexives
thus yield different LF-representations, as in (23):

(23)a. zibun$_i$-o [NP$_i$-ga t$_i$]   b. [NP$_i$-ga zibun-zisin$_i$]
    [+op]   mizukara$_i$

In (23a), there are two conceivable violations; (i) the trace is
A-bound by NP$_i$, violating Principle (C), and (ii) zibun does not
have a requisite antecedent. In (23b), these violations are
reconciled as a result of reconstruction, and the intended
interpretation is readily available. In short, the absence vs.
presence of conncectivity effects is reducible to the single
factor described in (20): whether a given anaphor is an operator
or not.
    Before moving on, I would like to clarify other aspects of
reconstruction revealed by the binding of zibun. It does not seem
to be the case that the reconciliation of any grammatical
principle violation triggers reconstruction. To illustrate,
consider (24), where zibun in the locally scrambled phrase
displays connectivity:
(24) John$_1$-ga Mary$_2$-ni [[zibun$_1$/*$_2$/$_3$ -no hahaoya]$_4$-o [Bill$_3$-ga t$_4$
    SB   IO   GN mother-DO   SB
    semeta to]] itta.   `John told Mary that zibun's mother,
    blamed that told   Bill blamed t.´

In (24), there are no violations involved: the trace is A-free,
and zibun has a requisite antecedent John from its scrambled
position. Nevertheless, the phrase undergoes reconstruction;
otherwise, zibun would not be able to refer to the lower subject
Bill. This leads to the following conclusion:
(25) Reconstruction is a general property of non-operators.

    Parameters in Connectivity Effects: So far, I clarified the
adequacy of assumption (21), repeated below:

(21)a. Operators can and must remain in A´-position.
   b. Non-operators in A´-positions must undergo reconstruction.

(21) is a rather strong claim and should be assessed cross-linguistically. The immediate challenge to (21) can be drawn from English, where himself contained in a WH-phrase displays multiple ambiguity:

(26) [Which picture of himself$_{i/j/k}$] [does John$_i$ want [t [
       Frank$_j$ to ask Martin$_k$][t [PRO$_k$ to publish t]
       (Weisler 1982 cited in Barss 1986)

My analysis predicts that which picture of himself does not undergo reconstruction since a WH-phrase is an operator. Consequently the sentence should be ruled out because himself does not have a requisite antecedent. My analysis makes the wrong prediction. My solution to this problem is to invoke parametrization. Unlike traces left by scrambling in Japanese, traces left by cyclic WH-movement in (26) are visible for the purpose of binding in English, and as was shown in Barss (1986), Chain Binding takes care of the multiple ambiguity displayed by himself. In other words, Reconstruction Theory and Chain Binding do not replace each other; they are rather complimentarily shared binding phenomena across languages. The following parametrization allows (21) to hold universally:

(27)a. Reconstruction takes place in Japanese.
   b. Chain Binding takes place in English.

More on Scrambling and Subject-Orientation: Consider cases of long-distance scrambing. As long as the scrambled elements undergo reconstruction, the reflexives display ambiguous binding:

(28) [Zibun$_{i/j}$ -no hahaoya]-o [dareka$_i$-ga [John$_j$-ga t
      Zibun-zisin$_{i/j}$ GN mother DO someone SB   SB
      Mizukara$_{i/j}$
      semeta to] itta.]   `Self´s mother, someone said that
      blamed that said   John blamed t. ´

In (28), zibun-zisin and mizukara can potentially pick every grammatical subject, even though they are local anaphors in nature. This fact suggests that binding in reconstruction takes place cyclically, which in turn supports the cyclic application of scrambling at S-structure (Saito 1985).
   There is some evidence that an operator anaphor raises after reconstruction takes place. This point can be seen in (29), where scrambled reflexives exhibit subject-orientation:

(29) [Zibun$_{i/*j}$ -no koto]-o [John$_i$-ga Bill$_j$-ni t hanashita.]
      Zibun-zisin$_{i/*j}$ GN matter-DO SB   IO   told
      Mizukara$_{i/*j}$ `Self´s matter, John told Bill t. ´

   Furthermore, locally scrambled reflexives display orientation toward a higher subject, and this fact is significant to the grammar of Logical Form. Observe the following:

(30) [Taro$_i$-ga Hanako$_j$-ni [zibun$_{i/*j/?*k}$ -o [Ziro$_k$-ga t
        SB   IO   zibun-zisin$_{i/*j/k}$ DO   SB
                            mizukara$_{i/*j/k}$

    semeta to] itta.]
    blamed that told `Taro told Hanako that self, Ziro blamed t. ´

In (30), the locally scrambled bare form zibun refers to a higher subject Taro; the non-subject Hanako cannot bind zibun. Since zibun does not undergo reconstruction, the higher subject-orientation must be the effect of anaphor-raising from the scrambled position. Similarly, we see that scrambled zibun-zisin and mizukara also exhibit a higher subject-orientation. If anaphor raising applies after these local reflexives reconstruct to an A-position, they should display a lower subject orientation only. Therefore, it must be the case that anaphor raising takes place from the scrambled A´-position in (30). This would argue against the nature of movement suggested in Huang (1981/82):

(31) Every chain of movement must originate from an argument
     position.

which is a weaker version of (32) proposed in Aoun, Hornstein, and Sportiche (1981):
(32) Wh-R (LF Wh Movement) only affects wh-phrases in argument
     position.

4. Limited vs. Non-Limited Interaction with the Pronominal Kare
    Aoun and Hornstein (1986) refer to the following contrast in (33) and (34), which indicates that the presence of zibun limits the coreference reading possibilities of kare:

(33) John$_i$-ga [kare$_i$-ga kare$_i$-no hahaoya-o semeta to] itta.
        SB   he SB he-GN   mother-DO blamed that said
     `John said that kare blamed kare´s mother. ´

(34) John$_i$-ga [zibun$_i$-ga kare$_{?*i}$-no hahaoya-o semeta to] itta.
        SB   SB he-GN   mother-DO blamed that said
     `John said that zibun blamed kare´s mother. ´

In (33), two occurences of kare can refer to John, however, this option disappers when the first occurence of kare is replaced by zibun as in (34).
    They relate this fact to the assumption that zibun raises at LF and a general property of kare, given in Saito and Hoji (1983):
(35) Kare cannot be bound by a quantifier.

If zibun raises at LF to an A´-position, then zibun shares a common property with quantifiers, which undergo universal quantifier raising at LF (May 1979; 1985); they both are in A´-positions at LF, as (36) illustrates:
(36) * ... QP$_i$/WH$_i$/zibun$_i$ ... [... kare$_i$ ...]

Since zibun is not a quantifier in the standard sense, the Disjointness Requirement on kare, formulated in Aoun and Hornstein (1986):

(37) Kare must be A´-free.   (hereafter the DRK)

which refers to the position, and not the content, of the binder,
subsumes (35) and explains why zibun cannot bind kare.
    Their analysis is not only consistent with my raising analysis
that   explains   subject-orientation,   but   also   has   a   great
significance to the claim that zibun is an operator.   That is, if
the proposal (21), repeated below:
(21)a. Operators can and must remain in A´-positions at LF.
    b. Non-Operators in A´-positions must undergo reconstruction.

is a reasonable one,   then LF is the level of grammar where only
operators are found in A´-positions.   The DRK (37) is thus another
way of saying:
(38) Kare cannot be bound by an operator.

If the fact that zibun cannot bind kare is due to the violation of
the DRK,   zibun must be an operator.   In other words, the limited
interaction of   zibun with kare must be reducible to   my   central
proposal that zibun is an operator.
    The   following fact   supports   the   raising   mechanism   I
formulated in section 2.   That is, the replacement of the second
occurence of kare in (33) with zibun does not seem to limit the
behavior of the subject kare; thus kare in (39) and zibun can both
refer to John, unlike in (34):

(39) (Aoun and Hornstein 1986)
    John$_i$-ga [kare$_i$-ga zibun$_i$-no hahaoya-o hihanshita to]
        SB   he   SB self GN mother-DO criticize   that
    itta.
    said   `John said that kare criticized zibun´s mother.´

(39) indicates that kare in subject position can escape from being
A´-bound by zibun.   This shows that zibun raises to a position
which does not c-command subject position.   The fact observed in
(39) is thus perfectly consistent with the raising mechanism that
explains subject-orientation.

    Assuming that the DRK (37) is a primitive principle operating
in the grammar of Japanese, we now have an excellent way of
testing whether a given element is in an A´-position or not.   My
analysis in section 2 predicts that anaphors involving raising
(zibun, zibun-zisin and mizukara) do not allow kare to bear the
same index, while non-raising reflexive (kare-zisin) has no such
effect.   This prediction is in fact borne out.   Consider the
following, in which we can see whether the DRK (37) is violated or
not:

(40) John$_i$-ga [zibun$_i$ -ga kare?*$_i$ -no hahaoya-o
        SB   zibun-zisin$_i$ kare???$_i$ GN mother-DO
        mizukara$_i$ kare???$_i$
        kare-zisin$_i$ kare$_i$ <--
    hihanshita to] itta.
    criticized that said
    `John said that self criticized kare´s mother.´

(40) shows the three-way contrasts denoted by the subscripts on kare, ?*, ???, and no ?. I feel, however, that the major contrast lies between zibun/zibun-zisin/mizukara on the one hand and kare-zisin on the other, indicated by an arrow (<--). To clarify, the three-way contrasts are reduced to one in the following coordinate constructions:

(41)a. John$_i$-ga [zibun$_i$ -no kustu] to [kare*$_i$-no fuku]-o
       SB   zibun-zisin$_i$ GN shoes and kare*$_i$ GN clothes-DO
            mizukara$_i$ kare*$_i$
            kare-zisin$_i$ kare$_i$ <--
       katazuketa.
       put-away   `John put away self's shoes and kare's clothes.'

    b. John$_i$-ga [kare*$_i$-no kutsu] to [zibun$_i$ -no fuku]-o
       SB   kare*$_i$ GN shoes and zibun-zisin$_i$ GN clothes-DO
            kare*$_i$ mizukara$_i$
            kare$_i$ <--   kare-zisin$_i$
       katazuketa.
       put-away   `John put away kare's shoes and self's clothes.'

In either order, zibun[7], zibun-zisin, and mizukara fall under a type of expressions that limit the behavior of kare. Kare-zisin does not belong to this type. Thus, I independently come to the conclusion that the first three reflexives involve raising, but kare-zisin does not.

5. Anaphors in Controlled Constructions
     There are some cases where the three reflexives do not display subject-orientation. Consider the following, where the reflexives appear in an object controll position:

(42) Taro$_i$-ga Ziro$_j$-ni [zibun*$_{i/j}$ -ga kaigi-ni deru yoo]
         SB   IO   zibun-zisin*$_{i/j}$ SB meeting attend that
                         mizukara*$_{i/j}$
     itta.   pro*$_{i/j}$/PRO*$_{i/j}$
     told   `Taro told Ziro to attend the meeting.'

In (42), the binder of the reflexives corresponds to the object controller Ziro, suggesting the possibility that the reflexives are object controlled. Since subject-orientation is not operating here, I must say that the reflexives do not undergo LF-raising. To confirm this possibility, let us apply an operational test that utilizes the DRK (37):

(43) Taro$_i$-ga Ziro$_j$-ni [zibun$_j$ -ga kare$_j$-no hahaoya-o
         SB   IO   zibun-zisin$_j$ SB he   GN mother DO
                         mizukara$_j$
     taisetsu-ni-suru yoo] itta.   `Taro told Ziro to treat
     treat with care that told   his mother with care.'

The fact that kare can bear the same index as that of the reflexives shows that the DRK (37) is not violated. This means that the reflexives are not in an A'-position, which implies that LF-raising does not take place.

When the reflexives appear in a subject controll position, subject-orientation re-emerges:

(44) Taro$_i$-ga Ziro$_j$-ni [zibun$_i$/*$_j$ -ga sono kuruma-o kau
         SB   IO   zibun-zisin$_i$/*$_j$ SB that car DO buy
                           mizukara$_i$/*$_j$
                           pro$_i$/*$_j$/PRO$_i$/*$_j$
     koto-o] yakusokushita.
     COMP   promised   `Taro promised Ziro to buy that car.´

However, the familiar operational test, applied in (45) below, shows that the reflexives in these cases do not raise at LF:

(45) Taro$_i$-ga Ziro$_j$-ni [zibun$_i$ -ga kare$_i$-no heya-de
         SB   IO   zibun-zisin$_i$ SB he   GN room-in
                           mizukara$_i$
     benkyoosuru koto-o] yakusokushita.   `Taro promised Ziro
       study   COMP   promised   to study in his room.´

Subject-orientation of the reflexives in (44) – (45) is thus not a consequence of LF-raising, but rather an accidental correlation with the possibility that the reflexives are subject controlled. I thus arrive at the following general conclusion:

(46) Operator anaphors do not raise when they appear in
     obligatory controll positions.

The significance of this phenomenon is that when the DRK (37) indicates no movement of the reflexives, subject-orientation breaks down. The reduction of subject-orientation to LF-raising of anaphors is thus quite convincing.

6. Conclusion

I have demonstrated that subject-oriented binding is a semantic property of anaphors that intersects with the syntax of LF-representation. In doing so, I have shown the necessity of a three-way classification of anaphors, which may be reduced to two factors, [±operator] and [±lexical]:

(47) Three-way classification of anaphoric expressions.
     (a) Raising anaphors   [+op, +lex]: zibun
     (b) Local-Raising anaphors [+op, -lex]: zibun-zisin, mizukara
     (c) Non-Raising anaphors   [-op, -lex]: kare-zisin
                                 ([-op, +lex]) non-attested[8]

There are some discriminant properties that would determine the three types of anaphors. We have discussed three such properties:

(48) (I) Long-Distance vs. Local Subject Orientation:
         a discriminant between (a) and (b).
    (II) The Absence vs. Presence of Connectivity Effects:
         a discriminant between (a) and (b)/(c).
   (III) Limited vs. Non-Limited Interaction with Kare:
         a discriminant between (a)/(b) and (c).

In the course of the discussion, I suggested another classificational property; namely:

(IV) The Presence vs. Absence of Subject-Orientation:
a discriminant between (a)/(b) and (c).

The availability of the second and the third discriminants may be specific to only Japanese, but I suggest the possibility that the first and the fourth discriminants apply cross linguistically.

Notes

*   I wish to thank Joseph Aoun, Mürvet Enç, Hajime Hoji, Osvaldo Jaeggli, Audrey Li, and Hiroaki Tada for valuable suggestions and criticisms. All shortcomings are mine.

1   This finding is indebted to L.S. Yeh´s (1985) observation on behavior of taziji (he-self) in Chinese.
    It should be noted that, to some speakers, zibun-zisin and mizukara can also refer to a subject across the specified subject. This interpretation is readily available especially when they appear in a specifier of NP.

2   There are some notable exceptions to subject-orientation, however, this paper does not discuss such cases.

3   Generally, morphologically simplex anaphors are lexical anaphors, and compound anaphors are non-lexical anaphors.

4   I wish to thank O. Jaeggli for his suggestions.
    This structure is only one of the possibilities, and it leaves some unsolved problems (see note 5 below). For an alternative analysis, see Katada (in preparation).

5   This is one of the unsolved problems in this paper.

6   I wish to thank H. Hoji for this observation.

7   The fact that a subject cannot bind both kare and zibun in coordinate constructions is noted in Fukui (1984).

8   This type of anaphor, if attested in some language, should be morphologically simplex, yet acts as a local anaphor which is not necessarily subject-oriented.

References

Akatsuka, N. (1976) Reflexivization: A Transformational Approach. Shibatani (eds.), Syntax and Semantics 5: Japanese Generative Grammar, Academic Press, New York, 55-116.

Akmajian, A. (1970) Aspects of the Grammar of Focus in English. PhD Dissertation, MIT, Cambridge, Massachusetts.

Aoun, J. and Clark, R. (1985) On Non-Overt Operators. Gilligan, Mohammad, and Roberts (eds.) Southern California Occasional Papers in Linguistics 10, USC, 17-36.

Aoun, J. and Hornstein, N. (1986) Bound and Referential Pronouns. ms.

Aoun, J., Hornstein, N. and Sportiche, D. (1981) Some Aspects of Wide Scope Quantification. Journal of Linguistic Research 1, 69-95.

Barss, A. (1986) Chains and Anaphoric Dependence: On Reconstruction and Its Implications. PhD Dissertation, MIT Cambridge, Massachusetts.

Chomsky, N. (1981) Lectures on Government and Binding, Foris.

Chomsky, N. (1986a) Knowledge of Language: Its Nature, Origin and Use, Praeger, New York.

Chomsky, N. (1986b) Barriers, MIT Press, Cambridge.

Fukui, N. (1984) Studies in Japanese Anaphora I: The Adjunct Subject Hypothesis and zibun. ms., MIT Cambridge, Massachusetts.

Giorgi, A. (1984) Towards a Theory of Long Distance Anaphors: A GB Approach. Linguistic Review 3, 307 - 361.

Higgins, F.R. (1973) The Pseudo-Cleft Construction in English. PhD Dissertation, MIT, Cambridge, Massachusetts.

Huang, J. (1982) Logical Relations in Chinese and the Theory of Grammar. PhD Dissertation, MIT, Cambridge.

Huang, J. (1981/82) Move Wh in a Language without Wh Movement. The Linguistic Review 1, 369 - 416.

Inoue, K. (1976) Reflexivization: An Interpretive Approach. Shibatani (eds.), Syntax and Semantics 5: Japanese Generative Grammar, Academic Press, New York, 117-200.

Kitagawa, Y. (1986) Subject in Japanese and English. PhD Dissertation, U. Mass, Amherst, Massachusetts.

Kuno, S. (1973) The Structure of the Japanese Language, MIT Press, Cambridge, Massachusetts.

Kurata, K. (1986) Asymmetries in Japanese. ms. University of Massachusetts, Amherst.

Kuroda, S.-Y. (1965) Generative Grammatical Studies in the Japanese Language. PhD Dissertaion, MIT, Cambridge.

Kuroda, S.-Y. (1986) Whether We Agree or Not; Rough Ideas about the Comparative Syntax of English and Japanese. ms. UCSD.

Lasnik, H. and Saito, M. (1984) On the Nature of Proper Government. LI 15.2, 235 - 289.

Lebeaux, D. (1983) A Distributional Difference between Reciprocals and Reflexives. LI 14.4, 723-730.

May, R. (1977) The Grammar of Quantification. PhD Dissertation, MIT Cambridge, Massachusetts.

May, R. (1985) Logical Form: Its Structure and Derivation, The MIT Press, Cambridge, Massachusetts.

Muraki, M. (1979) On the Rule Scrambling in Japanese. in G. Bedell, et al., eds.

Nakamura, M. (1986) Anaphora in Japanese. ms. MIT Cambridge.

Pica, P. (1987) On the Nature of the Reflexivization Cycle. Proceedings of NELS 1987, 483-499.

Saito, M. (1985) Some Asymmetries in Japanese and Their Theoretical Implications, PhD Dissertation, MIT Cambridge, Massachusetts.

Saito, M. and Hoji, H. (1983) Weak Crossover and Move @ in Japanese. Natural Language and Linguistic Theory 1.2.

Non-Canonical Argument Identification[*]

Judy Kegl and Christiane Fellbaum
Princeton University

0. Introduction

A Predicate Argument Structure (PAS) is used to indicate the number and types of arguments a particular verb requires for a sentence to be well-formed. A survey of numerous articles devoted to the topic of PAS (Belletti and Rizzi, 1986; Marantz, 1984; Perlmutter, 1978; and Kegl and Levin, 1988) yields a typology which recognizes not only a distinction between external and internal arguments (following Williams, 1981), but a distinction between two types of internal arguments as well: the direct argument (the one directly licensed by the verb via government and adjacency) and an indirect argument (canonically licensed by a preposition, but in some cases occurring in the PAS without a licenser).

Modifying a convention for representing PASs proposed in Levin and Rappaport (1986) and Rappaport, Laughren and Levin (1987), we use variables to indicate arguments of a verb. For purposes of exposition, we will always use x to indicate the external argument, y to indicate the direct argument, z to indicate the indirect argument and w to indicate an obligatory adjunct. In the following list, each PAS is followed by the label for a prototypically associated syntactic construction and an example sentence. The labels for constructions are not exhaustive. Thus, we argue that the PAS for a passive is identical to that of the unaccusative, $< y>$, and that the PAS of a psych-verb, $< yz>$, is identical to that of the passive of a double object verb.

Typology of Predicate Argument Structures

x< y>	transitive	The dog bit the boy.
x< >	unergative	The woman slept.
< y>	unaccusative	The bottle broke.
	passive	The baseball was hit.
x< y Pz>	ditransitive	The man gave the book to the woman.
x< yz>	double object	The man gave the woman the book.
< yz>	psych-verb	The play amused the children.
< >	weather verb	It rained.
< y> w	measure verb	The chicken weighed 3 lbs.
	copular	Mary is a doctor.

A PAS distinguishes itself from a subcategorization frame by not encoding the structural relations that hold between a verb and its arguments. For an argument to be identified, a government relation must hold between it and some licenser (previously referred to as a "theta-role assigner").[1] The manner of argument identification ultimately determines the mapping between

---

* Kegl's research was supported in part by a grant from the James S. McDonnell Foundation to Princeton University. Fellbaum's research was funded by contract N00014-86-K-0492 between the Office of Naval Research and Princeton University. The views and conclusions contained herein are those of the authors and should not be interpreted as representing official policies, either expressed or implied, of the Office of Naval Research, the McDonnell Foundation, or Princeton University.

[1] ARGUMENT IDENTIFICATION serves the same role as the process which is frequently referred to as "theta-marking" (Chomsky, 1981:37). In agreement with Rappaport, Levin and Laughren (1988), and Kegl and Levin

the grammatical relations held by NPs in the syntax and their corresponding variables in the PAS. Unlike subcategorizations which assume the presence of a subject NP in the surface realization of the sentence, the PAS does not require the presence of an external argument or any argument which might eventually be associated with the surface subject.

0.1. Canonical Argument Identification

Arguments are identified in several ways. The canonical means of argument identification, HEAD LICENSING, requires government by a lexical category (a verb or preposition) capable of licensing an argument. The prototypical configuration for argument identification involves sisterhood and adjacency between a verb and its direct argument. This is paralleled by the relation between a preposition and its NP argument.

Standard Government and Binding (GB) accounts license the external argument in a different manner, identifying it via a modified form of head licensing that applies leftward, indirectly theta-marking a subject by the V head of VP despite an intervening I' (see Chomsky 1981:37; 1985; 1986:13-14). Alternatively, one might adopt Williams' (1980) analysis of subject licensing by predication, thus admitting the possibility of other means of licensing arguments. We reject both approaches, arguing instead that the external argument is base-generated internal to VP as a sister to V' and is thus identified structurally through indirect licensing by the verb.

0.2. Non-Canonical Argument Identification

Sometimes, a verb selects for a second internal argument without a prepositional licenser (x< yz>). This argument, non-adjacent to the verb and thus "stranded", is licensed non-canonically by one of several options. In this paper, we propose three non-canonical licensing devices: INTERNALIZATION of an unlicensable argument to a position adjacent to and governed by V, INCORPORATION of a non-adjacent direct argument to form a complex verb and eliminate the need for it to syntactically receive Case, and thematic EXTERNALIZATION of a stranded internal argument to SPEC of VP (the position of base-generated external arguments) where it can be licensed.

0.3. Arguments vs. Adjuncts

Verbs select for not only arguments, but other obligatory XPs (Grimshaw, 1988). We propose in our typology a < y> w PAS that is associated with measure verbs and copular constructions. Although measure verbs are included in the class of unaccusatives by Perlmutter (1978), we are aware of neither any previous arguments for this choice of classification nor of any discussions of the status of the obligatory quantificational phrase (QP) associated with these verbs (see Grimshaw, 1987b). In this paper we demonstrate that the QP does not pattern like either of the classical internal arguments and we argue that it holds an adjunct relation to the lowest VP

(1988), we reject labels which imply the involvement of theta-roles at this level of representation. Although theta-roles have proved relevant to lexical semantics and play a systematic role with respect to the characterization of lexical conceptual structure, the term "theta-role" as it is frequently used in discussions of PAS is synonymous with the term "argument." While theta-roles may aid us in identifying particular lexical semantic classes of verbs which have characteristic PASs, the semantic status of the argument at the syntactic level of representation is irrelevant and eludes any systematic characterization. When we speak of "argument identification" we are really saying that the argument is licensed, or identified, and is therefore required by the Projection Principle to be present at all subsequent levels of representation.

dominating the measure verb--the same position resultatives and internal argument descriptors hold with respect to their verbs.

We distinguish adjuncts selected for by the verb from those which are truly optional by assuming the former (resultatives, descriptors, QPs) to be adjoined to VP and the latter (depictives) to be adjoined to IP. Scope distinctions on depictives vs. obligatory adjuncts also supports this structural distinction. AP adjuncts such as resultatives and internal argument descriptors might seem to be optionally present in a PAS: *The lake froze* vs. *The lake froze solid*. Instead, we can view these as two different PASs, one requiring an obligatory AP adjunct and the other not. The lexical idiosyncracy of resultatives and internal argument descriptor constructions and the semantic restrictions they place on their adjuncts support the postulation of two PASs.

The relation an adjunct holds to a VP differs from the relation held by an argument and is generally assumed to be a predication relation. The characterization of predication we propose strays quite a bit from that proposed in both Williams (1980,1983) and Rothstein (1983). With respect to Williams, we assume predication in only a subset of his cases. We do not, for example, assume that subjects are licensed by predication. Like Rothstein (1983) and Simpson (1983), we recognize that predication on internal vs. external arguments needs to be distinguished, but we also assume that the configuration in which predication applies is structurally consistent, namely XPs that are Chomsky-adjoined to VP or to IP are in a **PREDICATION** relation with them. We differ from Rothstein in not using predication as a relation between some XP and an already theta-marked NP, although this interpretation follows from scope properties of the adjunct. Resultatives and internal argument descriptors are selected by the verb and hold a predication relation to VP; depictives hold a predication relation to IP.

The diagram below illustrates the configurations in which we find external (x), direct (y), and indirect (z) arguments as well as the various types of adjuncts (w).

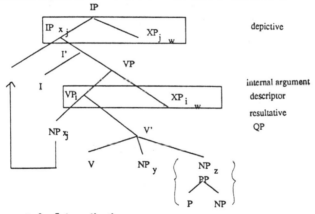

1. Arguments for Internalization

Evidence for internalization comes from constructions involving multiple internal arguments, where the indirect argument does not appear with a canonical licenser (a preposition). Consider sentences (1) and (2).

1. The man gave the book to the woman. x< y Pz>
2. The man gave the woman the book.   x< z y>

The order of internal arguments in the PASs corresponds to their surface syntactic arrangement. Notice the difference in argument ordering which correlates with the presence vs. absence of a prepositional licenser for the indirect argument. The z argument is an indirect argument and must be identified. The three-place predicate construction in (1) has the direct argument first, followed by the PP; whereas the double object construction in (2) has a surface ordering where the y and z arguments are inverted.

Internalization of a Stranded Indirect Argument:

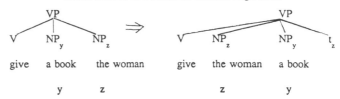

This inversion is significant and actually reflects a process of internalization that moves an NP from a non-lexically headed position that is non-adjacent to V, to a position adjacent to and directly governed by V. The internalization of an indirect argument is motivated only when the argument is stranded. In instances where the indirect argument is not canonically licensed by P it moves adjacent to the verb where it can be licensed directly. Of course, such a movement strands the original direct argument and it must be licensed by some other means.

Consideration of these constructions is by no means a novel idea, and many analyses have been proposed. A number of recent accounts (Baker, 1988 [1985]; Barss and Lasnik, 1986; Marantz 1984) assume the ordering of the indirect argument (z) before the direct argument (y) to be basic in double object constructions. Yet, in each instance their analyses run into problems.

Stowell's (1981) analysis assumes that strict subcategorization frames are unordered and that the order of arguments is imposed by principles of Case theory. He proposes incorporation of the indirect argument in double object constructions:

3. Wayne [V'[V sent[Robert]$_i$] [a telegram] [e]$_i$]

The incorporated object as part of the verbal complex absorbs Case, analogous to clitics in Romance. The second NP is the true syntactic object of the verb and it gets Case under adjacency from the verbal complex formed by the verb and the incorporated indirect object. Stowell recognizes the major problem with his analysis, namely, that it incorrectly predicts that the direct object, which he assumes to be unincorporated, should be able to passivize, while also incorrectly predicting that the indirect object, which he assumes to be incorporated, should not passivize. Stowell's own examples, which appear in (4) and (5), stand as counterexamples to his predictions.

4. *A telegram was sent Robert (by Wayne). (Stowell, 1981:325, ex. 47a.)
5. Robert was sent a telegram (by Wayne).

Baker (1988 [1985]), who correctly observes that crosslinguistically only themes (in this case direct arguments) incorporate, nevertheless resorts to a different account of English double object constructions that is based on his analysis of applicative constructions. Double object constructions, he argues, involve the incorporation of the preposition from the indirect object PP adjacent to the verb, yielding a verb *give* which functions like "give-to."

Structure from Baker (1988):

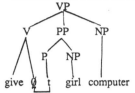

The trace of this invisible, incorporated preposition licenses the indirect argument; and somehow, despite non-adjacency, the verb can assign Case to the stranded direct argument. Despite the problem with how *a computer* receives Case, Baker's analysis is subject to the same criticism as Stowell's. Neither can explain why the incorporated NP can passivize, and why the free NP cannot.

Larson (1987, based on Chomsky 1975 [1955]) proposes an inversion operation that maintains the D-structure ordering of *y* before *z*. Larson's attempt at a transformational account of the dative alternation despite the well know objections of Dowty (1978), Green (1974), and Oehrle (1975), is motivated by an attempt to maintain Baker's (1985) Uniformity of Theta-Assignment Hypothesis (UTAH) that states: "Identical thematic relations are represented by identical structural relations between the items at the level of D-structure." His D-structure representation appears below:

Larson's D-Structure for Double Object Constructions:

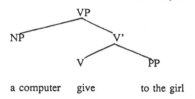

Larson maintains that the direct argument, *computer*, is in SPEC of VP verb, rather than in a position adjacent to and governed by the verb. The indirect argument, *the girl* appears originally under V' with a prepositional licenser which disappears when a process analogous to Passive absorbs Case. The direct argument spontaneously demotes, making its position non-thematic, and it consequently adjoins to V', its Theta-role assigner. Although Larson's account does not fall prey to the passivization problem, it provides no motivation for these spontaneous demotion and dethematization processes.

Finally, Barss and Lasnik (1986) demonstrate that, in a double object construction, the second NP must be in the domain of, and be bound by, the first NP, but not vice versa. This is shown by a number of anaphoric asymmetries such as those in (6) - (9) below, where NP_z must c-command NPy.

     6. I gave each man the other's watch.
     7. *I gave the other man each watch.
     8. I showed John himself in the mirror.
     9. *I showed himself John in the mirror.

Many current analyses predict the hierarchical relation between the NPs to be symmetrical or to predict scope relationships exactly opposite of what the data reveal. Barss and Lasnik (1986:352) propose a phrase structure where the 2 inverted NPs are sisters of each other and of V under VP. The asymmetries are successfully predicted using a new definition of domain: "Y is in the domain of X iff X c-commands Y and X precedes Y." While they account for the asymmetries, their analysis does not predict the passivization facts.

    Our analysis, which involves a combination of internalization of the indirect argument to a verb-adjacent and governed position and incorporation of the original direct argument, avoids the problems posed by transformational accounts of dative alternation by positing two distinct PASs: $x< y\ Pz>$ for the ditransitive and $x< yz>$ for the double object construction. We gain the benefits of Baker's UTAH by assuming the order of arguments in the PAS to be consistent with their argument status (external, direct, indirect), and by allowing this distinction to be structurally reflected by the D-Structure projection of VP configurations from the PAS to the syntax. One way in which we differ from Baker is by assuming that although indirect arguments are consistently associated with the same position in the PAS and will consistently link to the same theta-roles in the Lexical Conceptual Structure (LCS) of verbs sharing membership in the same lexical semantic classes, some multiple internal argument PASs can lack a prepositional licenser. The absence of a prepositional licenser has syntactic consequences triggered by the need for argument identification which parallel S-structure reconfigurations associated with the need to receive Case. It is the need for an argument to be in an acceptable configuration which motivates both the processes of inversion and incorporation and avoids the unmotivated spontaneous demotions and movements found in Larson's account. Finally, we provide a more coherent analysis of incorporation in two ways. Once the indirect argument has moved to verb-adjacent position in order to be identified, there is little motivation for incorporating it into the verb. It is the direct argument which is then stranded, and it is this argument which incorporates. Through incorporation the argument becomes part of a complex verb, thereby obviating the need for licensing or Case assignment. (The non-incorporated argument is canonically licensed by the verb.)

Proposed Formulation of Incorporation:

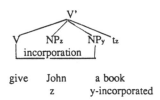

         give   John   a book
                z   y-incorporated

We avoid the passivization problem by assuming this direct argument to be the one which is incorporated, and the incorporation of the direct argument also fits with the cross-linguistic observation that it is themes which tend to incorporate. An abstract incorporation which leaves the complex verb discontinuous at S-structure does not seem problematic to us, particularly in view of the fact that it makes the correct prediction with regard to the passivization data.[2] Finally, our account handles the Barss and Lasnik (1986) asymmetries, since it meets the domain requirements. Furthermore, the presence of the trace of the indirect argument is in the domain of the direct argument.

Summary. Positing a rule of internalization yields 1) a systematic account of the inversion of direct and indirect arguments in double object constructions which is motivated by the stranding of the unlicensed indirect argument; 2) a VP configurational structure which fits with the anaphoric asymmetries noted in Barss and Lasnik (1986); and 3) an account of incorporation which correctly predicts the passivization facts. The availability of a thematically motivated internalization process offers an interesting solution to the locative alternation problem discussed in Levin and Rappaport (1986). Sentences like (10) and (11) have been assumed to have similar PASs, both of the type x< y Pz> .

10. John loaded the hay on the truck.   x< y Pz>
11. John loaded the truck with hay.   x< Py z>

The direct arguments *the hay* and *the truck* are linked to different theta-roles (theme vs. goal) which obscures the semantic relation between the two constructions. However, let us assume that not only the indirect, but also the direct arguments, can be associated with prepositional licensers. The availability of internalization allows movement of the stranded indirect argument in (11) adjacent to V, thereby allowing a consistent association of theta-roles and argument positions, as well as placing the indirect argument in a position directly governed by the verb where it plays a central role with respect to the aspectual interpretation of the construction--it is holistically affected by the action of the verb (see Anderson, 1971, 1977; Tenny, 1987).

2. Arguments for Externalization

Under our analysis, VP internal phrase structure is a direct D-structure projection from the PAS. In the canonical form, an external argument is a sister to V', a direct argument is adjacent to and governed by V, and an indirect argument is internal to a PP which is a non-adjacent sister of V. The head of that PP governs the indirect argument and licenses it. Non-canonically, a direct argument can occur with a prepositional licenser (cf. *with hay* in (11)) and an indirect argument can occur without one (the double object construction). When a licenser is absent, a stranded indirect argument internalizes in order to be in a position where it can be identified. If the process of internalization strands the original direct argument, as in the double object construction, that argument must be identified non-canonically, usually via incorporation. In this section we will introduce a second licensing device, THEMATIC EXTERNALIZATION, which moves a stranded argument to a position where it is a sister of V' where it can be licensed via indirect government by V. In thematic externalization, as in thematic internalization, the theta-role borne by an argument is a consequence of the lexical semantics of the verb (reflected consistently in the D-structure projection from the PAS). It does not follow structurally from the configuration in which an argument is eventually licensed.

---

[2] We would like to argue that English allows structures with discontinuous verbal material (such as in verb particle constructions), but at this point we have not mustered the syntactic arguments yet to substantiate this claim.

It is necessary to distinguish the syntactic externalization of a direct argument to SPEC of IP[3], which is motivated by the need for the argument to receive Case (as in unaccusatives, passives and raising constructions), from the thematic externalization of a stranded internal argument to SPEC of VP, which permits identification of the stranded original direct argument (as in psych-verb constructions).

Although we follow Belletti and Rizzi (1986, to appear) in positing a $< yz>$ PAS for psych-verbs, we propose a more complicated account of how these arguments are identified.[4] Under our analysis, psych-verb constructions involve three operations: thematic internalization of the z argument, thematic externalization of the y argument to external argument position (sister of V'), and, finally, syntactic externalization of the y argument to SPEC of IP in order to get Case. Although the psych-verb construction seems more complicated, the 3 processes involved can all be independently motivated. Furthermore, the added complexity of the psych-verb construction fits with its late acquisition. Examples of syntactic vs. thematic externalization for unaccusatives and psych-verbs appears below:

Unaccusative: The bottle broke.
(syntactic externalization
for Case assignment)

Psych-verb: The play amused the children.
(thematic externalization (argument identification); syntactic externalization (Case)

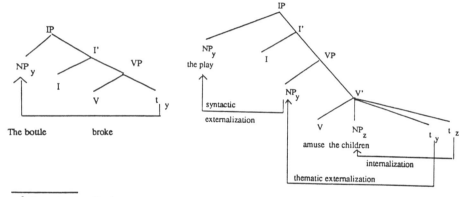

---

[3] Syntactic externalization must move an argument directly to SPEC of IP. Movement via SPEC of VP (sister to V') would result in double identification (a violation of the theta-criterion). Movement via adjunction to VP (the WH-movement case), would result in movement to an A'-position and back to an A-position and should be ruled out.

[4] Belletti and Rizzi (1986, to appear) argue for an analysis of psych-verbs which patterns them after double object constructions except for the fact that they lack an external argument. However, they recognize neither a rule of thematic internalization which inverts the arguments nor the possibility of thematic externalization to allow the stranded original direct argument to be licensed. Instead they argue for direct syntactic externalization of the direct argument to SPEC of IP and inherent Case assignment to the indirect argument separated from the verb by an intervening trace: $*y < t_z>$. Avoidance of an exceptional rule of inherent Case assignment provides additional motivation for the rule of internalization. (See Grimshaw (1987a) for an alternative analysis that also requires inherent Case assignment.)

In the psych-verb example, the NP_y is stranded by internalization. By virtue of being non-adjacent to the verb it is unable to be identified via direct licensing. This argument must move to external argument position to be licensed. Thematic externalization can apply only when the external argument position is empty; therefore, externalization would not be an option in double object constructions. Similarly, incorporation is possible only in PASs containing an external argument and, as (12) shows, it cannot account for licensing in intransitive psych-verb constructions, $< yz>$. (13), where the direct argument is sentential, reveals that both arguments are internal.[5]

 12. *It amused the children the play.
 13. It amused the children that we didn't know the answer.

Summary. This section has argued for a distinction between syntactic externalization, which is triggered by case requirements, and thematic externalization, which is triggered by the need for an argument to be identified. It was noted that thematic externalization can only apply when the external argument position inside VP is empty. The psych-verb construction is particularly interesting because its analysis requires internalization, as well as both syntactic and thematic externalization. Thus far, the base-generation of the external argument as a sister of V' has merely been stipulated. In the next section we consider the benefits to be gained from making such an assumption.

4. Arguments for base generating the external argument as a sister to V'

The Case Filter (Chomsky, 1981:49, 1986:74) states, too strongly, that every phonetically realized NP must be assigned (abstract) Case. Problems with this filter are pointed out in both Chomsky (1986) and Postal and Pullum (1987). Basically, there are NPs in the sentence which need not (do not) receive Case.

 14. John nominated Bill [president].
 15. The chicken weighed [3 pounds].
 16. I consider John [a fool].

A weaker alternative, the Visibility Condition, is formulated in Chomsky (1986:93) as follows: "a noun phrase can receive a θ-role only if it is in a position to which Case is assigned or if it is linked to such a position." Somehow, this seems circular.

An NP's presence in or its linking to a Case position is tied to whether or not that NP receives a θ-role. But, what determines that an NP must be in a Case position? If θ-roles are part of the lexical entry of a verb, why are they only assigned at S-structure? First, θ-roles were used as a diacritic to code which NPs got Case, and now Case is being used to identify which NPs get θ-roles.

---

[5] Sentential complements seem to be immune to the visibility condition which accounts for their appearance in non Case marked positions. But, are they identified as arguments? If Psych-verbs are unaccusative in nature, then what allows the verb to assign accusative Case to the internalized indirect argument? Either we also need some sort of inherent Case marking, or we need to assume that the sentential complement undergoes thematic externalization comparable to its NP counterpart and then has the option of either syntactic externalization to SPEC of IP or heavy NP shift. In the latter instance, the Extended Projection Principle would require the presence of a pleonastic in subject position.

4.1. A unified account of what an argument is

Basically, we need to know what NPs require Case. The content of the θ-roles with which these NPs are associated is a property of their lexical semantic representation and has little to do with the syntactic operations which move them into Case positions. Which of these D-structure arguments is the external, direct and indirect argument needs to be coded in the structural realization of these arguments at D-Structure. In fact, the PAS directly projects the D-structure phrase marker for these verbs up to the level of VP, with a few readjustments (thematic internalization, thematic externalization, and incorporation) on non-canonical projections.

An NP that requires Case or must be linked to a Case position at S-structure is an argument. The base-generation of the external argument in SPEC of IP makes it difficult to give any systematic structural characterization of what an argument is and how it can be distinguished from an adjunct (or NP which doesn't need to get Case). It even posed problems to the approach which tried to identify arguments through θ-role assignment, leading to elaborate formulations of predication which could assign a θ-role to the subject NP and to indirect licensing of subjects by a verb via I'.

Because the external argument shares with internal arguments the need to receive Case, we argue that it is base generated as a sister of V', namely, totally internal to VP. The assumption that all NPs that must receive Case are base-generated under VP allows us to simplify the GB account of indirect licensing and to provide a structurally motivated and unified characterization of the notion **ARGUMENT**--an NP base-generated fully internal to VP, which must receive Case at S-Structure. This definition allows us to distinguish arguments from sentential complements which differ only in the sense that they need not receive Case at S-structure. In all other respects they are indistinguishable from direct arguments (see Kegl and Levin 1988). In addition, this definition of argument excludes adjuncts, which, even though they are sometimes NPs, are not required to receive Case.

Since the external argument is external to V' while the direct and indirect arguments are dominated by it, the internal/external distinction, and the associated asymmetry, is maintained. The direct argument is distinguished from an indirect argument by the fact that it is both a sister of and adjacent to V. An indirect argument, then, is any constituent dominated by V' which is not both a sister and adjacent. This leaves NPs dominated by PP as well as NP sisters of the direct argument, which are themselves not adjacent to V.

Remembering the earlier discussion of the locative alternation with the verb *load*, we hasten to add that the presence or absence of a preposition may be irrelevant to the characterization of direct vs. indirect argument. If we accept examples like *John loaded the truck with hay* as having the PAS x< Py z> , thus admitting the presence of prepositional licensers for the direct argument, we find that there is never an indirect argument in the absence of a direct argument. The apparent exceptions to this observation, as far as we are able to determine, can be analyzed as adjuncts.

4.2. A cleaner account of predication

With external arguments licensed within VP, there is no longer a need to license subjects via predication. As a result, the surface subject position can remain athematic, only being associated with a θ-role when an argument externalizes to this position to get Case. Movement to SPEC of IP is then motivated solely to get Case, and the Extended Projection Principle inserts pleonastic *it* only when an overt subject is needed.

Base-generation of VP suggests an alternative analysis of *There*-constructions which captures the thematic properties of the dummy *there*. Notice that the set of unaccusative verbs is mixed between those that allow the causative/inchoative alternation (e.g., change-of-state verbs) and those that do not (e.g., verbs of appearance).

17. John broke the bottle./The bottle broke. (change of state)
18. *The train arrived three men./Three men arrived. (appearance)

Those that do not participate in the causative/inchoative alternation tend to allow the Presentational *There*-construction:

19. There arrived three men.
20. There arose a clamor.
21. There appeared on the horizon a herd of elephant.
22. There bloomed a blossom on the bush.

Furthermore, a subset of the class of copular constructions which we will also argue to be unaccusative allow *there*.

23. There is a mouse in the tub.
24. There is a Santa Claus.

We propose that *there* is a dummy external argument, which by virtue of its presence as sister to V' allows the verb to assign Case (see Burzio, 1986) to the direct argument, thereby explaining its ability to remain in direct object position. *There* then externalizes to SPEC of IP to get case. As we examine more and more of the lexicon from this perspective, we begin to see that most verbs participate in some sort of transitivity alternation, and *there*-external arguments seem to fill a gap. Thus, we see a distinction between the dummies *there* (thematic) and *it* (athematic). For discussions along these line see Davis (1984).

With an external argument as sister to V', we can avoid complicated definitions of predicates which include material from INFL and can provide a less complicated account of the argument-like qualities of *there*. In fact, the only remaining predication relations occur between VP and a Chomsky-adjoined XP. We will examine these adjuncts in the next section.

5. Adjuncts

With a strict definition and set of tests for arguments which includes being totally internal to VP, being able to move to argument positions, or alternating on the surface with respect to which argument position they receive Case in, we find that there are still a set of XPs obligatorily selected by the verb that elude identification as arguments. These VP internal adjuncts, not being arguments, are non-thematic and immune from the Case Filter. Furthermore, in addition to adjuncts obligatorily selected by the verb, which we presume to be specified as part of the PAS (probably better termed the Functional Structure once expanded in this way[6]), there are also non-selected adjuncts which are adjoined to IP.

Both types of adjuncts are licensed by the predication relation that holds between them and and the IP/VP. Of course, this relationship is now structurally unique, and what we call the co-indexing of predication might simply be a scope interpretation that follows from an adjoined configuration. Adjuncts have properties distinct from internal arguments (they cannot passivize,

---

[6] We thank Emmon Bach for pointing out this terminological discrepancy to us.

nor can they externalize like the direct argument of psych-verbs or passives).

One class of adjuncts is represented by depictives, which we argue are adjoined to and in a predication relation with IP (cf. the figure on p. 3). The structural predication relationship between the XP and the IP is reflected in the paraphrase relations that show the scope of the XP over the external argument of the IP. Depictive XPs can be APs, NPs, or PPs, as illustrated below:

25. The boy played the game nude.
26. John died a broken man.
27. John played the game with enthusiasm.

Note that in each case, the adjunct modifies and has scope over the entire IP. The inclusion of the subject in this scope relationship is indicative of the IP adjunct relationship. Notice that the NP adjunct can appear on the right of a copular construction and the adjectival adjunct can appear as a prenominal adjective. These are both characteristic of adjunction structures.

28. A nude boy played the game.
29. John was a broken man when he died.

The second class of adjuncts is represented by XPs that are adjoined to the highest VP and stand in a predication relation to the lower VP. While outside of V' (and therefore not arguments), these adjuncts are partially internal to VP. Such adjuncts are selected for by the verb and have distinct PASs reflecting their obligatory status.[7] Resultatives, internal argument descriptors, and copular constructions include the kind of adjunct that has scope over the internal argument (for a discussion of the scope relations and the semantics of resultatives and internal argument descriptors see Simpson (1983)). Resultatives can be AP, NP or PP:

30. John hammered the nail flat.
31. The committee appointed Bill chairman.
32. Sue pushed the thumbtack into wall.

Again, the structural relation and the co-indexation are reflected in the possible adjectival and copular paraphrases (*The flat nail/Bill was chairman/The thumbtack is in the wall.*)[8] Compare the following structurally identical internal argument descriptors with the resultatives just discussed.

33. John ate the meat raw.
34. Igor met Rosa pregnant

The third kind of construction that shares the predicative structure above is the unaccusative with a QP (a measure phrase)[9]:

---

[7] Although VP internal adjuncts like resultatives or internal argument descriptors may not seem to be obligatory in the way that their QP counterparts in measure verbs are, we still feel that the semantic restrictions that they inherit from the verb support the postulation that a VP adjunct belongs to a PAS that alternates with a non-adjunct taking counterpart.

[8] Notice that a sentence like (32) and a sentence like *John put the book on the table* seem to be identical not only in structure but also in the scope of the PP. We suggest that both the resultatives with PP and verbs like *put* share the same PAS. This supports our claim that resultatives with an adjunct PP have their own PAS distinct from resultatives without an adjunct and offers one case in which the PP adjunct is clearly obligatory.

[9] Space limitations force us to present only a reduced discussion of measure verbs. A detailed discussion of their argument-taking properties and implications for the typology of PASs appears in Kegl and Fellbaum (1988).

35. The chicken weighed 3 lbs.

Again, the QP can appear as a prenominal modifier of the internal argument (*the 3 lb. chicken/the 12ft. rug*, etc.). Moreover, measure phrases are also paraphrasable as copular constructions, parallel to resultatives and external argument descriptors.. The only difference between resultatives and internal argument descriptors is semantic and follows from the inherent aspectual properties of the two verb classes (cf. Simpson (1983)).

36. John hammered the nail flat./The nail became flat.
37. John ate the meat raw./The meat was raw.
38. The lake froze solid./The lake became solid.
39. The chicken weighed 3 lbs./The chicken was 3 lbs.

Note that cases where the verb and the predicate behave as a unit (such as *hammer flat, eat raw*, etc.) can be attributed to heavy NP shift:

40. John hammered flat {*the nail/every nail that stuck out more than 2 inches}.
41. John eats raw {*the meat/any fish you put in front of him}.

Finally, we claim that copular constructions such as the one below also share the predication structure of the sentences above. (Copular constructions allow a wide range of XPs; we will give only one example where XP is NP.):

42. Mary is a doctor.

Notice that the semantic emptiness of the verb in copular constructions accounts for the fact that the XP associated with a copular PAS has no semantic restrictions placed upon it. In this respect, copular constructions differ from resultatives, internal argument descriptors, and the measure constructions to be discussed below, where the verb more or less constrains the choice of XP. The structural representations involving copular constructions are not yet established in the linguistic literature, but see Rapoport (1987), Higgins (1973), Akmajian (1970) and Rothstein (1983) for extensive discussions of equative and copular sentences. The tree below illustrates the three cases of VP adjuncts:

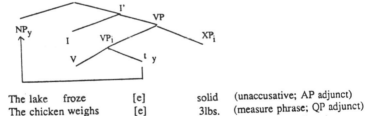

We now examine in more detail the class of measure verbs exemplified by *weigh* above. Many measure verbs have two distinct PASs. One is transitive with an external and a direct argument, where passivization is possible:

43. The butcher weighed the chicken./The chicken was weighed by the butcher.
44. The salesman measured the rug./The rug was measured by the salesman.

The second PAS involves an unaccusative which additionally selects for an obligatory QP adjunct and prohibits a passive:

45. The chicken weighed 3 lbs./*3 lbs. were weighed by the chicken.
46. The rug measured 9x12 ft./*12 ft. were measured by the rug.

Notice that in this second set of examples the QP is obligatory.

47. *The chicken weighed.
48. *The rug measured.

The QP behave neither as direct nor as indirect arguments. In contrast with the direct argument of a psych-verb, the QP cannot externalize:

49. *Three pounds weighed the chicken.
    z?   y

Unlike the direct argument in a double object or psych-verb construction, the QP never appears inverted (i.e., it never internalizes). This is another consequence of the fact that QP constructions have no indirect argument. While QPs never externalize to subject position or move to an argument position, they can move to an A' position:

50. *3lbs. weighed the chicken.
51. *3lbs. was weighed by the chicken.
52. How much did the chicken weigh?
53. What did the chicken weigh?

In both the transitive and the unaccusative PAS, *the chicken* bears the same argument relation to the verb. In the unaccusative, however, the direct argument undergoes syntactic externalization to SPEC of IP in order to get Case.

Finally, we note an interesting asymmetry between the obligatory adjunct structures in the two possible PASs. It turns out that the obligatory x and w constituents are in complementary distribution, when the adjunct XP, the w, is an NP.

54. The chicken weighed 3 lbs.
55. John weighed the chicken.
56. *John weighed the chicken 3 lbs.

External arguments seem unable to cooccur with NP predicates of the lowest VP: $*x< ..> w$. Thus, two possible configurations are in complementary distribution: $x< y>$ and $< y> w$. The existence of this complementary distribution further strengthens our assumption of two distinct PASs.

6. Conclusion In this paper, we argued for a number of non-canonical licensing devices: internalization, incorporation, externalization. By structurally distinguishing arguments from adjuncts, as well as VP adjuncts from IP adjuncts, we are able to provide a series of tests which distinguish three types of arguments (external, direct and indirect) from a variety of adjuncts--those selected by the verb (resultatives, internal argument descriptors, copular adjuncts, and obligatory QP), and those not selected by the verb (depictives).

References

Akmajian, Adrian. 1970. On Deriving Cleft Sentences from Pseudo-cleft Sentences. LI 1.12.149-168.

Anderson, Stephen. 1971. On the Role of Deep Structure in Semantic Interpretation. Foundations of Language. 7.387-396.

Anderson. Stephen. 1977. Comments on the Paper by Wasow. Formal Syntax, ed. by Peter Culicover et al., 361-377. New York: Academic Press.

Baker, Mark. 1988 [1985]. Incorporation: A Theory of Grammatical Function Changing. Chicago: The University of Chicago Press.

Barss, Andrew and Howard Lasnik. 1986. A Note on Anaphora and Double Objects. LI 17.2.347-354.

Belletti, Adriana and Luigi Rizzi. 1986. Psych-Verbs and Th-Theory. (Lexicon Project Working Papers 13.) Center for Cognitive Science, MIT, Cambridge, MA.

Belletti, Adriana and Luigi Rizzi. (to appear) Notes on Psych-Verbs, θ-Theory, and Binding. Proceedings of the Princeton Workshop on Comparative Grammar, ed. Robert Freidin. Cambridge, MA: The MIT Press.

Burzio, Luigi. 1986. Italian Syntax: A GB Approach. Dordrecht: D. Reidel.

Chomsky, Noam. 1975 [1955]. The Logical Structure of Linguistic Theory. Chicago: University of Chicago Press.

Chomsky, Noam. 1981. Lectures on Government and Binding. Dordrecht: Foris Publications.

Chomsky, Noam. 1985. Knowledge of Language: Its Nature, Origin and Use. New York: Praeger.

Chomsky, Noam. 1986. Barriers. Cambridge, MA: The MIT Press.

Davis, Lori. 1984. Arguments and Expletives. Doctoral dissertation. University of Connecticut, Storrs.

Dowty, David. 1978. Governed Transformations as Lexical Rules in a Montague Grammar. LI 9.393-426.

Green, Georgia. 1974. Semantics and Syntactic Regularity. Bloomington: Indiana University Press.

Grimshaw, Jane. 1987a. Psych Verbs and the Structure of Argument Structure. Unpublished manuscript, Linguistics and Cognitive Science Program, Brandeis University, Waltham, MA.

Grimshaw, Jane. 1987b. Subdeletion. LI 18.4.659-669.

Grimshaw, Jane. 1988. Adjuncts and Argument Structure. Occasional Paper # 36 , Center for Cognitive Science, MIT. Cambridge, MA.

Higgins, Roger. 1973. The Pseudocleft Construction in English. Doctoral dissertation. MIT, Cambridge, MA.

Kegl, Judy and Christiane Fellbaum. 1988. Properties of Measure Verbs. Unpublished manuscript, Princeton University. Princeton, NJ.

Kegl, Judy and Beth Levin. 1988. Entries in the GB Lexicon. Towards a Polytheoretical Lexical Database, ed. by Don Walker et al. Pisa, Italy: Instituto di Linguistica Computazionale, CNR.

Larson, Richard. 1987. On the Double Object Construction. (Lexicon Project Working Papers 16.) Center for Cognitive Science, MIT, Cambridge, MA.

Levin, Beth and Malka Rappaport. 1986. The Formation of Adjectival Passives. LI 17.4.623-661.

Marantz, Alec. 1984. On the Nature of Grammatical Relations. Cambridge, MA: MIT Press.

Oehrle, Richard. 1975. The Grammatical Status of the English Dative Alternation. Doctoral

Dissertation, MIT, Cambridge, MA.

Perlmutter, David. 1978. Impersonal Passives and the Unaccusative Hypothesis. Berkeley,CA: Proceedings of the Fourth Annual Meeting of the Berkeley Linguistics Society.

Postal, Paul and Geoffrey Pullum. 1987. Expletive Noun Phrases and Movement to Subcategorized Positions. Proceedings of WCCFL VI, ed. by Megan Crowhurst, 247-264. Stanford Linguistics Association, Stanford University.

Rapoport, Tova. 1987. Copular, Nominal, and Small Clauses: A Study of Israeli Hebrew. Doctoral dissertation, MIT, Cambridge, MA.

Rappaport, Malka and Beth Levin. 1988. What to Do with Theta-Roles. Thematic Relations, ed. by Wendy Wilkins, 7-36. (Syntax and Semantics 21.) New York: Academic Press.

Rappaport, Malka, Beth Levin, and Mary Laughren. 1988. Niveaux de Representation Lexicale. Lexique 7. [An English version appears as Rappaport, Malka, Mary Laughren and Beth Levin. 1987. Levels of Lexical Representation. (Lexicon Project Working Papers 20.) Center for Cognitive Science, MIT, Cambridge, MA.]

Rothstein, Susan. 1983. The Syntactic Forms of Predication. Doctoral dissertation, MIT, Cambridge, MA.

Simpson, J. 1983. Resultatives. Papers in Lexical Functional Grammar, ed. by Lori Levin, Malka Rappaport and Annie Zaenen. Bloomington, IN: Indiana University Linguistics Club.

Stowell, Tim. 1981. Origins of Phrase Structure. Doctoral dissertation, MIT, Cambridge, MA.

Tenny, Carol. 1987. Grammaticalizing Aspect and Affectedness. Doctoral Dissertation. MIT, Cambridge, MA.

Williams, Edwin. 1980. Predication. LI 11.1.203-238.

Williams, Edwin. 1981. Argument Structure and Morphology. The Linguistic Review 1.81-114.

Williams, Edwin. 1983. Against Small Clauses. LI 14.2.287-308.

On Inherent Case-marking

Paula   Kempchinsky
University of Iowa

0.   Introduction

According to Chomsky's (1986) revision of Case theory, there
is a basic distinction between structural Case, assigned by verbs
and tensed INFL, vs. inherent Case, assigned by nouns, adjectives
and prepositions. The latter is constrained by the uniformity
condition linking θ-marking and Case assignment, while the former
is not. Belletti and Rizzi (1986) argue that the class of inherent Case assigners should be extended to include certain groups of
verbs, even in languages where Case assignment by the verb is
usually structural, as in Italian. This suggests that the ability
to assign inherent Case is a property of particular lexical items,
rather than being derivable from the categorial nature of the
head. In this paper I will examine another class of apparent inherent Case assigning verbs in Romance. I will argue that the
Case assigning properties of these verbs can be accounted for only
if we make a distinction, following Baker (1988), between semantic
Case, linked to a specific θ-role assigned by the head, and inherent Case, which is unlinked to any particular θ-role, although
subject to uniformity. The class of verbs to be examined are the
pronominal verbs in Romance.

1.   Case properties of pronominal verbs

The class of pronominal verbs in the Romance languages includes both those verbs which obligatorily appear with a reflexive
clitic (the so-called 'inherently reflexive' verbs), and those
verbs which may appear with a reflexive clitic, i.e. pronominal
verbs with a non-pronominal counterpart. Examples from Spanish
are given in (1):

(1)   a.   Los estudiantes siempre se quejan de su trabajo.
           'Students always complain of their work'
      b. *Los estudiantes siempre quejan (de) su trabajo.

(2)   a.   Como siempre, Reagan se olvidó de los datos concretos.
           'As always, Reagan forgot (about) the concrete facts'
      b.   Como siempre, Reagan olvidó los datos concretos.

As is well-known, these verbs differ from transitive verbs used
reflexively in that no reflexive action is implied (hence the term
'pronominal verb' from the French traditional grammarians). Furthermore, in Spanish doubling of the reflexive clitic is disallowed with these verbs, although such doubling is fully grammatical with transitive verbs used reflexively:

(3)   a.   Los estudiantes siempre se quejan (*a sí mismos) de
           su trabajo.
      b.   Reagan se olvidó (*a sí mismo) de los datos.

cf. c. Como siempre, Reagan sólo se hablaba a sí mismo.
          'As always, Reagan was only talking to himself'
     d. La gata se miraba a sí misma en el espejo.
          'The cat was looking at herself in the mirror'

Burzio (1986) notes that the subjects of these verbs prove to be
derived subjects with respect to ne-cliticization and auxiliary
selection in Italian, as shown in (4) with the Italian pronominal
verb sbagliarsi:

(4) Se ne sono sbagliati molti.
     'Many of them have been mistaken'

Further proof of the derived status of the subject comes from the
fact that a third person plural form with pro as the subject cannot be given an indefinite interpretation (cf. Jaeggli, 1986a):

(5) a. Se jactaron (*a sí mismos) de la victoria.
         'They (def/*indef) boasted of the victory'
cf. b. Dijeron que la victoria estaba asegurada.
         'They (def/indef) said that the victory was assured'[2]

The data of (4) and (5) thus seem to indicate that the subject of
these verbs is generated as a sister to V. Some pronominal verbs
may also appear with PP complements which in some cases are obligatory, as shown by the Spanish examples of (6a,b) and the Italian
examples of (6c,d):

(6) a. Ana se quejó (de la clase).
         'Ana complained about the class'
     b. Pepe se mofó *(de Juan).
         'Pepe mocked/made fun of Juan'
     c. I bambini non si ricordano della guerra.
         'The children don't remember the war'
     d. Giovanni si vanta di tutto.
         'Giovanni boasts about everything'

I propose that the apparent PP complements in (6) are more accurately characterized as NP complements which receive inherent Case
from the verb via the preposition. That is, we can take the presence of the reflexive clitic as a diagnostic[3] for the verb's inability to assign structural accusative Case. As one piece of
evidence for this, consider synchronic pronominal/nonpronominal
pairs such as ricordarsi/ricordare in Italian, which differ systematically in the presence vs. lack of the preposition:[4]

(7) a. Giovanni si ricorda della guerra.
         'Giovanni remembers the war'
     b. Giovanni ricorda la guerra.   (from Burzio, 1986)

Furthermore, pronominal verbs which lack a synchronic nonpronominal counterpart historically showed the same pattern as ricordarsi/
ricordare. Thus the Spanish verb jactarse, which like quejarse
must always appear with the reflexive clitic, was at one time a

simple transitive verb assigning accusative Case:

(8) a. Se jacta de sus hazañas.
         '(S/he) boasts of her/his deeds'
     b. *Jacta sus hazañas.

(9) Que no jacto valor de mis pasados ...
     'That I don't boast (the) worth of my ancestors...'
         (Ruiz de Alarcón, La cueva de Salamanca, early 17th C.)

A second piece of evidence for considering the prepositions in (6)
as realizations of inherent case is related to the process of gapping a head N in Spanish. As several linguists have noted, such
gapping is not possible before a following preposition, with the
exception of de:

(10) a. *Los argumentos a favor de esa propuesta son mejores
         que los Ø (en) contra la otra.
         'The arguments in favor of that proposal are better
         than the (ones) against the other'
     b. *Los estudios en esta universidad son más serios que
         los Ø en esa otra.
         'The fields of study in this university are more
         serious than the (ones) in that other one'
     c. *Los informes sobre Nicaragua y los Ø sobre El Salvador
         son igualmente falsos.
         'The reports about Nicaragua and the (ones) about El
         Salvador are equally false'
  cf.   d. Los linguistas de España no tienen los mismos juicios
         que los Ø de Chile.
         'The linguists of/from Spain don't have the same
         judgements as the (ones) of/from Chile'

Torrego (1985) suggests that this asymmetry between de and other
prepositions may be attributed to some thematic dependency between
the head noun and prepositions other than de which prevents gapping of the head noun in those circumstances. In this light, it
should be noted that gapping is not possible before de when it is
not interpreted as genitive:

(11) a. *La huida de la cárcel y la Ø de la prisión fracasaron.
         'The escape from the jail and the (one) from the
         prison failed'
  cf.   b. Los prisioneros huyeron de la cárcel.
         'The prisoners fled from the jail'

Now observe that gapping of the nominal forms of pronominal verbs
is possible before de:

(12) a. Las quejas de que hay demasiado trabajo no son tan
         serias como las Ø de que los sueldos son demasiado
         bajos.
         'The complaints (of) that there is too much work
         aren't as serious as the (ones) (of) that the
         salaries are too low'

    b. No es el mismo el arrepentimiento de los pecados
        capitales que el Ø de los pecados veniales.
        'The repentance of mortal sins isn't the same as the
        (one) of venial sins'

The data examined thus far show that the subject of pronominal
verbs are derived subjects, i.e. the [NP,IP] position is non-
theta, and that the complements of these verbs do not receive
(structural) accusative Case. I would now like to turn to another
set of data related to the behavior of dative clitics in Spanish.

    As is well-known, Spanish dative clitics may double the a-NP
complement; furthermore, this clitic doubling is obligatory when
the indirect object does not bear a θ-role (usually goal) assigned
directly by the verb. Compare (13 and (14):

(13) a. (Le) entregué el sobre al empleado.
        '(I) handed the envelope to the employee'
    b. (Les) vendí el coche a mis vecinos.
        '(I) sold the car to my neighbors'
    c. (Le) compré el coche a Pepe.
        '(I) bought the car from Pepe'

(14) a. Le duele la cabeza a Ana.
        'Ana's head hurts'
    b. Les robaron el coche a los vecinos.
        '(They) stole the neighbors' car'
    c. El niño le comió la manzana a Lola.
        'The child ate Lola's apple/ate the apple on Lola'

As noted by Jaeggli (1986b), the θ-role borne by the indirect object in examples such as those of (14) can informally be viewed as
possessor, although in fact that is not the only possibility (note
the English glosses on (14c)). He argues that the clitic is
obligatory in these cases because it contributes the relevant
θ-role to the verb. That is, the argument co-indexed with the
clitic is not a true argument of the verb and is not linked to a
θ-role in the verb's θ-grid.

    The question now is whether the dative-marked NPs in (13) and
(14) differ in terms of the nature of the Case assigned. The
usual assumption is that dative Case is distinct from both
nominative and accusative in that it is only assigned to argments
θ-marked by the verb. In that sense it is an inherent Case since
it obeys the uniformity condition. However, here I want to make a
distinction between inherent Case and semantic Case. While inherent Case may only be assigned by the relevant Case assigning head
to an argument which receives some θ-role from the head, semantic
Case is associated with a specific θ-role. We will see below evidence from nominals which supports this distinction of inherent
vs. semantic Case. For the moment, let us assume that the dative
Case borne by the a-NP arguments is inherent in the examples of
(13) and semantic in the examples of (14), taking the obligatory
(vs. optional) presence of the dative clitic as a diagnostic for
semantic Case. This is somewhat along the lines of Yip et. al.

(1987), who make a distinction between the "lexical" dative borne by (typically goal) arguments of ditransitive verbs in Icelandic such as <u>segja</u> 'say', and the "quirky lexical" dative borne by the second internal argument of a ditransitive verb such as <u>lofa</u> 'promise'.

Now observe that an indirect object appearing with a pronominal verb is obligatorily doubled by the clitic and does not receive the usual θ-role of goal, a fact first noted, in slightly different terms, by Strozer (1976):

(15) a. Por fin el niño se *(le) arrepintió (de lo que había hecho) a Lola.
          'Finally the child repented (of what he had done) on/for Lola'
      b. El niño se *(le) murió a Lola.
          'The child died on Lola'

In those cases where a pronominal verb seems to allow a PP complement bearing the θ-role of goal, the clitic may not appear, regardless of whether the <u>a</u> NP complement is present or not:

(16) a. ?Los estudiantes se quejaron (de la clase) al profesor.
          'The students complained (about the class) to the professor'
      b. *Los estudiantes se le quejaron de la clase (al profesor).

Similar facts may be observed in French and Italian with the pronominal/nonpronominal pairs <u>vanter</u>/<u>se</u> <u>vanter</u> and <u>vantare</u>/<u>vantarsi</u> respectively:

(17) a. J'ai vanté ses talents à son pere.
          'I praised his/her talents to his/her father'
      b. ?Je lui ai vanté ses talents.

(18) a. Je me suis vanté de ses talents à son pere.
          'I boasted of his/her talents to his/her father'
      b. *Je me lui suis vanté de ses talents

(19) a. Gianni ha vantato i talenti degli studenti al professore.
          'Gianni praised the students' talents to the professor'
      b. Gianni gli ha vantato i talenti degli studenti.

(20) a. ?Gianni si è vantato dei suoi talenti al professore.
          'Gianni boasted of his talents to the professor'
      b. *Gianni si gli è vantato dei suoi talenti.

In fact, the <u>a</u>-NP phrase appearing with the pronominal verbs is more accurately characterized as an adjunct, rather than as a complement of the verb. This accounts both for the marginal status of the prepositional phrase in the Spanish and Italian examples, and the inability of the phrase to cliticize as a dative

clitic. In addition, these phrases behave like adjuncts with
respect to extraction from a wh-island:[5]

(21) a. ?Me pregunto [por qué los estudiantes se quejaron al
               profesor]
           '(I) wonder why the students complained to the
           professor'
      b. *A quién te preguntas por qué los estudiantes se
               quejaron [e]
           'To whom do you wonder why the students complained'

cf.   c. Me pregunto [por qué mandaron el paquete a Ana]
           '(I) wonder why (they) sent the package to Ana'
      d. A quién te preguntas por qué mandaron el paquete [e]
           'To whom do you wonder why (they) sent the package'

A summary of the properties of pronominal verbs examined thus far
is given in (22):

(22) i.   The surface subject is derived from VP-internal position.
      ii. Surface VP-internal arguments receive inherent Case marking
           from V.
      iii. There are no dative-marked arguments directly θ-marked
           by the V.

The co-occurrence of properties (i) and (ii), i.e. the link
between inherent Case marking and the non-θ nature of the subject
position, has been noted by Belletti and Rizzi (1986) for psych
verbs in Italian. Consider (23):

(23) Questo preoccupa Gianni.
      'This worries Gianni'

They argue that the surface subject _questo_ is base-generated as a
sister to V, while _Gianni_ is base-generated as a sister to V'.
Preoccupare does not assign structural accusative Case; hence
questo moves to subject position. However, _preoccupare_ does
assign inherent accusative Case to the argument bearing the experiencer θ-role. This analysis forces them to reformulate Burzio's
generalization as follows:

(24) V is a structural Case assigner iff it has an external
      argument.

The obvious question here is why the link between a verb's Case-
assigning properties and its ability to assign an external θ-role
should be sensitive to the inherent/structural Case distinction.
In particular, let us examine the part of Burzio's generalization
which states "If V assigns an external θ-role, then V assigns
(accusative) Case to its object".   This is ultimately reducible
to θ-theory considerations, since the θ-marked object needs Case
in order to satisfy visibility. If a verb lacked the capacity to
assign Case, its θ-marked object would need to satisfy visibility
in some other fashion; however, movement to subject position would
be ruled out just in case that position were also θ-marked. Since

visibility requirements are equally satisfied by structural or inherent Case, the type of Case assigned by the verb should have no obvious effect on its ability to θ-mark an external argument. In fact, Belletti and Rizzi themselves provide an example of a verb which assigns inherent, non-structural Case to an internal argument and θ-marks an external argument, the Italian example of (25a). A similar Portuguese example is given in (25b):

(25) a. Gianni gioisce _di_ questo.
          'Gianni rejoices of this'
      b. A Maria gosta _dos_ pastéis.
          'Maria likes the pastries'

The statement in (24), then, is too strong as it now stands. Nevertheless, it does seem to accurately characterize the difference between pronominal and non-pronominal counterparts such as vantare/vantarsi.

     The key to the pronominal/nonpronominal differences, I would like to argue, lies in property (23iii). Assume that at D-structure the VP-internal subject is generated not in the sister to V position, as argued by Burzio, but rather in the sister to V' position, assuming a strictly binary branching view of phrase structure. The argument which receives inherent Case via the preposition is generated as a sister to V. Thus we have the following configurations for the Italian pair vantare/vantarsi, where I am using the label "Gen(itive)" to represent the inherent Case assigned by the verb:

(26) a. vantare: NP_1 [V NP_2 NP_3]
                    θ   θ   θ
                                  Acc   Dat

      b. vantarsi: NP_1 [V NP_2 NP_3]
                    -θ   θ   θ
                                  Gen   -Case

Consider now the logically possible configurations which these verbs do not show:

(27) a. NP_1 [V NP_2 NP_3]
          -θ   θ   θ
                        Gen   Dat

      b. NP_1 [V NP_2 NP_3]
          -θ   θ   θ
                        Gen   Gen/Semantic Case

      c. NP_1 [V NP_2 NP_3]
          θ   θ   θ
                        Gen   Dat

      d. NP_1 [V NP_2 NP_3]
          θ   θ   θ
                        Gen   Gen/Semantic Case

(27a) and (27b) can immediately be ruled out. Since the two VP-internal arguments are both Case-marked in some fashion, then NP_1 must also be θ-marked, since otherwise, as a non-θ position, it would have to enter into a chain with either NP_2 or NP_3, violating the condition on CHAINs proposed by Chomsky (1986):

(28) If $C = (x_1 \ldots x_n)$ is a maximal CHAIN, then x_n occupies its unique θ-position and x_1 its unique Case-marked position.

What about (27c) and (27d)? Since all of the θ-marked positions are Case-marked, visibility and ultimately the θ-criterion is satisfied. Since they each contain one argument which receives semantic Case, they would of course be ruled out by (24); nevertheless we have seen that, given the existence of examples such as (25), the assignment of an external θ-role is not incompatible with the assignment of some VP-internal semantic Case. Let us first focus attention on (27d), according to which the verb assigns two semantic Cases to its internal arguments, with the argument in subject position receiving, presumably, nominative Case. It doesn't seem a priori impossible for a verb to have two internal arguments receiving semantic Case. Nevertheless, to this point I have not found any such examples. Similar facts are reported by Yip _et. al._ (1987) on the basis of an examination of ditransitive verbs in Icelandic, a language with relatively rich Case morphology. Assuming the distinction discussed earlier between "thematically related" dative Case (what I have been calling inherent Case) and "quirky lexical" Case (what I have been calling semantic Case), they found that in no case did a ditransitive verb assign two quirky lexical Cases, although there are verbs which assign two dative Cases, the first of which is assumed to be thematically predictable (usually associated with a goal argument) and the second of which is lexically idiosyncratic. Thus it appears to be the case that a verb which assigns semantic Case may assign one and only one semantic Case. This restriction, which is at this point merely a descriptive generalization, will account for the absence of configurations such as (27d).[6]

The non-existence of cases such as (27c) is more problematic. Given the restriction just discussed, the dative assigned to NP_3 cannot be semantic. Suppose that inherent dative Case, like structural accusative Case, is not linked to a specific θ-role in the verb's θ-grid; assignment of this Case to the appropriate NP argument is both a function of the θ-role borne by the NP, as argued by Yip, _et. al._, and of the structural position sister to V'. Then we might assume that the ability to assign unlinked (i.e. non-semantic) dative Case is a function of the verb's ability to assign structural accusative Case. The only crucial assumption that we need to make here is that if one Case assigned by the verb is linked to a particular slot in the θ-grid, then it may not have other, unlinked Cases. However, such a restriction, although it accounts for the Romance pronominal verbs, is too strong as it now stands, since it would rule out any combination of semantic Case and non-semantic Case (either structural or inherent). This fails to account for the existence of Icelandic verbs which assign both accusative and genitive (e.g. krefia 'demand'), inherent dative and semantic dative (kofa 'promise') and inherent dative and genitive (óska 'wish').

Nevertheless, there is a subgeneralization lurking in the Icelandic data discussed by Yip et. al. which also holds true for the Romance pronominal verbs. In all of the combinations of semantic and non-semantic Case which they discuss, the non-semantic Case (either accusative or thematically linked dative) is assigned to the first VP-internal argument, with semantic Case assigned to the second. I.e., in terms of the configurations of (27), NP_2 receives accusative or dative and NP_3 receives genitive or semantic dative. There are no instances of the order semantic Case--non-semantic Case, i.e. semantic Case on NP_2 and accusative or thematically linked dative on NP_3. Thus, it does seem to be the case that if the θ-role assigned to NP_2 is linked to a specific Case, then the other Case assigned by the verb must also be linked. This would entail, however, that the verb assign more than one semantic Case, violating the restriction discussed above. Thus the NP_3 position can only be Caseless, forcing movement to subject position, which consequently must be non-theta, as in (26b).

Why such restrictions should exist on semantic Case assignment is unclear at the moment. It is nonetheless striking that similar Case assignment patterns should hold in languages as dissimilar as Spanish and Italian, on the one hand, and Icelandic on the other. This suggests that the representation of lexical Case and the relationship between Case and θ-roles is more complex than has been assumed. In particular, the distinction between inherent and semantic Case appears to be crucial. I want to therefore look briefly at some related facts within nominals which support this distinction.

2. Case effects in NP

Chomsky (1986) proposes that assignment of inherent Case is a function merely of the head's categorial identity; thus all nouns, regardless of the Case-assigning properties of their related verbs (when these exist) would be expected to have similar Case-assigning properties. However, Torrego (1985) suggests the possibility that nouns and verb may be related not only by their thematic complement structure but also by their Case assignment properties. She notes that the complements of the nominal forms of ergative verbs such as llegar 'to arrive' show the same type of 'definiteness effect' as their verbal counterparts (cf. Belletti, 1987). It was argued above that the Case assigned by the pronominal verbs to the complement in the sister to V position is more accurately characterized as semantic rather than inherent. The question here then is what types of Case effects may be observed with nominals corresponding to verbs which assign semantic Case.

By the uniformity condition, a noun may not assign Case to an

element which it does not θ-mark, hence the ungrammaticality of
(29):

(29) *John's belief [[e] to have won the election]

Nevertheless, Torrego (op. cit.) argues that within NP genitive
Case may be assigned by the head N to an adverbial phrase just in
case there is no subject present, thus licensing extraction of
that adverbial:

(30) a. *[De qué siglos] has leído [varias novelas de
              autores españoles [e]]
              'From what centuries have you read various novels
              of Spanish authors'
      b. [De qué siglos] has leído [varias novelas [e]]
              'From what centuries have you read variouis novels?'

Similarly, in French an adverbial phrase in NP may cliticize as <u>en</u>
when no genitive Case-marked complement of the noun is present,
although this is marginal for some speakers:

(31) a. Elle a vu [les photos de cette maison]
              'She has seen the photos of that house'
      b. Elle <u>en</u> a vu les photos.

(32) a. Elle a vu [les photos du XIXeme siècle]
              'She has seen the photos from the 19th century'
      b. ??Elle <u>en</u> a vu les photos.

Interestingly, this relative freedom of genitive Case assignment
does not seem to be evidenced by the nominal counterparts of inherent Case-marking verbs:

(33) a. Los estudiantes se quejaron del curso el semestre
              pasado.
              'The students complained about the course last
              semester'
      b. No sabía de las quejas (sobre el curso) del semestre
              pasado.
              '(I) didn't know about the complaints about the course
              from last semester'
      c. *[De que semestre] no sabías de [las quejas [e]]
              'From what semester didnt you know about the complaints'

(34) a. On n'ecoute plus les vanteries de l'annee dernier
              (sur l'economie)
              'One no longer hears the boasts of last year (about
              the economy)'
      b. *On n'<u>en</u> ecoute plus les vanteries.

This contrast is just what we would expect, if the Case assigned
by the pronominal verbs (and, by hypothesis, their corresponding
nominal forms) is semantic. Since that Case is linked to a
specific θ-role, it may only be assigned to an argument bearing
that θ-role, ruling out the possibility of assignment to, for

example, adverbial phrases.

Note that if nouns do in fact assign semantic Cases linked to specific θ-roles, then we must assume that they, like verbs, have both a θ-grid and a Case grid. In the case of nouns which lack semantic Case, the Case grid will simply contain genitive Case, to be assigned to some argument of the noun, as required by uniformity. Nouns which assign semantic Case are also subject to uniformity, but vacuously, since that Case by its nature is already linked to a θ-role assigned by the verb.

Notes

[1]The verb <u>olvidar</u> (as versus <u>olvidarse</u>) implies an intentional forgetting on the part of the subject, i.e. the subject is interpreted as agentive. This follows from the underived nature of the subject of the nonpronominal, given current assumptions about D-structure representations of certain θ-roles. Because of this, a sentence such as (2b) is, for many speakers, somewhat infelicitous (since one does not usually purposefully forget the facts of a certain situation). Compare with (i):

> (i) A veces hay que olvidar el pasado.
>   'At times one must forget the past'

[2]Belletti and Rizzi (1986) point out that the contrast between the indefinite and the definite interpretations is very sharp in the context of a specific event (as, for example, when the preterite (definite) tense is used). The contrast is weaker in generic contexts such as the following:

> (i) (Aquí) siempre dicen que son los mejores.
>   '(Here) they always say that they are the best'

> (ii) ??(Aquí) siempre se jactan de la calidad de los
>   estudiantes.
>   '(Here) they always boast about the quality of
>   the students'

[3]In Campos and Kempchinsky (1988) we argue that the clitic <u>se</u> in fact absorbs the verb's structural accusative Case in the lexicon. This is based on an examination both of the pronominal verbs discussed here and of pronominal verbs such as <u>quemarse</u> 'to get burned' which assign lexical (inherent) rather than structural accusative Case to their complements.

[4]Burzio (op. cit.) presents the paradigm of (7), in particular the preposition of (7a), as a straightforward consequence of the derived nature of the subject of pronominal verbs. Since these verbs do not assign an external θ-role, they cannot, by Burzio's generalization, assign accusative Case to their complements. Below I will suggest an account which derives the relationship -external θ-role <--> -accusative Case in the opposite

direction: the lack of an external θ-role is a necessary consequence of the lack of structural accusative Case.

[5]Note that if the dative-marked NPs of the examples in (14)
and (15) receive their θ-role from the clitic rather than the
verb, as proposed by Jaeggli, then we might expect that these too
behave like adjuncts rather than complements with respect to
extraction from a wh-island. This prediction turns out to be
untestable, however, due to the obligatory nature of the clitic.
Suñer (1988) gives data from Spanish showing that in clitic-
doubled constructions the clitic serves as an antecedent governor
of the associated empty category, thus licensing extraction from
structures where extraction would otherwise be ungrammatical:

(i) *A quién$_1$ no sabías qué diccionario$_2$ había devuelto

[$_S$ Celia [$_{VP}$ t$_V$ e$_2$ e$_1$]]

(ii) A quién$_1$ no sabías qué diccionario$_2$ le$_1$ había devuelto

[$_S$ Celia [$_{VP}$ t$_V$ e$_2$ e$_1$]]

[6]Examples of pronominal verbs in Spanish with both inherent
genitive complements and dative-marked NPs, such as (15), may appear to be counterevidence to this restriction. Recall, however,
that these dative-marked NPs do not receive their θ-role from the
verb, but rather from the clitic itself. Therefore, the restriction on linking only one of the verb's arguments to a semantic
Case will not apply here. It is not implausible to suppose that
the dative citic here is the source not only of the relevant
θrole but also of the dative Case. Note, for example, that this
type of clitic-NP chain is possible with verbs which are otherwise
intransitive, as shown by the example of _morirse_ 'to die' in
(15b).

References

Belletti, A. and L. Rizzi. 1986. Psych-Verbs and Th-theory.
    mss., MIT. (to appear, NLLT).

Baker, M. 1988. Incorporation: A theory of grammatical function
    changing. Chicago: University of Chicago Press.

Burzio, L. 1986. Italian Syntax. Dordrecht: Reidel.

Campos, H. and P. Kempchinsky. 1988. Case absorption, theta
    structure and pronominal verbs. Paper presented at the 18th
    Linguistic Symposium on Romance Languages, University of
    Illinois, Urbana.

Chomsky, N. 1986. Knowledge of language: Its nature, origin and use. New York: Praeger.

Jaeggli, O. 1986a. Arbitrary plural pronominals. NLLT 4.43-76.

Jaeggli, O. 1986b. Three issues in the theory of clitics: Case, doubled NPs, and extraction. In H. Borer, ed. Syntax and Semantics. Vol. 19: The syntax of pronominal clitics. New York: Academic Press.

Strozer, J. 1976. Clitics in Spanish. Doctoral dissertation, UCLA.

Suñer, M. 1988. Two properties of clitics in clitic-doubled constructions. Paper presented at the 18th Linguistic Symposium on Romance Languages, University of Illinois, Urbana.

Torrego, E. 1985. On empty categories in nominals. mss., University of Massachusetts, Boston.

Yip, M., J. Maling and R. Jackendoff. 1987. Case in tiers. Language 63.217-250.

Syllable weight and quantity in Dutch

Aditi Lahiri and Jacques Koreman

Max-Planck-Institut für Psycholinguistik
Nijmegen, The Netherlands

0. Introduction

The stress system of Dutch is quite obviously sensitive to syllable weight; however, the interaction between syllable weight and vowel quantity is not quite straightforward. This paper addresses two issues. We first discuss the pros and cons of representing weight and quantity by the same phonological unit, as proposed in a moraic theory. Next, we present an analysis for Dutch stress, claiming that unless a non-isomorphic weight-quantity relationship is assumed, it is impossible to adequately account for the relevant facts.

1. Weight and quantity - general considerations

Syllable weight is known to play an important role in the phonological systems of natural languages, not just for stress assignment rules, but also for segmental processes. Some examples of rules sensitive to syllable weight are given below.

(1) a. Khalka Mongolian: stress falls on the first heavy
       syllable; otherwise stress is on the initial syllable
       (Hyman 1985).
    b. Uradhi: stress the first heavy syllable; otherwise
       stress the antepenultimate syllable (Crowley 1983).
    c. Hawaiian: stress the final syllable if it is heavy,
       otherwise stress the penultimate syllable (Prince 1983).
    d. Old English: final high vowels are deleted after a
       heavy syllable (Lahiri & Dresher 1983).
    e. Gothic: glides are vocalized when preceded by a heavy
       syllable (Lahiri 1982).

The distinction between heavy and light, however, appears to differ from language to language. What is crucial is the fact that languages that use this distinction in a productive way do not treat all syllables as being equal; rather, syllable-based rules differentiate between types of syllables, and this is the distinction that has traditionally been referred to as a 'heavy/light' contrast. A typological summary of the types of heavy/light contrasts recognized in different languages is given under (2).

(2) a. Syllables with long vowels are heavier than syllables
       with short vowels.
    b. Open syllables with long vowels and closed syllables
       with short vowels are both heavy.
    c. Closed syllables are heavier than open syllables.

    d. A sequence of two open syllables with short vowels count
       as a single heavy syllable.

It is apparent from the above summary that onsets do not play
any crucial role in determining syllable weight; the relevant
syllable constituent is the rhyme. Furthermore, within the
domain of the rhyme, although there is an obvious
correspondence between vowel quantity and the weight of a
syllable, the relationship isn't quite transparent. Two issues
need to be clarified. First, is it obligatory for a language
recognizing distinctions in syllable weight to have a phonemic
vowel length contrast? That is, does a distinction in syllable
weight presuppose vowel length contrast? There are
contradictory statements in the literature with respect to this
question.

(3) a. No language lacking -VV rhymes, but having -VC rhymes,
      treat the latter as heavy (Hyman 1985).
   b. Ilocano has no phonemic vowel length, but stress refers
      to syllable quantity, considering -VC rhymes to be
      heavier than -V rhymes (Hayes 1988).

According to Hyman, closed syllables (-VC rhymes) can only be
heavy in a language which also has underlying long vowels (and
thus -VV rhymes). Hayes, however, claims that a language
without underlying vowel length contrasts can distinguish
syllable weight; in such a language, closed syllables are
heavier than open syllables. If we accept the latter claim,
then we come to the second aspect of the relationship between
weight and quantity: In a language with phonemic vowel length
and syllable weight contrast, does length always contribute to
weight? Again, there are contradictory statements:

(4) a. No language counts -VC rhymes as heavy, but a -VV rhyme
      as light (Hyman 1985).
   b. In Seneca closed syllables are heavier than open
      syllables, length of vowels not playing any role in
      weight considerations (Stowell 1979).

Stowell's analysis of Seneca stress shows that, regardless of
the fact that the language has long vowels, closed syllables
are heavier than all open syllables - even those that contain
long vowels. Thus, available linguistic analyses leave the
relationship between vowel quantity and weight to be somewhat
unclear. This unclarity is also reflected in the attempt to
relate rhyme geometry to weight.

(5) Rhyme geometry and syllable weight - a synopsis

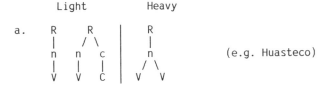

(e.g. Huasteco)

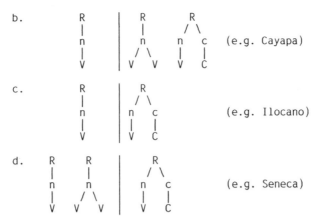

One way of capturing weight via rhyme geometry is to say that a branching rhyme is heavy. Such a statement is clearly suitable for representations like 5b and 5c. However, 5a and 5d are clearly contradictory. In the latter representation only a 'true' branching rhyme is heavy, while in the former only a branching nucleus contributes to the weight. One might argue that typologically speaking, types 5a and b are the ones that are most common. But even within that distinction, relating the 'branchingness' of the rhyme to weight is not very satisfactory, since what is common in both is the branching nucleus. In both 5a and 5b, the branching nucleus is heavy; in addition, a rhyme with a coda is heavy in the latter type.

Arguing against the heavy/light distinction being at par with the branching/nonbranching character of the rhyme, Hyman (1985) takes the position that 'heaviness' is actually a property of segments - first a quality of vowels and secondarily a property of some consonants in the coda. He proposes that there should be a 'weight tier', where weight is represented directly and not projected from any branching rhyme. In the same vein, Hayes (1988) and McCarthy & Prince (1986) argue in favour of a tier representing weight units, or morae, which replaces the skeletal tier. In the next section, we discuss briefly the details of such a representation and the consequences of such a move.

2. Moraic representation

In a moraic theory, the prosodic tier consists of morae. This tier replaces the skeletal tier (CV theory or X theory) with the result that each moraic unit not only represents weight, but also counts as a phonological position. Hence, weight and abstract phonological timing slots are represented by the same unit (Hyman 1985; McCarthy and Prince 1986; Hayes 1988). In the following discussion, we will be referring to the details as spelt out in Hayes' proposal. The representation of long segments in the two theories are given under (6).

(6) a.   Moraic representation

   b.   Skeletal representation

There are two important points which are relevant for our discussion. First, the difference between a short and a long vowel is that the latter has two morae and therefore will always be heavy. The bimoraic representation of a long vowel suggests that long vowels are intrinsically heavier than short vowels. Second, a long or geminate consonant is distinguished from a single consonant by the fact that it comes with a weight unit. Such a representation has very different implications from a skeletal representation where the difference was only on the level of abstract timing units and not weight. Here, the distinction between long and short segments makes a direct reference to the weight they may contribute to the syllable. Before we discuss further implications, we should mention another mechanism by which a syllable may become heavy; Hayes refers to this as 'weight by position', where optionally a consonant in the coda of a syllable is given a mora. Under (7) we give schematic syllable structures showing the various possibilities with the moraic representations.

(7) Weight either obtained directly from a long vowel or, optionally, from the coda - 'weight by position' (Hayes 1988). Schematic syllable structure assignment:

   (a) underlying long vowels

   (b) coda not contributing to syllable weight

(c) weight by position

(d) underlying geminates

The two major consequences of representing weight and quantity by the same phonological unit are as follows:

(8) a. If a language has vowel length contrast and recognizes distinctions in syllable weight, syllables with long vowels must be heavy.
   b. A language with underlying long vowels and geminates must treat (traditional) -VV and -VC rhymes as equally heavy.

The first point implies that languages with long vowels will not allow closed syllables to be heavier than open syllables containing a long vowel (cf. 4). We will address this issue in the following section. As for (8)b, since geminates must come with a mora, this implies that syllables closed by geminates must be as heavy as syllables with long vowels. The 'weight by position' is optional for consonants in the coda - but the geminate consonant in a coda adds weight to the syllable by default (see derivation under (7)d). This appears not to be the case in languages like Malayalam (with long vowels and geminates), where heavy syllables attract stress, but the weight of a syllable is determined by vowel length only, consonants closing the syllable not adding to its weight (Mohanan 1986). Since a geminate normally closes the syllable, it should automatically add a mora and make the syllable heavy, giving incorrect results for Malayalam. It is not within the scope of this paper to discuss this point in more detail although we will briefly come back to it at the end. Of more immediate concern is the interaction between vowel length and syllable weight with specific reference to stress in Dutch. We will begin the next section with a brief discussion of the stress facts in Dutch showing that stress is indeed sensitive to syllable weight.

3. Dutch Stress

Dutch contrasts vowel length in closed syllables, short vowels not being allowed in open syllables. Some minimal pairs are given under (9).

(9)   kap 'hood'   : kaap 'cape'
       mal 'foolish' : maal 'time'
       bek 'beak'   : beek 'brook'

The rhyme in Dutch tautomorphemic words is obligatorily and maximally -VX (-VV or -VC); thus, a single consonant following a short vowel must close the preceding syllable. The only exceptions to the -VX rhyme occur word-finally; in this position, a single consonant can be added to a -VX rhyme, so that minimal pairs can occur of words containing a short and a long vowel followed by a single consonant (-VC vs. -VVC) in the final syllable. Syllables of the type -VXC (-VVC or -VCC) are called 'superheavy' (for detailed discussion, see van der Hulst 1984; Kager & Visch 1983; Trommelen 1983).

The stress assignment rule in Dutch is as follows:

(10) Stress assignment: stress the penultimate syllable unless this syllable is open and the final syllable is closed; then stress the antepenultimate syllable.

Examples (rhyme projection):

Penultimate:

VV VV VV   <u>valuta</u>   [va:lu:ta:]   'currency'
VC VV VV   <u>bombarie</u> [bomba:ri:]   'hullabaloo'
VV VC VV   <u>kwitantie</u> [kwi:tansi:] 'receipt'
VC VC VV   <u>injectie</u> [injeksi:]   'injection'
VV VC VC   <u>detector</u> [de:tektor]   'detector'
VC VC VC   <u>Wilhelmus</u> [wilhelmus]   'William'

Antepenultimate:

VV VV VC   <u>monitor</u>   [mo:ni:tor]   'monitor'
VC VV VC   <u>festival</u> [festi:val]   'festival'

In other words, stress usually falls on the penultimate syllable; however, if the final syllable is closed (-VC rhyme) stress falls on the penultimate syllable only if it is closed, otherwise it falls on the antepenultimate syllable. Clearly, the stress assignment rule makes reference to weight distinctions between closed and open syllables. Within the mora theory, if there is a weight distinction in a language which has long vowels, the only feasible hypothesis is to assume that syllables with long vowels are heavy. Let us assume that -VV syllables are heavy. Also assume foot construction following Hayes (1987) where the only relevant foot types for weight-sensitive languages would be the moraic trochee or the iamb, both of which are summarized under (11).

(11) (H= heavy syllable, L= light syllable, S= any syllable)

                   (x)   (x .)   (.)
  moraic trochee   H   L L, else   L

```
            (. x)          (x)  (.)
iamb        L  S ,  else  H or  L
```

Main stress assignment by End Rule Right/Left

The assumption that syllables with -VV rhymes are heavy does not capture the stress facts correctly. Some incorrect analyses listed under (12) show the futility of this line of approach.

(12) a. Foot construction with the iamb:
     with final syllable extrametricality stress incorrectly falls on the antepenultimate syllable for kwitantie and on the penultimate syllable for monitor;

```
(x     )                    (     x)
(x) (.)                     (x) (x)              ERR
kwii tan sii                moo nii tor
```

And ERL gives incorrect results for valuta although monitor gets the right stress assignment.

```
(x     )
(x) (x)
vaa luu taa
```

With no extrametricality it is a futile exercise.

  b. Foot construction with the moraic trochee: with or without final syllable extrametricality, left to right, incorrect initial stress for wilhelmus;

```
(x    .) (x)
wil hel mus
```

Right to left, with or without extrametricality (of any sort) incorrect stress patterns for injectie.

```
(x    .) (x)
in jek sii
```

Clearly, the closed syllables are the ones that are heavy, and this is reflected in the fact that a closed penult is never skipped over. Earlier analyses (van der Hulst 1984; Kager, Visch & Zonneveld 1987) also accept this to be the case. Van der Hulst, who assumes a direct relationship between branching rhymes and syllable weight, attributes the distinction to a weight scale of the type

$$V \ \to \ VV \ \to \ VC$$

Kager, Visch & Zonneveld relate it to branching nucleus vs. branching rhyme with a coda. The first proposal is purely a descriptive statement; and the second has all the difficulties mentioned before (Hyman 1985).

To account for the stress facts in Dutch, we have to accept the fact that closed syllables (with short vowels) are indeed heavier than open syllables (with long vowels). In the next section we first present an analysis which provides a coherent account of these facts. This still, however, leaves open the question of how one should represent underlying vowel length contrasts in a moraic theory if length does not directly contribute to weight. We end section 4 with a proposal of an alternative representation which takes into account the non-isomorphic relationship between weight and quantity.

4. An alternative proposal

Assuming that -VC rhymes are heavier than -VV rhymes, the appropriate metrical structures to account for Dutch stress are as follows:

(13) Foot construction: from right to left parse a word into moraic trochees.
Extrameticality: mark the rightmost monosyllabic foot extrametrical.
Main stress: assign /x/ by End Rule Right

Penultimate:
```
                                             (    x    )
(.) (x) (x)      (.) (x) (x)      (.) (x) (x)
 VV  VC  VC  ->   VV  VC  VC  ->   VV  VC  VC
dee tek tor                         ‾‾       ‾‾

                                             (    x    )
(x) (x) (x)      (x) (x) (x)      (x) (x) (x)
 VC  VC  VC  ->   VC  VC  VC  ->   VC  VC  VC
Wil hel mus                         ‾‾       ‾‾
                      (    x    )
(.) (x   .)      (.) (x    .)
 VV  VV  VV  ->   VV  VV  VV
vaa luu taa
                      (    x    )
(x) (x   .)      (x) (x    .)
 VC  VV  VV  ->   VC  VV  VV
bom baa rii
                                             (    x    )
(.) (x) (.)      (.) (x) (.)      (.) (x) (.)
 VV  VC  VV  ->   VV  VC  VV  ->   VV  VC  VV
kwii tan sii                        ‾‾       ‾‾
                                             (    x    )
(x) (x) (.)      (x) (x) (.)      (x) (x) (.)
 VC  VC  VV  ->   VC  VC  VV  ->   VC  VC  VV
in jek sii                          ‾‾       ‾‾
```

Antepenultimate:

```
                               (x         )
(x   .) (x)      (x   .) (x)    (x   .) (x)
 VV  VV  VC  ->   VV  VV  VC  ->  VV  VV  VC
moo nii tor
```

```
                               (x         )
(x) (.) (x)      (x) (.) (x)    (x) (.) (x)
 VC  VV  VC  ->   VC  VV  VC  ->  VC  VV  VC
fes tii val
```

Now we come to the problematic question of the representation of quantity in Dutch. To maintain the underlying length distinction, one must maintain separate representations for weight and quantity; the fact that closed syllables are heavier than open syllables shows that weight is not in a one-to-one correspondence with quantity. If underlying long vowels are represented as bimoraic, they will be equal in weight to closed syllables. Reverting back to the branching nucleus vs. branching rhyme controversy does not really solve the problem; Hyman's arguments are rather convincing that weight is a property of segments, not of the rhyme projection. However, it appears that a single phonological unit cannot adequately represent weight as well as count as an abstract timing slot. One must, then, assume that in some languages all vowels, long or short, have a single unit of weight. Syllables can only become heavy by weight-by-position. Syllabification rules in Dutch require a word-internal syllable to have maximally and obligatorily two phonological positions. Relevant derivations are given below:

(14)

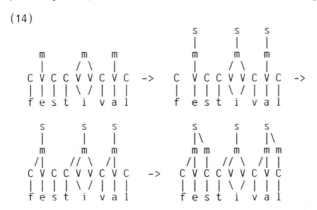

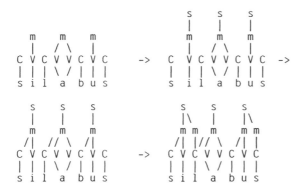

Not only does this provide an adequate account of Dutch, where the relationship between syllable weight and vowel quantity is clearly not isomorphic, representing weight and quantity separately has other advantages. Under this hypothesis, geminate consonants do not have any underlying moraic value and are therefore not intrinsically heavy. They can close syllables (as they usually do), but still not add weight to the preceding syllable. This predicts that languages may differ as to whether geminates can add weight to a syllable or not.

(15)

```
                    s    s
                    |    |
      m      m      m    m      (no weight added)
      |      |      |\   /|
(i)  X X X X       X X X X
     | \ / |  ->   | \ / |
     a p a         a p a


              s    s
        OR   |\    |
        ->   m m   m          (weight by position)
             | |  /|
             X X X X
             | \ / |
             a p a
```

Under the moraic theory, the possibility also remains that a language may not have 'weight by position', so that ordinary consonants do not get a mora in the coda, but syllables closed by geminates are heavy. To our knowledge, such languages do not exist.

5. Conclusion

We have argued that representing weight and abstract timing positions by the same phonological units causes problems for both long vowels and geminate consonants. In a language like Dutch, which has contrastive vowel length, but where closed syllables are heavier than open syllables, a moraic representation is unsuccessful in capturing the facts. An alternative hypothesis for Dutch would be to assume that vowels are underlyingly all short and that there is a contrast between single and geminate consonants. There are several arguments against this. First, there are more long vowels than short ones, whereas the consonant 'ambisyllabicity' is predictable. If the vowels were all underlyingly short, some form of neutralization would be necessary to obtain the correct surface forms. Second, the long vowels in closed syllables would have to be lexically marked since there is a contrast in this position. Finally, to get the surface long vowels in open syllables, after stress assignment, all vowels, even those in weak positions, would have to be lengthened - a process which appears to be quite undesirable. A proposal on these lines has been put forward recently by van der Hulst and van Lit (1988). We feel that, given the above facts, the assumption that Dutch has phonemic vowel length is appropriate, and the analysis we have proposed adequately accounts for the facts and makes correct typological predictions.

Acknowledgements:
We wish to thank several colleagues and participants at WCCFL for their valuable comments; of course, not all of them agree with our point of view: Bruce Hayes, Doug Pulleyblank, Larry Hyman, Jennifer Cole, Paul Kiparsky, Harry van der Hulst, Sharon Inkelas, Junko Ito, Moira Yip.

References

Crowley, T. 1983. Uradhi. Handbook of Australian Languages, ed. by R.M.W. Dixon & B. Blake, Vol. III, 307-430. Amsterdam: John Benjamins

Hayes, B. 1987. A revised parametric metrical theory. NELS 17.

Hayes, B. 1988. Compensatory lengthening in Moraic Phonology. Ms., UCLA.

van der Hulst, H. 1984. Syllable Structure and Stress in Dutch. Dordrecht: Foris.

van der Hulst, H. 1988. Lettergreepstructuur. Ms., Leiden University.

Hyman, L. 1985. A Theory of Phonological Weight. Dordrecht: Foris.

Kager, R. & E. Visch. 1983. Een metrische analyse van ritmische klemtoonverschijnselen. Doctoraalskriptie, Utrecht University.

Kager, R., E. Visch, & W. Zonneveld. 1987. Nederlandse woordklemtoon. Ms., Utrecht University.

Lahiri, A. 1982. Theoretical implications of analogical change: evidence from Germanic languages. PhD dissertation, Brown University.

Lahiri, A. and B.E. Dresher. 1984. Diachronic and synchronic implications of declension shifts. Linguistic Review 3, 141-163.

McCarthy, J. & A. Prince. 1986. Prosodic Morphology. Ms., Brandeis University.

Mohanan, K. 1986. The theory of lexical phonology. Dordrecht: D. Reidel Publishing Company.

Prince, A. 1983. Relating to the grid. LI 14, 19-100.

Stowell, T. 1979. Stress systems of the world unite. MIT Working papers in Linguistics, ed. by K. Safir, Vol. I, 51-76.

Trommelen, M. 1983. The syllable in Dutch: with special reference to diminutive formation. Dordrecht: Foris.

Subtractive Morphology as Dissociation

JACK MARTIN

University of California, Los Angeles

1. While classical structuralist morphology as represented by Hockett (1954) was concerned largely with distinctions between what were termed ITEM AND PROCESS and ITEM AND ARRANGEMENT as models of grammatical description, generative morphology, with its emphasis on rules and rule systems, has uniformly abandoned position classes for various versions of process-based morphology. Within generative morphology itself, a separate dispute has centered on the types of rules required to describe word formation in natural language, much as syntacticians have disputed the power of the rules needed to describe sentence grammar. These two views can be summarized as follows:

Phrase Structure Morphology (PSM)	*Transformational Morphology (TM)*
a. a set of morphemes	a. a set of roots
b. a set of PS rules combining morphemes (or projection of lexical subcategorization)	b. i. a set of T rules modifying roots ii. a set of PS rules combining stems
c. semantics based on items and arrangements	c. semantic rules paired with morphological rules

Proponents of versions of PSM include Selkirk (1982) and Di Sciullo and Williams (1987), while proponents of versions of TM include Anderson (1983,1987), Janda (1983), and Zwicky (1988).[1]

The principal empirical claim of PSM is that rules of word formation are strictly affixal, a requirement entailed by the use of PS rules. Arguments against PSM involve attempts to show that word formation requires rules with transformational power. TM, on the other hand, with its greater expressive power, is attacked for being too unconstrained and for allowing formal descriptions of phenomena that are unattested in natural language.[2] The situation is made more complex by the fact that theories such as Autosegmental Morphology (AM; McCarthy 1979), which otherwise would appear to share more of the characteristics of a TM than a PSM, nonetheless have explicit restrictions requiring that morphology be affixal.

As noted by Anderson (1987), one of the especially problematic areas for affix-only morphology (including now PSM and AM) is SUBTRACTIVE morphology, in which a morphological rule *deletes* a portion of the base rather than *adding* to it.[3] The best known examples of subtractive morphology are: 1) Icelandic deverbal action nouns (Orešnik and Pétursson 1977, Kiparsky 1984); 2) Danish imperatives (Anderson 1975, 1987, and sources therein); and, 3) Pluralization in Hessian German (Wurzel 1981, Dressler 1987). Of these, the first two examples have been discussed in detail elsewhere. The last example appears in the literature with only one form cited, and is therefore suspect pending further research.

This paper discusses two cases in the Muskogean literature of subtractive morphology, arguing that they are best described as *dissociation of a prosodic element*, an operation that is claimed by McCarthy and Prince (1986) not to exist. Such a description is fully compatible with the basic tenets of AM, but is in-compatible with PSM and with the claim that morphology is purely affixal. As a response to the increased descriptive power of TM over PSM, two conditions on morphological rules are advanced with the goal of reintroducing much of the desired parsimony of PSM.

   2. The Muskogean family (a group of languages indigenous to the southeastern United States) contains several languages showing evidence of subtractive morphology. These include Koasati (Kimball 1983,1985), Alabama (Hardy and Montler 1986), Chickasaw, and Choctaw (Broadwell 1987). Consider the Koasati forms in Table 1 based on data from Kimball (1985):[4]

TABLE 1: Koasati singular-plural alternants

	Singular	Plural	Gloss
af ~ ø			
	pitáf-fi-n	pít-li-n	to slice up the middle
	akoláf-ka-n	akol-ká:ci-n	to erode and collapse
	socáf-fi-n	sós-li-n	to strip skin off something
	tosáf-fi-n	tos-lí:ci-n	to cut a piece out of
	latáf-ka-n	lát-ka-n	to kick something
	kaláf-fi-n	kál-li-n	to mark something
	taɬáf-ka-n	táɬ-ka-n	to whittle something
	baháf-fi-n	báh-li-n	to stab something
ap ~ ø			
	tiwáp-li-n	tíw-wi-n	to open something
	wilap-lí:ci-n	wil-lí:ci-n	to tear up the earth
	yiɬáp-li-n	yíɬ-ɬi-n	to tear something down
	ɬomáp-li-n	ɬóm-mi-n	to whip something
	lasáp-li-n	lás-li-n	to lick something
	kaháp-li-n	káf-fi-n	to dip something up
a: ~ ø			
	ataká:-li-n	aták-li-n	to hang something
	icoktaká:-li-n	icokták-li-n	to open one's mouth
	acokcaná:-ka-n	acokcán-ka-n	to quarrel with someone
i: ~ ø			
	albití:-li-n	albít-li-n	to place on top of
	atiní:-li-n	atín-ni-n	to burn something
	acití:-li-n	acít-li-n	to tie something
ip ~ ø			
	ciɬíp-ka-n	cíɬ-ka-n	to spear something
	misíp-li-n	mís-li-n	to wink
	obakhitíp-li-n	obakhít-li-n	to go backwards
o: ~ ø			
	facó:-ka-n	fás-ka-n	to flake off
	apoɬó:-ka-n	apóɬ-ka-n	to sleep with someone
ay ~ ø			
	aponáy-li-n	apon-ní:ci-n	to wrap something up
	onasanáy-li-n	onasan-ní:ci-n	to twist something on
op ~ ø			
	iyyakohóp-ka-n	iyyakóf-ka-n	to trip
	fotóp-ka-n	fót-ka-n	to pull up something

$of \sim \phi$			
	koyóf-fi-n	kóy-li-n	to cut something
	ʔobóf-fi-n	ʔob-bi-n	to pierce something
$as \sim \phi$			
	tipás-li-n	típ-li-n	to pick something off
$at \sim \phi$			
	simát-li-n	sím-mi-n	to cut up tanned skin
$aʔ \sim \phi$			
	kawáʔ-ʔi-n	káw-wi-n	to snap something
$ot \sim \phi$			
	akocofót-li-n	akocóf-fi-n	to jump down

Each of the forms in Table 1 consists of a verb root followed by one of the auxiliary suffixes -*ka* or -*li* and a suffix -*n*. Of special interest is the morphological rule or rules responsible for relating the singular and plural forms.

There are several imaginable rule types for describing the facts in Table 1. The first is to take the plural forms as basic, deriving the singular forms by adding a singular suffix {af,ap,a:,i:,ip,o:,ay,op,of,as,at,aʔ,ot}, as lexically determined. This approach requires thirteen rules and lexical classes, and tends toward duplicating the occurring rhymes in the language. The second approach takes the singular forms as basic, and forms the plural by deleting the final rhyme of the root. The second approach is clearly preferable from the viewpoint of economy, since one need posit only one rule to account for all of the alternations in Table 1. Moreover, the second approach allows one to state the rule more naturally as *pluralization* rather than as *singularization*.[5]

It thus appears desirable to describe the singular-plural alternations in Table 1 as *subtraction* of a prosodic constituent. 'Deletion of the final rhyme' can be described autosegmentally as follows:

(1) *Koasati Rhyme Deletion:*

```
     ⚹
  r |
```
(where 'r'=rhyme and '|' is the edge of a form)

The rule in (1) operates to dissociate the final rhyme of the root, with the stranded element subject to stray erasure.[6] The following derivations exemplify this process:

(2)
```
   σ  σ
   |  ⚹
   |  / r
  la t  af     +ka+n   --->   lat-ka-n 'to kick something' (pl.)
                              (cf.  lataf-ka-n 'to kick something' (sg.))
```

(3)
```
   σ  σ
   |  ⚹
   |  / r
  ci ʔ ip      +ka+n   --->   ciʔ-ka-n 'to spear something' (pl.)
                              (cf.  ciʔip-ka-n 'to spear something' (sg.))
```

(4) σ σ σ
     | | A̹
     | | / r
     a ci t i: +li+n   —>   acit-li-n 'to tie something' (pl.)
                                (cf. aciti:-li-n 'to tie something' (sg.))

Dissocation of a rhyme occurs at the right edge of a root in examples (2-4), before other suffixes are added. Plurals are thus formed from singulars in Koasati by application of an *additional process* that happens not to be additive in form. If this analysis is correct, then the requirement that morphology be described purely through affixation of phonological material must be abandoned.

There is another rule in Koasati (as well as in closely related languages) that operates to delete the final coda of a verb. These alternations can be seen in Table 2:

TABLE 2: *Koasati coda deletion*

	Singular	Plural	Gloss
$t \sim \emptyset$			
	famót-ka-n	famó:-ka-n	to wave
	libát-li-n	libá:-li-n	to get burned by a hot solid
	asipát-li-n	asipá:-li-n	to get a splinter
	tabát-ka-n	tabá:-ka-n	to catch something
	topát-ka-n	topá:-ka-n	to recede
$s \sim \emptyset$			
	akapós-ka-n	akapó:-ka-n	to be pinched
	labós-li-n	labó:-li-n	to extinguish something
	alabós-li-n	alabó:-li-n	to close up (of flowers)
	ɬibós-li-n	ɬibó:-li-n	to squash something
$f \sim \emptyset$			
	ɬatóf-ka-n	ɬató:-ka-n	to melt
	yicóf-ka-n	yicó:-ka-n	to shrivel
	ɬicóf-fi-n	ɬicó:-li-n	to chip by accident
	kocóf-fi-n	kocó:-li-n	to pinch something
$p \sim \emptyset$			
	asikóp-li-n	asikó:-li-n	to breathe
$ɬ \sim \emptyset$			
	kacáɬ-ɬi-n	kacá:-li-n	to bite something

While the rule responsible for the alternations in Table 2 is related historically to the rule creating the alternations in Table 1 (the forms in Table 1 arose from coda deletion followed by syncope), synchronically it seems best to distinguish two lexical classes of verbs: those in which the final rhyme deletes, and those in which the final coda deletes.

Given only the facts in Table 2, it would appear that deletion results in compensatory lengthening of the preceding vowel. If this were the case, one would probably wish to state the rule as deletion of the segmental material without deleting the segmental timing slot. However, Koasati has an independent rule lengthening a penultimate light syllable in the indicative, so that lengthening in the plural forms in Table 2 may result from this rule rather than from coda deletion. In the absence of additional data, I will assume that the lengthening seen in Table 2 is a result of the rule of penultimate lengthening. One may now posit the following rule to derive the plural forms in Table 2:

(5) *Koasati Coda Deletion:*

　✳
　c |　　　　　　　　　　　　　　(where 'c'=coda and '|' is the edge of
　　　　　　　　　　　　　　　　　　a form)

The above rule operates to dissociate the final coda in a root. As with Rhyme Deletion, the stranded element is then subject to stray erasure. The following derivation exemplifies the rule in (5):

(6)　σ　σ
　　　|　 /\
　　　|　/ /✳c
　　 fa mo t　　+ka+n　　　—>　　　/famo+ka+n/

　　　　　　　Lengthening:　—>　　　famo:-ka-n 'to wave' (pl.)
　　　　　　　　　　　　　　　　　(cf. famot-ka-n 'to wave' (sg.))

Coda Deletion operates in (6) to delete the final consonant of the root before additional suffixes are added. After suffixation, Lengthening applies to create the surface form.

As with Rhyme Deletion, it is difficult to see how one could describe these data as affixation. One could posit a class of singular formatives {t,s,f,p,ɬ} that are suffixed to lexically determined sets of verbs, but this would involve a substantial increase in rule complexity and memorization of lexical classes. Alternatively, one could posit a phonological rule of consonant deletion before a zero plural morpheme, but this would evacuate the interesting restrictiveness of affix-only theories of morphology, and would fail to extend to examples involving rhyme deletion. Far simpler is to allow application of the normal operations found in autosegmental phonology to higher prosodic units in the morphology.

The same formalism can be extended to cover examples of subtraction in Scandinavian languages. Thus, deletion of a final vowel in the Danish imperative (Anderson (1975)) can be described with the following rule:

(7) *Danish Imperative:*

　　　✳
　[+inf .... V]

The above rule operates on a verb in the infinitive to *morphologically* delete the final vowel. Thus from *bade* [bæ:ðə] 'to bathe' one can derive an imperative *bad!* [bæʔð] 'bathe!'. As a result, the imperative will show the normal lengthening (or *stød*) characteristic of infinitives in Danish.

3. McCarthy and Prince (1986) reduce several apparent examples of subtraction to an additive process that they call templatic truncation. Consider the following examples of Japanese hypocoristic formation from Poser (1984a):

TABLE 3: *Japanese hypocoristics*

Name:	Derived hypocoristic:
akira	aki+tyan
taroo	taro+tyan
aasa(a)	aa+tyan
ti	tii+tyan
hiro+ko	hiro+tyan *or* hii+tyan
kayo+ko	kayo+tyan *or* kaa+tyan

As noted by Poser (1984a,1984b) a description of hypocoristics in Japanese must be capable of describing the fact that the base for the suffix *-tyan* in the derived forms in Table 3 is uniformly two morae in length. For the first three examples, this involves deleting the final mora. In the case of the fourth example, the base form must be *lengthened* to meet this requirement. Finally, in the fifth and sixth examples, the final mora is either deleted, or alternatively the last two morae are deleted and the first vowel lengthened.

The Japanese examples in Table 3 provide evidence that a bimoriac template is associated to the left edge of the base forms, with subsequent lengthening or deletion to meet the requirements of the template. Poser's (1984b) and McCarthy and Prince's (1986) treatment in terms of a template thus accounts for apparent subtraction in morphologically additive terms. The Muskogean phenomenon, however, has properties that differ from the Japanese example and that make a similar treatment difficult.

One difference between templatic truncation and subtraction is that the former involves deletion of a string of variable length, while subtraction involves deletion of a fixed prosodic unit. Conversely, whereas the portion saved in templatic truncation has a fixed prosodic structure, the portion saved in subtraction may vary in length and shape. Third, templatic truncation shows properties of a template, as evidenced by lengthening or shortening in Japanese hypocoristics depending on the shape of the base. No such lengthening is found with subtraction. Finally, while templates are generally associated to the *left* edge of the word, the prosodic requirements of subtraction are met in the examples above by alignment to the *right* edge of the word. This last difference might be eliminated by a convention that deletion occur on the right, whether through truncation or subtraction.

It thus appears that there are important differences between subtraction and templatic truncation that are better described by allowing two sources for deletion in morphological theory. By allowing dissociation *as well* as templatic truncation in an autosegmental morphology, one is able to better constrain each process, and extend the range of descriptive coverage to include morphological processes in Alabama, Koasati, Choctaw, Chickasaw, Danish, and Icelandic. Further, while the constraint that morphology be additive is a highly restrictive addition to autosegmental morphology, it does not follow from anything in the theory (as it would in PSM's), and amounts to a stipulation. In fact, it emerges as something of a paradox within autosegmental morphology that the operations needed for phonology are *less* constrained than the operations needed to describe morphology, so that while association, dissociation, and metathesis are presumably allowed in phonological descriptions, only the first is allowed in the morphology. If anything, work on morphology over the past fifteen years has revealed that rules in that component are less constrained than the more familiar territories of sound and sentence structures, or at least constrained in different ways.

4. While I have argued that theories of word formation must recognize dissociation as a morphological process, it is clearly not the case that subtraction is a common phenomenon among the world's languages or even within those languages showing evidence for subtraction. We must leave it to a theory of markedness to determine whether Universal Grammar is a theory of possible languages (and hence possibly acquired rules), or a theory accounting for the relative frequency of different grammatical processes. It seems likely, however, that the relative infrequency of subtractive morphology may be due entirely to principles outside of acquisition theory, so that all children have the *potential* to learn morphological rules of deletion, even if they are not often given the opportunity to use it. Dressler (1987) suggests that the infrequency of subtractive morphology can be explained by a semiotic principle of iconicity. Since, as he observes, morphological rules are typically additive semantically, the use of subtraction to represent additional meaning is 'anti-diagrammatic'. Alternatively, one could avoid positing vague psychological principles (that are clearly violated in some cases) by observing that morphology derives most often from fusion of independent formatives; the historical chain of events leading to the creation of a word formation rule would therefore rarely allow for reinterpretation along subtractive lines. The likeliest source for a subtractive rule on this alternative account would come from morphologization of a phonological rule of deletion.

However, the observation that morphology is semantically additive even when morphologically subtractive offers interesting possibilities for reconstraining transformational morphology. Interpreting Dressler's observation as a condition on morphological rules, one can posit the condition in (8):

(8) *Condition on Morphosemantics:*
    Morphological rules are semantically additive.

The condition in (8) has the effect of requiring that every morphological rule be accompanied by a corresponding morphosemantic rule adding meaning to the semantics of the base. In this way, the *signifiant* of structuralist interpretations of Saussure (see Anderson 1983, 1985) moves from the 'morpheme' to the rules of word formation and their bases. The condition in (8) thus represents the transformational equivalent of the claim that every formal morphological unit have an accompanying meaning.

While the condition in (8) is able to recreate much of the restrictiveness of a PSM, it does so in transformational terms, so that a wider variety of rule types (including subtraction) are possible. Clearly, however, if transformational morphology is ever to gain explanatory adequacy, some attempt must be made at restricting the formal operations available. One suggestion pursued by Zwicky (1988) is that Universal Grammar contains a list of possible morphological operations (where by 'operation' I mean rule *type* rather than specific rules). Following this line of research, a suggestion that fits fairly well with ideas underlying AM is that the morphological operations available in language are related formally to the operations available in autosegmental phonology. In the work of McCarthy (1979), it was suggested that the operations available in morphology form a subset of the operations available in phonology, consisting of exactly association.

However, metathesis has been described as a morphological rule in Salish languages (see Anderson 1987), and evidence has been presented in this paper for morphological subtraction. Interestingly, the relative infrequency with which one encounters morphological metathesis in the world's languages might follow from the same hypothesis discussed above that morphologization of phonological rules is rare relative to fusion of independent formatives. If these descriptions are correct, then a natural modification of AM is to pursue connections with phonology and limit the set of possible morphological operations to exactly the set of possible phonological operations, whatever this set turns out to be. This condition is stated in (9):

(9) *Condition on Morphological Operations:*
The operations available to morphology are exactly the
operations available to phonológy.

While it is apparently not the case that the organization, the specifics of rules, or the domains to which phonological rules apply are necessarily identical to morphological rules, the claim in (9) is that rule *types*, e.g. association, metathesis, and dissociation, are the same. On this view, it may well be the case that transformational-generative morphology is best described by means of PS rules combined with T rules (in autosegmental guise), with the former describing desyntactic word formation processes and the latter describing dephonological processes. Where transformational-generative morphology differs from Chomsky's (1957) model of syntax is that in morphology the T rules may (and generally do) precede PS rules (see footnote 2).

5. An interesting question is the historical origin of the subtractive morphology seen in the Southwestern Muskogean languages Choctaw, Chickasaw, Alabama, and Koasati. Kimball (1985:266) attempts to reconstruct meanings associated with the elements undergoing deletion. Broadwell (1987) adopts Kimball's suggestions and argues that the posited formatives (or at least their loss) are a shared innovation in Southwestern Muskogean. The vague nature of the semantics associated with these putative formatives and their lack of productivity would appear to suggest an origin predating Southwestern Muskogean, however, if they are indeed isolable.[7]
A simpler approach is to assume that the prosodic dissociation seen in Southwestern Muskogean derives from *templatic truncation*. Historically, the singular roots in Table 1 appear to be of the shape (prefix+)CVCVC (assuming that vowel length (:) is consonantal), while the plural roots are probably all of the shape (prefix+)CVC. As noted by Munro (1987a), initial *a-* derives from a prefix in some Chickasaw verbs; the same element may be responsible for *a*-initial trisyllabic Koasati verbs in Tables 1-2. Kimball (1985:117) mentions an 'archaic motion prefixes' *cok-* and *ako-* that may help account for some additional trisyllabic stems in Table 1. The multisyllabic verb *iyyakohóp-ka-n* 'to trip' almost certainly includes the word *iyyi* 'foot', perhaps followed by one of the archaic directional prefixes. If these etymologies can be substantiated and extended, then it appears likely that the alternations in Table 1 can be reduced to the following pattern in Pre-Koasati:

(10)   **Singular**   **Plural**
         $C_1 V_2 C_3 V_4 C_5$ $C_1 V_2 C_3$

This alternation is much more easily described in additive terms; Rhyme Deletion in Pre-Koasati can be described as *association* of a monosyllabic template to the left edge of the verb root, a process identical in form to the formation of English hypocoristics (*Tom* from *Thomas*, *Mike* from *Michael*, etc.). As Koasati developed from Pre-Koasati, certain prefixation processes became opaque, and templatic association was reanalyzed as subtraction.

Applying the same etymologies to the forms in Table 2, we arrive at the following alternations in Pre-Koasati verb roots showing modern Coda Deletion:

(11)   **Singular**   **Plural**

$C_1V_2C_3V_4C_5$ $C_1V_2C_3V_4$

If the alternations in Table 2 can all be reduced historically to the pattern in (11), then the alternation in (11) can be described in Pre-Koasati as association of a bimoraic template to the left edge of a CVCVC root, much as in Japanese hypocoristics.[8]

It is further possible to speculate on the relation between the alternation in (10) and the alternation in (11) in Pre-Pre-Koasati, and the origin of the two lexical verb classes. There is independent evidence for a rule of syncope operating in Koasati, creating e.g. *toklo* 'two' from Proto-Muskogean *tokolo. Imagine that the singular-plural alternations in (10) and (11) were all originally like that in (11). If some final vowels (but not others) were then deleted before the auxiliaries, the result would be a surface contrast like that in (10-11).

In fact, additional data lend support to the idea that rhyme deletion arose from (what amounts to) coda deletion followed by syncope (or apocope, depending on the status of the auxiliary suffixes at the time). Note that a fairly common restriction on syncope is that it fails to occur between certain types of consonants. If a restriction of this kind applied to syncope in Pre-Pre-Koasati, then there should be examples of these consonants in Table 2, and no examples in Table 1. Stated another way, if $C_1V_2C_3V_4$+li/ka represents the output of plural formation in Pre-Pre-Koasati, one might expect that V_4 would be preserved for certain values of C_3. The prediction is that one would find examples of this particular value for C_3 in Table 2 but never in Table 1. Reexamining Table 2, one notes that a full one-third of the examples have /b/ as C_3, while none of the examples in Table 1 do. These facts can be explained if syncope was blocked after a /b/ and in certain other contexts. Where it was blocked, the original pattern was preserved. When it applied, and when syncope ceased to be productive, a new class of verbs emerged.

The result of these layers of phonological rules and reanalyses is a modern system displaying all the properties of subtractive morphology. It is rare only because the chain of events leading to its development are rare, not because of a universal constraint against subtraction. Morphological theory can be broadened by allowing for morphologization of phonological rules, and hence for a full range of phonological operations in morphology (9). In turn, the highly restricted pairing of form and meaning inherent in the notion of morpheme can be replaced by a pairing between form *change* and meaning (8).

Notes

I am grateful to Stephen R. Anderson, G. Aaron Broadwell, Eugene Buckley, David Cline, Abigail Cohn, John Colton, Bruce Hayes, and Pamela Munro for useful discussion of ideas expressed in this paper. All mistakes are mine.

1. Anderson (1987) and Zwicky (1988) refer to PSM as 'item-based' and 'morpheme-based', and to TM as 'process-based'. Since all generative approaches would probably be considered process-based under Hockett's (1954) classification, I have chosen instead to use standard generative terminology. Lieber (1980), who I have left unclassified, makes explicit reference to the need for transformational rules in morphology. The bulk of her work, however, is cast in terms of a PSM, and she argues explicitly for affix-only approaches to morphology.

2. In principle, there are additional arguments for distinguishing T rules and PS rules in morphology. For example: 1) T rules are almost always ordered before PS rules; 2) T rules are not structure building, though PS rules may be; 3) T rules may not access structural information, though PS rules may.

3. More precisely, an operation is called SUBTRACTIVE just in case the set of articulatory operations in the output is a *subset* of the set of articulatory operations of the base, and ADDITIVE just in case the set of articulatory operations in the output is a *superset* of the set of articulatory operations of the base. For example, a rule that voices, rounds, or nasalizes an element of the base is additive, while a rule that devoices, unrounds, or oralizes an element of the base is subtractive.

4. Kimball (1985) groups the verbs in Tables 1-2 differently based on his own analysis. On his account, six separate ordered rules are responsible for the data, allowing for a certain amount of residue. The forms in Tables 1-2 contain several rules of allomorphy that are irrelevant for the current discussion. See Kimball (1985) for a description.

5. In this respect, the Muskogean examples differ from the Polynesian examples discussed by Hale (1973), where final consonants occurring in underlying representations and derived forms were reanalyzed as part of the derivational suffix. It seems likely that the 'primacy' of singular forms over plural forms in acquisition (however this is to be measured) has kept the Muskogean examples from being reanalyzed, while primacy works in exactly the opposite direction in Maori.

6. An alternative subtractive account of the phenomenon pointed out to me by Stephen Anderson is to assume that the final *syllable* of the root is deleted. On this account, portions of the dissociated syllable would be saved by reassociation to the intact structure on the left. Since only the onset would fit the preexisting structure, the effect would be to delete the rhyme without requiring reference to the rhyme as a prosodic constituent. An empirical claim made by this second theory is that the entire syllable might delete in cases where reassociation of the onset is blocked by syllable structure requirements. Interestingly, there appear to be no cases of roots of the shape ...CCVC showing subtraction, a fact perhaps related to the historical description below.

7. Some comparative evidence supports Kimball's internal reconstruction. Thus, one can compare Creek *lo:f-ita* 'to skin, remove the hair' and Western Muskogean *lof-fi* 'peel' directly with Koasati *lofap-li* 'chip (sg. obj.) lengthwise'/*lof-fi:ci* 'chip (pl. obj.) lengthwise' to suggest Koasati addition of a formative *-ap. The same formative is suggested by Creek *la:s-ita* 'to lick' and Choctaw *holakši* 'lick' against Koasati *lasap-li* 'lick once'/*las-li* 'lick several times' (both sets from Munro *et al.* (1987)). More examples are needed for firm

conclusions, however, especially given that Western Muskogean (Choctaw and Chickasaw) patterns with Creek in these sets rather than with Koasati, and since deletion of final consonants and vowels is common in the family.

8. Alternatively, one might suppose that singular and plural verb forms were distinguished accentually, with deletion of a final consonant tied to accent pattern. Such an account might explain why the alternation in Table 2 is limited to verbs of the shape CVCVC (see Martin (1987) for some possibly related accent facts).

References

Anderson, Stephen R. 1975. On the Interaction of Phonological Rules of Various Types. JL 11.39-62.

Anderson, Stephen R. 1983. Rules as 'Morphemes' in a Theory of Inflection. MALC.

Anderson, Stephen R. 1985. Phonology in the Twentieth Century: Theories of Rules and Theories of Representations. Chicago: Univ. of Chicago Press.

Anderson, Stephen R. 1987. Morphological Theory. In F. Newmeyer, ed., Linguistics: The Cambridge Survey.

Broadwell, George A. 1987. Subtractive Morphology in Southwest Muskogean. Presented at the 40th Annual Kentucky Foreign Language Conference.

Chomsky, Noam. 1957. Syntactic Structures. The Hague: Mouton.

Di Sciullo, Anna Maria and Edwin Williams. 1987. On the Definition of Word. Cambridge, MA. MIT Press.

Dressler, Wolfgang U. 1987. Subtraction in a Polycentristic Theory of Natural Morphology. In E. Gussman, ed., Rules and the Lexicon: Studies in Word-Formation. Lublin: Katolickiego Uniwersytetu Lubelskiego.

Hale, Kenneth. 1973. Deep-Surface Canonical Disparities in Relation to Analysis and Change: An Australian Example. Current Trends in Linguistics, 11, 401-458.

Hardy, Heather and Timothy Montler. 1986. Alabama Radical Morphology: H-infix and Disfixation. Presented at the Haas Festival Conference, UCSC.

Janda, Richard. 1983. 'Morphemes' Aren't Something that Grows on Trees: Morphology as More the Phonology than the Syntax of Words. In J. Richardson , eds., Interplay, CLS, pp. 79-95.

Kimball, Geoffrey. 1983. Verb Pluralization in Koasati. MALC 1982:401-11.

Kimball, Geoffrey. 1985. A Descriptive Grammar of Koasati. Doctoral dissertation, Tulane University.

Kiparsky, Paul. 1984. On the Lexical Phonology of Icelandic. Elert et al., eds.

Lieber, Rochelle. 1980. On the Organization of the Lexicon. Doctoral dissertation, MIT. Reprinted through Indiana University Linguistics Club, 1981.

Marantz, Alec. 1982. Re Reduplication. LI 13:435-82.

Martin, Jack. 1987. Vowel Lengthening in Hitchiti and Mikasuki and its Relation to Proto-Muskogean Metrical Structure. In P. Munro, ed., pp. 111-118.

McCarthy, John J. 1979. Formal Problems in Semitic Phonology and Morphology. Doctoral dissertation, MIT.

McCarthy, John J. and Alan S. Prince. 1986. Prosodic Morphology. MS.

Munro, Pamela. 1987a. The Muskogean II Prefixes and Their Significance for Classification. Presented at the 40th Annual Kentucky Foreign Language Conference.

Munro, Pamela, ed. 1987b. Muskogean Linguistics. UCLA Occasional Papers in

Linguistics 6.

Munro, Pamela; George A. Broadwell; Emanuel J. Drechsel; Geoffrey D. Kimball; Jack Martin. 1987. Muskogean Cognate Sets. MS.

Munro, Pamela and Catherine Willmond. 1986. Chickasaw-English: An Analytical Dictionary. MS.

Orešnik, Janez and Magnus Pétursson. 1977. Quantity in Modern Icelandic. Arkiv för Norjisk Filologi 92:155-71.

Poser, William J. 1984a. The Phonetics and Phonology of Tone and Intonation in Japanese. Doctoral dissertation, MIT.

Poser, William J. 1984b. Hypocoristic Formation in Japanese. Proceedings of WCCFL 3. Stanford, CA: Stanford Linguistics Association.

Selkirk, Elisabeth O. 1982. The Syntax of Words. Cambridge, MA: MIT Press.

Wurzel, W. U. 1981. Problems in Morphonology. In W. U. Dressler; O. E. Pfeiffer; J. R. Rennison, eds., Phonologica 1980. Innsbruck: Institut für Sprachwissenschaft der Universität Innsbruck.

Zwicky, Arnold M. 1988. Morphological Rules, Operations, and Operation Types. Proceedings of ESCOL 4.

On the Parallelism Between IP and DP
M. A. Mohammad
University of Southern California

Introduction:
    The construct state in Semitic languages has a clustering
of properties that pose some interesting questions as to how
to best account for these properties. In this paper, I will
provide an analysis that will solve the problems posed by the
construct state. This paper is organized as follows: in
section 1, I provide a description of the properties of the
construct state; in section 2, I give an analysis of the
construct state by borrowing and extending ideas from Baker
(1985) and Abney (1987); and finally in section 3, I discuss
briefly SPEC-to-SPEC movement in IP and DP Arabic.

1. Properties of the construct state

    Although the data to be discussed in this paper is
derived exclusively from Classical Arabic, it is applicable
to all the modern Arabic dialects, and to the very best of
my knowledge, to Hebrew.

    First what is the construct state? It is a construction
that roughly corresponds to the genitive NP in English both
with possessive 's and the "possessive" of in English. To get
a feel of the construct state, consider the following
examples:

(1)   kitaab-u   l-walad-i
       book-NOM   the-book-GEN
       'the boy's book'
       'the book of the boy'
(2)   hajmu   l-qamar-i
       size-NOM   the-moon-GEN
       'the size of the moon'

(3)   intixaabaat-u   r-ri?aasat-i
       elections-NOM   the-presidency-GEN
       'the election of the presidency =presidential
       elections"

1.1. Definiteness/ Indefiniteness

    The definiteness or indefiniteness of the entire
construct state NP is determined solely by the genitive NP
(i.e. that NP corresponding to the possessor in English).
Compare the following examples:

(4)   kitaab-u   l-walad-i
      book-NOM   the-book-GEN
      'the boy's book'
      'the book of the boy'
      '*a book of the boy '

(5)   kitaab-u   walad-in
      book-NOM   boy-GEN
      'a boy's book'
      'a book of a boy'

In (4) the head of the construct state <u>kitaabu</u> appears in
its "bare" from. Its definiteness is determined by that of
the possessor, namely <u>lwaladi</u> "the boy". By contrast, in
(5) the head is interpreted as indefinite despite the fact
that its shape is identical to that in (4). Thus, its
indefiniteness is determined by the genitive NP. Word order
aside, the same thing is observed in English in that the
definiteness of the entire possessive NP is equally
determined by the possessor. To derive further nuances of
definiteness one must resort to other constructions such as
the use of <u>of</u> in English and <u>li</u> "for" in Arabic. In both
English and Arabic the possessed NP can never have the
definite article preceding it:

(6)* al-kitaab-u   l-walad-i
      the-boy-NOM   the-book-GEN
      '*the boy's the book'

1.2.THE FEMININE MARKER

   The construct state does create some kind of a unique
domain, found nowhere else in Arabic, where some
phonological processes, whose exact nature need not concern
us here, take place. Indeed, this property can be used to
determine whether an expression is a construct state or
something else. Compare the following examples:

(7)   saa9a   kahrubaa?
      clock   electricity
      'an electrical clock, i.e. a clock that is powered
      by electricity.'

(8)   saa9at   kahrubaa?
      clock   electricity
      'an electricity meter, i.e. the device used to measure
       electricity'

The crucial difference between (7) and (8) is the absence of
the feminine marker in (7) and its presence in (8).
Consider the following examples where the head of the
construct state has this "feminine" marker:

(9)(a) zawja<u>t</u>   ?ahmad
        wife   Aḥmed
        'Ahmed's wife'

   (b)* zawja   ?ahmad
        wife   Aḥmed
        'Ahmed's wife'

(10)(a) ?ixwa<u>t</u>   ?ahmad
         brothers   Ahmed
         'Ahmed's brothers'

    (b)* ?ixwa   ?ahmad
         brothers   Aḥmed
         'Ahmed's brothers'

Thus, it is clear from the above examples that the
construct state is the context where this marker can never
be absent.

1.3. <u>THE SOUND PLURAL -na AND THE DUAL -ni</u>

   Classical Arabic, unlike any of the modern Arabic
dialects, has a similar process to the feminine marker in
the construct state described in the previous section but
with an opposite effect: that is, instead of retaining some
element, this element is deleted in the construct state but
inserted everywhere else. Consider the following examples:

(11)   mu9allimuuna; mu9allimiina;   mu9allimaani;
        teachers NOM; teachers GEN/ACC; two teachers NOM

Examples (11) provide citation forms of some nouns in the
so-called sound plural and the dual. When the head of the
construct state is either a sound plural or a dual, the
respective -na and -ni endings are deleted (or not
inserted). Consider:

(12)(a) mu9allimuu   l-waladayni
         teachers-NOM   the-two boys GEN
         'the two boy's teachers'

    (b)* mu9allimuuna   l-waladayni
         teachers-NOM   the-two boys GEN
         'the two boy's teachers'

This phenomenon, together with that of the feminine marker, is observed nowhere else. That is, if the form of the head in (12a) appears in any context other than the construct state the resulting output is totally ungrammatical.

1.4.MULTIPLE EMBEDDING: ENDINGS, AND "CLOSURE"

It has been noted (Aoun 1978, Borer 1984, and Ritter 1987) that in case of multiply embedded construct states only the final member of such a construction can have the definite article. In a sense, this last NP closes the construct since once a definite article is introduced anywhere in the construct, no further embedding is allowed. Borer calls this "closure". As in the case of definiteness, word order and style aside, Arabic and English share this property. Consider the following examples:

(13)(a)   taawilat 9ammat   zawjat   ar-rajul
           table   aunt   wife   the-man
           'the man's wife's aunt's table'

   (c)* any instance of (a) when any of the feminine
        markers is deleted, or where the definite article
        appears anywhere but of the last NP

(14)(a)   mu9allimuu   bentay   šaqiiqay   ar-rajul
           teachers NOM two daughters GEN two brothers NOM the-man
           'the man's two brother's two daughters' teachers'
           'the teachers of the two daughters of the two brothers
            of the man'

   (b)* any instance of (a) when either the sound plural
        ending or the dual ending or both are inserted, and
        where the definite article appears anywhere but on the
        last NP .

Two things need to be noticed with regards to the above examples: first is that only and only the last member can have the definite article cliticized to it, and secondly, the contexts of the feminine marker and the sound plural and dual endings are met in every member. This latter point shows that the examples above do contain multiply embedded construct states.

1.5. INSEPARABILITY OF THE CONSTRUCT STATE MEMBERS

Members of the construct state, with multiple embeddings or not cannot ever be separated by anything. Consider:

(15)(a)   ?amsi   jaa?a   ?ibn-u   ar-rajul-i
           yesterday came 3sm son-NOM   the-man-GEN
           'Yesterday, the man's son came.'

(b) jaa?a   ?amsi   ?ibn-u   ar-rajul-i
     came 3sm   yesterday   son-NOM   the-man-GEN
     `Yesterday, the man's son came.'

(c) jaa?a   ?ibn-u   ar-rajul-i   ?amsi
     came 3sm   son-NOM   the-man-GEN   yesterday
     `Yesterday, the man's son came.'

(d)* jaa?a   ?ibn-u   ?amsi   ar-rajul-i
     came 3sm   son-NOM   yesterday   the-man-GEN
     `*The man's yesterday son came.'

Despite the freedom of word order tolerated in the above
examples, the construct state cannot be separated. This
means that if an adjective is to describe the head of the
construct it must follow the entire construct (adjectives
in Arabic follow the nominal they modify). Consider:

(16)(a) ?ibn-u   ar-rajul-i   l-qasiir-u
         son-NOM   the-man-GEN   the-short-NOM
         `the short son of the man'

(b)* ?ibn-u   l-qasiir-u   ar-rajul-i
     son-NOM   the-short-NOM   the-man-GEN
     `the short son of the man'

The adjective in (16a) shows an important property of the
construct state. Adjectives in Arabic agree with the
nominal they modify in number, gender, Case and
definiteness. In (16a) the head does not have the definite
article, but, given that the genitive Np is definite, the
head is taken to be definite, and this dictates the
appearance of the definite article of the adjective.

1.6. Modifiers Cannot Precede the Construct State

In Arabic, the demonstrative pronoun can either precede
or follow the NP it modifies. It can always follow, but in
order for it to precede, the NP modified must have the
definite article phonetically realized. Thus, the
demonstrative can never precede the construct state, since the
head of the construct state can never have the definite
article attached to it. Thus, the adjective is sensitive to
the abstract notion of definiteness, the demonstrative article
requires the phonetic presence of the definite article to
precede an NP. Consider:

(17)(a) haadaa   l-walad-u
         this   the-boy-NOM
         `this boy'

(b)   ?al-walad-u   haaδaa
       the-boy-NOM   this
       'this boy'

(18)(a)* haāTHaa   ?ibn-u   ar-rajul-i
         this   son-NOM   the-man-GEN
         'this son of the man'

(b)   ?ibn-u   ar-rajul-i   haaδaa
       son-NOM   the-man-GEN   this
       'this son of the man'

(c)* ?ibn-u   haaδaa   ar-rajul-i   this
     son-NOM   this   the-man-GEN   this
     'this son of the man'

Given the restriction of the inseparability of the construct
state, the only grammatical version is for the demonstrative
to follow the entire construct state. Thus, in the construct
state, the demonstrative can only appear in two positions, it
must follow the entire construct state, in which case it can
be taken to refer to either the head or the genitive NP as
long as they have identical features of number and gender, or
it can precede the last member in which case it can only
modify this member and nothing else. Thus, the (b) examples
are perfectly grammatical if the demonstrative is taken to
modify the genitive NP and not the head.

1.7.Relativizability of Both Members of the Construct State

   Unlike the English genitive NPs (with the possessive 's),
both members of the construct state are relativizable
without having to resort to alternative constructions.
Consider:

(19)   kitaab-u   walad-in   ra?aa-hu   ?ahmad-u
       book-NOM   boy-GEN   saw-him   Ahmed-NOM
       'a book of a boy who Ahmed saw'

(20)   kitaab-u   walad-in   mazzaqa-hu   ?ahmad-u
       book-NOM   boy-GEN   tore-it   Ahmed-NOM
       'a book of a boy that Ahmed tore'

In (19) the relative clause modifies the genitive NP in the
construct state, namely waladin "a boy", while in (20) the
relative clause modifies the head of the construct state.
Since both NPs are indefinite the relative pronoun is ∅.
Consider the following examples where the both the head and
the genitive NP are definite:

(21) kitaab-u   l-walad-i   llaðii mazzaqa-hu ?ahmad-u
     book-NOM   the-boy-GEN which   tore-it   Ahmed-NOM
     'the book of the boy that Ahmed tore'

(22) kitaab-u l-walad-i   llað ra?aa-hu   ?ahmad-u
     book-NOM the-boy-GEN   who   saw-him   Ahmed-NOM
     'the book of the boy who Ahmed saw'

Here the relative pronoun is obligatory in both examples.

1.8. THE ACTION NOMINAL ?al-masdar

In this section I will briefly describe the most
important sub-class of the construct state, as it will help
shed some light on the construction as a whole. This section
describes what the grammarians called ?al-masdar "the source
=action nominal ". Specifically, the one aspect of the masdar
that I will be concerned with, is what corresponds to the
English construction referred to as POSS-ING. Consider:

(23) [qatl-u   l-walad-i ad-dajaajat-a]   ?az9aja-nii
     killing-NOM the-boyGEN the-chicken-ACC   upset-me
     ' The boy's killing the chicken upset me.'

What (23) shows is (i) the action nominal retains the
argument structure of the corresponding verb, (ii) the
ability of the action nominal to assign accusative Case to
the object, (iii) the Case of the subject of the construct
state is genitive and NOT nominative as is generally
required in sentences, and finally (iv) unlike a
corresponding sentence with the verb, word order in the
construct state with the action nominal as the head is rigidly
NSO (where N is the action nominal). What needs to be
established is the internal structure of the construct state
in (23). We need to establish one of two things (i) either
the internal structure is flat in the sense the maximal
projection dominating the entire construct state immediately
dominates everything else (i.e. everything in the construct
state above c-commands everything else), or (ii) there is some
kind of an asymmetry between at least some of the elements
contained in the construct state in (23). In order to address
such alternatives, one must turn to the binding properties in
the construct state, assuming the notion of c-command to be
crucial to the formulation of the binding conditions (cf.
Chomsky 1981). Consider:

(24) [qatl-u   l-walad-i   nafs-a-hu]   ?az9aja-nii
     killing-NOM the-boy-GEN   self-ACC_his upset-me
     'The boy's killing himself upset me.'

(24) is a perfectly grammatical example. Since it contains
an anaphor, the anaphor must, therefore, be bound in a
certain domain whose exact determination need not concern
us. Thus, this means that the antecedent l-walaldi "the
boy" is in a position to c-command the anaphor. The
question that arises here is does the anaphor c-command the
antecedent? Presumably, it should not, since if it does a
violation of Principle C will result. To show that this
seems to be right conclusion consider the following example
where the subject of the construct is now the anaphor:

(25) *[qatl-u   nafs-i-hi l-walad-a] ?aza9aja-nii
        killing-NOM   self-GEN-his the-boy-ACC upset-me
        '*Himself's killing the boy upset me.'

The ungrammaticality of (25) suggests one of two things (i)
the antecedent does not c-command the anaphor (thus
resulting in a violation of Principle A of the binding
theory), or (ii) there is a mutual c-command which will result
in Principle C, although Principle A is satisfied. But if the
latter line of reasoning is correct, then the grammaticality
of (24) is inexplicable since there is no Principle C
violation. Thus it seems that the correct conclusion must be
that the genitive NP in the above two examples, asymmetrically
c-commands the accusative object.

The above line of reasoning, namely that the subject
(i.e. the genitive NP) asymmetrically c-commands the object
can be confirmed if we look closely at Principle C. Consider:

(26)   [qatl-u   l-walad-i   l-walad-a] ?az9aja-nii
         killing-NOM the-boy-GEN the-boy-ACC upset-me
         '*The boy's$_i$ killing the boy$_i$ upset me.'

(27)[qatl-u   ?ab-i   l-walad-i   l-walad-a] ?az9aja-nii
     killing-NOM father-GEN   the-boy-GEN the-boy-ACC upset-me
     'The boy's$_i$ father's killing the boy$_i$ upset me.'

If the object NP c-commands the subject NP, it follows
(given Principle C) no referential NP inside the subject
could be ever taken as coreferential with the object. If
it does not c-command it, then we expect that if an NP is
found in the subject which does NOT c-command the object,
the resulting example should be perfectly grammatical. This
is indeed the case as (27) shows. Thus, (27) provides
direct evidence that the object does not c-command the
subject NP. In (26), therefore, the subject
asymmetrically c-commands the object. Having said that,
the above examples can now be ruled out with no structural
ambiguity. The co-indexation between the subject NP and the

object NP are allowed (or barred) by appealing to the binding Principles because the subject asymmetrically c-commands the object.

To conclude this section, let me summarize what has been established. The Construct state constitutes an opaque domain for the binding theory. There is a structural asymmetry between the subject NP and the object NP (when the latter is present). In the next section, I will turn my attention to deriving the above facts.

2. ANALYSIS

Leaving open the question whether D in Arabic is the equivalent of determiner, I assume, following Abney (1987), that the structure of classical category NP is as given in (28): below.

(28) $[_{DP}$ SPEC $[_{D'}$ D $[_{NP}$ SPEC $[_{N'}$ N]]]]

I further assume that in (28) N is in a -CASE position. Given the assumption in the literature, that a Case assigner that governs the maximal projection of a Case assignee governs the head, I assume that D is the recipient of the Case assigned to DP. I assume further, following Aoun (1978), that the genitive NP of the construct state is base-generated in the SPEC of NP. As first step in the derivation of the construct state, N must move into D to get Case. This movement will accomplish two things simultaneously: move N into a position where it will be assigned Case (thus avoiding a violation of the Case Filter); and it will create the configuration under which the genitive Case is to be assigned. Consider first how a simple NP will be derived under the assumptions I have just spelled out.

(29) $[_{DP}$ SPEC $[_{D'}$ D $[_{NP}$ $[_{SPEC}$ al] $[_{N'}$ $[_N$ walad]]]]]

Let us make the assumption that the definite article in (29) has to cliticize to a category that can "host" it. In this instance this host is an N. The cliticization must take place before N moves into D. Otherwise there will remain a clitic with no host. A trace, since it is phonetically empty, is not a suitable host. Thus, in the final step the N and the cliticized <u>al-</u> raise into D.

Consider now the construct state. The subject of the construct (i.e. the possessor) is base-generated under SPEC of NP. N must move into D to receive Case, and create the .pa structural conditions under which the genitive Case will be assigned the NP <u>l-walad</u> "the boy". This movement will derive (31) from the underlying (30):

(30)

[$_{DP}$SPEC [$_{D'}$D[$_{NP}$[SPEC[$_{DP}$ al-walad]][$_{N'}$[$_N$ kitaab]]]]]

(31)
[$_{DP}$SPEC [$_{D'}$[$_D$kitaab[$_{NP}$[SPEC[$_{DP}$ al-walad]][$_{N'}$[$_N$ t]]]]]]

Let us turn our attention now to the gerunds in the construct state and address the title of this paper, namely the parallelism between IP and DP. Recall first that we have established that the subject of the gerund asymmetrically c-commands the object (if there is one); the gerund retains the argument structure of the verb; the word order is rigidly VS(O) (where V in the construct state under discussion is the gerund); and finally, and perhaps most importantly, the Case that appears on the object is the accusative Case, a Case that is typically assigned by verbs (but never by nominals). Before establishing the internal structure of the gerund in Arabic and discussing ways of deriving its properties, it is important that we digress briefly to discuss the internal structure of IP in Arabic.

Following Mohammad (1987a), I assume that Arabic is underlyingly an SVO language. Adopting the proposals suggested in Koopman and Sportiche (1985) and Kuroda (1986), the following structure can be assumed to be the underlying structure of Arabic.

(32)[$_{IP}$[SPEC [$_{I'}$I [$_{VP}$SPEC [$_{VP}$ V DP]]]]]

There are compelling empirical reasons supporting the configuration in (32) above as the structure underlying the Arabic sentence. The problem of subject-verb agreement in Arabic can be argued to support (32). This is the position argued for in Mohammad (1987a). Here I summarize the salient points in that paper. The problem of agreement is its apparent dependence on word order: if the verb precedes the subject, the verb is third person singular (regardless of the number associated with the subject_; but if the verb follows the subject, the verb agrees fully with the subject. I claim that in the former case, there is no agreement whatsoever between the verb and the thematic subject; but the verb is in actual fact agreeing with an expletive subject. Looking at (32), the claim put forward is that the SPEC of IP is the position where the expletive subject is found, while the SPEC of VP is where the thematic subject is generated. Consider:

(33)(a) jaa?a   l-walad-u   w-al-bent-u
         came 3sm   the-boy-NOM   and-the-girl-NOM
         'The boy and the girl came.'

    (b) ?al-walad-u   w-al-bent-u   jaa?aa
         the-boy-NOM   and-the-girl-NOM came 3dm
         'The boy and the girl came.'

    (c)* jaa?aa   l-walad-u   w-al-bent-u
         came 3dm   the-boy-NOM   and-the-girl-NOM
         'The boy and the girl came.'

    (d)* ?al-walad-u   w-al-bent-u   jaa?a
         the-boy-NOM   and-the-girl-NOM came 3dm
         'The boy and the girl came.'

Thus, when the subject precedes the verb, the verb necessarily agrees fully with the subject; when the subject follows, the verb necessarily shows singular agreement. Examining the properties of the expletive pronominal in Arabic, we find that it too is in the third person singular. For lack of space I will give only one representative example:

(34)(a) yabduu   ?anaa   l-?awlaad-a   saafaruu
         seem 3sm   that   the-boys-ACC   departed 3pm
         'It seems that the boys departed.'
         'Lit. pro seems that the boys departed.'

    (b)* ?al-?awlaad-u   yabduuna   ?anna   saafaruu
         the-boys-NOM   seem 3pm   that   departed 3pm
         'Lit. The boys$_i$ seem that pro$_i$ departed.'

    (c)* ?al-?awlaad-u yabduuna   ?anna-hum   saafaruu
         the-boys-NOM   seem 3pm   that   departed 3pm
         'Lit. The boys seem that they departed.'

    (d) ?al-?awlaad-u yabduu   ?anna-hum   saafaruu
         the-boys-NOM   seem 3sm   that   departed 3pm
         'Lit. The boys, pro seems that they departed.'

    (e) * any sentence in which the features associated
         with the verb yabduu are changed.

The examples above show us that there is no raising in Arabic with the seem type verbs. As the examples above show no subject, apart from the expletive pronominal can ever occupy the subject slot of such verbs. Of course, one can say that the third person singular agreement has nothing to do with the presence or the absence of such a pronominal; rather it is a default type of agreement .

Fortunately, there is direct evidence to support the claim
that such an expletive subject is indeed present. The
evidence comes from contexts when the above examples are
embedded:

(35)(a) ?idda9aa   ar-rajul-u ?anna-<u>hu</u> yabduu   ?anna
         claimed 3sm the-man-NOM that-<u>it</u> seems <u>3sm</u> that

         al-?awlaad-a   saafaruu
         the-boys-ACC   departed 3pm
         'The man claimed that it seems that the boys
         departed.'

    (b)* ?idda9aa   ar-rajul-u ?anna-pro yabduu   ?anna
         claimed 3sm the-man-NOM that-pro seems <u>3sm</u> that

         al-?awlaad-a   saafaruu
         the-boys-ACC   departed 3pm
         'Lit. The man claimed that pro seems that the boys
         departed.'

The expletive pronoun must be present. The presence of the
pronoun is expected, given a general constraint in Arabic
which states that empty pronominals of any kind cannot
occur in a non-nominative context. This is a context that
the complementizer <u>?anna</u> creates since it has the property
of assigning an accusative Case.

    If my claim about the structure of a simple
declarative sentence is as suggested above, it follows
that, if there is indeed an expletive in the SPEC of IP,
the expletive pronoun must show up if we embed the clause
under <u>?anna</u>. Indeed, it does:

(36) idda9aa ?ahmad-u ?anna-hu   jaa?a r-rijaal-u
     claimed 3sm Ahmed-NOM that-it came 3sm the-men-NOM
     'Ahmed claimed that the men came.'

(37)? idda9aa   ?ahmad-u   ?anna-hu r-rijaal-u jaa?-uu
      claimed 3sm Ahmed-NOM that-it the-men-NOM came-pm
      'Ahmed claimed that the men came.'

    The lexical presence of the expletive pronominal in
the above examples provide very strong evidence for the
presence of two subject positions in an Arabic sentence.
Recall that I have said that there seems to be no raising in
Arabic when it comes to the seem-type verbs. This suggests
that in Arabic there is no raising from SPEC of VP to SPEC of
IP. Thus, it seems that the following processes are at work
in IP in Arabic:

(38) Head-to-head Movement
      a. V to I
      b. I to V (Rule R)

(39) SPEC-to-SPEC Movement
      a. NO SPEC-to-SPEC Movt. in IP

    Having established that there is a need for two SPEC
positions in IP (one in IP and the other in VP), I turn now
to the gerund. We have seen that the gerund has sort of
dual character in that it shows both sentential and nominal
properties. Crucially, it was noted that the gerund,
unlike a sentence, has a rigid word order. Combining
proposals made in Baker (1985) and Abney (1987), we might
propose that the configuration underlying the gerund is
something like (40):

(40)
[$_{XP}$ SPEC [$_{X'}$ [X [$_{VP}$ [[$_{SPEC}$ al-walad] [$_{VP}$ [[$_{V}$QTL] [$_{DP}$nafashu]]]]]

I leave the question concerning is the nature of XP. That
is, whether it is base-generated as IP, or DP, or whether it
is base-generated as IP but later changed by percolation
into DP (assuming for the latter that there is some
nominalizing element present (corresponding to ING in
English in I (cf. Baker 1985). Consider first how the VP
portion at least can now give us all the properties of the
gerund. First, the subject is in a structural position to c-
command the object. Thus, the subject cannot ever be an
anaphor with the object as its antecedent. Nor can the
subject bind a pronominal object, now can the subject bind a
referential object. Second, we now have an element , namely
V, which is capable of assigning accusative Case. V can now
move into I with the nominalizing element (or this
nominalizing element is lowered into V, where it will change
this V into N, thus forcing it raise into D to receive Case).
It should be clear to the reader familiar with GB theory how
easily does the above configuration give the correct results
with reference to the binding facts mentioned earlier.

    One problem remains with the above analysis. Namely,
how can we prevent the movement of the NP in the SPEC of VP
to the SPEC of IP (DP)? Recall that I have suggested that
there is reason to believe that there is no such movement
from the SPEC of VP to the SPEC of IP. Thus, it is
reasonable to suggest that whatever is barring is also
barring it in our gerunds. Note that even if we allow
movement from the SPEC of VP to the SPEC of IP, we can find
a way, admittedly still stipulatory in nature, to block this
movement within DP. We can stipulate that the genitive Case
context must be maintained at the relevant levels.

The parallelism between DP and IP seems to involve the
following properties: (i) the apparent lack of raising from
SPEC of VP to SPEC of IP and the absence of the same from the
SPEC of NP to the SPEC of DP; (ii) the availability of V to I,
and N to D; (iii) the binding properties in both make a
crucial reference to the notion of c-command; (iv) the
possibility of lowering in both (i.e. Rule R); (v) the
rigidity of word order in the construct state may be
attributed to the presence of the genitive Case which, unlike
nominative, requires strict adjacency to be maintained at all
relevant levels (possibly at SS and PF, but not at LF).

References

Abney, S.P. The English noun phrase in its stentential
aspect. Doctoral Dissertation, MIT.

Aoun, J. Structure interne du groupe nominal en arabe,
l?idaafa. Analyses Theorie 1, Paris VIII, Vincennes.

Baker, Mark. 1985. Syntactic affixation and English Gerunds.
Proceedings of WCCFL 7, 1-11.

Borer, H. 1983. Parametric syntax: case studies in Semitic
and Romance. Dordrecht: Foris.

Chomsky, Noam. Lectures on government and binding.
Dordrecht: Foris.

---1982. Some concepts and Consequences of the theory of
government and binding. Cambridge (Mass): MIT   Press.

--- 1986. Barriers. Cambridge (Mass): MIT Press.

Koopman, H. and D. Sportiche. 1985. GLOW Newsletter.

Kuroda, Y. Whether we agree or not. ms., UCSD.

Mohammad, M.A. 1987a. Subject-object asymmetries and word
order in Arabic, LSA Annual Meeting, San Francisco

--- 1987b. The problem of subject-verb agreement in Arabic:
towards a solution, First Annual Symposium on Arabic
Linguistics, Salt Lake City.

Ritter, E. NSO noun phrases in Modern Hebrew. Proceedings of
NELS 17.

Ascription of Responsibility in Propositional Attitudes

M.G. Moser
University of Pennsylvania

1. Introduction

In uttering a sentence, a speaker assumes responsibility for its accuracy, felicity, and subjective expressions. Within the propositional attitudes, these responsibilities may be shared between the speaker and the attitude subject. For instance, to understand a simple statement, we may need to explicitly recognize a difference between the speaker's point of view and our own. To take a famous example, if a man is drinking water from a martini glass, the referent of the noun phrase in (1) is clear to everyone, even those who know there is no martini. It is debatable exactly what truth conditions should apply to the sentence containing this description. The speaker has failed to make her description match the world in the right way, an unintentional violation of Grice's maxim of quality. While the description amounts to failed responsibility on the part of the speaker when it is used in a simple statement, it has quite a different status within a propositional attitude. That is, we could describe the situation using (2) without committing the same error, the same noun phrase determines the right person in this context.

(1) The guy with the martini laughs loudly.
(2) Marie believes that the guy with the martini laughs loudly.

In this paper, I suggest that the subjectivity of each phrase be explicitly represented in model theoretic semantics via a person index, or p-index. Then, for nonattitude utterances such as (1), the speaker's Gricean responsibility requires her description to match reality, i.e. to be true of its intended referent. First, I will elaborate on the treatment of these cases in Montague grammar, and the inclusion of a p-index within that system. Then I will cite analyses of other phenomena, semantics of self-knowledge and logophoric pronouns, which further support the use of a p-index. Then an example derivation will demonstrate how the p-indices are introduced and manipulated. Finally, I look at the consequences of this approach where p-indices may facilitate an accurate description of certain other phenomena.

2. Referring expressions in attitudes

Within the Montague framework, the object of an attitude will be a proposition, the set of possible worlds where the attitude expression is true. So *hope* is a relation between hopeful people, the hopers, and propositions, the hopes. Consider the sentence (3). In (Montague 1973), this is given two readings, considered to be a scopal ambiguity. In (5) a model with four individuals is given by showing which sentences are true at each possible world.

(3) Beth hopes that the neighbor visits distant lands.

(4) The neighbor visits distant lands.

(5) *Sample model, current index w1*

A={b,c,d,e} named Beth, Cal, Dan, Eve

w1:	*w2:*	*w3:*
Neighbor'(c)	**Neighbor'**(e)	**Neighbor'**(e)
VDL'(c)	**VDL'**(e)	**VDL'**(c)
VDL'(e)	**VDL'**(d)	**VDL'**(d)

Using the notation introduced by (Dowty et al. 1981), the logic translation for the de dicto reading is shown in (6). Below it is the ordered pair that belongs in the hope relation. Here we have the non-referential reading, it concerns no particular individual. The proposition is the set of worlds at which the neighbor at that world travels. So Cal at w1 and Eve at w2, visit distant lands.

(6) **Hope'**(b,$^\wedge\exists$y($\forall$x[**Neighbor'**(x) $\leftrightarrow$ x=y] & **VDL'**(x)))
<b,{w1,w2}> (*de dicto*)

Consider (7), the standard referential or de re reading. In this case, the referent of the noun phrase is fixed at the current index, so it is Cal. The proposition shown is the set of possible worlds at which Cal travels, w2 and w3. One way to establish the truth of (3) is to ask Beth about (4). Imagine that Beth would like for Cal to take frequent trips abroad, but she happens not to know that he is also the neighbor. Now if we ask Beth about her wish for (4) she will object. We might call it speaker substitution, that allows us to take (3) as true even though Beth objects. The idea is that even though Beth would not choose *the neighbor* as a description for Cal, the speaker may do so.

(7) $\exists$y($\forall$x[**Neighbor'**(x) $\leftrightarrow$ x=y] & **Hope'**(b,$^\wedge$**VDL'**(x)))
<b,{w1,w3}> (*de re*)

But there is another referential reading where the noun phrase refers to whoever Beth thinks is the neighbor. I call this this the de re2 reading. The referent of *the neighbor* is fixed at w1, but with respect to Beth's point of view. I notate this with a superscript as shown in (8), a sentence I am adding to the model in (5) at w1. Here we imagine that Beth is mistaken. She thinks that Dan, who visits distant lands, is the neighbor. She may believe that Cal, the real neighbor, never goes anywhere.

(8) **Neighbor'**^{b}(d)
$\exists$y($\forall$x[**Neighbor'**^{b}(x) $\leftrightarrow$ x=y] & **Hope'**(b,$^\wedge$**VDL'**(y)))
<b,{w2,w3}> (*de re2*)

The proposition shown in (8) is different from both previous readings. The noun phrase picks out Dan, the neighbor according to Beth, and so we take the set of possible worlds in which Dan travels, w2 and w3. We have to allow that the sentence is true in the de re2 circumstances because Beth would express her hope with the assertion (4). We, as omniscient beings, may realize that her assent is based on an error. But (3) is undeniably true.

Without a semantic account of the de re2 reading, there is no logical referential reading for (9). Unless we allow multiple ways to fix the referent, Beth hopes of the same person that they both travel and stay home. But we have seen that this sentence is true, because Beth mistakenly believes that Dan is the neighbor.

(9) Beth hopes the neighbor visits distant lands while Cal putters in his yard.

The de re2 reading of (3) is an embedded version of the martini example. For the simple assertion, the speaker has made a mistake and it is debatable exactly what truth conditions apply. But for the attitude report, the speaker is not responsible for the hoper's mistake; Beth herself would have chosen the description. In the embedded instance, the reference is successful using an inaccurate description. That is, under one reading, the truth conditions are determined with respect to Beth's intended referent. So there are two readings with a fixed referent for the noun phrase, but the point of view that fixes it is ambiguous. This ambiguity is independent of the issue of scope of the intensional operator.

Basically, we must explicitly represent the variation from person to person of the intended referent of an expression. I suggest that this should be directly represented in the model by adding a third index, the p-index. The two referential readings are distinguished by p-index. The classical de re reading has the speaker p-index for the noun phrase, while the de re2 has the hoper p-index. With this amendment, all predicates in the model have an extension relative to a self or speaker as well as a world-time.

Because the p-index is independent of scope, this approach implies there should also be a de dicto2 reading. If the description is the way the attitude subject represents the referent to himself, then it is a de dicto2 reading. On the other hand, the description may be a speaker substitution. The speaker, knowing the intensional equivalence of two descriptions, e.g. *the mayor* and *the highest official in town*, may ignore the subject's lack of knowledge of this equivalence.

(10) Andrew hopes that the mayor gets arrested.

For example, in (10), Andrew's desire may concern no particular individual, maybe he just thinks this turn of events would be dramatic. If he entertains the desire via the noun phrase *the mayor*, it is a de dicto2 reading. If it is via the noun phrase *the highest official in the city*, it is the de dicto reading, speaker substitution has occurred.

3. Self-knowledge

The notion of a p-index to represent the self or speaker of an utterance is also suggested in (Cresswell 1986) to account for special properties of self-knowledge. As discussed in (Lewis 1979), (Perry 1979), and others, knowledge about oneself, or self-attributive knowledge, is different in character than propositional knowledge. For me to know (11) is to know something different than (12). My knowledge of (11) entails its propositional form (12). While many people can know the proposition (12), I am unique in being able to know it in virtue of self-attributing the property expressed in the indexical form (11).

> (11) I wrote a paper (*self-attributive*)
>
> (12) Megan wrote a paper (*propositional*)
>
> (13) Megan knows that she wrote a paper (*ambiguous*)

This is a fairly straightforward account of the meaning of *I*. The distinction between these two is clearly expressed by a contrast in grammatical person, *I* vs. *Megan*. Within the scope of *know*, a report of knowledge, this contrast is collapsed. In (13), my knowledge could either be in the form of a self attribute like (11) or simply the proposition (12). The weaker form of knowledge would occur in a situation where I know the proposition but, for whatever strange reason, do not realize that I am Megan. So, I know a proposition about myself, but in a third person way rather than a first person way.

The p-index ambiguity is similar to the two modes of self-knowledge. In the de re reading, the referent is fixed in the third person way, a description by the speaker. Beth does not necessarily realize that the description holds of the referent, i.e. that Cal is the neighbor. In the de re2 reading, the referent is fixed in the first person way. Whoever fits the description according to Beth is the referent. For Beth this is "the neighbor according to me". Another way to see the relationship is to imagine the description of Beth herself which would be produced by each p-index value. With the speaker as p-index, Beth would be described as *Beth* or *she*. While with Beth as p-index, the description would be *I*.

4. Logophors

Other recent work, on the semantics of logophors, supports the use of a p-index. Logophors are a distinct pronoun paradigm or a special, non-clause-bound use of reflexives found in many languages. West African languages, Italian, Icelandic, Japanese. Logophors are used to refer to someone whose thoughts or feelings are being reported. (Sells 1987) analyses logophors as what he calls role oriented anaphora, oriented to the discourse role of SELF. Roughly, logophors function to refer to whoever is the SELF at that point in the sentence.

When multiple embeddings occur, the referent of a logophor may be ambiguous, as for (14) an example from Icelandic. Here, SELF can refer to any of the attitude subjects:

Jon, Maria, or Harold. Each attitude verb may set the role referent for the logophor. So the ambiguity indicates that either the role setting is optional or all the role fillers in dominant clauses are accessible. To choose between these two possibilities, we could consider sentences with multiple logophors.

(14) Jon segir ad Maria viti ad Haraldur vilji ad Billi heimsaeki sig$_{j/m/h}$.

Jon says that Maria knows that Harold wants that Bill visits SELF$_{j/m/h}$.

Logophoric pronominals grammaticize the influence of subjects of attitudes. Within attitudes, the referent of the form SELF may also be responsible for a referring expression. It would be too strong to claim that logophor referents and p-index values are always identical. This could only be established by a more extensive investigation of both logophors and p-indices in all the propositional attitudes.

To summarize so far, it is natural for a hearer to recognize the effect of the speaker as the framer of a description, as when *the guy drinking a martini* succeeds in referring. This process is compounded within attitude reports because multiple agents, the speaker and the subject, can be the framer of the description. So, constituents may be ascribed to subject (de re2) or speaker (de re), via p-indices. The work on self-knowledge and logophors further demonstrates the ambiguity of self or speaker in this context.

5. Grammar fragment

To demonstrate how the p-indices are introduced and set, I will present an example derivation in Montague grammar. Extensions to Montague PTQ are needed in the structure of the model and the compositional rules.

Predicates are assigned extensions with respect to a person, a world, and a time. Intuitively, at each world-time, several points of view may be represented. A model will be defined in the usual way, an ordered quintuple $<A,W,T,<,F>$. The difference is that the assignment function F must assign denotations to non-logical constants for a world-time-person index, an element of $W \times T \times (A \cup \{R\})$. The possible values of the p-index are the elements in A, the set of entities. In addition, stipulate a special objective person, an omniscient point of view, called "R" or "the reality".

In the tree derivation, the indices are introduced as free variables at the leaves and then carried up the tree. Each predicate in the lexicon has a free variable as an argument, the p-index for that predicate. Accordingly, the index is defined as in (15). This allows for the binding of point of view, as in (16).

(15) $\|Q(x)\|^P =_{df} \|Q(p,x)\|$

(16) Every student believes that the mayor is a crook.

I will use a Saenz-Ross phrase structure grammar, as explicated in (Partee&Bach 1981). Each phrase structure rule specifies syntactic composition, e.g. S = NP VP, and semantic composition, e.g. 0' = 1'(^2'). In the semantic rule, each constituent in the syntactic rule is referred to by the number of its left to right order, 0 for S, 1 for NP, etc. The "'" indicates the translation of that constituent, 0' for the translation of S, etc.

The rules needed to generate the sentence (3) are given below. For simplicity, the details of quantifying in are omitted. In (R4), a variable for the attitude subject is introduced and lambda bound. Any free variable which matches the lambda variable will also be bound, setting the p-index for its predicate to the attitude subject. The other rules are the standard compositional rules.

(R1) S = NP VP
  0' = 1'(^2')
(R2) XP = X
  0' = 1'
(R3) NP = Det CN
  0' = 1'(^2')
(R4) VP = V S
  0' = 1'(^2')
  $0' = \lambda x_i [1'(^2')(x_i)]$

Below is a partial derivation tree with just the relevant nodes. For each node is displayed an English expression and its logic translation. At the leaves, a predicate is inserted from the lexicon with the p-index variable as an argument. So, the **Neighbor'** predicate, at the middle node on the bottom, has the argument w, a free variable. Similarly, the variables v and u are introduced for the visiting predicate, **VDL'**, and **Hope'**.

When an attitude VP is constructed, as at the first right daughter in the tree, then a variable for the subject is introduced and lambda bound. Here, the subject variable is w which also happens to be the p-index variable for **Neighbor'**. In this way, the predicate acquires the attitude subject as a p-index.

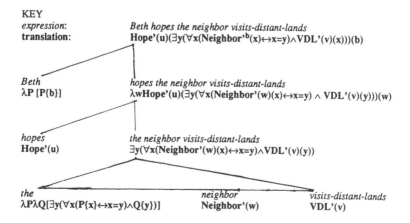

6. Speaker responsibility

Finally, what about v and u, the free variables at the root of the derivation tree? All remaining free variables must be set to a default point of view. The two candidates are the speaker and the omniscient-R, the reality. First consider the speaker-default possibility, in reference to the simple statement (17). A possible model is shown in (18). The convention used here is superscripting the p-index. The 'm' is for Megan, the speaker in this case, and R is the reality. With this solution, Megan must be in A, the set of model entities.

(17) The neighbor visits distant lands.

$\exists y(\forall x[\text{Neighbor}'^{m}(x) \leftrightarrow x=y] \wedge \text{VDL}'^{m}(y)$

(18) *Simple model for assertion*

w1:	*w2:*	*w3:*
Neighbor$'^{R}$(d)	Neighbor$'^{R}$(b)	Neighbor$'^{R}$(e)
Neighbor$'^{m}$(c)	Neighbor$'^{m}$(e)	Neighbor$'^{m}$(e)
VDL$'^{R/m}$(c)	VDL$'^{R/m}$(e)	VDL$'^{R/m}$(c)
VDL$'^{R/m}$(e)	VDL$'^{R/m}$(d)	VDL$'^{R/m}$(d)

Notice that in reality, as represented by the R p-index, the statement is false. That is, the real neighbor is Dan who does not travel at w1. However, Megan made the assertion based on her mistaken belief that Cal is the neighbor and so the statement is true from her point of view. I think this is a fair account of what happens when a speaker unintentionally says something false. At least one of their terms does not have the same referent as reality. Like in the martini example, if the audience recognizes that the speaker does not match reality, then the utterance is successful even though in error.

So, except for lying, all statements are true from the speaker's point of view. With the speaker as the default p-index, an assertion of X is interpreted to mean something like *I believe that X*, which is trivially true.

In order to get truth conditions, we must both have a truth standard, the R, and invoke a Gricean maxim of quality: do not say what you believe to be false. This pragmatic principle commits the speaker to matching her description to the reality. Since we expect the speaker to be responsible for the truth of the utterance, we can take the default point of view to be the reality, R. Now we are not required to include the speaker in the model.

Notice that R represents what was in the model before I added the p-index. So, any sentence which has only default p-indices is interpreted in the standard Montagovian style. For instance, a belief sentence which does not have any p-indices set to the believer will have the classical de re reading.

I want to point out that no parallel line of reasoning will reduce the attitude subject's point of view to the reality. First, the subject cannot be held directly accountable for the description because she is not present. Second, the speaker is not held accountable on the subject's behalf. There is no burden on the speaker to choose only subject descriptions which match reality. In fact, the function of an attitude report may be just the opposite. By ascribing a proposition to someone else, the speaker is absolved of responsibility. That is, an obvious reason for choosing to utter (3) rather than (4) is that one is not committed to the truth of (4).

7. Substitution of equivalents

Now I want to turn to implications and consequences of the p-index for other phenomena. First, an obvious question is how the substitution of equals into attitude expressions is affected. That propositional attitudes do not preserve truth under this operation is an ancient problem.

A model which includes p-indices has an additional parameter with which to define the right sort of equivalence. However, p-indices do not in general provide a solution to the problem, for reasons which have been noted by (Partee 1979). Basically, if we relativize intensional meaning to each individual, there is no way to assert that people share an attitude.

I want to talk about extensional meaning only. Consider the inference of (19)c given a,b. The substitution is valid only when equivalence obtains at the same p-index. So, for the standard de re reading, the inference is valid because all the noun phrases are from the same point of view, as indicated by the superscripted R p-index in (20). For the de re2 reading in (21), the inference is not valid. In (21)a, the description is from Ann's point of view. But the statement (21)b cannot possibly be from Ann's point of view. It does not occur in the right configuration to have a non-default p-index. Even though (21)b is a fact about someone, the descriptions in a,c do not necessarily refer to the same someone under the de re2 reading.

(19) a. Ann believes that the neighbor jogs.

    b. The neighbor is the mayor.

    c. Ann believes that the mayor jogs.

(20) a. [Ann believes that the neighbor^R jogs.]

    b. [The neighbor^R is the mayor^R.]

    c. $\Rightarrow$[Ann believes that the mayor^R jogs.]

(21) a. [Ann believes that the neighbor^a jogs.]

    b. [The neighbor^R is the mayor^R.]

    c. $\not\Rightarrow$[Ann believes that the mayor^a jogs.]

    c'.$\not\Rightarrow$[Ann believes that the mayor^R jogs.]

(22) a. [Beth insists that Cal is not the neighbor^b.]

    b. [Cal is the neighbor^R.]

    c. $\Rightarrow$[Beth insists that the neighbor^R is not the neighbor^b.]

Now consider an inference like (22). In this case, we attribute a seemingly illogical insistence to Beth by using the same description with two distinct p-indices. Such sentences do occur in describing situations of mistaken identity like that in the previous section. Given the proper context, we can use the sentence (22)c to express Beth's mistake.

8. Evaluatives

Now I will consider some constructions which are speaker centered and how the notion of p-indices can accommodate them. First, consider evaluative statements such as (23). (Kuno 1987) notes that such expressions are attributable to a self entity, and (Sells 1987) makes use of this as a diagnostic for the referent of discourse roles. The p-index makes this attribution explicit. With the account given so far, the only possible p-index is R. But there is no meaning of *nifty* in the reality which the speaker is taking responsibility for matching. Instead, this kind of expression conveys an inherently subjective idea.

(23) The neighbor^R is nifty^m.

(24) Joe realizes the neighbor is nifty.

The definition of the default point of view could be extended naturally to give the right results for this sentence. These predicates would have an undefined extension for the R p-index. So, for these predicates, the default point of view would be the speaker. Consequently, the speaker becomes part of the model when she gives evaluations. Now the default point of view is the R or, when undefined, the speaker.

Within an attitude context, this account would predict that an evaluative ambiguity would arise. And it does. In (24), the evaluation can be due either to Joe or to the speaker. That is, Joe may have actually used the word *nifty* in speaking of the neighbor. Or he may have expressed beliefs about the neighbor which include characteristics the speaker takes to be nifty. The grammar fragment already given will provide both readings via two distinct p-index settings.

9. Center of deixis

Finally, consider the phenomenon of center of deixis. The lexical choice between *go* and *come* involves location of the speaker, either physically or in a more abstract sense. Imagine Dan calling up Eve, who is not home. Beth answers the phone and tells him that Eve was home after work but then went out again. In a simple assertion of this fact, Dan is constrained in his lexical choice as shown in (25). He can say *Eve went home* but not *Eve came home* because he is not there at Eve's house.

(25) Eve went/*came home.

(26) a. Beth believes that Eve came home.

b. **Believe'^{R}**(b, ^**Came**^{b}(e,Home))

(27) a. Beth believes that Eve went home.

b. **Believe'^{R}**(b, ^**Went**^{R}(e,Home))

However, if he reports the fact as Beth's belief, he may choose either lexical item. This can be accounted for as a p-index ambiguity. In (26), *came* is ascribed to Beth. In

(27), on the other hand, *went* is ascribed to Dan, the speaker.

To summarize, I have tried to establish the validity of a p-index based on facts about definite referring noun phrases in propositional attitudes. Other work on the semantics of self-knowledge and logophoric pronominals also supports such a view. The p-index may also be applied to other speaker-centered phenomena, and serves to describe their ambiguity within the attitudes.

References

Cresswell, M.J. 1985. **Structured Meanings.** Cambridge:MIT Press.

Dowty, D., R. Wall and S. Peters. 1981. **Introduction to Montague Semantics,** Dordecht:Reidel.

Kuno, S. 1987. **Functional Syntax.** Chicago:The University of Chicago Press.

Lewis, D. 1979. *Attitudes De Dicto and De Se.* **The Philosophical Review.** 88:4. 513-544.

Montague, R. 1973. *The proper treatment of quantification in ordinary English.* **Approaches to Natural Language: Proceedings fo the 1970 Stanford Workshop on Grammar and Semantics,** ed. by J. Hintikka et al., 221-242. Dordecht:Reidel.

Partee, B. 1979. *Semantics-- Mathematics or Psychology?* **Semantics from Different Points of View,** ed. by R. Bäuerle et al., 1-14. Springer-Verlag:Berlin.

Partee, B. and E. Bach. 1981. *Quantification, pronouns and VP anaphora.* **Formal Methods in the Study of Language,** part 2, ed. by J.A.G. Groenendijk et al, 445-482. Amsterdam:Mathematisch Centrum.

Perry, J. 1979. *The Problem of the Essential Indexical.* Noûs 13. 3-21.

Sells, P. 1987. *Aspects of Logophoricity.* **Linguistic Inquiry.**

(In)definiteness in the Absence of Articles:
Evidence from Hindi and Indonesian*

Leslie Porterfield and Veneeta Srivastav
Cornell University

Discourse Representation Theory treats definite and indefinite noun phrases as variables that differ in their relation to discourse entities: definites presuppose a referent while indefinites introduce one. In Heim (1982) this distinction is formalised in the conditions that check the felicity of utterances. Sentences are evaluated with respect to files; the Novelty Familiarity Condition requires every definite NP to bear an index familiar to the file and every indefinite to have an index novel to it. On the basis of this distinction the interpretation rules derive the different behavior of definite and indefinite variables in quantified structures.

Heim's discussion is concerned with the semantics of singular NPs in English, a language in which definiteness is identifiable through the articles a and the. There are many languages, however, which do not have articles and allow bare singular NPs. For a theory that relies so heavily on the familiar-novel distinction, it is pertinent to ask what the status of such NPs would be. Heim suggests that they may be either definite or indefinite or even ambiguous (1982:229). In this paper we present evidence from Hindi and Indonesian, two unrelated languages, to argue against the ambiguity hypothesis.

What would it mean, in terms of DRT, for an NP to have both + and - values for definiteness ? The way the felicity conditions are defined, it would follow that such NPs could never be infelicitous, modulo pragmatic plausability. Potentially two readings should be possible. Under one interpretation (the definite one) the NP would bear an old index and behave like any other definite, under another interpretation it would bear a new index and behave like any other indefinite. Thus, there would always be at least one felicitous reading and in many cases two. In essence, then, the felicity conditions would not apply. The theory predicts a total lack of definiteness effects with respect to such NPs. However, the difference between given and new information, which the felicity conditions are supposed to formalise, is an important principle of language organization. As such, to the extent that a theory relies on a feature such as definiteness in the interpretation of NPs, we claim, that feature should be obligatorily and uniquely specified in all languages.

We shall argue that the ambiguity hypothesis makes the wrong predictions for Hindi and Indonesian. The Hindi bare NP appears to have two functions: it is a referential definite and a generic. The Indonesian bare NP, which at first glance appears to be indefinite, turns out to have only a generic reading.[1] The generic character of bare NPs in both languages is to be analyzed, we propose, in terms of reference to kinds, following Carlson (1977). In the course of our analysis we will also discuss an interesting subject-object asymmetry that both languages display.

Let us now turn to a discussion of the Hindi facts.[2] The behavior of bare singular NPs in Hindi is represented in (1) and (2). In (1) the indefinite [a movie] introduces a discourse referent to which the following bare NP [movie] is anaphoric. It cannot have an interpretation in which it refers to another movie, as the indices indicate.

(1) kal   mẼne **ek film**₁ dekhi: **film**₁/*₂ bahut acchi: thi:
     yesterday I   one movie saw. movie   very good was

"Yesterday I saw a movie. The movie was very good."

(2) is a presentational type sentence that introduces the location and the main character of a story. As such, it presupposes the non-familiarity of such entities, and in fact, the bare NPs are inappropriate here.

(2) *bahut din pahle, **desh-mẽ**₁ **ra:ja:**₂ rahta: tha:
     many days back, country-in king   lived

"A long time ago, in some country there lived a king."

The above suggests that the bare NP is +definite. We expect, then, that in a pragmatically neutral context it should behave like the definite behaves in English. (3) is a discourse in which we could either have a definite in sentence (d) or an indefinite.

(3) (a) Yesterday, I witnessed a bizarre scene in the lounge, involving
         some people.
     (b) A man₁ was wearing a skirt;
     (c) a woman₂ was singing;
     (d) **a man**₃ / **the man**₁ was listening to her and
     (e) another man₄ was standing on the table.

If we look at the Hindi counterpart of this discourse, given in (3'), we can see that the bare NP indeed behaves like the English definite. Thus [man] in sentence (d) refers anaphorically to the referent introduced in sentence (b). If a disjoint reading is required an indefinite has to be used.

(3') (a) kal,   la:unj-mẽ   mẼne ek aji:b   drishya dekha:
          yesterday, in the louge I   a strange scene   saw

          wahã: kuch log   the
          there some people were

      (b) ek a:dmi:₁ sa:Ri: pahne tha:
          one man   sari   was wearing

      (c) ek Orat₂   ga:na: ga: rahi: thi:
          one woman was singing

      (d) **ek a:dmi:**₃/**admi:**₁ ga:na: sun raha: tha: Or
          one man   man   song was listening and

      (e) ek Or a:dmi:₄ tebal par kha:Ra: tha:
          another man   table on was standing

Thus it seems clear that Hindi bare NPs are definite, which in Heim's theory means that their index must already be present in the file.

The data so far provide evidence that the Hindi bare singular is analogous to the English definite NP. But there are two kinds of possible counterexamples. Bare NPs seem to be universally bound in the antecedent of conditionals, and they seem to be in variation with the indefinite in object position. In what follows we would like to show that these instances can be systematically linked to genericity. We claim that the Hindi bare singular NP has a second meaning which refers to 'kind'. This is illustrated in (4):

(4) **a:dmi: Orat**-se   ta:katwar hE
     man   woman-than strong   is

     "The man is stronger than the woman."
     "Man is stronger than woman."

(4) has two readings, one is the definite referential reading, which presupposes the existence of a uniquely salient man and woman; the other is the generic, which relates men and women as a class rather than as specific individuals. It seems clear, then, that the bare NP is also generic. But what kind of a generic is it and what is its connection with definiteness ?

A distinction that we think is relevant was made in recent work by Manfred Krifka. Building on the work of Heim and Carlson, Krifka distinguishes between indefinite generics (I-generics) and definite generics (D-generics). I-generics are the generic counterparts of indefinites, as illustrated in (5):

(5) (a) A dog barks   (if it is hungry).
     (b) I like a good cup of coffee.

Krifka analyses these as unselectively bound variables. Prototypical D-generics are generic uses of the definite article, as illustrated in (6):

(6) (a) The dodo is extinct.
     (b) In Alaska Bill photographed the grizzly.

Krifka suggests that these are names of kinds. He proposes further, that English bare plurals have both an I-generic and a D-generic reading. While we do not know whether this is the right analysis, we will use Krifka's distinction as descriptive labels and note that the Hindi bare NP appears to behave like a D-generic.

Our first diagnostic shows the behavior of generics in the antecedent of a conditional. The English definite generic in (7) gets a universal reading only when the tense is generic.

(7) (a) If **the child** has a toy, (s)he is happy. (universal)
     (b) Yesterday, whenever **the child** had a toy, (s)he was happy.
         (not universal)

This contrasts with the way English bare plurals behave, as illustrated in (8). Here the sentences get a universal interpretation despite the tense.

(8) (a) If **dogs** are hungry, they bark. (universal)
     (b) Yesterday, whenever **dogs** felt hungry, they barked.
                                                    (universal)

The Hindi bare NP in (9) is like the English definite generic in that it can be universally bound only when the tense is generic; when the tense is episodic, it behaves like a referential definite.

(9) (a) agar **bacce**-ke pa:s **khilOna** ho,   to   wo khush rahta: hai
         if   child-with   toy   have, then he   happy remains

     "If a child has a toy, he is happy" (universal)

     (b) kal   ek-se do ke-bi:ch-mẽ jabbhi: **chor ghar**-mẽ ghusa:
         yesterday one two between   whenever thief house-in entered

         pulis-ne   us-ko parkaR liya:
         police   him   caught

     "Yesterday, between one and two, whenever the thief entered the house, the police caught him." (not universal)

The only possible reading of (9b) is an anomalous one where a particular thief entered a particular house several times and was caught by the police (presumably, each time the thief was caught, he was released). While we do not at present have an explanation for this phenomenon, it is clear that the universal reading of the bare NPs in (9a) does not require us to posit a - definite feature specification. Rather, it calls for a closer examination of the relations between definite and indefinite generics.

A second property that the Hindi generic shares with the English definite generic has to do with the notion of <u>natural kinds</u>. Carlson notes that English bare plurals tolerate reference to any kind whatsoever while <u>the</u> - generics are more restricted. Consider (10):

(10) (a) John photographed the grizzly.
      (b) John photographed fat ugly grizzlies.
      (c) ?? John photographed the fat ugly grizzly.

While the definite in (a) and the bare plural in (b) can receive kind readings, it is difficult to give such an interpretation to the definite generic in (c).

The generic use of the Hindi bare NP is similarly constrained, as we see in (11):

(11) (a) wo **da:kTar** / **ek da:kTar** se sha:di: kar rahi: hE
          she doctor   / a doctor with   marriage is doing

      "She is marrying a doctor."

      (b)wo ***Ø/ ek lambe, gari:b da:kTar** se sha:di: kar rahi: hE
          she *Ø / one tall,   poor doctor with marriage is doing

      "She is marrying a tall, poor doctor."

In (11b) the bare NP can only be used if it refers to somebody whose existence is presupposed, i.e. if it is used as a referential definite. When it refers to a kind, the bare NP is not an option since the properties tall and poor are not the natural properties of the kind doctor.

So it seems that bare NPs in Hindi are either definites or kind-level D-generics.

So far we have considered occurences of kind-level NPs in generic sentences. If we look at what happens to them in episodic sentences, we notice an interesting asymmetry. In object position they are perfectly felicitous, as in (12):

(12) jOn   Or meri: **kita:b** paRh rahe hẼ
      John and Mary   book   are reading

      "John and Mary are reading one or more book(s)"

Here we see that the bare NP does not have any essential quantification. We can either have one book or more. The quantification is inferred, much as in the case of English bare plurals, depending on pragmatic factors.

By contrast, for bare NPs in subject position, only the definite reading is possible, as shown in (13):[3]

(13) kal   **a:dmi:** chiTThi: laya: tha:
      yesterday man   letter   brought

      "Yesterday, the man brought letters."
      *"Yesterday, a man brought letters."

This is similar to what happens, to a limited extent, in English:

(14) (a) Jack photographed the lion in Africa.
      (b) The lion appeared suddenly.

The most natural interpretation of the definite in (14a) is that of a representative of the class of lions. In (14b), however, it must refer to a contextually defined unique individual lion. We will see later, that this subject-object asymmetry also exists in Indonesian.

How is this range of facts to be analyzed? We propose an explanation along the following lines. Let us assume that relations are analyzed as functions from entities into one-place predicates. So for instance, read maps x into the property of reading x. These functions can take both individuals and kinds.[4] Thus consider sentence (15):

(15) jOn **kita:b** paRh raha: hE
      John book   is reading

      "John is reading a book."

This sentence is ambiguous, due to the ambiguity of 'book'.[5] If book is an individual-level referential NP, the VP in (15) has the logical form:

(15) (a) [read (x)] (j)

(15a) says that j has the property of reading x, felicity here is dependent upon x being the variable associated with a familiar book, following Heim. The second reading of (15) ensues if we take book to be a kind-level NP. In such a case we get:

(15) (b) [read (B)] (j)

(15b) attributes to j the property of book-reading; he may be reading one or more book(s).   Thus 15 (a) and (b) would have distinct DRSs:

(15) (a)
```
| u=john    |
| x         |
| book(x)   |
| read(u,x) |
```

(15) (b)
```
| u=john    |
|           |
| read(u,B) |
```

To account for the ungrammaticality of (13), under the generic reading, we assume that predicates (unlike functions from entities into predicates) are sorted as to the type of arguments they can take. When the tense is non-generic, predicates take individuals as arguments. Thus, [bring(x)] in (13), like [read(x)] above, is an individual-level predicate and infelicity arises when it is predicated of an argument which refers to a kind. When the tense is generic predicates are able to take kind-level arguments due to the presence of a generic operator. Thus the logical form and DRS associated with a generic sentence like (4) would be the following, where man, a kind-level term, is an appropriate argument:

(4') [stronger-than (W)]$_{Gn}$ (M)   stronger-than (M,W)

This analysis of the subject-object asymmetry in (12) and (13) has a further consequence of interest with respect to anaphora. In Hindi anaphora to a kind-level NP is possible but less natural than anaphora to individual-level NPs. Thus, if (11a) were to be continued with a description of the doctor, it would be more likely to have an overt indefinite rather than a bare NP in the first sentence:

(11) (a') wo ? **da:kTar / ek dakTar** se sha:di: kar rahi: hE
            she   doctor / a doctor with marriage is doing

            uska: na:m ravi: hE
            his   name ravi is

            "She is marrying a doctor. His name is Ravi."

This is explained under our assumption that only individual-level NPs (referential indefinites) introduce discourse referents; for a kind-level NP a semantic operation is required to produce an individual-level realization, which can then be represented on a file card and be accessible for anaphora. Thus to the extent that anaphora to a kind-denoting NP is at all possible, it is the result of accommodation and therefore less natural than anaphora to a referential indefinite.

In a sentence like (16), accommodation is complicated by the fact that the set of people reading has many members and we are likely to infer that there are many books. And anaphora is, indeed, impossible:

(16) *ravi:, va:ni: Or shi:la: **kita:b** paRh rahe h$\tilde{\text{E}}$ **we** acchi: h$\tilde{\text{E}}$
       Ravi, Vani and Shila book are reading. They good are

       "Ravi, Vani, and Shila are reading book(s). They are good."

x=ravi:
y=va:ni:
z=shi:la:
read (x & y & z, B)   read (x,b) & read (y,b) & read (z,b)

The present analysis predicts the marginal status of (11a') and the ungrammaticality of (16), since we are claiming that anaphora to bare NP is possible only by resorting to some kind of accommodation that introduces discourse referents by an inferential process of some sort.

To sum up the Hindi facts, we can be sure that the Hindi bare NP is a referential definite as shown by (1) through (3). We have also shown, in (4) through (16), that it is a kind-denoting term that does not presuppose a discourse referent. In object position, it is possible to interpret it as an indefinite but facts about quantification and anaphora show that it does not introduce an individual-level discourse referent. We see no way in which a theory that assumes a bare NP to be ambiguous between + and - definite could account for the array of facts presented above.

Now let us consider the Indonesian data.[6] Indonesian also has bare singular NPs. The question we must ask is whether the bare NP is definite or indefinite. If we look at (17) and (18) we are inclined to call it indefinite:

(17) Saya melihat **pohon**.
       I   see   tree

       "I see a tree."   *"I see the tree."
(18) *Seekor anjing₁ masuk. **Anjing** ₁ berbaring di bawah meja.
       one-clf dog   enter   Dog   lie down below   table

       "A dog came in. The dog lay down under a table."

In (17) the bare NP does not refer to any particular tree and in (18) it cannot be anaphorically related to a previously introduced discourse referent, i.e. it cannot bear a familiar index. Further, it also occurs in presentational contexts i.e. with the predicate <u>ada</u> in (19):

(19) Ada   **anjing** di luar.
       There is dog   outside

       "There is a dog outside."

However, there are two problems with claiming that the bare NP is indefinite. The first concerns the fact that bare NPs are used to refer to unique entities--exactly the kind of thing for which English uses the definite article. So in (20) the interpretation of <u>presiden</u> is <u>the President</u>. This has to be a familiar referent:

(20) **Presiden** mau datang.
President want come

"The President will come."

And in (21) <u>matahari</u> refers to the unique entity, the sun. Since it is a part of our perceptual world, it is represented at the topmost level of the file and is therefore familiar:

(21) Saya melihat **matahari**.
I see sun

"I see the sun."

The second problem concerns the fact that bare NPs cannot occur with an indefinite reading in subject position. Thus (22) is ungrammatical:

(22) ***Anjing** masuk.
Dog enter

"A dog entered."

(22) is only acceptable when <u>dog</u> is preceded by a classifier, i.e. when the subject is clearly an indefinite. However, there is nothing in the theory of indefiniteness that predicts such a difference.

In light of these facts we cannot claim that the Indonesian bare NP is indefinite or ambiguous. The account that we propose here is that it is only a generic, i.e. it names a kind just as the bare NP in Hindi does. This claim is substantiated by the fact that it occurs in generic sentences such as (23):

(23) (a) **Beruang** suka **ikan**.
Bear like fish

"Bears like fish."

(b) **Anjing** makan **tulang**.
Dog eat bone

"Dogs eat bones."

The contrast between (22) and (23) follows from the fact that predicates are sorted with respect to the level of arguments they may take. [Entered] in (22) is sorted to take an individual-level argument such as [seekor anjing] while the predicates in (23) take kind-level NPs such as [beruang] and [anjing]. The sentences become ungrammatical when the argument is of the wrong type.

Given the present approach to generics, the reading in (17) need no longer be taken as evidence of a referent-introducing indefinite. The indefinite quantification could be inferred, just as we have argued for Hindi examples like (12). In fact, given these facts about the behavior of generic NPs in Hindi and Indonesian, it seems to be an open question at this point whether bare NPs in any language are indefinite in the specific sense defined above.

Treating the Indonesian bare NP as generic predicts differences in the quantificational forces of bare NPs and classifier NPs in object positions. Consider (24):

(24)   John dan Mary membaca **buku** /sebuah buku.
      John and Mary read   book/ clf   book

   "John and Mary are reading one or more book(s)/ a book."

The sentence will have the DRS in (24a) if the bare NP is used and the DRS in (24b) if the Classifier NP is used:

(24)   (a)

$$x=j$$
$$y=m$$
$$read(\ x\ \&\ y,\ B)$$

(b)

$$x=j$$
$$y=m$$
$$z$$
$$book(z)$$
$$read(\ x\ \&\ y,\ z)$$

It does not follow from (24a) that John and Mary are reading the same book, but in (24b) the introduction of a discourse referent with the descriptive content book entails that they must be reading the same book. This is indeed true. One is a case of inferred quantification while the other is a case of variable binding. These facts are representative of the different behavior of bare and classifier NPs in the language. (25) is another example of the same phenomenon:

(25)   Saya mendengar **anjing** / seekor anjing menggonggong.
      I   hear   dog   / clf   dog   bark

   "I hear one or more dog(s)/ a dog barking."

The different readings, we have shown, arise from different representations.

Treating the bare NP as generic seems to explain some rather troubling facts in the language but how does this account deal with the problematic cases in (20) and (21) ? In these sentences an individual-level predicate seems to be predicated of a kind-denoting term. Recall, however, that this only happens when the common noun names a kind that is uniquely instantiated at the individual-level. Clearly, some kind of a type-shifting operation is involved. A natural formulation of this operation would be in terms akin to Partee's (1984) "iota" function. In rough terms, $f_\iota(X)$, where X is a kind, will yield the unique individual that instantiates X. We assume that f_ι is a freely available option that comes into play whenever the standard interpretation process is blocked. In (20), for example, function application is blocked since the predicate requires an individual-level term but the argument denotes a kind. $f_\uparrow$ allows for an individual-level interpretation of the argument:

(20') [will come] $(f_\uparrow(P))$ The president will come.

While $f_\uparrow$ is always available, it becomes vacuous when the set denoted has more than one member. In (22), for example, the predicate [entered] is sorted to take an individual, but the argument names a kind. Even though the type shifting rule applies, since the kind dog is not uniquely instantiated, $f_\uparrow(D)$ is undefined. The sentence remains uninterpretable.

This type-matching is a restriction on predicate-argument structure and not on thematic roles. Consider the active-passive pairs in (26):

(26)   (a) **Seekor anjing** /*anjing menggigit kaki saya.
          Clf dog   / dog   bite   leg   I

       "A dog bit my leg."

     (b) Kaki saya digigit   **seekor anjing/ anjing**.
          Leg   I   was bitten clf dog   / dog

       "My leg was bitten by a dog."

Since the agent is internal to the VP in the passive, it is felicitous as a bare NP. As we have already seen, an individual-level referent is not crucial for VP interpretation. However, since the predicate is sorted to take only individual-level arguments, the subject has to be of the right type, i.e. an individual-level entity, whether it is active or passive.

To sum up, we have shown that the bare singular NP in Hindi is an individual-level definite and a kind-level generic. The bare NP in Indonesian is only a generic. Kind-denoting NPs do not have any essential quantification since they do not introduce individual-level referents into the discourse. Anaphora is sensitive to this. Further, the subject-object asymmetry displayed by generic NPs is explained by recognizing that predicates are sorted with respect to the level of argument they can take. On the basis of the data we have looked at we suggest that bare singular NPs are never ambiguous. The ambiguity perceived in their interpretation has to do with genericity and the semantic operations involved in shifting from kind-level to individual-level entities. The data we have analyzed here strongly argue for the need to combine a Kamp-Heim style theory of (In)definiteness with a Carlson-style theory of generics.

Notes

* We are very grateful to Gennaro Chierchia for his crucial help at every stage in the preparation of this paper. We would also like to thank Gita Martohardjono for important discussion of the Indonesian data, and Fred Landman for clarification of related issues in DRT. We alone are responsible for any errors that remain.

1 The observation that bare NPs have generic functions has been made before, for example by Verma (1971) for Hindi and by Dardjowidjojo (1983) for Indonesian.

2 Overt definites in Hindi are marked by the demonstrative wo "that". Indefinites are preceded by the numeral ek "one". When unstressed it is akin to "a", when stressed to "one".

3 There is a possible "indefinite" reading of this sentence. In a situation where the speaker knows that mail is brought by people of both sexes, (13) could be used to assert that yesterday the mail was brought by a man (as opposed to a woman). A more accurate translation would be "It was a man who brought the mail". The sentence still presupposes the existence of a discourse referent. We consider such readings to be related to the issue of focus. An analysis of such focus related interpetations is beyond the scope of this paper.

4 Our use of "individual-level" corresponds to Carlson's "object-level". We do this to avoid confusion between the object-level term and the syntactic object position.

5 The generic reading is more prominent, though the referential reading is also available. Intonation helps in disambiguating the sentence. Pending an analysis of focus, we treat the bare NP here as representing simple ambiguity.

6 Overt definites in Indonesian are marked by the demonstrative itu "that" or by the morpheme -nya. Overt indefinites are preceded by classifiers.

References

Carlson, G. 1977. Reference to kinds in English. Doctoral dissertation, University of Massachusetts, Amherst.

Dardjowidjojo, S. 1983. Beberapa aspek linguistik Indonesia. Jakarta: Djambatan

Heim, I. 1982. The Semantics of Definite and Indefinite Noun Phrases. Doctoral dissertation, University of Massachusetts, Amherst.

Kamp, H. 1981. A theory of truth and semantic representation in Truth, interpretation and information: selected papers from the third Amsterdam colloquium, 1984 ed. by J. Groenendijk, T.Janssen and M. Stokhof. Dordrecht: Foris Publications

Krifka, M. 1987. A typology of generics. University of Tuebingen Ms.

Partee, B. 1984. NP interpretation and type-shifting principles. Paper presented at the fifth Amsterdam conference on formal semantics.

Verma, M.K. 1971. The Structure of the Noun Phrase in English and Hindi. Delhi: Motilal Banarasidas.

The Representation of Prenasalized Consonants*

Sam Rosenthall
McGill University

0. Introduction

This paper investigates the representation of prenasalized consonants in the feature hierarchy framework introduced by Clements (1985). Sagey (1986) proposes that prenasalized consonants have the representation shown in (1).

(1) Prenasalized consonants (Sagey 1986)

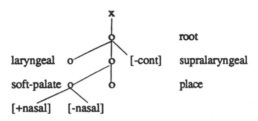

The following facts concerning Sagey's representation are interesting: 1. prenasalized consonants have one root node, and 2. the features [+nasal] and [-nasal] dominated by a single soft-palate node represent the fact that prenasalized consonants consist of a nasal and an oral segment. Furthermore, Sagey proposes that affricates, which also consist of two segments, are represented by the features [-cont] and [+cont] dominated by the same root node. Prenasalized consonants and affricates (called contour segments) are subject to the following restriction.

(2)   Contour segments may branch for terminal features only.
       No branching class nodes are allowed. (Sagey 1986:50)

This paper shows that Sagey's representation of prenasalized consonants and the restriction on contour segments cannot be correct. This paper claims that class nodes are allowed to branch provided a certain condition on representation is satisfied. Furthermore, prenasalized consonants are shown to be represented as one skeletal point dominating two root nodes. The condition on representation and the representation of prenasalized consonants are based on the hierarchical arrangement of features proposed in section 1. A two root node representation of prenasalized consonants and the theory of underspecification in Archangeli (1984), Archangeli and Pulleyblank (1986) and Steriade (1987) are used to account for post-nasal voicing, post-nasal hardening, nasal deletion, and coalescence which occur in situations where prenasalization is expected (henceforth prenasalization environments).

This paper is in four sections: 1. the hierarchical arrangement of features, 2. the evidence for a two root node representation of prenasalized consonants, 3. the condition on representation, and 4. an account of the phenomena in prenasalization environments.

1. Feature Geometry

The hierarchical arrangement of features proposed here is based on the hierarchies given in Archangeli and Pulleyblank (1986) (henceforth A&P), Clements (1985), Piggott (1987), Sagey (1986), and Schein and Steriade (1986).

Clements and A&P show the supralaryngeal node dominating the features [cont], [son], [nasal], and [strident], but no features are directly linked to the root node. Sagey and Schein and Steriade have [cont], [strident], and [son][1] linked directly to the root node and the supralaryngeal node (the soft-palate node in Sagey) dominating [nasal]. Piggott (1987) argues [nasal] must be linked directly to the root node to account for nasal stability phenomena. The feature hierarchy proposed here has the root node dominating [nasal] and [son] (also [cons] and [vocalic][2]) and the supralaryngeal node dominating [cont] and [strident].

(3) Proposed hierarchy (relevant features above the place node[3])

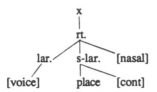

The feature hierarchy in (3) is consistent with other proposals in the literature. Furthermore, Sagey (1986) admits the precise positioning of the major class features seems to be irrelevant. Therefore, the hierarchical arrangement here does not entail the loss of any generalizations based on previous proposals.

2. Evidence for Two Root Nodes

There is nothing inherent in the hierarchy in (3) that prohibits Sagey's hypothesis concerning contour segments. The values [+nasal] and [-nasal] of a prenasalized consonant can both link directly to the root node.

(4)
```
        x
        |
        rt.
       / \
 [+nasal]  [-nasal]
```

The alternative to Sagey's hypothesis is to propose there are two root nodes dominated by one skeletal point. Each root node then dominates one specification for [nasal].

(5)

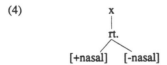

There are empirical and conceptual reasons for preferring the representation in (5) rather than (4). The empirical evidence is provided by compensatory lengthening and interaction with syllabification and the conceptual evidence is provided by the theory of autosegmental spreading.

2.1 Compensatory Lengthening

Many languages have a process by which a vowel becomes long when followed by a prenasalized consonant. Clements (1985a) and Sagey (1985) account for this process in Luganda and Kinyarwanda, respectively, by proposing there is a rule of prenasalization which delinks the nasal from its skeletal point (C-slot in Clements) and attaches the segment to the obstruent's skeletal point. The skeletal point which had been previously linked to the nasal is now linked to the vowel thus producing a long vowel.

(6) Luganda (adapted from Clements 1986) /mu+ ntu/ --> [muu^{n}tu]

```
x  x  x  x  x        x  x x x  x
|  |  |  |  |         |  V/\  |
m  u  n  t  u   -->  m  unt  u
```

Clements' account of compensatory lengthening crucially depends upon the fact that the nasal segment is associated with a skeletal point. For the nasal to have an independent skeletal point, the nasal must also have a root node to which the skeletal point can attach. Therefore, the delinking and relinking of the nasal to the skeleton must involve the root node, hence the prenasalized stop [^{n}t] is derived from two root nodes attached to a single skeletal point.

2.2 Sinhalese Syllabification

Prenasalized stops in Sinhalese alternate with a corresponding nasal-stop cluster.

(7) Sinhalese (Feinstein 1979)

	singular	plural	root	gloss
a.	kandə	ka^{n}du	kandw	hill
b.	hombə	ho^{m}bu	hombw	chin

Feinstein (1979) claims the prenasalized stop in the plural is derived from an underlying nasal-stop cluster. Since the prenasalized stop is phonemically a cluster, the two discrete segments must have independent root nodes.

The rule of prenasaliztion in Feinstein (1979) is somewhat antiquated and is replaced by the process discussed in Rosenthall (1988). According to Rosenthall (1988), the obstruents /d/ and /b/ in the roots of /kandw/ and /hombw/, respectively, are not underlyingly associated with a skeletal point. Prenasalization is the result of linking the obstruent to the skeletal point dominating the nasal during plural formation.

The proposed underlying representation of /kandw/ and /hombw/ is consistent with other aspects of Sinhalese phonology. There is an alternation between single and geminate consonants in the plural and singular.

(8) Gemination (Feinstein 1979)

	singular	plural	root	gloss
a.	pottə	potu	potw	core
b.	reddə	redu	redw	cloth

The prenasalized consonants of the plurals in (7) and the simple segments in the plurals in (8) are one segment with respect to the skeletal tier. The patterning of geminates and nasal-stop clusters is expected since Schein and Steriade (1986) argue that nasal-stop clusters are quasi-geminates because they can behave as geminates, e.g. with respect to inalterability. Given a theory of Sinhalese singular formation based on gemination (Rosenthall 1988), it is expected that the prenasalized consonants in the plurals of (7) should geminate as ^{N}C^{N}C, but this does not occur.

(9) C ≈ CC

N_C ≈ NC

≈ *$N_C N_C$

If prenasalized consonants have one root node, then $N_C N_C$ sequences would be predicted. In fact, prenasalized consonants never geminate as $N_C N_C$ (Herbert 1986). The nasal-stop cluster in the singular is predicted by the representation of the singular morpheme -*a* given in Rosenthall (1988). The singular morpheme introduces a skeletal point that must link to the root node tier in accordance with one-to-one, left-to-right association. Since the post-nasal obstruents in the roots of (7) are not associated with a skeletal point, these segments will associate with the introduced skeletal point. The obstruents /t/ and /d/ of /potw/ and /redw/, respectively, are underlyingly linked to skeletal points but also link to the introduced point hence forming a geminate.

(10)

An account of prenasalization in Sinhalese which is consistent with other aspects of Sinhalese phonology is possible only when prenasalized consonants are represented as two root nodes. The single root node analysis cannot account for the behaviour of prenasalized consonants with respect to clusters and in gemination environments.

2.3 Autosegmental Spreading

The representation of prenasalized stops in Sagey (1986) is partially motivated by the interaction of prenasalization and nasal spreading. Consider the derivation of prenasalization in Guarani taken from Goldsmith (1976) and thereafter repeated in Van der Hulst and Smith (1982) and Sagey (1986).

(11) Guarani (Van der Hulst and Smith 1982)

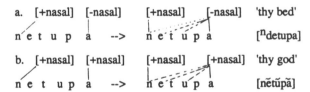

The traditional analysis of prenasalization in Guarani (and other languages in which prenasalization is a consequence of nasal spreading) is incompatible with the nature of autosegmental spreading. Consider the representation of autosegmental spreading shown in (12).

(12)

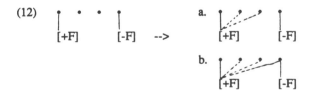

The structural description in (12) usually produces the autosegmental spreading shown in (12a), where the opposite value for the spreading feature blocks further spreading. Prenasalization in Guarani is considered to be the result of autosegmental spreading as shown in (12b). The problem with (12b) is that the opposite value of the spreading feature does not block spreading onto the opposite value segment. Furthermore, (12b) is used only for the spreading of [nasal] (and possibly [cont]). The fact that no other feature spreads as shown in (12b) exposes an inconsistency in the nature of autosegmental spreading. Any principled account of autosegmental spreading must be based on spreading as shown in (12a).

Piggott (1987a) proposes that autosegmental spreading is subject to the following constraints.

(13) Spreading Constraints (in part) (Piggott 1987a)
    a. the spreading of a [feature] (X) may spread
    only to a position not specified for X.
    b. the spreading of a [feature] (X) may be
    arrested only by a position specified for (X).

Piggott (1987a) reanalyzes Guarani so that a principled account of autosegmental spreading is used. Piggott proposes that the /n/ of the morpheme *no* is represented as one skeletal point dominating two root nodes, one of which (the leftmost) is specified as [+nasal] and the other (the rightmost) is not specified for nasality. The leftward spreading of nasality spreads to the unspecified root node creating a configuration where one skeletal point dominates two [+nasal] root nodes. The two identically specified root nodes are then reduced to one by the OCP. Prenasalization occurs as a consequence of the absence of nasal spreading: the oral stem does not spread. Therefore, the unspecified root node is specified as [-nasal] by redundant feature value insertion.

3. The Representation of Prenasalized Consonants

Having established that prenasalized consonants must be represented as one skeletal point dominating two root nodes and using the hierarchical arrangement of features proposed in section 1, prenasalized consonants have the following representation.

(14)

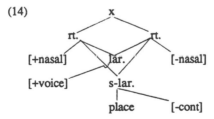

Sagey's (1986) objection to branching class nodes is motivated by the nonexistence of a constraint to limit possible contour segments. For example, if the root node can form a contour, then any two segments can be dominated by one skeletal point. It is possible to propose a restriction concerning possible contour segments using feature hierarchy given in section 1. Notice that the two root nodes are linked to the same set of subordinate nodes in the representation of prenasalized consonants in (14). This representation reflects the fact that the nasal and oral components of a prenasalized voiced stop (the least marked prenasalized consonant) must agree for place of articulation, voicing, and continuancy. The following condition on representation captures these phonetic agreements.

> (15) Contour Node Condition (CNC) (first approximation)
> Class nodes A and B on tier T form a contour when A and B dominate the same set of non-null subordinate class nodes.

The CNC ensures prenasalized stops agree for voicing, continuancy, and place of articulation. The CNC also predicts the following contour segments are possible.

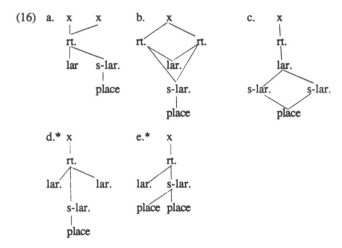

The CNC states that only class nodes may form contours, thus excluding the articulator nodes. The exclusion of the articulator nodes is not as stipulatory as it might appear. Sagey (1986) offers evidence for claiming a natural distinction between class nodes and articulator nodes.

(16a) is the representation of a geminate. The skeletal point is subject to the CNC although the skeleton is usually considered a node of syllable structure (Levin 1985 and Piggott and Singh 1985). A&P, however, have a class node called the "macro node" which is equivalent to the skeletal point. Furthermore, geminates by definition must dominate the same set of subordinate nodes therefore the representation naturally conforms to a condition such as the CNC. (16b) is the representation of prenasalized consonants as previously discussed and (16c) is the representation of affricates.

(16d and e) are ill-formed contours which are excluded by the CNC's requirement that the subordinate set of class nodes cannot be null. The laryngeal and place nodes are terminal class nodes hence do not dominate other class nodes.

Prenasalized affricates in Venda and Zande, for example, contradict the CNC.

(17)

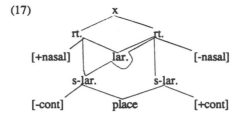

Although the [-nasal] root node dominates the same supralaryngeal node as the [+nasal] root node, the latter root node does not dominate the [+cont] supralaryngeal node. The CNC, on the other hand, correctly predicts the following contour segment is not possible.

(18)

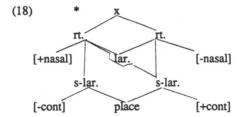

The [-nasal] root node in (18) does not dominate the [-cont] supralaryngeal node and such a segment is excluded by the CNC. However, (17) must be permitted, thus creating an asymmetry for which the CNC cannot account.

Paradis (1987), based on Kaye, Lowenstamm, and Vergnaud (1987), argues that the notion of headedness is relevant for geminate configurations. The right-hand skeletal point of a geminate is considered to be the head of the geminate.[4] The notion of headedness can be extended to other contour segments generated by the CNC. All contour segments are right-headed. This means that the right-hand root node of a prenasalized consonant and the right-hand supralaryngeal node of an affricate are the heads of the respective segments. The CNC can now be stated in terms of headedness.

> (19) Contour Node Condition (final form)
> Class nodes A and B on tier T can form a contour when the head dominates the same set of non-null class nodes as the non-head.

The asymmetry shown in (17) and (18) is now accounted for by the CNC. Prenasalized affricates are licit segments because the [-nasal] root node is the head and it dominates the same set of subordinate nodes as the [+nasal] root node which is the non-head. (18) is ill-formed because the [-cont] supralaryngeal node is dominated by the non-head but not by the head.

4. Prenasalization Environment Phenomena
4.1 Post-nasal Voicing
Many languages have a process that voices obstruents (particularly stops) when the obstruent is preceded by a nasal. This voicing assimilation process is called 'post-nasal voicing' (Herbert 1986) when it occurs in a prenasalization

environment.

Post-nasal voicing follows from the theory of underspecification in Archangeli (1984), A&P (1986) and Steriade (1987). Consider the phonemic inventory of obstruents in Kikuyu (Armstrong 1940) and the proposed underlying specification for [voice].[5]

(20) Kikuyu (obstruents only)

	p	t	c	k	β	₹	ɣ
[voice]					+	+	+

Stops are not specified for [voice], but fricatives are specified as [+voice] and the default value in Kikuyu is [-voice]. The specification for [voice] given here is consistent with Kikuyu phonology since stops are voiced only in prenasalization environments.

(21) Kikuyu (Armstrong 1940)
  a. /tem-a/   [ⁿdemeete]   'cut 1p. perf. ind.'
  b. /tom-a/   [ⁿdomeete]   'send'
  c. /kom-a/   [ŋgomeete]   'sleep'
  d. /ker-a/   [ŋgereete]   'cross'

Two assumptions concerning underlying representation must be made before discussing post-nasal voicing. Since Kikuyu stops are voiced only when preceded by a nasal and stops are not specified for [voice], then [+voice] must spread from the nasal to the stop. However, nasals are redundantly [+voice] because all [+son] are [+voice], hence nasals should not be specified for [voice]. This paper assumes nasals are redundantly specified as [+voice]. It might be possible to eliminate this assumption, but this option is not explored here.

Rosenthall (in prep) proposes a restricted theory of Node Generation, based on A&P, which states that nodes are generated only when features to be dominated by the node are present. As a result of node generation, no laryngeal node is generated for stops in Kikuyu because there is no feature, i.e.[voice], to license it. Post-nasal voicing, therefore, is simply the spreading of the laryngeal node from the nasal to the obstruent.

(22) Post-nasal Voicing (relevant structure only)

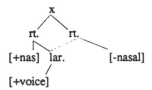

4.2 Post-nasal Hardening

Many languages have a process called 'post-nasal hardening' that despirantizes fricatives in a prenasalization environment. Post-nasal hardening, like post-nasal voicing, can be accounted for by underspecification. Consider the data from Kikuyu in (23).

(23) Kikuyu (Armstrong 1940)
    a. /βor-a/   [ᵐbureete]   'lop off 1p. perf. ind.'
    b. /ɣor-a/   [ᵑgoreete]   'buy'

Since the labial and velar fricatives become stops only post-nasally, these segments are not specified for [cont]. The specification for Kikuyu obstruents is given in (24).

(24) Kikuyu[6]

p t c k β ծ ɣ
[voice]   + + +
[cont]

    The feature [cont] is absent from the underlying representation of Kikuyu obstruents as a consequence of the default rule [] --> [-cont] and the co-occurrence redundancy rule (Steriade 1987) [+voice] --> [+cont]. These two rules render the value for [cont] completely predictable. Post-nasal hardening, like post-nasal voicing, is a case of assimilation as spreading. This paper assumes that nasals are redundantly specified as [-cont] as well as [+voice]. Furthermore, node generation as discussed in Rosenthall (in prep) ensures that fricatives do not have a supralaryngeal node. Therefore, post-nasal hardening is simply the spreading of the supralaryngeal node from the nasal to the fricative.

(25) Post-nasal Hardening (relevant structure only)

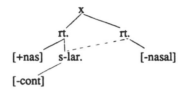

4.3 Nasal Deletion

    Nasal segments delete in a prenasalization environment when followed by a nasal or by certain obstruents. Consider the following data from Ndali and Kikuyu.

(26) Ndali (Vail 1972)
    a. /iN+ puno/   [iᵐbuno]   'nose 9/10 class'
    b. /iN+ tunye/   [iⁿdunye]   'banana'
    c. /iN+ kunda/   [iᵑgunda]   'dove'
    d. /iN+ β ale/   [iᵐbale]   'plate'
    e. /iN+ fuwa/   [ifuwa]   'hippo'
    f. /iN+ satu/   [isatu]   'python'
    g. /iN+ nyenye/   [inyenye]   'bee'
        Kikuyu (Armstrong 1940)
    h. /meñ-a/   [meñeete]   'know 1p. perf. ind.'

The two deletion processes are given in (27).

(27) Nasal Deletion
   a. /N+ m,n, ŋ/   -->   [m,n,ŋ] ex. (26 g,h)
   b. /N+ f,s,š/   -->   [f,s,š] ex. (26 e,f)

(27a) is explained by the OCP. The adjacent [+nasal] root nodes violate the OCP (McCarthy 1986) hence one root node (the left one) deletes. The deletion process described in (27b) seems quite natural. Since Ndali has only prenasalized voiced stops (Vail 1972), then fricatives cannot be prenasalized and the nasal deletes to avoid creating an illicit Ndali segment. Although deletion seems natural, there is no explanation for the fricatives /f,s,š/ to trigger deletion and the fricatives /β,γ/ to trigger hardening. Another problem is to explain the lack of obstruent triggered deletion in Kikuyu.[7]

The deletion facts in Ndali are accounted for by the interaction of underspecification and the CNC. (28) shows the proposed specification of Ndali obstruents.

(28) Ndali (obstruents only)

	p	t	c	k	f	s	š	β	γ
[voice]								+	+
[cont]				+	+	+			

default insertion: [ ] --> [-voice]
                      [ ] --> [-cont]
co-occurrence rule: [+voice] --> [+cont]

The feature value [+voice] is necessary to distinguish the phonemically voiced segments (/β/ and /γ/) from stops and other fricatives, and [+cont] is necessary in the specification in Ndali to distinguish the voiceless fricatives from the stops.

This paper assumes the theory of underlying representation in Piggott (1985) and Rosenthall (in prep). Root nodes (represented here as segments for simplicity) are linked to skeletal points in underlying representation. Affixes are allowed to have unattached root nodes or skeletal points, but roots cannot have unattached skeletal points. The underlying representation of the Ndali 9/10 class marker and the root /fuwa/ are given in (29).

$$(29) \quad \begin{bmatrix} x \\ | \\ i \quad N \end{bmatrix} \begin{bmatrix} x & x & x & x \\ | & | & | & | \\ f & u & w & a \end{bmatrix}$$

The root node of the archiphoneme /N/ links to the skeletal point dominating the /f/ in /fuwa/ by one-to-one, left-to-right association creating the configuration for a prenasalized consonant since two root nodes are attached to one skeletal point. Nasal deletion is represented as the delinking of the nasal's root node from the skeleton. Now, this delinking in Ndali must be related specifically to /f, s, š/. Given the specification of Ndali obstruents, /f, s, š/ are the only [+cont] segments. Therefore, post-nasal hardening cannot occur. Since there is no spreading from the nasal, then the linking of the nasal root node to the skeletal point dominating the /f/ creates a configuration where the two root nodes do not dominate the same supralaryngeal node, which violates the CNC. The nasal delinks, thus deletes, to avoid violating the CNC.

(30)

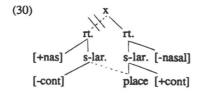

The absence of obstruent-triggered nasal deletion in Kikuyu is explained by the specification of Kikuyu obstruents. The feature [+cont] is predictable, therefore, it is unnecessary in the representation. Hence the nasal can always spread its supralaryngeal node ensuring the CNC is satisfied since there will be only one supralaryngeal node for the nasal and the obstruent.
Nasal deletion can also be triggered by voiceless stops.

(31) Venda (Ziervogel et al. 1972)
    a. /N+ pala/   [pala]   'scratching'
    b. /N+ kako/   [kako]   'fault'
    c. /N+ tsumbulo/   [tsumbulo]   'rolling in dust'

The deletion facts in Venda follow from the CNC provided that stops are specified as [-voice] and that [+voice] is the default value, unlike Kikuyu and Ndali. Changing the default feature value for a specific language is consistent with the Complement Rules in A&P which allow for language-specific specification. Since Venda stops are specified as [-voice], the [+voice] laryngeal node of the nasal cannot spread to the stop. The two root nodes in this case do not dominate the same laryngeal node, hence the nasal delinks to avoid a violation of the CNC.

4.4 Coalescence

Schadeberg (1982) claims that voiced stops in Umbundu only occur when a fricative is followed by a nasal, i.e., the voiced stop of a prenasalized consonant is the result of post-nasal hardening.

(32) Umbundu (Schadeberg 1982)
    a. /N+ vanya/   [ᵐbanya]   'I look'
    b. /N+ fela/   [fela]   'I dig'
    c. /N+ seva/   [seva]   'I cook'
    d. /N+ popya/   [mopya]   'I speak'
    e. /N+ tuma/   [numa]   'I send'
    f. /N+ kwata/   [ŋwata]   'I take'

Post-nasal hardening is seen in (32a). (32b&c), on the other hand, are cases of nasal deletion which is expected when fricatives occur in a prenasalization environment. (32d,e,&f) are interesting. Voiceless stops should either undergo post-nasal voicing, as seen in Kikuyu and Ndali, or trigger nasal deletion, as seen in Venda. Instead, voiceless stops in Umbundu trigger coalescence, which is shown here to follow from underspecification and the CNC. (33) shows the specification of features in Umbundu from which the hardening and deletion/coalescence facts can be derived.

(33) Umbundu (obstruents only)

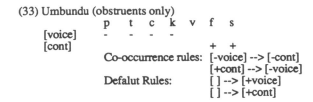

```
              p   t   c   k   v   f   s
[voice]       -   -   -   -
[cont]                        +   +
```
Co-occurrence rules: [-voice] --> [-cont]
                      [+cont] --> [-voice]
Defalut Rules: [ ] --> [+voice]
                      [ ] --> [+cont]

The fricative /v/ is not specified for [cont] hence it can undergo post-nasal hardening. The fricatives /f/ and /s/ are specified as [+cont] therefore a CNC violation occurs and the nasal deletes as expected.

Coalescence, like nasal deletion, is the result of delinking a root node from the skeleton. The [-voice] specification of the stops creates a CNC violation because the [-nasal] and [+nasal] root nodes do not dominate the same laryngeal node. Since prenasalized consonants consist of two root nodes linked to one skeletal point, then there are two association lines that may delink to avoid a CNC violation. Coalescence is the result of two processes: 1. nasal-stop assimilation, which is obligatory (Rosenthall in prep), and 2. the delinking of the [-nasal] root node from the skeleton. The [+nasal] root node, which is associated with the skeleton by the association convention, remains with the place features of the obstruent.

(34) Coalescence (relevant structure only)

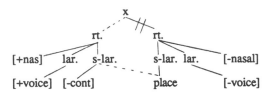

The fact that there are two ways to resolve CNC violations implies languages might be divided with respect to nasal deletion or coalescence. Obviously this is not the case since Umbundu exhibits both phenomena, therefore, nasal deletion/ coalescence cannot be attributed to a parameter which would state which association line delinks. This paper proposes, without exploring the details, that nasal deletion is the unmarked process by which CNC violations are resolved. Coalescence, therefore, must be a language specific process, at least in Umbundu, which applies when the configuration in (34) arises, i.e., two laryngeal nodes are in a prenasalization environment.

5. Parameters

It is possible to introduce a parameter for prenasalization based on the proposal that prenasalized consonants are represented as two root nodes. Languages which lack prenasalization simply do not allow the root node to form a contour.

(35) Prenasalization Parameter
     Root nodes form contours (yes/no)

The CNC is too strong insofar as it predicts the occurrence of only prenasalized voiced stops, which are not the only attested class of prenasalized consonants. The Luganda example in section 2.1 has a prenasalized voiceless stop and prenasalized fricatives are discussed in Herbert (1986). Prenasalized consonants other than voiced stops can be permitted given certain parametric variations of the CNC.

There is a markedness hierarchy within the range of prenasalized consonants (Herbert 1986). Prenasalized voiced stops are the least marked then the prenasalized voiceless stops follow which are in turn followed by the prenasalized fricatives which are the most marked. Herbert (1986) notes that languages with prenasalized voiceless stops also have prenasalized voiced stops. The markedness hierarchy and the necessary co-occurrence of prenasalized voiceless stops and voiced stops are predicted by the parameters of the CNC. As stated above, the CNC predicts only prenasalized voiced stops (and affricates), therefore, the CNC predicts that prenasalized voiced stops are the least marked of the prenasalized consonants.

Prenasalized voiceless stops are accounted for by a parameter that excludes the laryngeal node from the set of mutually dominated subordinate nodes required by the CNC. Since the two root nodes need not dominate the same laryngeal node, it is possible for the [-nasal] root node to dominate a [-voice] laryngeal node.

(36) Prenasalized Voiceless Stop Parameter
Exclude the laryngeal node from the set of mutually dominated nodes (yes/no)

This parameter also explains the necessary occurrence of prenasalized voiced stops in languages with prenasalized voiceless stops. If the laryngeal node is excluded from the set of subordinate nodes indicated in the CNC, then it is possible that both laryngeal nodes can be [+voice], which will then reduce to one node by the OCP. Parameter (36) necessitates the existence of prenasalized voiced stops when prenasalized voiceless stops occur because (36) cannot prohibit the former.

Prenasalized fricatives are similarly explained. In the case of fricatives, the parameter concerns the supralarnygeal node.

(37) Prenasalized Fricative Parameter
Exclude the supralaryngeal node from the set of mutually dominated subordinate nodes (yes/no)

Parameters (36) and (37) predict a limited range of prenasalized consonant inventories, some of which might not be attested. Given here are some possibilities which require more study. Parameter (37) predicts that languages with prenasliazed fricatives must have prenasalized stops because the occurrence of two [-cont] supralaryngeal nodes cannot be prohibited. Parameters (36) and (37) together predict that prenasalized voiceless fricatives are very marked since two parameters must be set and such a language also must allow for the full range of prenasalized consonants because there would no criteria, other than homorganicity, for prenasalization. Herbert (1986) claims Rundi is one language in which all obstruents have a prenasalized counterpart. Parameter (37) predicts a language can have prenasalized voiced fricatives and voiced stops but not prenasalized voiceless stops because (36) and (37) are indepedently activated. This prenasalized consonant inventory exists in Zande (Herbert 1986).

6. Conclusion
Representing prenasalized consonants as two root nodes dominated by one skeletal point accounts for the behaviour of prenasalized consonants with respect

to gemination and derivation from nasal-stop clusters. A principled account of autosegmental phonology dictates that prenasalized consonants derived from nasal spreading also must be represented as two root nodes.

The CNC and the theory of underspecification account for post-nasal voicing, hardening, nasal deletion, and coalescence in prenasalization environments. Post-nasal voicing and hardening are the result of the spreading the laryngeal and supralaryngeal nodes from the nasal to the obstruent. Nasal deletion and coalescence occur by delinking the [+nasal] root node or the [-nasal] root node, respectively, when the aforementioned spread processes are blocked and a CNC violation ensues.

The CNC accounts for the claim that prenasalized voiced stops are the least marked prenasalized consonants. The range of possible prenasalized consonant inventories, the prenasaliztion markedness hierarchy, and prenasalization co-occurrence facts are all derived from parameteric variations of the CNC.

Footnotes
*   I thank G.L. Piggott and J. Lowenstamm for many useful comments and suggestions. I also thank Henrietta Hung whose comments prevented the appearance of potentially embarrassing earlier drafts. Any remaining embarrassments are my responsibility.
1.   Sagey (1986) does not include [son] in the hierarchy.
2.   The position of [son], [cons], and [vocalic] is not clearly presented in the literature. Some authors only include [son] whereas others only include [cons]. I propose these features, if relevant, link to the root node. For the purposes of this paper, the major class features are not included in the hierarchy. The point here is that the major class features are not dominated by the supralaryngeal node, as proposed by Clements (1985).
3.   The place node dominates a set of articulator nodes (Sagey 1986). The internal structure of the place node is not germane to this paper.
4.   Paradis claims the right hand point is the head of geminate consonants and the left hand point is the head of geminate vowels. Since all contour segments discussed in this paper are consonants, the right hand headedness is consistent with Paradis' notion of headedness.
5.   This paper discusses alternations concerning obstruents only. See Rosenthall (1988a) for a discussion of glides in prenasalization environments.
6.   /ʒ/ may be anomalously specified as [+cont] since it triggers nasal deletion. See 5.3 for discussion of nasal deletion.
7.   Except for /ʒ/.

References
Archangeli, D. 1984. Underspecification and Yawelmani phonology and morphology. Doctoral dissertation. MIT.
Archangeli, D. and D. Pulleyblank. 1986. The content and structure of phonological representations. ms. U. Arizona & USC.
Armstrong, L.E. 1940. The phonetic and tonal structure of Kikuyu. Cambridge: C.U.P.
Clements, G.N. 1985. The geometry of phonological features. Phonology Yearbook. 2. 225-252.
Clements, G.N. 1985a. Compensatory lengthening and consonant gemination in Luganda. In Wetzels and Setzer. eds.

Feinstein, M. 1979. Prenasalization and syllable structure.
    Linguistic Inquiry. 10. 245-278.
Goldsmith, J. 1976. Autosegmental phonology. Doctoral dissertation.
    MIT.
Herbert, R.K. 1986. Language universals, markedness theory, and
    natural phonetic processes. Berlin: Mouton de Gruyter.
Kaye, J.D., J. Lowenstamm, and J-R. Verngaud. 1987. Constituent
    structure and government in phonology. ms. UQAM &
    U. Maryland.
Levin, J. 1985. A metrical theory of syllabicity. doctoral dissertation.
    MIT.
McCarthy, J. 1986. OCP effects: gemination and antigemination.
    Linguistic Inquiry. 17. 207- 263.
Paradis, C. 1987. On phonological constraints.
    McGill University Working Papers in Linguistics. 4.2.
Piggott, G.L. 1985. Deletion in multi-tiered phonology. ms. McGill.
Piggott, G. L. 1987. On the autonomy of the feature nasal.
    Proceedings of the Chicago Linguistic Society. 23.
Piggott, G. L. 1987a. Parameters of nasalization. Paper presented
    at the MIT Colloquium. MIT.
Piggott, G. L. and R. Singh. 1985. The phonology of epenthetic
    segments. Canadian Journal of Linguistics. 30. 415-451.
Rosenthall, S. 1988. Syllabification and Sinhalese phonology.
    McGill University Working Papers in Linguistics. 5.1.
Rosenthall, S. 1988a. Post-nasal voicing, hardening, and nasal
    deletion. Presented at the 19th annual African Linguistics
    Conference, Boston.
Rosenthall, S. in prep. The representation of nasal-stop
    assimilation. McGill.
Sagey, E.C. 1985. On the representation of complex segments and their
    formation in Kinyarwanda. In Wetzels and Setzer. eds.
Sagey, E. C. 1986. The representation of features and relations in
    non-linear phonology. Doctoral dissertation. MIT.
Schadeberg,T. 1982. Nasalization in Umbundu. Journal of African
    Languages and Linguistics. 4. 109-132.
Schein, B. and D. Steriade. 1986. On geminates.
    Linguistic Inquiry. 17. 691-744.
Steriade, D. 1987. Redundant values. Proceedings of the Chicago
    Linguistic Society. 23.
Vail, L. 1972. The noun classes of Ndali. Journal of African
    Languages. 11:3. 21-47.
van der Hulst, H. and N. Smith. 1982. Prosodic domains and opaque
    segments in autosegmental theory. The Structure of phonological
    representations II, ed. by H. van der Hulst and N. Smith.
    Dordrecht: Foris.
Wetzels, L. and E. Sezer. eds. 1985. Studies in compensatory
    lengthening. Dordrecht: Foris.
Zeirvogel, D., P.J. Wetzel, and T.N. Makuya. 1972. A Handbook of the
    Venda Language. Pretoria: U. of South Africa Press.

Thematic and Grammatical Hierarchies:
Albanian Reflexivization

Peter Sells
Stanford University

Introduction

This paper looks at certain interactions of the effects of a thematic hierarchy (stated in terms of underlying or thematic structure) and a grammatical hierarchy (stated on final grammatical relations). There is fairly clear evidence in Albanian that reflexivization obeys the familiar thematic hierarchy (Jackendoff (1972)). In addition, there seems to be a need for a grammatical distinction between terms and obliques, familiar from Relational Grammar.

1. Albanian

All the Albanian data in this paper is taken from Hubbard (1985).[1]

1.1. Final Term Reflexivization

The examples (1)a/c indicate that a subject in Albanian can be the antecedent of an object reflexive or indirect object reflexive. Hubbard (1985) shows that word order does not affect binding possibilities, as in (1)b.

(1) a. Agimi   pa   veten   nə pasqyrə.
       Agim-NOM see-3sPDAct self-ACC in mirror
       'Agim saw himself in the mirror.'

    b. Veten   e pəlqen   Agimi   nə pasqyrə.
       self-ACC A see-3sPDAct Agim-NOM in mirror
       'Agim saw himself in the mirror.'

    c. Drita   i dərgon   letra   vetes.
       Drita-NOM D send-3sPrAct letters-ACC self-DAT
       'Drita sends letter to herself.'

On the other hand, an object or indirect object cannot antecede a subject reflexive.

---

[1] Abbreviations in the verb-forms are: Pr=present, P=past, D=definite, Act=active, N Act=non-active, with person and number agreement for the subject also indicated. Clitics, which precede the verb if present, also bear agreement in some instances; a clitic also agrees in case with the NP that it is grammatically linked to, A=accusative, D=dative. Hubbard argues that the presence or absence of clitics is not relevant to the reflexivization facts.

(2) a. *Vetja   pa   Agimin   nə pasqyrə.
       self-NOM see-3sPDAct Agim-ACC in mirror
       'Himself saw Agim in the mirror.'

    b. *Vetja   i dərgon   Dritəs   letra.
       self-NOM D send-3sPrAct Drita-DAT letters-ACC
       'Herself sends letter to Drita.'

In the next set of examples, we see that an indirect object may antecede a direct object, while a direct object may not antecede an indirect object (though direct objects may antecede obliques, as will be shown below).[2]

(3) a. Artisti   i a tregoi   veten   Dritəs.
       artist-NOM D A show-3sPDAct self-ACC Drita-DAT
       'The artist showed herself$_i$ to Drita$_i$.'

    b. Gazetari   i a pərshkroi   veten   Agimit.
       journalist-NOM D A describe-3sPDAct self-ACC Agim-DAT
       'The journalist described himself$_i$ to Agim$_i$.'

(4) a. *Artisti   i a tregoi   Dritən   vetes.
       artist-NOM D A show-3sPDAct Drita-ACC self-DAT
       'The artist showed Drita$_i$ to herself$_i$.'

    b. *Gazetari   i a pərshkroi   Agimin   vetes.
       journalist-NOM D A describe-3sPDAct Agim-ACC self-DAT
       'The journalist described Agim$_i$ to himself$_i$.'

Hubbard proposes that the binding here observes a (somewhat exceptional) relational hierarchy, $1 > 3 > 2$. However, I would like to claim that the hierarchy is thematically based, being Agent > Goal > Theme (Jackendoff (1972)). There are clear precedents for such a hierarchy governing reflexivization; Jackendoff claims that it applies in English, and other languages are known to have similar properties (Kiparsky (1987)).[3]

Under passive, an indirect object may antecede the (derived) subject, indicating that initial (that is, thematic) relations are relevant for the binding, as in the examples (5).

(5) a. Vetja   i u tregua   Dritəs   prej artistit.
       self-NOM D show-3sPDNAct Drita-DAT by artist
       'Herself$_i$ was shown to Drita$_i$ by the artist.'

    b. Vetja   i u pərshkrua   Agimit   prej gazetarit.
       self-NOM D show-3sPDNAct Agim-DAT by journalist
       'Himself$_i$ was described to Agim$_i$ by the journalist.'

---

[2] In some cases, I will not show all the possible readings of the example, indicating (where necessary) the relevant interpretation by coindexing.

[3] In some examples, the subject may be receiving the Experiencer role rather than Agent (e.g., (1)a). I will assume that Experiencer comes right below Agent on the hierarchy, and will omit it from subsequent presentations of the hierarchy.

Recall that in an active, the subject (Agent) cannot be bound by the indirect object (Goal); here the grammatical binding involves Goal anteceding Theme.

Themes, however, are not totally excluded as antecedents: the following examples illustrate a Theme as antecedent of a passive oblique phrase, in (6)a, and a locative oblique in example (b); in (c) the Goal is the antecedent of the passive oblique.

(6) a. Kapedani   u ftua   prej vetes.
       captain-NOM invite-3sPDNAct by self-ABL
       'The captain was invited by himself.'

    b. Presentova   Agimin   ne njə vajzə pranə vetes.
       introduce-1sPDAct Agim-ACC to a   girl   beside self-DAT
       'I introduced Agimᵢ to a girl beside himᵢ.'

    c. Libri   i u dərgua   Agimit   prej vetes.
       book-NOM D send-3sPDNAct Agim-DAT by   self-ABL
       'The book was sent to Agim by himself.'

On the other hand, the passive oblique cannot antecede any of the term arguments, indicating that it is lower on the hierarchy than any term.

(7) a. *Vetja   u ftua   prej kapedanit.
        self-NOM invite-3sPDNAct by   captain-ABL
        'Himself was invited by the captain.'

    b. *Libri   i u dərgua   vetes prej Agimit.
        book-NOM D send-3sPDNAct self-DAT by Agim-ABL
        'The book was sent to himself by Agim.'

The inability to antecede terms is true of all obliques, as with the 'about' phrase in (8).

(8) *Vetja   i foli   Dritəs   mbi Agimin.
      self-NOM 3sD speak-3sPDAct Drita-DAT about Agim-ACC
      'Himselfᵢ spoke to Drita about Agimᵢ.'

Overall, then, we find evidence for the following hierarchy (really, two hierarchies, one thematic and one grammatical):

(9)   Agent > Goal > Theme   . . . .
       ‿‿‿‿‿‿‿‿‿‿‿‿‿‿‿‿‿‿‿‿   ‿‿‿‿‿‿‿‿‿‿‿‿‿‿
           final terms   > final obliques

There are two apparently independent conditions here: one, the target must not grammatically outrank its antecedent (therefore obliques cannot antecede terms); and two, the antecedent must thematically outrank the target. As the diagram indicates, the grammatical hierarchy predominates: any term can antecede any oblique, but among terms the thematic hierarchy must be respected.

1.2. Hubbard's Analysis

Hubbard's (1985) relational analysis is given in (10); it accounts for all the data.

(10) a. Final Term Reflexivization
   A nominal A heading a final term arc with tail c may antecede a reflexive nominal B heading a final term arc with tail c only if the R-sign of the arc headed by A outranks the R-sign of the arc headed by B on the hierarchy $1 > 3 > 2$ at the initial level.

   b. Final Non-Term Reflexivization
   A nominal A heading a term arc with tail c may antecede a reflexive nominal B heading a final non-term arc with tail c.

The ability of the passive oblique to be an antecedent is guaranteed by the fact that (10)b does not require A to be a final term arc, but rather, just a term arc at some level. What is puzzling about (10) is why there should be two somewhat independent conditions on reflexivization.

1.3. Extending the Hierarchy

In certain circumstances, benefactives can appear as final datives (indirect objects), though these cannot antecede Themes (objects). Assuming that Benefactive is lower than Theme on the hierarchy, the present approach predicts this.

(11) *I   rruajta   Agimit   veten.
      3sD shave-1sPDAct Agim-DAT self-ACC
      'I shaved himself$_i$ for Agim$_i$.'

On the other hand, these benefactive datives can antecede obliques, as in (12), though they cannot do so when appearing themselves as obliques, as seen in (13).

(12) I   bleva   prezidentit   njə libər   mbi   veten.
      3sD buy-1sPDAct president-DAT a   book-ACC about self-ACC
      'I bought (for) the president$_i$ a book about himself$_i$.'

(13) *Bleva   pər prezidentin   njə libər   mbi   veten.
      buy-1sPDAct for president-ACC a   book-ACC about self-ACC
      'I bought for the president$_i$ a book about himself$_i$.'

The benefactive dative may also antecede a passive oblique, as in (14), but may not be anteceded by a passive oblique, as in (15).

(14) Libri   i u ble   prezidentit   prej vetes.
      book-NOM 3sD buy-3sPDNAct president-DAT by   self-ABL
      'The book was bought (for) the president$_i$ by himself$_i$.'

(15) *Libri   i u ble   vetes   prej prezidentit.
      book-NOM 3sD buy-3sPDNAct self-DAT by   president-ABL
      'The book was bought (for) himself$_i$ by the president$_i$.'

The same range of behavior is shown by raised possessors, which are also surface datives. Such possessors cannot antecede Themes, as in (16).

(16) *Bija   mə pa   veten.
      daughter-the-NOM 1sD see-3sPDAct self-ACC
      'My$_i$ daugher saw myself$_i$.'

However, they can antecede obliques, as in (17)a, though not when they are themselves obliques, as in (17)b.

(17) a. M' a   vuri   bijən   pranə veten.
         1sD 3sA place-3sPDAct daughter-the-ACC beside self-ABL
         'He placed my$_i$ daughter beside myself$_i$.'

     b. *Agimi   e   vuri   bijən   time pranə veten.
         Agim-NOM 3sA place-3sPDAct daughter-the-ACC my   beside self-ABL
         'Agim placed my$_i$ daughter beside myself$_i$.'

Finally, the raised possessor may antecede a passive oblique, though the reverse is bad.

(18) a. Shtəpia   mə əshtə lyer   dy herə prej vetes.
         house-the-NOM 1sD be-1sPr paint-Prt two times by self-ABL
         'My$_i$ house has been painted twice by myself$_i$.'

     b. *Shtəpia   mə əshtə lyer   vetes   dy herə prej maje.
         house-the-NOM 1sD be-1sPr paint-Prt self-DAT two times by me-ABL
         'My(self's)$_i$ house has been painted twice by me$_i$.'

From this last example it is clear that the grammatical hierarchy (terms > obliques) must be relevant, for the raised possessors bear no thematic relation to the matrix predicate and would therefore be absolutely lowest on any thematic hierarchy relative to that predicate.

The idea that the 'ascended' possessors are indeed raised and hence non-thematic may be somewhat controversial, in that such ascensions are only possible with animate possessors, a fact which may suggest an analysis in terms of a lexical rule altering a predicate's argument structure. However, the ungrammaticality of (16) shows that even if the raised argument were thematic, the role assigned to it would have to be lower than Theme, as the raised argument cannot antecede the Theme argument. This in turn would leave the grammaticality of (18)a unexplained, if the thematic hierarchy were the only relevant factor, for the raised argument *can* antecede an passive oblique, but could not possibly outrank it thematically (as the passive oblique realizes the highest thematic role).

From this evidence we can extend the composite hierarchy to that shown in (19).[4]

(19)
$$\text{Agent} > \text{Goal} > \text{Theme} > \text{Benef.} > \bar{\theta} \quad \dotsb$$
$$\underbrace{\hspace{6cm}}_{\text{final terms}} \quad > \underbrace{\text{final obliques}}$$

---

[4] As an alternative to placing Benefactive below Theme on the hierarchy, it may be that examples (11)–(15) illustrate another case of a phrase which is formally non-thematic: the dative Benefactives might be adjuncts (semantically speaking) with respect to the matrix predicate, and therefore bear no thematic relation to that predicate.

1.4. Evidence for Final Terms

Evidence that the raised possessors and benefactives are final terms comes from floating of the quantifier *tə gjithə* ('all'). This quantifier may float off final terms, such as a subject in (20).

(20) a. Tə gjithə burrat   mə panə.
        all-NOM   men-the-NOM 1sA see-3pPDAct
        'All the men saw me.'

     b. Burrat   mə panə   tə gjithə.
        men-the-NOM 1sA see-3pPDAct all-NOM
        'All the men saw me.'

With datives, *tə gjithə* may float off regular indirect objects, or dative subjects, as seen in (21).

(21) a. Burrave   tə katundit   u   fola   tə gjithəve.
        men-the-DAT village-the-GEN 3pD speak-1sPDAct all-DAT
        'I spoke to all the men of the village.'

     b. U   dhimsen   unə tə gjithəve.
        3pD care for-1sPrNAct I   all-DAT
        'All of them care for me.'

It may also float off dative benefactives and possessors.

(22) a. Djemve   u   bleu   bileta   Agimi   tə gjithəve.
        boys-the-DAT 3pD buy-3sPDAct tickets-ACC Agim-NOM all-DAT
        'Agim bought all the boys tickets.'

     b. Qeni   u   pa   çupave   macet   tə gjithəve.
        dog-the-NOM 3pD see-3sPDAct girls-the-DAT cats-the-ACC all-DAT
        'The dog saw the cats of all the girls.'

Note, however, that the oblique benefactive does not license *tə gjithə*-float, as shown in (23).

(23)   *Pər djem   bleu   bileta   Agimi   tə gjithə.
        for boys-the-ACC buy-3sPDAct tickets-ACC Agim-NOM all-ACC
        'Agim bought tickets for all the boys.'

1.5. Final Oblique Reflexivization

Despite the fact that obliques cannot generally be antecedents, the passive oblique is not fully excluded in this role: it can antecede other oblique reflexives. This property is restricted to just those obliques that are 'logical subjects'—for example, the object of *afər* ('near') in (24) is not a potential antecedent for anything.

(24)   Afər drejtorit u vu   prej Agimit   libri   mbi   veten.
        near director put-3sPDNAct by   Agim-ABL book-NOM about self-ACC
        'The book about himself$_{i/*j}$ was placed by Agim$_i$ near the director$_j$.'

The examples in (25) again demonstrate that obliques cannot be antecedents, with the one exception just noted.

(25) a.   Agimi   vuri   librin   mbi   drejtorin   afər vetes.

          Agim-NOM put-3sPDAct book-ACC about director-ACC near self-ABL

          'Agim$_i$ put the book about the director$_j$ near himself$_{i/*j}$.'

     b.   Agimi   vuri   librin   mbi   veten   afər drejtorit.

          Agim-NOM put-3sPDAct book-ACC about self-ACC near director-ABL

          'Agim$_i$ put the book about himself$_{i/*j}$ near the director$_j$.'

There is more than one kind of analysis possible here. Given the fact that the passive oblique will bear the role that is highest on the hierarchy among the arguments of the particular predicate in question, we might say that any highest argument can be an antecedent, so long as it is not grammatically outranked by its target (a kind of 'logical subject' condition on reflexivization). However, there is no obvious reason why such a 'logical subject' condition should only hold for obliques.

Pursuing a different line, I will say here that passive obliques are alone among obliques in being subcategorized (in the sense given below), and that final obliques can be anteceded by any subcategorized argument. This latter approach generalizes the conditions on antecedent-hood to all subcategorized phrases: only those can be antecedents. We are left with the conditions in (26).

(26) a.   Any subcategorized argument may be antecedent

     b.   AND, the target must not outrank its antecedent grammatically (terms > obliques)

     c.   AND, the antecedent must outrank its target thematically if it does not outrank it grammatically

Passive obliques will antecede other obliques in virtue of condition (a), being subcategorized; they will always satisfy (c).

1.6. Locality Constraints on Reflexivization

There is presumably a locality constraint of a familiar kind on reflexivization, though presently there is no data available to me which demonstrates this. However, it seems implicit in Hubbard's analysis that there is a 'clause-mate' constraint, and I will assume this: that the reflexive and its antecedent should be in the same S.

2. The Term/Oblique Distinction

In order that the grammatical condition (26)b is respected, the grammar must represent the distinction between terms and obliques.

In some theories, such as Relational Grammar, terms are defined as the relations 1, 2, and 3. In Lexical-Functional Grammar, terms are similarly defined as the functions SUBJ, OBJ, OBJ2. However, it is not obvious that there is anything particular about such definitions which indicates why terms should have the properties that they do.

In standard Government-Binding theory, the representation of terms appears to be somewhat problematic; for example, one might think of terms as the verb's thematic arguments, but thematic structure alone cannot be the crucial factor, as we have seen. This would suggest that surface case-marking properties are relevant; the problem is that the subject is a term, yet is not case-marked by the verb.[5]

Here, adopting some basic ideas and notation from Head-Driven Phrase Structure Grammar (Pollard and Sag (1987)), we will define terms to be phrases whose form is dictated in the lexical entry, following the intuition that terms are the 'core' syntactic dependents of a predicate. Each predicate will specify the form of the syntactic realization of certain such dependents, and the linking of those dependents to its thematic roles. Subcategorized phrases may also lack a thematic role, as in the case of raising, for example. Oblique phrases will be any remaining lexically specified thematic roles, which are mapped by general principles onto syntactic structures. In a sense, terms are inherited subcategorizations, while obliques are instantiated subcategorizations. In contrast, adjuncts will be extra phrases, both thematically and grammatically.

Under this conception a given predicate will have a list of associated semantic roles and a list of dependents. Let us assume for the purposes of discussion that in the sentence *John broke the window with a rock*, the *with*-PP is an oblique. Then the lexical entry for *break* will contain the following information:

(27)   *break*, SUBCAT: $< NP_k \ NP_i >$
          ROLE: $< Theme_k \ Instrument_j \ Agent_i >$

The lists encode obliqueness from left-to-right; so NP_i is the least oblique phrase (the subject), and Agent is the highest thematic role.

The Instrument argument is syntactically unlinked at this stage; it will be realized as a PP by general default principles. It may be that only PPs are subject to such principles; that is to say, it might be that NPs and APs and S's are always terms. If that is so, a verb like *tell*, which can appear in two frames (*tell Sue about Jack* or *tell Sue that Jack is here*), will optionally have S' as a dependent linked to the Theme argument. The choice of preposition to head the PP in question when there is no S' will be semantically driven (e.g., *about* is for PPs realizing arguments that are Themes of propositional content). Some of these general principles are discussed in Foley and Van Valin (1984); I have nothing new to add to the existing wisdom on this matter in the present paper.

Adopting some new terminology, I will refer to subcategorized phrases as DEPENDENTS and roles as ARGUMENTS; and I will assume that the thematic hierarchy is encoded in the order in the ARGUMENTS list. (27) will now have the structure shown in (28).[6] There clearly are generalizations covering the linking of ARGUMENTS to DEPENDENTS, but I ignore those here (see the following section), and just show the linkings.

(28)   *break*, DEPENDENTS: $< NP_k \ NP_i >$
          ARGUMENTS: $< Theme_k \ Instrument_j \ Agent_i >$

Lexical rules will apply to these lexical entries of this form. One consequence of this approach, for example, will be that there can be no raising or ascension to

---

[5] Williams (1988) discusses the problems that the Albanian data pose for the standard GB binding theory.

[6] This kind of lexical entry is, I think, compatible with the general assumptions of Government-Binding Theory, if one assumes that lexical items specify both semantic- and categorial-selection, and that the Projection Principle applies to both.

oblique, for such operations require a non-thematic dependent, while obliques (by definition) are all thematic; thus raising will be restricted to the (term) dependents.[7] The structure of the lexical entry of a raising verb (for something like *John seems to sing well*) is shown in (29); note that the NP is not linked to any thematic role.[8]

(29) V, DEPENDENTS: $< VP_i\ NP >$
         ARGUMENTS: $< Theme_i >$

Passive, as another example, would involve deletion of the syntactic part of the subcategorization for the logical subject (here, just the removal of an NP position).

(30) a. V, DEPENDENTS: $< NP_j\ NP_i >$
          ARGUMENTS: $< Theme_j\ Agent_i >$

     b. $V\text{-}pass$, DEPENDENTS: $< NP_j >$
          ARGUMENTS: $< Theme_j\ Agent_i >$

The Agent is still part of the verb's role structure, and is therefore an argument, in the sense intended here, though it is not lexically linked to a particular syntactic realization, and is thus an oblique. A *by*-PP optionally realizes the thematically highest role of a predicate, if it is unlinked in the lexical entry, by general principles.

The Oblique Law of Relational Grammar (Perlmutter and Postal (1983)), which blocks demotion to oblique, suggests that in the case of passive, among other lexical operations, what is necessary is chômage, rather than deletion of the position; chômage leaves the DEPENDENT in the list, but marks it ineligible for linking to a term position in the surface structure. If that were adopted, the present approach would mirror that given in Kiparsky (1987), and the output of passive would be the entry shown in (31). The notation on NP_i indicates that it is syntactically inert.

(31) $V\text{-}pass$, DEPENDENTS: $< NP_j\ \widehat{NP}_i >$
         ARGUMENTS: $< Theme_j\ Agent_i >$

In this representation then, the difference between a chômeur and an oblique is that the latter has no corresponding item on the DEPENDENTS list, while the former corresponds to a position on the DEPENDENTS list which is marked to be ignored by whatever principles link lexical entries and syntactic structures.

Given this approach to grammatical relations, in which they are hierarchically rather than directly encoded (following the terminology of Johnson (1987)), the property of stratal uniqueness is guaranteed; each predicate can only govern one subject, one direct object, and so on. Presumably each language must set a limit on the maximum number of terms (i.e., maximum size of the DEPENDENTS list), and possibly on what can be a term: in some languages, perhaps only NPs are terms.

The distinction between terms and non-terms also seems to be relevant for stating word order facts; for example, Sag (1986) suggests that while relative order requirements holds beween terms, they do not between non-terms.

---

[7] Raising to indirect object has been claimed to exist in Irish (McCloskey (1984)) and Italian (Chierchia (1984)). Joseph (1979) presents evidence of raising to "oblique" in Greek, data which would constitute a counterexample to the present proposal if indeed the raised phrase is a surface non-term.

[8] I am assuming here that the propositional argument of *seem* is assigned the Theme role; it is not crucial here to know exactly what the role is, as there is only one, and so no hierarchy is involved.

3. The Term/Oblique Distinction and Reflexivization

The thematic hierarchy will be relevant for terms as it is known from much recent work that general principles which relate to thematic structure (in particular, the thematic hierarchy) govern the linking of thematic arguments to subcategorization frames. That is, principles relating to thematic structure govern the linking of arguments to dependents.[9]

Returning to the original topic of this paper, in the terminology introduced in the previous section the conditions on Albanian reflexivization can be restated as follows:

(32) a. Any ARGUMENT or DEPENDENT may be an antecedent

    b. AND, the target must not outrank its antecedent grammatically (DEPENDENTS > NON-DEPENDENTS)

    c. AND, the antecedent must outrank its target thematically if it does not outrank it grammatically

We see that any phrase encoded in the lexical entry may in principle be an antecedent, from (a). In (b), the final termhood requirement comes in—DEPENDENTS outrank ARGUMENTS grammatically. Finally in (c) we see that a DEPENDENT target (which from (b) requires a DEPENDENT antecedent) must be thematically outranked.

These requirements do not seem all that unusual; something like (c) has been claimed to hold in English (for example, in Jackendoff (1972) and Wilkins (1988)). Additionally, there is evidence that (b) holds; for example, it seems that the passive oblique (a non-term) can antecede only non-terms, though the English data in (33) is somewhat marginal and variable.

(33) a. *John was introduced to herself by Maxine.

    b. ??John was shown a picture of herself by Maxine.

    c. ??A lot of bad things have been said about herself by Maxine.

    d. *A lot of bad things have been said to herself by Maxine.

I would conjecture that condition (32)b holds for all languages where surface relations matter at all in reflexivization. There are many languages in which the antecedent is the "logical subject", regardless of final relations (Kiparsky (1987)); but there seem to be no languages in which pure thematic outranking is all that is relevant (e.g., no languages in which Goal antecedes Theme regardless of final relations).

In conclusion, on the basis of the facts of Albanian reflexivization I have suggested that what is needed is a representation from which differences in the behavior of terms vs. obliques is predictable, and to accomplish this it would seem that what is required is a view of terms as being directly subcategorized in a way that obliques are not. Clearly the remarks in section 2 are only suggestive, but I hope that they will lend themselves to more detailed and concrete development.[10]

---

[9] See for example Belletti and Rizzi (1987), Bresnan and Kanerva (1988), Foley and Van Valin (1984), Grimshaw (1987), Kiparsky (1987), Pesetsky (1987), among others.

[10] I am grateful to Ivan Sag and Wendy Wilkins for helpful input with respect to the issues discussed here. This paper was written while I was a visitor at the University of California, Santa Cruz, and was supported in part by the Syntax Research Center.

References

Belletti, Adriana and Luigi Rizzi: 1987. Psych-Verbs and θ-Theory. *Natural Language and Linguistic Theory*, to appear.

Bresnan, Joan and Jonni Kanerva: 1988. Locative Inversion in Chicheŵa: A Case Study of Factorization in Grammar. Ms. CSLI, Stanford University.

Chierchia, Gennaro: 1984. *Topics in the Syntax and Semantics of Infinitives and Gerunds*. Doctoral dissertation, University of Massachusetts at Amherst.

Foley, William and Robert Van Valin: 1984. *Functional Syntax and Universal Grammar*. New York, Cambridge University Press.

Grimshaw, Jane: 1987. Psych Verbs and the Structure of Argument Structure. Ms. Brandeis University.

Hubbard, Philip: 1985. *The Syntax of the Albanian Verbal Complex*. New York, Garland Publishing.

Jackendoff, Ray: 1972. *Semantic Interpretation in Generative Grammar*. Cambridge, MIT Press.

Johnson, Mark: 1987. Grammatical Relations in Attribute-Value Grammars. In Megan Crowhurst (ed.), *Proceedings of WCCFL* 6. Stanford, Stanford Linguistics Association, 103–114.

Joseph, Brian: 1979. Raising to Oblique in Modern Greek. In C. Chiarello et al. (eds.), *Proceedings of the 5th Annual Meeting of the Berkeley Linguistics Society*, 114–128.

Kiparsky, Paul: 1987. Morphology and Grammatical Relations. Ms. Stanford University.

McCloskey, James: 1984. Raising, Subcategorization and Selection in Modern Irish. *Natural Language and Linguistic Theory* 1, 441–485.

Perlmutter, David and Paul Postal: 1983. Some Proposed Laws of Basic Clause Structure. In David Perlmutter (ed.), *Studies in Relational Grammar 1*. Chicago, University of Chicago Press, 81–128.

Pesetsky, David: 1987. Binding Problems with Experiencer Verbs. *Linguistic Inquiry* 18, 126–140.

Pollard, Carl and Ivan Sag: 1987. *Information-Based Syntax and Semantics*. Stanford, CSLI, and Chicago, University of Chicago Press.

Sag, Ivan: 1986. Grammatical Hierarchy and Linear Precedence. CSLI Report No. 60, Stanford University. Also in Geoffrey Huck and Almerindo Ojeda, 1987, (eds.), *Discontinuous Constituency (Syntax and Semantics Vol. 20)*. New York, Academic Press, 303–340.

Wilkins, Wendy: 1988. Thematic Structure and Reflexivization. In W. Wilkins (ed.), *Thematic Relations (Syntax and Semantics Vol. 21)*. New York, Academic Press, 191–213.

Williams, Kemp: 1988. Exceptional Behavior of Anaphors in Albanian. *Linguistic Inquiry* 19, 161–168.

The expletive verb <u>be</u>

Tineke Scholten
University of Maryland

1. introduction

The proper characterization of the meaning of the verb <u>be</u> has been a prime subject of debate among logicians, linguists, and philosophers. It has been proposed that there are multiple <u>be</u>s, each with its own inherent semantics; alternatively, it has been argued that <u>be</u> has one meaning in all its occurrences and that interpretational differences follow from properties of the context in which the verb appears. Finally, there is a recurring idea in the literature that <u>be</u> is essentially meaningless.[1]

Notice that the distribution of the passive auxiliary supports an analysis of <u>be</u> as a grammatical rather than lexical formative. As (1) demonstrates, the distribution of the passive auxiliary cannot be predicted solely on the basis of selectional properties of either <u>be</u> or the passive participle, since not every passive participle combines with an auxiliary verb. This means that the syntactic context of the participle determines at least to some extent whether <u>be</u> must appear.

(1)a.   Mary was attacked by the dogs
   b.   Mary considers herself (*be) fired
   c.   The (*be) attacked woman

The same applies to perfective <u>be</u>. In most Germanic and Romance languages, perfective <u>be</u> is selected as the auxiliary in sentential structures headed by an ergative verb. Again, the syntactic context of the ergative participle is essential in determining whether the ergative participle must be accompanied by an auxiliary verb. Ergative participles in small clauses or modifier positions do not trigger <u>be</u> as (2) demonstrates for Dutch.

---

[1]<u>be</u> lacks an obvious semantic interpretation. This in combination with the fact that in many languages, semantic relations expressed in constructions containing <u>be</u> can be expressed without a verb, has led to the hypothesis that <u>be</u> is a grammatical formative. For instance, Lyons (1977) showed that copula <u>be</u> is absent in Russian; Rapoport (1987) demonstrated the same for copula <u>be</u> in Hebrew, which is optional in all present tense copula constructions.

(2)a.   Marie is/*heeft gearriveerd
             'Mary is/has   arrived'
  b.   Ik beschouw de trein gearriveerd (*zijn)
             'I consider the train arrived   (be)'
  c.   De gearriveerd(e) (*zijnde) trein
             'the arrived   (being)   train'

In this article, I will explore the idea that the distribution of be is completely determined in the syntax. I intend to show that an analysis of be as a grammatical formative can provide an answer to the following questions:

1.   why do sentential passives require the presence of an auxiliary verb in Romance and Germanic?
2.   why do most Germanic and Romance languages distinguish between ergative and non-ergative constructions in the choice of perfective auxiliary?
3.   why is be, as opposed to have, consistently the chosen auxiliary for ergatives and passives?[2]

2. be as an expletive

Let's assume that be is an expletive verb on a par with, for instance, the expletive preposition of in nominalizations, which must assign case to the object of the nominalized head. 'Supportive' do in English is also generally assigned a purely grammatical status and provides the verbal root for tense and agreement morphology. Contrary to standard assumptions about the insertion of do or of, I will not propose to insert be through a late process of lexical insertion.[3] Instead, let's assume that be appears in the lexicon with the minimal specification that it is a verb, i.e., that it bears the features [+V,-N]. What makes it an expletive is the fact that it bears no selectional or subcategorizational specification.

The Projection Principle stipulates that lexical features must be projected onto syntactic structures;

---

[2]The situation described here is somewhat simplified. In some languages other verbs can perform a role very similar to that of the passive auxiliary be. Examples are get in English and werden ('become') in German. I will not discuss the status of these verbs here.

[3]I will argue that the V-projection in which be appears plays a role in the mapping of D-structures onto S-structures. Be can be inserted by a late rule of lexical insertion if it involves the lexicalization of a V-position that is already present at D-structure.

X-bar-theory requires these representations to conform to a specified format. Given these principles, no phrase structure rules need to be assumed to realize the syntactic representation of argument structure. The Projection Principle will not guarantee the generation of be in D-structure, however, if be does not bear selectional features. We may assume that categorial representations can be freely generated, hence that V-projections, as long as they conform to X-bar-theory, can be generated, even if no lexical verb heads the projection. In order to prevent the system from widely overgenerating, a general principle is then needed that prohibits the creation of unnecessary structure. Specifically for the expletive verb be, we must prevent the generation of a string of expletives where its members serve no grammatical purpose.

Though the precise formulation is not without problems, it does not seem unlikely that an economy principle of some sort is operative in Universal Grammar that prevents the unnecessary complication of syntactic structures. The intent of this restriction is expressed in the Principle of Full Interpretation (Chomsky 1986a):

(3)   Every element at PF and LF must receive an appropriate interpretation

An appropriate interpretation for arguments is that they receive a θ-role, for operators that they bind a variable; for expletives, a specific grammatical function must license its occurrence in a grammatical representation.[4]

Be, by virtue of its categorial features, can head a maximal projection labelled VP. Since it does not assign θ-roles, tense, or case, it will never be the sister of a constituent that needs any of these features. Be can be the sister of a maximal projection that does not require semantic or case features from the verb. If, as does not seem unlikely, VPs do not need case, tense, or a θ-role, be could appear as a sister of VP.

---

[4]One of the questions that must be decided is at what level this principle operates. The principle might allow the generation of an endless string of expletives, but ultimately exclude the 'unnecessary' ones at a later level. Presumably the principle must in some form operate at S-structure or at PF. If expletives are prohibited at LF on general grounds, this may imply that be is absent at LF.

3. passive and ergative <u>be</u>

Burzio (1986) has presented convincing evidence for the following derivation of ergative verbs in Italian:

(4)a.   Le due navi$_i$ arrivano t$_i$
         'the two ships arrived'
   b.   e$_i$ arrivano le due navi$_i$
         'arrived the two ships'

The ergative verb <u>arrivare</u> assigns a θ-role but no case to the direct object position. In order to receive case, the object NP must be coindexed with the subject position. In (4a) this is realized through NP-movement, in (4b) coindexing is realized in some other manner, presumably obeying the same locality conditions that apply to NP-movement.

As Burzio has pointed out, the trigger for the occurrence of the passive and the ergative auxiliary <u>be</u> can be defined in an identical fashion. Two factors must be satisfied in order to trigger <u>be</u>: 1. the verb must take on the participle form, and 2. an A-chain must be formed including the subject of the sentence and the direct object.[5] In (4), there is an A-chain including the direct object, but no participle; in (5a), there is a participle, but no proper A-chain; in (5b) and (6), both conditions are satisfied and <u>be</u> must appear:

(5)a.   The enemy has destroyed the city
   b.   the city$_i$ was destroyed e$_i$ by the enemy
(6)a.   Le due navi$_i$ sono arrivato t$_i$
         'the two ships are arrived'
   b.   e$_i$ sono arrivato le due navi$_i$
         'are   arrived the two ships'

3.1. the A-chain

A number of authors have argued that clausal subjects originate under the VP.[6] Following proposals along these lines, I will assume that the D-structure of (5b) and (6) is as in (7).

Sportiche (1987) incorporates this analysis of clausal subjects in a reworking of the Barrier Theory of Chomsky (1986b) and shows that it permits an elegant account of locality principles applying to NP-movement.

---

[5]I will assume that perfective and passive <u>be</u> will appear if and only if these two factors are satisfied. Since small clauses do not trigger <u>be</u>, a movement analysis for (1b) or (2b) must be excluded. For discussion, see Scholten (1988).

[6]See Sportiche (1988) and reference cited there.

Sportiche adopts (8) as the definition of what
constitutes a barrier.[7]

(7)

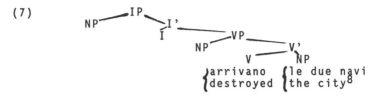

(8)   If X_n dominates α, α does not equal X_0,
        and X_n is not L-marked, then X^{max} is a
        barrier for α.

Contrary to Chomsky (1986b), Sportiche assumes that VPs
are L-marked.
    Notice that X' is never L-marked since only maximal
projections can be L-marked. This means that for any
constituent dominated by X', with the exception of the
head, X^{max} will be a barrier. Extraction of an object
out of its maximal projection can therefore only take
place through adjunction, an option only available for
A'-moved constituents, or by moving the object first to
a transparent position within its X^{max}, i.e., to SPEC of
XP.[9] Movement out of the maximal projection in one swoop
would yield an (antecedent) government violation at LF.
    It is the crucial role of the subject position for
NP-movement that I will exploit when proposing an
explanation for the obligatory appearance of <u>be</u> in
passive and ergative participle constructions.

3.2. syntactic categories and their subject positions
    Sentential structures realize a subject position
irrespective of θ-role assignment. The obligatory
appearance of an expletive <u>it</u> in (9a) and <u>there</u> in (9b)
can be explained in this manner:

---

[7](8) replaces both the permissive barrier
definition that Chomsky adopts for syntactic movement as
well as the more restrictive barrier definition based on
minimality.

[8]Another way in which this idea can be implemented
is by adjoining the clausal subject to the VP. If we
were to take this position, the argument presented will
hold with some minor modifications.

[9]Sportiche assumes that NP-movement to SPEC of I is
an instance of A-movement, even though SPEC of I is a
θ'position. A'-movement is defined as movement to a
position that can contain an operator.

(9)a.   It seems that Bill is sick
   b.   I believe there to be a good reason for his refusal

The obligatory realization of the subject position was considered a property of verbal predicates in Chomsky (1986a), and taken as an instance of the Principle of Full Interpretation. As opposed to sentential constructions, presence of the subject position in APs, NPs, or PPs depends on lexical properties of the head. The subject position of APs, NPs, and PPs will only be realized when a θ-role is assigned to the position. If no θ-role is assigned, no argument position will be projected at D-structure.

If clausal subjects originate under the VP, there are two subject positions in a simplex sentence. The occurrence of expletive subjects in clauses can therefore indicate that either the VP or the IP allows or demands the presence of a θ'-subject-position. Let's assume that VPs, and only VPs, must realize a subject position irrespective of θ-role assignment:

(10)   If an XP is headed by α, where α = +V,-N, then XP contains a position [NP,XP]; if XP is headed by β, where $\beta \neq$ +V,-N, then *[NP, XP], unless NP is a θ'-position.

3.3. participles

In the early transformational literature, the perfective or passive participle suffix is attached to a verbal root by a syntactic transformation of 'Affix Hopping'. I will assume instead that the derivation of participles and possibly the combination of all derivational affixes with a verbal root takes place outside the syntactic component. Participle formation is hence a context free process. Adopting standard assumptions of feature neutralization,[10] participles will bear the feature [+V] but not [-N]. Participles will be projected from the lexicon as heads of VPs where the head bears the feature [+V].

3.4. the role of be

Now notice that given the assumptions in 3.1, 3.2, and 3.3, sentential passive and ergative participle constructions cannot be derived. (11) demonstrates the structure in which an ergative or passive participle is

---

[10]See Muysken & Van Riemsdijk (1986) for an overview of the literature on feature neutralization.

incorporated in an IP; the structure corresponds to (5b) and (6) in which <u>be</u> has been omitted:

(11)

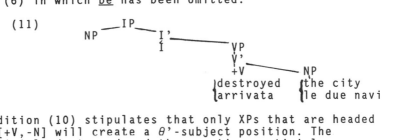

Condition (10) stipulates that only XPs that are headed by [+V,-N] will create a θ'-subject position. The participle <u>destroyed</u> and the ergative participle <u>arrivata</u> will only realize a subject position if the subject is assigned a θ-role. Ergative participles will therefore never realize the position [NP,VP], and only the active participle <u>destroyed</u> will project a subject position. The object in (11), however, must be coindexed with SPEC of I in order to receive case. Since this coindexing can only be established through the presence of an intermediate subject, cf. (8), sentential ergative and passive participle constructions cannot be derived.

We have assumed that <u>be</u> is an expletive solely bearing phonetic and categorial features in the lexicon. Now suppose that <u>be</u>, simply by lexicalizing a [+V,-N] position, realizes an accessible SPEC position for the object of the participle, thereby allowing the proper constitution of the A-chain.

(12) $[_{IP}NP_i \ I \ [_{VP_1}t_i \ be \ [_{VP_2} \ V\text{-}ed \ t_i]]]$

Since <u>be</u> has the categorial features [+V,-N], it will realize a position [NP,VP]; since <u>be</u> has no θ-marking properties, [NP,VP] will be a θ'-position. What is left to explain is why the subject of <u>be</u> is accessible to the object of the participle in (12).

3.4.1. segments of maximal projections

In Chomsky (1986b) the notion 'maximal projection' was given a new interpretation with respect to the definition of locality conditions on movement. In order to allow wh-movement of a constituent dominated by the VP, Chomsky proposed to allow A'-movement out of a maximal projection through adjunction to the VP. Extraction out of VP_2 in (13) is allowed since VP_1 and VP_2 are treated as segments of the same maximal projection.

(13) $[_{VP_1} \ wh\text{-}phrase \ [_{VP_2}...t...]]$

The identity of VP_1 and VP_2 in (13) is attributed to the
fact that the wh-phrase is in an adjoined position.
In (14) this interpretation of what constitutes a
distinct maximal projections is given a slightly more
general interpretation:[11]

(14)   In a structure of the form
         $[XP_a...[XP_b...]]$,
         XP_a and XP_b are segments of the same
         maximal projection when there are no
         selectional or subcategorizational
         features assigned to members of XP_a that
         do not apply to members of XP_b.

Now notice that (14) is satisfied in (12). Be,
since it is an expletive, does not assign any features
to members of its projection. The subject position is a
θ'-position, and its VP-sister is not a complement in
the usual sense: it is not c-selected or s-selected by
be. Given (14), VP and VP* in (12) are therefore
segments of the same maximal projection. This makes SPEC
of be accessible for the object of the passive or
ergative participle.

3.5. have
Why can perfective have not replace be in
sentential ergative and passive participle
constructions?[12] Notice that have, as opposed to be in
English, has a main verb variant that does not undergo
inversion in questions and does not appear to the left
of quantifiers, sentence adverbials, and negation. Have
also has a causative interpretation, in which case it
assigns case to the subject of its complement. In other
Germanic and Romance languages, have has a comparable
possessive and sometimes also causative function. Let's
therefore assume that have is a lexical verb, bearing c-
selectional and/or s-selectional features.

---

[11]An extension of the theory of what constitutes a
distinct maximal projection to base-generated structures
is necessary for independent reasons. Base-generated
adverbials do not affect the opacity of the domain which
they modify. Notice that the constituent dominating
certainly must not be interpreted as an independent
barrier for extraction of the subject.

(i) $Frank_i$ [certainly [NP_i seems [t_i to stay]]].

[12]The same question must be asked for do. In
Scholten (1988) I argue that do must assign an agentive
θ-role when generated outside INFL.

If <u>have</u> is a lexical verb, it cannot provide an accessible subject position for the object of its participle complement. Being a lexical verb, VP$_1$ and VP$_2$ in (15) do not represent segments of the same maximal projection, and the direct object of the participle would have to cross a barrier in order to move to the SPEC of <u>have</u>:

(15)   *[$_{VP_1}$NP$_i$ have [$_{VP_2}$*V-ed t$_i$]]

The subject position of <u>have</u> is not accessible to the object of the passive participle. As a result, a passive participle in the complement of <u>have</u> is prohibited. <u>Have</u> does take an active participle in its complement cf. (6a). In that case, the participle assigns a θ-role to its subject position and the derivation will be as follows:

(16)   *[$_{VP_1}$NP$_i$ have [$_{VP}$t$_i$ V-ed ...]]

There is some interesting evidence supporting this analysis of participles, <u>have</u>, and <u>be</u>. Sportiche (1988) has argued that displaced quantifiers such as <u>tous</u> in (17) are left behind when the subject moves to SPEC of I.

(17)   Les enfants$_i$ [$_{VP}$t$_i$ ont [$_{VP}$tous t$_i$ parti]]
         'the children   have   all   left'

Notice that, given this derivation, the presence of a displaced quantifier is indicative of a subject position immediately to its right. If we accept this analysis and, as Sportiche has suggested, its applicability to English <u>all</u>, the unwellformedness of (18b) in comparison to (18a) indicates that passive participles as opposed to active participles do not project a subject position.

(18)a.   They$_i$ must have [$_{VP}$all t$_i$ examined the patients]
    b.   *They$_i$ must have [$_{VP}$t$_i$ been [$_{VP}$all t$_i$ examined by the doctor]]

This confirms the predictions made by principle (10), which stipulates that participles can only project a subject position if this position receives a θ-role.

3.6. thematic properties of participles

The dependence of the projection of a subject position on the categorial features of the head as expressed in restriction (10) permits a minimal analysis of the morphological process of participle formation. Zubizarreta (1985), following Manzini (1980) and Marantz (1984), has drawn attention to the fact that the agent θ-role of a verb in sentential passives is never suppressed, but merely dissociated from the subject position. Zubizarreta notes that purpose adverbials and adverbs such as <u>voluntarily</u> and <u>intentionally</u> can only modify agentive predicates. In verbal passive constructions, these adverbs can occur regardless of the syntactic realization of the <u>by</u>-phrase.

(19)a.   The boat was sunk intentionally
   b.   The house was burned in order to collect
          the insurance

The examples contrast with similar ergative constructions that do not allow modification by agentive adverbs:

(20)a.   The boat sunk (*intentionally)
   b.   The house burned (*in order to collect
          the insurance)

(20) indicates that no agent θ-role is assigned in ergatives. I take it that ergatives optionally assign an agent θ-role. Following Jaeggli (1986), let's assume that the agent θ-role in passives is assigned to the passive participle suffix.
    Suppose we adopt a filter on representations of argument structure. Filter (21) is formulated as a condition on wellformed D-structures.

(21)   A syntactic representation of θ-
        structure is unwellformed if it contains
        a position α and a θ-role β, where α is
        the designated position for β, and β is
        not assigned to α.[13]

I will assume that the designated position for the agent θ-role is the position [NP,XP].
    Filter (21) in combination with (10) makes the following predictions: 1. it predicts that participles can, but need not relocate their agent θ-role to a position distinct from the subject position; 2. it predicts that verbal roots must assign their agent θ-role to the subject position. Starting with the latter, verbal roots are [+V,-N]. When inserted in a syntactic

---

[13]A similar constraint preventing the assignment of the external θ-role to a position other than the subject in active verb constructions is adopted in Zubizarreta (1985):

(i)   If the head of the VP has a lexically
       designated external argument, the VP must be
       predicated of this argument. Zubizarreta (1985:256).

structure, they will hence realize a subject position
(cf. 10). Since the subject position is always present,
the verb must assign its agent θ-role to that position.
A sentence such as (22) in which the agent θ-role is
assigned to the <u>by</u>-phrase is filtered out by (21).

(22)   *It arrests Mary by the police

   The participle <u>arrested</u>, however, bears the
categorial feature [+V]. Given (10), it will not create
a θ'-subject position. Therefore, filter (21) can be
circumvented, since the designated position for the
agent θ-role need not be present. This explains why
participles can, but need not assign their agent θ-role
to a position other than [NP,VP]. When the agent θ-role
is assigned to a <u>by</u>-phrase or to the participle suffix,
the position [NP,VP] will not be realized, and the
structure will not violate filter (21); this is the
passive participle interpretation. On the other hand,
the participle can assign its agent θ-role to the
[NP,VP] position, since all categories can project a
subject position as long as this position receives a θ-
role; in that case the participle is an active
participle. Only the following correlation must
therefore be expressed in the grammar:

(23)   [+V,-N]   <—>   [+V]+ed

   Levin & Rappaport (1986) have shown that the
externalization of an internal argument in adjectival
passive participle constructions is a by-product of the
category conversion from verbal participle to adjectival
participle, and need not be stipulated as part of the
rule. They hypothesize that rules defining the
externalization or internalization of a particular θ-
role (e.g., the theme in lexical passives) can be
dispensed with altogether in the grammar, allowing for a
more restrictive theory of morphological change.
The proposal for participle formation in this section
takes this approach just one step further. If the
analysis presented here is correct, not only the
relation between a verbal passive and an adjectival
passive can be stated simply in terms of category
change, but the change from verb to (verbal) participle
can as well. A tempting hypothesis that emerges is an
even more restrictive theory of morphology precluding
any type of rule that stipulates a change in syntactic
category in combination with a change in lexical
properties of the target.

4. parametrization
   There appears to be a gradual decline in the use of
<u>be</u> in ergatives with Italian at one end of the scale,

and English and Swedish at the other. In Italian, all
ergative constructions trigger be; in French, and also
in Danish, Dutch, and Norwegian, only certain ergatives
trigger be, the others take have. English and Swedish
ergatives consistently take have. In this section I will
discuss certain differences in the use of auxiliary be
in French and Italian,[14] and propose a parameter.

The distribution of perfective and passive be in
French and Italian is listed under (24). (24) shows
that, as opposed to Italian ergatives, only a subclass
of the ergatives in French are preceded by be. French
raising verbs are preceded by have, and so is the
participle form of be itself; passives consistently
trigger auxiliary be in French and Italian.

(24)		French	Italian
	ergatives	be/have	be
	seem	have	be
	be	have	be
	passives	be	be

Suppose that the difference between French and
Italian is an effect of the categorial interpretation of
the participle. Let's assume that French speakers will
interpret participles as [V,-N], unless there is an
overriding grammatical principle forcing them to do
otherwise. Italian speakers on the other hand will
interpret every participle as [+V]. We may assume that
the unmarked categorial interpretation of participles is
[+V,-N] and that French represents the unmarked
variant.[15]

This parameter predicts that French raising verbs
and be, also a raising verb, do not trigger be-
insertion. The participle form of seem and be is
[+V,-N]. NP-movement of constituents from the complement
of the participle can therefore take place through the
subject position that is realized in all XPs headed
by [+V,-N]:

(25)a.   Marie$_i$ [t$_i$ a [t$_i$ été [invitée t$_i$]]]
         'Mary   has   been invited'
   b.   Maria$_i$ [t$_i$ è [stata [invitata t$_i$]]]
         'Mary   is been   accused'

---

[14]This section is based on the data discussed in
Burzio (1986).

[15]This may not just apply to the interpretation of
participles but may apply to all lexical items of the
form [X+suffix]. It is possible that the language
learner will interpret all morphological affixation as
not affecting the categorial status of the root, unless
there is evidence to the contrary.

Now notice that principle (10) in combination with the filter on θ-role projection (21) forces French speakers to analyze passive participles as [+V] rather than [+V,-N]. Passive participles must assign their agent θ-role to a position distinct from the designated position [NP,VP]. Cf. filter (21), this can only be done if the position [NP,VP] is unrealized. VPs headed by [+V,-N] will generate a subject position irrespective of θ-role assignment. Assignment of an agent θ-role to a by-phrase or to the participle suffix will therefore force a categorial interpretation of the participle other than [+V,-N], which in turn will trigger the insertion of expletive be.

Finally, the case of ergatives. The theory presented here does not force a specific categorial interpretation on the ergative participle, since ergative participles do not assign agent θ-roles to a participle suffix or to a by-phrase. I do not exclude the possibility that other factors than the one discussed here determine the choice of auxiliary in ergatives. Possibly these factors translate into a specific categorial interpretation of the participle, a subject which requires further research.[16]

*I would like to thank Frank Drijkoningen, Hilda Koopman, Norbert Hornstein, David Lightfoot, Christer Platzack, Tim Stowell, and Jean-Roger Vergnaud for valuable comments on earlier drafts of this paper.

references
Burzio, Luigi. 1986. Italian Syntax, a Government-Binding Approach. Studies in Natural Language and Linguistic Theory. Dordrecht: Reidel.

Chomsky, Noam. 1986b. Barriers. Cambridge: MIT Press.

-------------- 1986a. Knowledge of Language: Its Nature, Origin and Use. New York: Praeger.

---

[16]Notice that English can be treated in the same manner as French. English speakers will interpret participles as [+V,-N], unless forced to do otherwise. This leads to the following paradigm:

(i)

	English
ergatives	have
seem	have
be	have
passives	be

Jaeggli, Oswaldo. 1986. Passive. LI. 17.587-622.

Levin, Beth & Malka Rappaport. 1986. The Formation of
    Adjectival Passives. LI. 17.623-62.

Lyons, John. 1977. Semantics. Cambridge: Cambridge
    University Press.

Manzini, Maria-Rita. 1980. On Control. MIT. Ms.

Marantz, A. 1984. On the Nature of Grammatical
    Relations. Linguistic Inquiry Monograph 10.
    Cambridge: MIT Press.

Muysken, Pieter & Henk van Riemsdijk. 1986. Features and
    Projections. Dordrecht: Foris Publications.

Rapoport, Tova. 1987. Copular, Nominal, and Small
    Clauses: A study of Israeli Hebrew. Doctoral
    Dissertation, MIT.

Scholten, Tineke. 1988. Universal Properties of Grammar
    and the Auxiliary Verb Phenomenon. Doctoral
    Dissertation, University of Maryland.

Sportiche, Dominique. 1987. Unifying Movement Theory.
    University of Southern California, Ms.

Sportiche, Dominique. 1988. A Theory of Floating
    Quantifiers and Its Corollaries for Constituent
    Structure. to appear in LI.

Zubizarreta, Maria-Luisa. 1985. The Relation between
    Morphophonology and Morphosyntax. The Case of
    Romance Causatives. LI 16.247-90.

Bare-Consonant Reduplication:
Implications for a Prosodic Theory of Reduplication
Kelly Sloan
M.I.T.

McCarthy and Prince (1986) proposes that all reduplicative
[1]
processes are prosodic. By this they mean that reduplicative
affixes are restricted to prosodic constituents - basically
syllable, foot and word. This is in contrast to the assumption,
standard since Marantz (1982), that reduplicative affixes
consist of a string of skeletal slots. Since skeletal slots are
not prosodic constituents, a reduplicative affix could not be
merely 'C' (or 'X' in the notation suggested by Levin (1985)).

This brings into question the status of bare-consonant
reduplication - the copy of one or more consonants to the
exclusion of vowels. Given, on the one hand, the difficulty of
accounting for bare-consonant reduplication in a prosodic
framework, and on the other, the tremendous coverage (as well as
appeal) of the prosodic account, it is important to study this
phenomenon in more detail.

In this paper I examine a group of languages for which
bare-consonant reduplication is well-documented and highly
productive. These are a branch of Mon-Khmeric languages spoken
primarily in Laos and the Malay Peninsula. All of these
languages exhibit a striking and unusual type of syllable
structure called 'sesquisyllabic' structure. I discuss three of
these languages - Semai, Temiar, and Kammu. I show that a
prosodic analysis can in fact handle the type of bare-consonant
reduplication evidenced in these three. In addition, Kammu
gives us a great deal of insight into the relationship between
affixation and copy. I will argue first that these processes
may be separated by other morphological operations and second
that they can occur independently.

I. Prosodic Affixes and Bare Consonant Reduplication

Examples of reduplication in each of these languages is shown
[2]
in (1). In Semai, a copy of the initial and the final
consonants is prefixed to the base. In Kammu a copy of the
final consonant is infixed into the base. Temiar shows both

----

1. I am indebted to Diana Archangeli, Jill Carrier-Duncan, Alan
Prince, and Donca Steriade for useful discussion of ideas
presented in this paper.

2. All Kammu data is from Svantesson (1983), Temiar from
Benjamin (1976), and Semai from Diffloth (1976a, b).

patterns. (The reduplicated portion is underlined.)

(1) <u>Semai</u>: dnoh   -> <u>dh</u>dnoh   'appearance of nodding
                                             constantly'
               ghup   -> <u>gp</u>ghup   'irritation on skin'
               cru:haw -> <u>cw</u>cru:haw   'the sound of water
                                             falling'
               sibi:t   -> <u>st</u>sibi:t   'squinting eyes'

    <u>Kammu</u>:   ṣté:ñ   -> s<u>n̄</u>te̞:ñ   'small steady still light'
               lmà:c   -> l<u>c̞</u>mà:c   'be stuck'
               k?ā́:w   -> k<u>w̞</u>?à:w   'open'
               r̀ŋìp   -> r<u>ṇ̞</u>ŋìp   'many people lie down'

    <u>Temiar</u>: kɔw   -> <u>kw</u>kɔw   'calling (cont.)'
               ca:?   -> <u>c?</u>ca:?   'eating (cont.)'
               lug   -> <u>lg</u>lug   'laughing (cont.)'

               slɔg   -> s<u>g</u> lɔg   'sleeping (cont.)'
               sluh   -> s<u>h</u> luh   'blow-piping (cont.)'

The unusual patterns of consonant clusterings in (1) result
from the sesquisyllabic structure these languages exhibit.
('Sesquisyllabic' meaning 'one and a half syllables'.) In
addition to what are termed 'major' syllables – normal syllables
in our view, basically (C)CV(V)C – there are 'minor' syllables –
a 'syllable' consisting of one or two consonants and no vowel.
In (2), I show the syllabic structure of Kammu (from Svantesson,
1983, p.3). The parentheses denote optionality. The example
word <u>cn.traas</u> is a maximal word in Kammu. Relevant differences
among the syllabic structures of Kammu, Semai, and Temiar will
be discussed below. Each of the languages, however, allows for
minor syllables.

(2)

Minor syllables are restricted to word-initial position. A
sesquisyllabic word thus contains a minor syllable followed by a
major syllable. In Semai minor syllables can be concatenated.
Thus, words can consist of a string of minor syllables followed
by a string of major syllables, as shown in (3) (the symbol '.'
delimits syllabic boundaries).

(3) kc.km.r.?ɛ:c   'short, fat arms'
    dl.d.yo:l.yo:l   'appearance of an object which goes on
                      floating down'

Minor syllables are clearly heard and perceived as distinct syllables. We can see this in the minimal pair k.lôok 'bamboo bowl' and k.lôok 'slit drum'. Another pair, p.cró:l 'bounce' and pc̀.rà:c 'mesentery', distinguishes minor syllables with one consonant from those with two. In Kammu, minor syllables with two consonants carry a tone. (The tone is usually carried by the consonant, particularly if it is sonorant, and sometimes by an epenthetic vowel.) The tone in pc̀.rà:c is taken as evidence that the 'c' is in the rhyme of the minor syllable.

There is much that is not understood about minor syllables. We do know that there are two distinct types of minor syllables − C and CC. From the tonal data of Kammu, it is reasonable to conclude that the former is nonmoraic and the latter monomoraic. In the diagrams below these two types of minor syllables are termed s0 and s1, respectively, as in (4).[3]

(4) Proposed minor syllable structure:

Notice in (1) that what is reduplicated in Semai is a minor syllable − two consonants at the beginning of the word. I propose then that the reduplicative affix is a monomoraic syllable − an s1. The major problem with reduplication in Semai is that it is the first and last consonants of the copy which are associated to the affix, an unusual association process. One clear generalization that can be made from (1), however, is that regardless of whether the initial consonant is reduplicated, the final consonant is always reduplicated in all three languages. Therefore, I propose the language-particular Special Association Principle given in (5).

(5) Special Association Principle (SAP)
    As the first step of association, associate the rightmost element of the copy to the affixal template.

The derivation of Semai gp.g.hup is then as shown in (6). An empty monomoraic syllable, s1, is prefixed to the base. Copy applies and then the SAP which will associate the final element of the copy, 'p', to the reduplicative affix. At this point association proceeds as normal. Since the unmarked direction of association for prefixes is left-to-right, the initial consonant, 'g', will associate to the affix as in (6)d. The

----

3. I shall not speculate on the odd notion of a 'nonmoraic syllable'. It is apparent that any analysis of Kammu will have to recognize and account for the existence of minor syllables. Once such syllables are recognized, they can be be utilized to account for reduplication, as I do below.

affix is then maximally satisfied and association ceases.

(6) Derivation of Semai gp.g.hup

a. Affixation
```
              s1   +   s0    s
                        |   /|\
                        g  h u p
```

b. Copy
```
              s1   +   s0    s
                        |   /|\
              g h u p   g  h u p
```

c. SAP
```
              s1   +   s0    s
                \        |   /|\
              g h u p   g  h u p
```

d. Association
```
              s1   +   s0    s
               /\        |   /|\
              g h u p   g  h u p
```

The continuative active in Temiar is formed by reduplication as was seen in (1). Monosyllabic roots, such as kɔw, reduplicate the first and last consonants, just as in Semai. kw.kɔw is thus derived in the same manner as gp.g.hup above, with affixation of s1 followed by copy and association.

Sesquisyllabic roots, such as s.lɔg show a different pattern, reduplicating as sg.lɔg. Since the continuative affix is an s1, as evidenced by kw.kɔw, I assume that the initial consonant of the sesquisyllabic roots is not syllabified underlyingly. (If it were not, we might expect a trisyllabic continuative form such as sg.s.lɔg.) The derivation of sg.lɔg[4] is given in (7).

----

4. Note that I am assuming that (1) segmental material is copied on the same plane as the base (2) only the syllabified material is copied, and (3) that the copy is prefixed directly to the syllabified portion of the base. None of these assumptions is crucial and each could be dropped. For example, the entire segmental melody could be copied and then the SAP and Association would apply as follows:

```
        s1    +    s
        /\        /\
      s l ɔ g   s l ɔ g
```

(7) Derivation of Temiar sɔ.lɔg

a. Affixation   s1   +   s
                                            /|\
                                          s l ɔ g

b. Copy   s1   +   s
                                            /|\
                                   s l ɔ g l ɔ g

c. SAP   s1   +   s
                                        \   /|\
                                   s   l ɔ g l ɔ g

d. Association   s1   +   s
                                        /\   /|\
                                   s   l ɔ g l ɔ g

We have thus accounted for the two distinct reduplicative patterns in Temiar using a single affix. The differences result from the syllabic structure — the extra consonant in the sesquisyllabic roots is available to associate to the affix without undergoing copy.

There are many different types of reduplication employed by Kammu. One of these, dubbed 'coda-copying' by Svantesson, shows the same pattern as sɔ.lɔg. Kammu has three word classes — noun, verb, and expressive. Expressive roots are monosyllabic and are marked for aspect by various morphological operations including reduplication. Coda-copying is used to express 'state' (as opposed, for example, to total reduplication of the root to express 'ongoing action').

Examples of coda-copying are given in (8). The root is first prefixed (the prefix is idiosyncratic and must be lexically marked, except for the prefix 'r' which marks plurality). Reduplication then applies. I assume that the reduplicative affix is s1, as in Semai and Temiar, and therefore that the prefix is not syllabified underlyingly.

(8) Kammu expressive reduplication ('coda-copying')

root	->	prefixation	->	reduplication
lɨp		k.lɨp		kp̬.lɨp
tèːñ		s.tèːñ		sñ̬.tèːñ
ʔàːw		k.ʔàːw		kw̬.ʔàːw

The derivation of kp̬.lɨp is given in (9). Note that it is the same as Temiar sɔlɔg except that the extrasyllabic element is prefixed rather than part of the root.

(9) Derivation of Kammu <u>kp.lip</u>

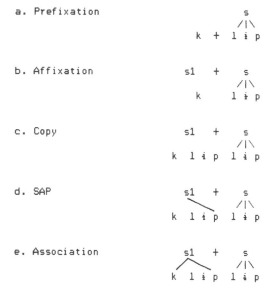

a. Prefixation

b. Affixation

c. Copy

d. SAP

e. Association

   Kammu differs from both Semai and Temiar in that it allows vowel-final roots. These roots have a distinctive pattern of reduplication as shown in (10).

(10) Kammu expressive reduplication in vowel-final roots

root	->	prefixation	->	reduplication	
ŋɔ́ɔ		c.ŋɔ́ɔ		cɔ́ɔ ŋɔ́ɔ	'white-skinned'
krò:		s.krò:		só: krò:	'downbent'
ŋə̀ə		t.ŋə̀ə		tə̀ə ŋə̀ə	'look upwards'

   Although this pattern appears radically different from the one in (8), it results from the same reduplicative affix, s1. Remember that s1 is a monomoraic syllable. Semai words and Temiar verbal roots are always consonant final. This fact, in combination with the SAP, which associates the rightmost element of the copy to the moraic position of the affix, ensures that affixation of s1 in Semai and Temiar always results in a minor syllable. In Kammu, however, V-final roots are allowed. In this case, the SAP will associate the vowel to the moraic position of the affix. Kammu has a restriction against light, open syllables. A general rule of lengthening then applies to lengthen the vowel. The derivation of <u>só: krðo</u> is given in (11).

(11) Derivation of Kammu sóo kròo

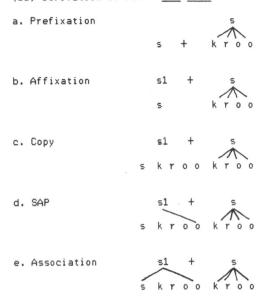

a. Prefixation

b. Affixation

c. Copy

d. SAP

e. Association

f. Lengthening   so kroo -> soo kroo

In this Section we have seen three different patterns of reduplication — prefix of initial and final consonant, infix of final consonant, and infix of vowel. I have shown that all three result from affixation of the prosodic affix s1, a monomoraic syllable. It is because of the unusual syllabic structure exhibited by these languages that we are able to account for bare-consonant reduplication without reference to the skeletal tier.

II. Separation of Affixation and Copy

Kammu shows an interesting interaction between expressive reduplication, discussed above, and intensive reduplication. Intensives in Kammu are formed by total reduplication. When a sesquisyllabic word is reduplicated, the major syllable rhyme is prespecified. (The prespecification is idiosyncratic and, I assume, lexically marked. There are certain tendencies, however; in particular an or Vn are common.) As we can see from the examples in (12), when a sesquisyllabic word reduplicates in the intensive its minor syllable always remains unchanged in the copy.

(12)   cm̀.ká:k cm̀.ké:n   from   cm̀.ká:k   'to stride across'
        cń.tràŋ cń.trìŋ   "   cń.tràŋ   'pillar'
        kr̀.ŋà:c kr̀.ŋìc   "   kr̀.ŋà:c   '(exp) spotted'

```
pr̠.kíp pr̠.káŋ      "    pr̠.kĭp   'swampy'
sm̥.pló? sm̥.plâŋ    "    sm̥.pló?  'to touch'
```

The exception to this is any word that has also undergone
coda-copying. Examples are shown in (13). Notice that while in
(12) the minor syllable codas of the base and copy are the same,
in (13) they are different - the minor syllable coda in the copy
is identical to the prespecified major syllable coda of the
copy.

(13)   cf̥.rì:t cŋ̥.ràŋ   from   cf̥.rì:t   '(exp) not hear'
        cw̥.ʔìaw ct̥.ʔò:t   "   cw̥.ʔìaw '(exp) talk much'
        kp̥.lĭp kŋ̥.làŋ   "   kp̥.lĭp   'to be noisy'
        kt̥.wàt kŋ̥.wàŋ   "   kt̥.wàt   'to wag'

It can be shown independently for Kammu that expressive
reduplication must precede the intensive (see Sloan 1987). We
would thus expect the coda-copied words in (13) to behave just
as any other sesquisyllabic word in the intensive - that is,
they should follow the pattern of (12). This problem is
resolved if we assume that intensive reduplication applies _after_
the affixation of s1 associated with expressive reduplication
and _before_ copy and association. This is demonstrated in (14).
Note that I have avoided the problem of prespecification (about
which I make no claims) and simply inserted the prespecified
material into the copy in the intensive.

First prefixation applies. Then, the s1 reduplicative affix
is prefixed - this is the morphological operation marking the
aspectual class 'state'. At this point, intensive reduplication
applies as in (14)c, which copies the entire representation,
with prespecification of the rhyme to _an_. Copy occurs,
independently in the base and copy as in (14)d. The SAP and
Association will then derive kp̥.lĭp kŋ̥.làŋ.

(14) Derivation of Kammu kp̥.lĭp kŋ̥.làŋ

a. Prefixation   s
                                       /|\
                                 k + l ɨ p

b. Affixation   s1 +   s
                                        /|\
                                 k   l ɨ p

c. Intensive   s1   s   +   s1   s
   (with prespecification)   /|\   /|\
                                 k   l ɨ p   k   l a ŋ

d. Copy   s1   s   +   s1   s
                                       /|\   /|\
                              k l ɨ p l ɨ p   k l a ŋ l a ŋ
```
```

e. SAP

```
        s1            s      +       s1            s
          \         /|\                \         /|\
        k   l i p  l i p             k   l a ŋ  l a ŋ
```

f. Association

```
        s1            s      +       s1            s
         /\          /|\              /\          /|\
        k   l i p   l i p            k   l a ŋ   l a ŋ
```

Even more interesting than the above is the interaction of expressive and intensive reduplication in V-final roots. From the root <u>rii</u>, we derive <u>cii</u> <u>rii</u> <u>ck.rak</u>. Though this is at first glance bizarre, I show in (15) that it follows quite naturally from the assumptions made thus far.

(20) Derivation of Kammu <u>cìi rìi ck.ràk</u>

a. Prefixation

```
                        s
                       /|\
                   c +  r i i
```

b. Affixation

```
                s1 +    s
                       /|\
                   c    r i i
```

c. Intensive
   (with prespecification)

```
                s1       s      +        s1            s
                        /|\                            /|\
                   c    r i i             c            r a k
```

d. Copy

```
                s1        s      +        s1            s
                         /|\                            /|\
              c  r i i   r i i          c  r a k       r a k
```

e. SAP

```
                s1        s      +        s1            s
                  \      /|\                 \          /|\
              c   r i i  r i i           c   r a k     r a k
```

f. Association

```
                s1        s      +        s1            s
                 /\      /|\                /\          /|\
              c   r i i  r i i           c   r a k     r a k
```

g. Lengthening

cì rìi ck.ràk ->   cìi rìi ck.ràk

III. <u>Phonologically Triggered Reduplication</u>

We know that affixation occurs independently of copy. I have just shown that affixation and copy can be separated in a derivation by the operation of distinct morphological processes. The obvious question to ask is whether copy occurs independently of affixation. I argue that it does.[5]

Kammu has a nominalizing prefix <u>rn-</u> and a causative prefix <u>pn-</u>, which are prefixed to monosyllabic roots as in (16).

(16) Nominalizing and Causative prefixes in Kammu

   a. Nominalizing /rn-/

rǹ.tèn	'chair'	from	tèn	'to sit'
rǹ.lùh	'pestle'	"	lùh	'to pound'

   b. Causative /pn-/

pǹ.pó:l	'to roll'	from	pó:l	'to roll (int.)'
pń.mah	'to feed'	"	mah	'to eat'
pǹ.kl5:k	'to whiten'	"	kl5:k	'white'

Reduplication often occurs in nominatives and causatives as in (17), where in place of the 'n' of the prefix we find a copy of the major syllable coda. This is an optional process (which Svantesson calls 'coda-assimilation' to distinguish it from coda-copying). Some roots always assimilate, some never do. Other roots can do either, leading to alternations like <u>rn.hɔm</u> /<u>rm.hɔm</u>.

(17) Reduplicated Codas in Nominatives and Causatives

   a. Nominalizing /rn-/

rk.sék	'cutting'	from	sék	'to cut'
rl.pèɛl	'wedge'	"	pèɛl	'to fix'
rỳ.wà:y	'fin'	"	wà:y	'to swim'

   b. Causative /pn-/

pś.rò:s	'to make angry'	"	rò:s	'angry'
pć.?ɨ̀:c	'to make silent'	"	?ɨ̀:c	'silent'
pt̂.klà:t	'to pass (tr.)'	"	klà:t	'to pass (itr.)'

Let us assume (as does Svantesson) that there is an optional rule in Kammu that delinks the 'n' of the prefix. The prefix is an s1, or monomoraic syllable. The derivation of <u>rk.sék</u> is given in (18).

----

5. A similar claim was made by Bat-El (1984) (though it was refuted rather convincingly by Prince (1987)). Bat-El's account differs from mine in that it applies to a templatic language, where it might be argued that choice of template implies a morphological operation.

(18) Derivation of r̆k.sék

a. Prefixation

```
        s1    +     s
       /\          /|\
      r  n        s e k
```

b. Delinking

```
        s1    +     s
       /x         /|\
      r  n        s e k
```

c. Copying

```
        s1    +     s
       /          /|\
     r s e k     s e k
```

d. SAP

```
        s1    +     s
      /‾‾‾‾        /|\
     r s e k     s e k
```

First there is prefixation, followed by delinking. At this point we have a template, an s1, that is not satisfied. Let us assume, along with McCarthy and Prince, that templates must be maximally satisfied. The obvious recourse for satisfying the template, one that is utilized by many languages, is to spread from an adjoining segment. Thus, either the 'r' of the prefix or the 's' of the root could spread into the position vacated by the delinked 'n'. However, geminates are not allowed in Kammu, so spreading cannot apply.

There is a process available in Kammu, namely copy, that will provide a means of filling the s1 template without violating the constraint against geminates. Copy therefore applies as in (18)c and the SAP as in (18)d to correctly derive r̆k.sék. This is a case of phonologically triggered reduplication – where copy is triggered not by a morphological rule but by the phonological rule of delinking.

To conclude, I have shown that bare-consonant reduplication in Kammu, Temiar, and Semai can be accounted for with a prosodic affix. This is directly related to the sesquisyllabic structure these languages exhibit, which allows for vowel-less syllables. In addition I have demonstrated that affixation and copy-and-association can be separated by other morphological operations, and indeed, that they can apply independently of each other.

References

Bat-El, Outi. 1984. Reduplication in Modern Hebrew. LSA Annual Meeting.

Benjamin, Geoffrey. 1976. An outline of Temiar grammar. Austroasiatic studies, ed. by P. N. Jenner, et. al. Honolulu: University Press of Hawaii.

Diffloth, G. 1976a. Minor syllable vocalism in Senoic languages. Austroasiatic studies, ed. by P. N. Jenner, et. al. Honolulu: University Press of Hawaii.

Diffloth, G. 1976b. Expressives in Semai. Austroasiatic studies, ed. by P. N. Jenner, et. al. Honolulu: University Press of Hawaii.

Levin, Juliette. 1985. A metrical theory of syllabicity. Doctoral dissertation, MIT.

Marantz, Alec. 1982. Re Reduplication. LI 13:435-482.

McCarthy, John and Alan Prince. 1986. Prosodic morphology. Manuscript, University of Massachusetts, Amherst, and Brandeis University.

Prince, Alan. 1987. Planes and Copying. LI 18:491-509.

Sloan, Kelly. 1987. Phonology generals paper. MIT.

Svantesson, Jan-Olof. 1983. Kammu phonology and morphology. Lund, Sweden, Liber Forlug.

On the Universality of X-Bar Theory: The Case of Japanese*

Koichi Tateishi
UMass/Amherst

0. Introduction

The universality of X-Bar theory has been a central issue in syntax
since Chomsky's (1972) "Remarks on Nominalization". One particular
focus of investigation has been the number of bar-levels per category.
This issue has been studied both cross-linguistically and
cross-categorially by Jackendoff (1977) and by Fukui (1986), among
others, and, in the context of languages like Japanese, is closely
related to the "non-configurationality issue" discussed by Chomsky
(1981) or by Hale (1983). In this paper, I will take up the issue of
cross-linguistic differences in X-bar theory, focusing on Japanese.
The central question for my paper is: Is X-bar theory parametrized?
   In particular, I will discuss the status of the SPEC position in
phrasal categories. Jackendoff (1977) and Chomsky (1986), among
others, have argued for the existence of a unique SPEC position in IP
and in DP (or NP), because of the apparent existence of one and only
one subject or determiner in these phrasal categories. Recent work by
Fukui (Fukui (1986)) proposes that this aspect of X-Bar theory is
subject to cross-linguistic variation. Fukui's argument is based
principally on two phenomena in Japanese: first, the existence of
multiple "determiners" in NP as in (1); and, second, the existence of
multiple subjects as in (2) (Kuno (1973)).

(1) John-no   MIT-Press-no   gengogaku-no   hon
    John-GEN MIT Press-GEN linguistics-GEN book
    '*John's MIT Press's linguistics' book
    = John's linguistics book from MIT Press'

(2) Nihon-ga   dansei-ga heikinjumyoo-ga   mijika-i.¹
    Japan-NOM man-NOM   average lifespan-NOM short-PRES
    'It is Japan where for men, their average lifespan is short.'

   Assume that each phrasal category has at most one SPEC position,
as Chomsky (1986) and Fukui (1986) argue. It follows that multiple
subjects in Japanese NPs and sentences are not instances of the SPEC
position. Following this reasoning, Fukui concludes that Japanese
entirely lacks a unique SPEC position in its phrasal categories. In
this paper, I will argue that X-bar theory is not parametrized. X-Bar
Theory is inviolable, at least for the functional categories (I, D,
C). The apparent non-uniqueness of Japanese determiners/subjects must
therefore be accounted for in another way, without rejecting the
hypothesis of a unique SPEC position. I will argue for NP that there
should be a SPEC position above an ordinary position of genitive
phrases to account for the distribution of Wh-phrases inside Japanese
NP. For the sentence, I will argue that some of the so-called
"multiple subjects" in Japanese are actually not instances of
"subjects" if we carefully consider their syntactic properties.

_____

* I am very grateful to Emmon Bach, Molly Diesing, Nobuko Hasegawa,
Hajime Hoji, Yasuo Ishii, Noriko Kawasaki, Masashi Kawashima, Yoshihisa
Kitagawa, Miori Kubo, Jack Martin, Yo Matsumoto, Shinobu Mizuguchi,
Maire Ni Chiosain, Yutaka Ohno, David Pesetsky, William J. Poser, Tim
Stowell, Mari Takahashi, Michiko Terada, Anne Vainikka, and Yasushi
Zenno for their comments, questions and encouragement. Remaining
errors are, of course, mine.

1. Some people do not accept multiple subjects because of the general
unnaturalness of ga as a subject marker. For such speakers, replacing
ga in the initial subject phrase with wa (the topic marker) does not
alter the point in this paper. An alternative way to improve
acceptability is to think of a situation where some emphasis is put on
each "subject".

To be sure, Fukui points out that some instances of Japanese subjects and determiners are not in the SPEC position. This conclusion appears to be right: the data in (1) and (2) almost force this conclusion on us. However, I think that there are some more questions that must be asked before we conclude, with Fukui, that there is no SPEC in Japanese. First, does the non-SPEC status of Japanese determiners lead us to the conclusion that there is no SPEC position in Japanese NP? Does every subject in (2) that is marked with *ga* really function as a subject?

1. NP

Let us consider NP's first.[2] Suppose that Fukui is right and no *no*-phrase inside NP is in SPEC position. Then the structure of (1) will be as in (3).

(3)

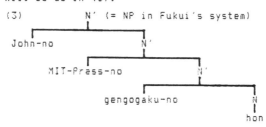

This conclusion does not in itself tell us that there is no SPEC in Japanese. Even if (3) is a structure for (1), we must still ask ourselves the following question: Is there a DP or N-double-bar immediately dominating this N-bar? If so, does *this* phrasal category have a unique SPEC position, as in (4)?

(4)

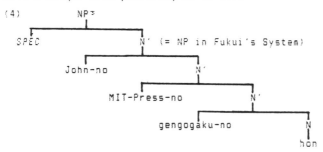

I will argue that the answer is yes: (4) is correct.

1.1. Multiple Interrogation in NP

Consider a sentence as in (5), with a subject NP that contains several *no*-phrases. In such an NP, either one of the two *no*-phrases can be replaced by a corresponding *Wh*-phrase: e.g. *dare* 'who', as in (6).

---

2. The work in this section could not have been accomplished without the benefit of discussions with Miori Kubo, to whom I am very grateful.

3. At this point, I will not commit myself to the question of whether NP in (4) is N" or DP (= Det Phrase) in the sense of Fukui (1986) and Abney (1987). I will briefly discuss this question later.

(5) [John-no Mary-no hihan-ga]   shuppan-s-are-ta.
    John-GEN Mary-GEN criticism-NOM publication-do-PASSIVE-PAST
    'John's criticism of Mary was published.'

(6) a. [Dare-no Mary-no hihan-ga] shuppan-s-are-ta-no(-ka)?
       who-GEN   -(nominalizer)-Q
       'Whose criticism of Mary was published?'
    b. [John-no dare-no hihan-ga] shuppan-s-are-ta-no(-ka)?
               who-GEN
       '*John's criticism of whom was published?'

However, if both of them are questioned as in (7), acceptability of the
sentence significantly decreases[4]:

(7)*?[Dare-no dare-no hihan-ga] shuppan-s-are-ta-no(-ka)?
     '*Whose criticism of whom was published?'

   The same paradigm can be reproduced with the *NP-no-Adjective-noun*
sequence in (8):

(8) Bill-wa   [John-no aka-i   shatsu-o] nusun-da.
    Bill-TOPIC John-GEN red-PRES shirt-OBJ steal-PAST
    'Bill stole John's red shirt.'

As in (9), either the genitive phrase or the adjective inside the
object NP can be questioned, but both can not be questioned at the same
time:

(9) a. Bill-wa [dare-no aka-i shatsu-o] nusun-da-no(-ka)?
              who-GEN   -(nominalizer)-Q
       'Whose red shirt did Bill steal?'
    b. Bill-wa [John-no nani-iro-no shatsu-o] nusun-da-no(-ka)?
                       what-color-PRES
       'What color shirt of John's did Bill steal?'
    c.*?Bill-wa [dare-no nani-iro-no shatsu-o] nusun-da-no(-ka)?
       '*Whose shirt of what color did Bill steal?'

Thus, there can not be any NP-internal multiple questions in Japanese.

1.2. NP-Internal Scrambling

To explain these facts, we must introduce some further data concerning
scrambling internal to NP. In Japanese, an adjective can be scrambled
to the front of NP over a genitive phrase, as in (10):

(10) Bill-wa [aka-i   John-no|shatsu-o] nusun-da.
             red-PRES John-GEN
     'Bill stole John's red shirt.'

Interestingly, in an NP with a scrambled adjective, only the *adjective*
can be Wh-questioned, as in (11a). With a scrambled adjective, nothing
to the right of the adjective in NP can be Wh-questioned. This can be
seen in (11b):

(11) a. Bill-wa [nani-iro-no John-no shatsu-o] nusun-da-no(-ka)?
                what-color-GEN   -(nominalizer)-Q
        'What color shirt of John did Bill steal?'
     b.*Bill-wa [aka-i dare-no shatsu-o] nusun-da-no(-ka)?
                      who-GEN
        '*A red shirt of whom did Bill steal?'
     c.*Bill-wa [nani-iro-no dare-no shatsu-o] nusun-da-no(-ka)?
        '*What color shirt of whom did Bill steal?'

---

4. Example (7) is possible as an echo question, but not as a multiple
Wh-question.

I will argue that these data can be accounted for if we assume that
there is a unique SPEC position in Japanese NP.[5]

1.3. Analysis

Let us assume, following Torrego (1985) and Longobardi (1987), that
Wh-movement out of NP is only possible through an unoccupied SPEC
position, as Ross's (1967) observation about English in (12) suggests:

(12) a. Who did you see [pictures of t]?
     b.*?Who did you see [John's pictures of t]?

If Wh-Movement out of NP always involves movement through SPEC, then we
can account for the prohibition against double Wh-phrases seen in (7)
and (9c) by arguing that only one of the two Wh-phrases can go through
the unique SPEC position at LF. (13) is the structure I am assuming
for (7):

(13)

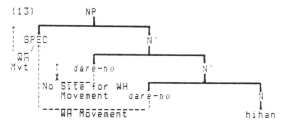

Either one of two instances of *dare-no* 'whose', can leave NP through
the SPEC position. The other Wh-phrase, however, can not be extracted
from the NP, because the SPEC position is already occupied by the trace
of the Wh-phrase which has moved out first. Even if the upper
Wh-phrase has moved out of NP first, the result is the same.

(13')

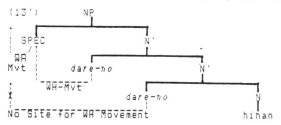

Therefore, multiple Wh-questions inside NP is ruled out.
     Turning to (11b), where an adjective is preposed over a
Wh-genitive phrase, I propose that Scrambling of an adjective moves the
adjective to the SPEC position. As a result, the path of Wh-movement
out of NP at LF is closed off. This is shown in (14).

---

5. See also Kubo (1987) for an account of the phenomenon in (11) in
terms of feature percolation of [+WH]. Kubo also reached the
conclusion that Japanese noun phrase has a SPEC position for
independent reasons. Nishigauchi's (1986) account of wh-movement and
LF-Pied-Piping also requires that there is a SPEC inside Japanese noun
phrase.

(14)

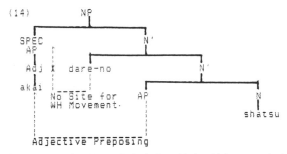

Adjective Preposing

Once an adjective (*akai* `red' in this case) has moved into the SPEC position of NP by Scrambling, there is no intermediate landing site for Wh-movement of *dare-no* in (14). The structure is ill-formed because Wh-word in the NP can not move out of the NP at LF.

Of course, a preposed adjective can itself be questioned as in (11a), since the adjective itself is in SPEC, and nothing prevents an element from moving out of the SPEC position at LF.

(14')

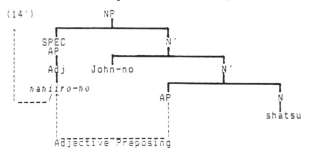

Adjective Preposing

Thus, by assuming a unique, leftmost SPEC position inside Japanese NP, we can immediately account for the distribution of Wh-phrases in Japanese NP. Note that this is also a strong argument for Wh-movement at LF in Japanese.

If this analysis is correct, we make a further prediction. Only one prenominal adjective should be able to precede a possessive *no*-phrase. Example (15) shows that this prediction is correct:

(15) a. John-no   aka-i   omoshiro-i   hon
        John-GEN red-PRES interesting-PRES book
        'John's red interesting book'
     b. i. omoshiro-i John-no aka-i hon
        ii. aka-i John-no omoshiro-i hon
     c. i. *omoshiro-i aka-i John-no hon
        ii. *aka-i omoshiro-i John-no hon

Two preposed adjectives are not allowed because there is only one SPEC position for the adjective to occupy.

1.3.1. D-Structure Order within NP

This subsection is an appendix to the Section 1.3. My argument in that section depended on the particular ordering relations among adnominal elements in the underlying structure[6]. For my hypothesis to be correct, genitive phrases inside Japanese NP must precede adjectives in the underlying structure, although they are all elements of N', a

---

6. Thanks to Tim Stowell for pointing out this problem.

non-maximal projection, which has no SPEC-complement distinction in principle. I have nothing to say about what produces this order, which is perhaps related to the semantic relations among adnominal elements, but I have some further syntactic evidence for my hypothesis (albeit weak evidence).

Consider (8) and (10) again.

(8) Bill-wa [John-no aka-i shatsu-o] nusun-da.
    Bill-TOPIC John-GEN red-PRES shirt-OBJ steal-PAST
    'Bill stole John's red shirt.'

(10) Bill-wa [aka-i John-no shatsu-o] nusun-da.
              red-PRES John-GEN
     'Bill stole John's red shirt.'
     or 'Bill stole John's shirt, which is red.'

As we can see from the gloss, there is a slight semantic difference between (8) and (10). An adjective in (8) can only be interpreted as a restrictive modifier of the head noun. However, in (10), it can be interpreted either as a restrictive or as a non-restrictive modifier[7]. Moreover, (8) is actually ambiguous. *John-no* in (8) has both restrictive and non-restrictive reading, and so does *John-no* in (10). (8) actually has two readings: "Bill stole a red shirt which John has." and "Bill stole that red shirt, which John has." The descriptive generalization is (16):

(16) A prenominal modifier can be interpreted as a non-restrictive modifier if another prenominal modifier follows it.

Let us explain what (16) means.

Suppose that the basic ordering relation among adnominal modifiers is that in (8)--Genitive-Adjective. Then the D-structure of the object NP in (8) will be the following:

(8')

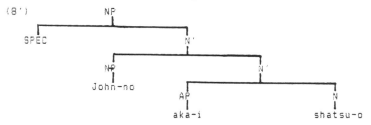

In (8'), only *John-no* can be interpreted as a non-restrictive modifier, since it precedes another prenominal modifier *aka-i*[8]. In (10), there

---

7. This fact was pointed out by Whitman (1981), although I don't necessarily agree with other judgements he presents. Hajime Hoji and Miori Kubo (p.c.) have pointed out this fact to me independently. We can see that (10) may be restrictive, since it is acceptable in the following context:

(i) Bill-wa naniiro-no John-no shatsu-o nusun-da-no?
    Bill-TOPIC what color-GEN John-GEN shirt-OBJ steal-PAST-Q
    'What color shirt of John did Bill steal?'

    --Aka-i John-no shatsu-o nusumi-mashi-ta.
      red-PRES John-GEN shirt-OBJ steal-ASSERTION-PAST
      '(he) stole red shirt of John's.'

8. Note that if we adopt the DP/NP (=N') distinction proposed by Fukui (1986), Abney (1987) among others, we can reduce the condition for the non-restrictive modification to the Predication relation as proposed by

are two candidates for the non-restrictive modifier, since both of the prenominal modifiers precede another prenominal modifier. *Aka-i* in (10') precedes *John-no*, and *John-no* precedes the trace of *aka-i*.

(10')

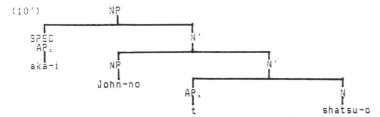

The restrictive/non-restrictive interpretation of prenominal modifiers can be accounted for if we assume the basic ordering relation among prenominal modifiers in this paper and adopt the movement analysis of NP-Internal Scrambling.
There is other independent evidence for the movement analysis of NP-Internal Scrambling. Consider the following contrast:

(17) a. John-no [aka-i   shatsu-to ao-i   booshi]
        John-GEN red-PRES shirt-and blue-PRES hat
        'John's red shirt and John's blue hat'

     b.*aka-i   [John-no shatsu-to Bill-no booshi]
        red-PRES John-GEN shirt-and Bill-GEN hat
        'John's shirt and Bill's hat, both of which are red'

In these conjoined NPs, the genitive NP can modify both conjuncts, as in (17a). However, in the case of NP-Internal Scrambling, the outermost prenominal modifier can not modify the second conjunct, as shown in (17b). Now, this exactly parallels the situation with sentential Scrambling. (18) is a relevant example.

(18) a. 'John went to the library and read a book.'
        John-ga [[toshokan-e iki] sosite [hon-o   yon-da]]
        John-NOM library-to go and   book-OBJ read-PAST
     b. 'John bought a book and Mary read it.'
        *Hon-o [[John-ga kai] sosite [Mary-ga yon-da]]
        book-OBJ John-NOM buy and   Mary-NOM read-PAST
     c. 'The book, John bought it and Mary read it.'
        Hon-wa [[John-ga kai] sosite [Mary-ga yon-da]]
            -TOPIC

If we assume, with Saito (1985), Hoji (1985) among others, that topic position in Japanese sentence is not necessarily filled by Move-Alpha, but may be base-generated, then we can account for the contrast in (18) in the following way. (18a,c) are acceptable because there is no movement involved. (18b) is ungrammatical because it involves Scrambling (a movement rule) out of the object position of both conjuncts, in an across-the-board fashion⁹. Given that (17b),

Williams (1980). If the SPEC in (8') is SPEC(DP) and N' is NP (= N') in Fukui, then the relation between *John-no* and the rest of N' will be the relation between DP and NP, the relation between two maximal projections which is required for the predication relation, including appositive relation, to be established. This I assume to be the source of non-restrictive relation.
    One problem with this analysis is what we assume as the head of DP. A possibility is that a case particle is a D (or some type of a functional head) in Japanese, as Fukui (1986) suggests (He does not pursue this possibility.).

across-the-board NP-Internal Scrambling, behaves like (18b), sentential
Scrambling, and given that there is much independent evidence for a
movement analysis of sentential Scrambling, we have a strong argument
for the movement analysis of NP-Internal Scrambling.

   I thus conclude that there is some evidence which suggests that
the basic ordering of prenominal modifier is Genitive NP-Adjective, and
that NP-Internal Scrambling is an instance of movement into the
SPEC(NP).

1.4. Summary

To summarize the discussion so far, we have seen that the prohibition
on multiple Wh-phrases inside NP follows if we assume that there is
only one position which can function as a landing site for Wh-movement
out of NP at LF. This uniqueness requirement lends initial support to
the hypothesis of a unique SPEC position in Japanese NP. We observed
next that no Wh-phrase can move out of NP across a Scrambled adjective
at the leftmost position of NP. This is accounted for by the
assumption that the landing site for Scrambling of nominal modifiers
and for Wh-movement out of NP is one and the same: the SPEC position.
This establishes the hypothesis that there is a unique leftmost SPEC
position in Japanese NP. This hypothesis is also supported by the fact
that more than one adjective can not be Scrambled across a genitive
phrase. Finally, the underlying ordering of adnominal elements which I
assume has independent syntactic motivation.

2. IP

In this section, I will argue for a unique SPEC of *IP*. I will claim
that the seemingly multiple subjects in examples like (2) are really
not so multiple. In particular, I will argue that the structure of the
ga-phrases in examples like (2) is not homogeneous.

   Consider the situation in (19). I will show that in the string of
ga-phrases in (19), X_3 and all preceding ones are actually *genitive
subconstituents* of X_2. They are marked with *ga* by a percolation
mechanism I will come back to later. X_2 itself occupies a unique
SPEC(I) position. X_1 is a VP-internal subject theta-marked by the verb
(as proposed by Kitagawa (1986), Kuroda (1986), Sportiche (1987) and
Fukui (1986)). I will give three arguments for this hypothesis.

(19) X_n-ga .... X_4-ga X_3-ga X_2-ga X_1-ga .... V.

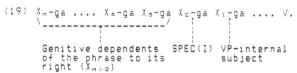

       Genitive dependents   SPEC(I)   VP-internal
       of the phrase to its   subject
       right ($X_{n>2}$)

(20)

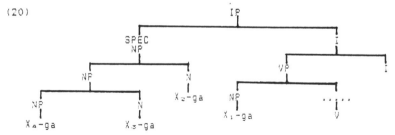

_____

9. Note that this explanation is independent of the issue of the
existence of an object empty pronominal in Japanese. See Hasegawa
(1985), Hoji (1985) and Kuroda (1965) for discussions.

2.1. Binding Theory (B)

The first argument for the analysis in (20) concerns a distinction
between the status of X_1 and X_2 with respect to Condition (B) of
Chomsky's (1981) Binding Theory, and is due to Kitagawa (1986).
Kitagawa (1986) showed that X_1 and X_2 are in different domains with
respect to this part of the Binding Theory. For example, Japanese
pronoun *kare* 'he' in object position must be free from X_1, but it can
be bound by X_2. This is shown in (21):

(21) John$_1$-ga chichioya$_j$-ga kare$_{i/*j}$-o nagut-ta.
     John-NOM father-NOM   him   hit
     'John's father hit him.'

This supports the assumption that X_1 is a VP-internal subject, if, with
Kitagawa, we take VP as the Binding Domain for Condition (B) in
Japanese.

2.2. Sentential Adverbs

The second argument distinguishes X_1 and X_2 from all ga-phrases further
to the left. That is, it distinguishes X_1 and X_2 from X_3 and up.
Sentential adverbs in Japanese, such as *totsuzen* 'suddenly', are
impossible between X_1 and X_2 or between any two ga-phrases to the left
of X_2, but they can occur at the sentence initial position or between
X_2 and X_1, as shown in (19):

(22) a. *Totsuzen* [$_{IP}$[$_{NP}$[$_{NP}$John-ga] computer-ga][$_{VP}$disk drive-ga
                      John-NOM computer-NOM   disk drive-NOM
        koware-ta]]
        break-PAST
        'John's computer's disk drive has suddenly broken.'
     b.*[$_{IP}$[$_{NP}$[$_{NP}$John-ga] *totsuzen* computer-ga][$_{VP}$disk drive-ga
        koware-ta]]
     c. [$_{IP}$[$_{NP}$[$_{NP}$John-ga] computer-ga] *totsuzen* [$_{VP}$disk drive-ga
        koware-ta]]

This argument shows that there is a major sentence boundary between X_1
and X_2, and (obviously) at the left periphery of the sentence, but
there is *no* major sentence-level boundary between X_2 and X_3. This is
what we expect, if X_3 and up are genitive dependents of X_2.

2.3. *Jibun* 'Self' and C-Command

Finally, the genitive hypothesis predicts that X_3 and preceding
ga-phrases can *not* bind an anaphoric expression in S. This is because
such genitive phrases do not c-command elements of S. The prediction
is correct. Consider (23).

(23) a. X_1
        John$_1$-ga *jibun*$_i$-o seme-ta.
        John-NOM self-OBJ blame-PAST
        'John blamed himself.'
     b. X_2
        John$_1$-ga hahaoya-ga *jibun*$_i$-o seme-ta.
        John-NOM mother-NOM self-OBJ blame-PAST
        'John's mother blamed self (= John).'
     c. X_3
        *John$_1$-ga hahaoya-ga tomodachi-ga *jibun*$_i$-o seme-ta.
        John-NOM mother-NOM friend-NOM self-OBJ blame-PAST
        'John's mother's friend blamed self (= John).'

X_3 can never bind *jibun* 'self' in (23c), supporting the genitive
hypothesis.

2.4. Case Copying Rule

So far, I have shown that the so-called "multiple subject construction"
is actually not so multiple and not so subject. There can only be two

"subjects"--a VP-internal initial subject and an IP-internal initial subject. Each subject is leftmost in its phrase, and is unique--exactly what we expect from a SPEC. If we are right, then we have to assume the existence of a unique SPEC position in IP, and in VP as well.

The final question to ask at this point will be: Why are X_0 and preceding subjects marked with ga, although they are in a genitive position? I do not have a complete answer to it at this point, but I will suggest the following. In my analysis, NP in a genitive position can be marked with ga only if it is dominated by NP in a SPEC(I) position and is the leftmost constituent of it. This gives us the schematic structure in (24).

(24)

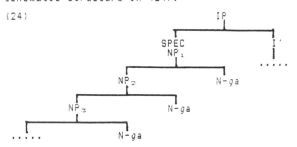

In (24), both NP_2 and NP_3 are the leftmost constituent of NP_1 in SPEC(I), so that they can be marked with ga (NOMINATIVE). Now, there is one other phenomenon in Japanese which is very similar to this "ga-chain" formation; I have in mind what is generally called Ga/No-Conversion. Ga/No-Conversion changes the normally ga-marked subject of adnominal clause into a no-marked phrase. (25) is an example of Ga/No-Conversion:

(25) [₁ₚJohn-{が}] eigo-ga   deki-ru] koto
      John-{ＧＥＮ} English-NOM able-PRES matter
      the fact that John can speak (write, etc.) English

Just like ga-marking in (24), this no-marking has an absolute peripherality condition. As in (26), it is blocked by the existence of an external subject, as in (26a), or a scrambled object as in (26b).[10]

(26) a.*[₁ₚJohn-ga eigo-no deki-ru] koto
     b.*[₁ₚeigo₁-ga John-no t₁ deki-ru] koto

The structure in which Ga/No-Conversion occurs is that in (27):

(27)

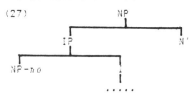

This exactly corresponds to (24), except that the IP which is probably in the SPEC position of NP can not be morphologically no-marked because of the morphological impossibility of Case-marking on IP. I suppose what is happening in these peculiar Case-marking process is a rule of Case-feature percolation process from the SPEC of IP and NP to the SPEC of them, as seen in (28).

---

10. Actually, there is dialectal variation in this phenomenon, which I will discuss in the next section.

(28) In the following configuration:

$[_{XP}[_{YP}[_{ZP}...]...]...]$
(where each of XP, YP, and ZP is either IP or NP, YP = SPEC(XP),
and ZP = SPEC(YP).)

A Case-feature assigned to YP in an XP-domain can optionally be
copied onto ZP.

If this rule holds, then this again is an argument for a SPEC position
in Japanese, especially in NP.

3. Dialectal Variation[11]

In this final section, I will discuss some dialectal differences with
respect to the multiple subject construction and *Ga/No*-Conversion. Let
us review the relevant examples.

(23) c. John$_i$-ga hahaoya$_j$-ga tomodachi$_k$-ga *jibun$_{i/j/k}$*-o seme-ta.
     John-NOM mother-NOM friend-NOM   self-OBJ   blame-PAST
     'John's mother's friend blamed self (= John).'

(22) a. *Totsuzen* $[_{IP}[_{NP}[_{NP}$John-ga] computer-ga]$[_{VP}$disk drive-ga
                    John-NOM computer-NOM   disk drive-NOM
     koware-ta]]
     break-PAST
     'John's computer's disk drive has suddenly broken.'
     b.*$[_{IP}[_{NP}[_{NP}$John-ga] *totsuzen* computer-ga]$[_{VP}$disk drive-ga
     koware-ta]]
     c. $[_{IP}[_{NP}[_{NP}$John-ga] computer-ga] *totsuzen* $[_{VP}$disk drive-ga
     koware-ta]]

(25) $[_{IP}$John-{ga} eigo-ga   deki-ru] koto
     John-{ga} English-NOM able-PRES matter
     'the fact that John can speak (write, etc.) English'

(26) a.*$[_{IP}$John-ga eigo-*no* deki-ru] koto
     b.*$[_{IP}$eigo$_i$-ga John-*no* t$_i$ deki-ru] koto

These judgements are basically mine and other people share them. Let
me add (29) as an example of multiple *Ga/No*-Conversion, which I don't
accept.

(29)*$[_{IP}$John-*no* eigo-*no* deki-ru] koto

     Also, let me add (30) as simple example of multiple subject
constructions:

(30) a. John-ga   byooki-da.
        John-NOM sick-PRES
        'John is sick.'
     b. John-ga chichioya-ga byooki-da.
                father-NOM
        'John, his father is sick.'
     c. John-ga chichioya-ga tomodachi-ga byooki-da.
                             friend-NOM
        'John, it is his father whose friend is sick.'

     There are at least 5 patterns of dialectal difference as far
as I know[12]. The pattern is summarized in (31):

_____

11. In writing this section, comments from Nobuko Hasegawa, Hajime
Hoji, Miori Kubo, Shinobu Mizuguchi, William J. Poser, Tim Stowell,
Michiko Terada, and Yasushi Zenno were very helpful.

12. There is another pattern of dialectal difference concerning
Ga/No-Conversion. Some people just don't like (25) and (29), where

(31)

	(30a)	(30b)	(30c)	(23c)	(22a)	(22b)	(22c)	(25)	(26a)	(26b)	(29)
A	OK	OK	OK	j,k[13]	OK	*	OK	OK	*	*	*
B	OK	OK	OK	i,k	OK	OK	*	OK	OK	*	OK
C	OK	OK	OK	i,j,k	OK	OK	OK	OK	OK	*	OK
D	OK	OK	*	*	*	*	*	*	*	*	*
E	OK	*	*	*	*	*	*	*	*	*	*

I have no account of the fact (26b) is ungrammatical for all speakers.
It presumably is related to the fact that there is an instance of
Scrambling across the *no*-converted phrase. Dialect A is mine; I have
already offered an account of it. Dialect B is different from Dialect
A in that only the first and the last subjects can bind *jibun* 'self' in
(23c), and *totsuzen* 'suddenly' in (22) can be at the sentence-initial
position and between the first and the second subject, but not between
the second and the third ones. These facts suggest the following
constituent structure for the multiple subject construction in Dialect
B:

(32)

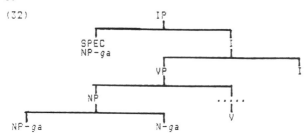

This means that the condition for the case-copying rule is different
from the Dialect A. Only a VP-internal subject can copy case to its
genitive modifier. I will formulate the Case-Copying rule for such a
dialect as follows:

(28') <u>Dialect B</u>

In the following configuration:

$[_{XP}[_{YP}....[_{ZP}...]....]....]$
(where $XP = VP$ or N' (= NP in the sense of Fukui (1986)), and
each of YP and ZP is either IP or NP (= N'').)

A default-case-feature (= $[+ga]$ or $[+no]$) assigned to YP in an
XP-domain can optionally be copied onto ZP, if both of YP and ZP
are in the default-case-position (= *ga* and *no* position).

Note that this rule can account for why (26a) and (29) are acceptable
for such a speaker, because it does not require any kind of

_____

another phrase is intervening between a *No*-converted phrase and the
verb. I will not discuss this, because it seems to act independently
from what I will discuss in this section. See Harada (1971, 1976),
Inoue (1976), Shibatani (1975) and Terada (1986) for discussions about
this point.

13. If there is an index in the space, it refers to the possible
antecedent of anaphor in (23c).

peripherality. We can copy the *no*-case feature to any one of NP_1 and NP_2, or both in the following structure:

(33)

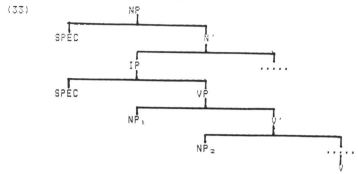

Dialect C is the union of the dialect A and the dialect B. Both IP-subject and VP-internal subject can copy the case feature. The rule will be as in (28"):

(28") Dialect C

In the following configuration:

[$_{YP}$....[$_{ZP}$...]....]
(where each of YP and ZP is either IP, VP, NP or N'.)

If YP bears a default-case-feature (*ga* or *no*), then this feature can be copied onto ZP.

This case-feature copying can copy the case-feature to anywhere unless some other non-default Case, e.g. Objective, is already assigned. Therefore, the structure of a sentence with three subjects can be ambiguous between the one in which the SPEC(IP) copies the case-feature and the other in which VP-internal subject copies it. This accounts for the freedom of binding for anaphors and the freer insertion of sentential adverbs.

The Dialects D and E are peculiar in that there is no case-copying, so that the maximal number of "subjects" is two, IP-subject and VP-subject, as in the Dialect D. These dialects systematically lack Ga/No-Conversion at all, because there is no case-copying.[14]

Such dialectal differences can not be predicted by the No SPEC Hypothesis, since there is no natural tool for making such differences. Furthermore, even with the dialectal variation described here, there is one sharp prediction made by our theory, in contrast to the No SPEC Hypothesis, which is testable in all dialects: There is no sentence with three subjects where a genitive-head relation between the two adjacent subjects is impossible:

(34) *Hana-ga   sakura-ga   yaezakura-ga   i-i.
     flower-NOM cherry blossom-NOM double cherry blossoms-NOM good-PRES
     'Flowers, especially in cherry blossoms, double cherry blossoms
     are good.'

This is ungrammatical for every dialect. In Dialects D and E, this is no problem, because there is no case copying, so that more than two

---

14. There was one speaker who does not have the multiple subject construction at all, but *does* have Ga/No-Conversion. I suppose that there is an independent process of Ga/No-Conversion for such a speaker, but it does not alter my point here.

"subjects" are not allowed. Why, then, is (34) ungrammatical in dialects with case-copying? Case-copying onto a given "subject" requires the genitive relation to the immediately following subject. However, in (34), such a relation is impossible:

(35) a.*hana-no sakura[15]
        -GEN
     '*flower's cherry blossom'
    b.*sakura-no yaezakura
     '*cherry blossom's double cherry blossoms'

(34) is ungrammatical because the basic requirement for case-copying can not be satisfied, so that the maximum number of "subjects" should be two and one of the three multiple "subjects" can not have a syntactic position.

Now, this is what the analysis in this paper can predict but No SPEC Hypothesis cannot predict. If we adopt the No SPEC Hypothesis for Japanese phrase structure, then (34) should be grammatical, since a chain of aboutness relations can be established by generating multiple VP-internal ga-subjects. In this sense, the account in this paper is superior to the No SPEC Hypothesis, because it can predict what never occurs in Japanese, while allowing the dialectal variations that is attested in Japanese.

4. Conclusion

I have considered multiple determiner and multiple subject constructions in Japanese and I have shown that the analysis of these constructions shown here crucially supports the hypothesis that the SPEC position for functional categories, and NP (if it is not DP), is universal and not subject to cross-linguistic variation. What *is* subject to variation are particular case-marking conventions, as shown by various dialects I have discussed. This is a very natural conclusion, since an apparent absense of *positive* evidence for SPEC position can not trigger the hypothesis that SPEC is totally absent, if we assume SPEC to be a part of universal equipment of syntactic structure. In this sense, the No SPEC Hypothesis for Japanese phrase structure is wrong and his theory cannot be supported--unless we find a true case of multiple subjects/determiners in another language.

REFERENCES

Abney, S. P. (1987) *The English Noun Phrase in Its Sentential Aspect.* PhD Thesis, MIT Cambridge.

Chomsky, N. (1972) "Remarks on Nominalization." in Chomsky, N. (1972) *Studies on Semantics in Generative Grammar.*, The Hague, Mouton, pp. 11-61.

_____ (1981) *Lectures on Government and Binding.* Dordrecht, Foris.

_____ (1986) *Barriers.* Cambridge, MIT Press.

Fukui, N. (1986) *A Theory of Category Projection and Its Applications.* PhD Thesis, MIT, Cambridge.

Hale, K. (1983) "Warlpiri and the Grammar of Non-Configurational Languages." *Natural Language and Linguistic Theory* 1.1., pp. 5-47.

Harada, S. (1971) "Ga-No Conversion and Idiolectal Variations in Japanese." *Gengo Kenkyu* 60., pp. 25-38.

---

15. Here we are dealing with the *no* which is a case particle, not the one which is a copular element. If *no* in (35) is a copula, then it is grammatical with the meaning like 'cherry blossom, which is a flower'.

_____ (1976) "Ga-*No* Conversion Revisited--A Reply to Shibatani." *Gengo Kenkyu* 70., pp. 23-38.

Hasegawa, N. (1985) "On the So-Called "Zero Pronouns" in Japanese." *Linguistic Review* 4.4., pp. 289-341.

Hoji, H. (1985) *Logical Form Constraints and Configurational Structures in Japanese.* PhD Thesis, University of Washington, Seattle.

Inoue, K. (1976) *Henkei-Bunpo-to Nihongo.* Tokyo, Taishukan.

Jackendoff, R. (1977) *X̄ Syntax: A Study of Phrase Structure.* Cambridge, MIT Press.

Kitagawa, Y. (1986) *Subjects in Japanese and English.* PhD Thesis, UMass, Amherst.

Kubo, M. (1987) "Wh-Movement in Japanese NPs." ms., University of Washington, Seattle. (Manuscript of the talk presented at the 17th Western Conference of Linguistics, University of Washington, Seattle.)

Kuno, S. (1973) *The Structure of the Japanese Language.* Cambridge, MIT Press.

Kuroda, S.-Y. (1965) *Generative Grammatical Studies in the Japanese Language.* PhD Thesis, MIT, Cambridge.

_____ (1986) "Whether We Agree Or Not: Rough Ideas about the Comparative Grammar of English and Japanese." ms., UCSD, La Jolla.

Longobardi, G. (1987) "Extraction from NP and the Proper Notion of Head Government." ms., Scuola Normale Superiore, Pisa.

Nishigauchi, T. (1986) *Quantification in Syntax.* PhD Thesis, UMass, Amherst.

Ross, J. R. (1967) *Constraints on Variables in Syntax.* PhD Thesis, MIT, Cambridge.

Saito, M. (1985) *Some Asymmetries in Japanese and Their Theoretical Implications.* PhD Thesis, MIT, Cambridge.

Shibatani, M. (1975) "Perceptual Strategies and the Phenomena of Particle Conversion in Japanese." Grossman, R. E., L. J. San and T. J. Vance (eds.) *Papers from the Parasession on Functionalism.*, Chicago, Chicago Linguistic Society, pp. 469-480.

Sportiche, D. (1987) "A Theory of Floating Quantifiers." *NELS* 17, pp. 581-594.

Terada, M. (1986) "Unaccusativity and QPs in Japanese." ms., UMass, Amherst.

Torrego, E. (1985) "On Empty Categories in Nominals." ms., UMass, Boston.

Whitman, J. (1981) "The Internal Structure of NP in Verb Final Languages." *CLS* 17, pp. 411-418.

Williams, E. (1980) "Predication." *Linguistic Inquiry.* 11.1., pp. 203-238.

Tone Contours as Melodic Units: Tonal Affricates
Moira Yip
Brandeis University

It is generally accepted that contour tones are made up of
sequences of level tones, and a number of arguments have been
adduced in support of this position (Woo 1969, Leben 1973,
Goldsmith 1976, Yip 1980, Pulleyblank 1986 and many others).
However, a contrasting viewpoint was once widely held (Wang 1967,
and others), although it has now fallen into disfavor. Wang and
others treated contour tones as units with features such as
[+rising], [+falling]. In this paper I shall argue that although
contour tones are on one level sequences of level tones, there is
also a need to recognize a level on which they can be treated as
units, and that this behavior is not contradictory or suprising,
but precisely parallel to the behavior of affricates in the
segmental domain. It does not imply the use of contour features,
but only the existence of branching structures within the Tonal
feature node . The arguments I shall use will be precisely parallel
to the arguments used to justify the treatment of affricates as
units: initial association, spreading behavior, and syllable
structure.

I shall begin by outlining the relevant properties of segmental
contour segments such as affricates and pre-nasalized stops. Then I
shall set out the general predictions about tonal behavior made by
a theory which cannot treat contours as units, versus one which
can. These predictions will then be shown to hold true of three
Chinese tone languages: Wuxi, Amoy and Danyang. A final section
will discuss various other implications of the proposal.

1. Segmental Contour Segments

Contour tones are usually represented as in (1)a , with the
segmental parallel shown in (1)b:

I shall argue that the appropriate characterization for underlying
contour tones is instead that given in (2)a, parallel to the
segmental (2)b:[1]

Both (1) and (2) have a single syllabic position associated with an
ordered sequence of elements, but only (2) allows reference to that
sequence as a melodic unit as well as a prosodic unit.[2] Sagey
(1986:69-92) gives a number of arguments that demonstrate the need
to assume the structure of (2)b, not (1)b. Similar arguments can be

found in McCarthy and Prince (1986: 89) First, affricates and other contour segments must have a single root node to account for their behavior in association with a template, since they associate as single melodic units. For example, in Ewe reduplication the affricate /ɕ/ and the labiovelars /kp,gb/ reduplicate as units, in contrast to clusters such as /fl/:

(3)   ɕi   'to grow'   ɕiɕii   'grown up'
         kplo   'to lead'   kpokplo   'leading'
but   fle   'to buy'   fefle   'bought'

Second, contour segments must be single root nodes because they spread as units. Modern Hebrew, for example, shows forms like <u>kicec</u> , 'he cut' derived as in (4)a. If the affricate [c] was made up of the sequence /ts/ branching directly off the skeleton we would wrongly derive *<u>kites</u>, as shown in (4)b:

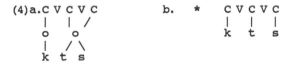

(4)a.C V C V C   b. *   C V C V C
     | | / | | |
     o   o   k t s
     | / \
     k t s

(The outcome of spreading a contour segment will be discussed in section 4 .)

It is clear from arguments of this kind that the branching in affricates takes place <u>below</u> the root node. (but see Hualde 1987,1988 for a different view).Sagey (1986:50-52) limits branching to the terminal feature level, so that affricates involve branching of the feature [continuant], and not, say, the Manner node. Sagey's examples include [continuant] /ts/, [nasal] /mb/, and [lateral] /tl/, and she also says (p51):
       "..contour tones must be represented as branching just for the features [stiff] and [slack], and not for the laryngeal or root nodes, because tone spreading is not blocked by intervening laryngeal or root nodes."

I shall not be concerned here with the issue of whether the Laryngeal node, some sub-node that we might call Tonal, or the particular tonal features [Upper], [High/Raised] (Yip 1980, Pulleyblank 1986) or [stiff], [slack] (Halle and Stevens 1971) are the branching entities, and will use L, H as a shorthand for the relevant elements. What I am interested in is whether tonal systems show the kind of behavior that is predicted by this model. Specifically, is there any evidence that contour tones are dominated by a single feature node, as affricates are?

If contour tones are analagous to segmental affricates, then they should show evidence of behaving as melodic units, both in initial association, and in spreading. Chinese languages show widespread evidence of just such behavior, as we shall see.

2. Initial Tone Association: Amoy

Consider first Initial Tone Association. Take a language with word-level tone association, one-to-one left-to- right of free tones and TBU's (Pulleyblank 1986:11). If a morpheme with a contour tone is followed by a toneless morpheme, and the contour tone is a melodic unit, then the contour will remain fixed on the root morpheme, as shown in (5):

(5)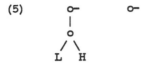

In the absence of spreading, the toneless suffix will show up with a default tone.[3] Contrast this with an analysis in which the contour tone is not a melodic unit. We would then expect the second part of the contour tone to show up on the suffix, not the root, as shown in (6):

(6)

Both these situations are found, and the division is more or less typological: most East Asian tone languages behave like (5), and most African tone languages behave like (6). Let us assume that African tone languages lack underlying tonal 'affricates' (although they may be produced by late association rules, primarily to final TBU's.) East Asian tone languages, on the other hand, exemplify exactly the behavior for tonal affricates shown in (5).

I will use Amoy as an example. (See Cheng 1973, Yip 1980:49-50;219-221).[4] Amoy has seven citation tones, two of which are variants restricted to short syllables closed by a stop. The five remaining citation tones are shown in (7):[5]

(7)   55   33   13   53   21

I will use the contour tones, 13 and 53, as examples. When followed by a neutral toned (ie toneless) syllable, morphemes show up with their citation tones, and the neutral toned syllable shows up as low level, [11]. Neutral toned syllables can be shown to be toneless, either underlyingly or as a result of a stress-conditioned tone deletion rule. For example, we have forms like (8):

(8) hou 53 a 11   'there you are'
    Tan 13 sian 11 sĩ 11   'Mr. Tan'
    bue 53 neng 11 sã 11 kin 11'buy two or three catties'

This is precisely the behavior shown in (5). Initial association of the contour tone as a unit, followed by insertion of default low [11] tones:

(9)

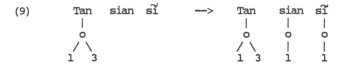

As usual, an alternative analysis of these data is initially plausible. If tone association is cyclic, and at the end of each cycle any extra tones are associated to the final TBU, we would arrive at the same result. Evidence that this is wrong comes from the rare instances of bisyllabic morphemes, such as pu3ltoul3 'grapes' (Lugan Coastal Dialect). Each syllable may bear a contour tone, not just the last, and there is no way to achieve this in a cyclic level-tone analysis unless each syllable constitutes a cycle, or tones are lexically pre-linked to syllables in these cases.

Many other Chinese languages show similar facts, although the toneless syllable may acquire its tone in other ways than by default rules. Some languages have spreading rules (Danyang), and in others no phonological tone is supplied, but rather phonetic interpolation rules produce the surface pitch. In each case there is strong evidence that contour tones associate as units.

3. Edge Association, and Phonetic Interpolation: Wuxi
3.1 General Predictions
So far I have discussed only a case in which the melody is a single contour tone. Now consider cases with more complex melodies, such as LHL. If branching tones are melodic units this melody could either be (LH)L, L(HL), or LHL.[6] The parentheses here define branching melodic units. Each of these would show quite different behavior in association to long domains, and the first two are found to contrast in Wuxi, as I shall show.

Before I do this, let me digress to discuss the principles of association in more detail. Association has been generally assumed to proceed from left-to-right, except in reduplication, when it works from LR in prefixes but RL in suffixes - in other words, from the outsides inwards (Marantz 1982, McCarthy and Prince 1986). However, I have argued (Yip 1987b) that association may work from the outside inwards in stems as well, and given evidence from Semitic morphology that this is indeed the case. Edge-In (EI) Association in stems (as opposed to affixes) anchors both ends of the domain, then fills in the middle by spreading, default, or phonetic interpolation. What I shall show is that EI association must have access to contour tones as melodic units, and that it is these contours that anchor to the edges of the domain. Medial syllables are never supplied with phonological tones, but rather acquire phonetic pitch as a result of non-binary interpolation rules of the kind discussed in Pierrehumbert and Beckman (1986). The result is a sort of contour stretching, a fixed envelope over different lengths of utterance.[7]

Consider the patterns in (10), in which the underlying melody of the first syllable is followed by one, two or three toneless syllables:

(10) /(LH)L/

```
      o- o-        o- o- o-        o- o- o- o-
      |  |         |     |         |        |
     (LH)L        (LH)   L        (LH)      L
```

/L(HL)/

```
      o- o-        o- o- o-        o- o- o- o-
      |  |         |     |         |        |
      L (HL)       L    (HL)       L       (HL)
```

/L(LH)/

```
      o- o-        o- o- o-        o- o- o- o-
      |  |         |     |         |        |
      L (LH)       L    (LH)       L       (LH)
```

Each of these melodies has a level part and a contour part, and each part anchors as a unit to one edge of the domain. The resulting patterns will show fixed rises, falls, and level target tones at the edges, but in between there will be gradual gradients whose steepness will vary with the length of the utterance. I will show below that this is exactly the situation found in Wuxi.

These patterns cannot be easily explained in a theory which associates only level tones as units. In (11) I show the patterns produced by associating /LH/ from left-to-right, accompanied by either (a) default L insertion or (b) spreading. In either case the rise will be restricted to the first two syllables, and will be followed by either an immediate fall to low level, or a level high tone:

(11a) Default L:

```
      o- o-        o- o- o-        o- o- o- o-
      |  |         |  |  |         |  |  |  |
      L  H         L  H  L         L  H  L  L
```

(11b) Spreading:

```
      o- o-        o- o- o-        o- o- o- o-
      |  |         |  |  /         |  |  /  /
      L  H         L  H            L  H
```

In (12) I show the patterns produced by associating /LH/ from the edges-in, with phonetic interpolation giving a single gradual rise over the entire domain:

(12)

```
  o- o-    o- o- o-    o- o- o- o-
  |  |     |     |     |        |
  L  H     L     H     L        H
           L           H
```

It should be apparent that neither theory can fix a rise or fall on the first syllable of the domain, although LR association could fix it on the first two syllables (and RL on the last two syllables). Making one tone extrametrical could fix a contour on <u>one</u> edge of the utterance, but not at different edges in the case of different tones, the situation seen in Wuxi and schematized in (10) above.

3.2 <u>Wuxi</u>
I now turn to the Wuxi data. Wuxi is a N.W. Wu dialect , spoken in

Wuxi city about 80 miles north-west of Shanghai. Chan and Ren
(1986) and Ren (1982) give an interesting and careful description
and analysis of the tonal system of Wuxi, accompanied by F_0
tracings. In what follows I depend entirely on their data, but
depart from their analysis on a number of points.[8] Wuxi has eight
phonetic tones on monosyllables, from four underlying patterns,
given in (13):[9]

(13)		Voiceless Onset		Voiced Onset	
			Glottal Coda		Glottal Coda
A:	L(LH)	T3 (313)		T6 (213)	
B:	(LH)L	T1 (52)	T7 (53)	T4 (131)	
C:	H	T5 (34)			
D:	L(HL)			T2 (213)	T8 (13)

Two segmental effects are apparent, and will be discounted in what
follows. Voiced onsets lower the pitch, especially at the start of
the syllable, and final glottal stops shorten the syllable. The
tones are grouped into four patterns A-D according to the patterns
they produce when they begin a long span. The groupings are Chan
and Ren's, the underlying melodies are mine. These patterns occur
in certain kinds of morpho-syntactic environments, where the tone of
the initial syllable determines the tone of whole domain. [10] This
is a familiar characteristic of Wu dialects, and I shall assume
that the tone of all but the first syllable (=morpheme) is deleted
in these environments, possibly conditioned by stress. My focus
here is on exactly how the tone of the first syllable is
instantiated over domains of different lengths. The relevant data
is given in (14). Only four possible pitch contours occur.

The first thing to notice about the patterns in (14) is that they
are invariant: they are squashed up or stretched out to fit the
domain, but the relative timing remains constant. In particular,
the position of the peak is fixed relative to one end of the
domain:

- A has a rise near the end
- B has a rise near the start
- D has a fall near the end
(- C will be discussed below)

Otherwise, the gradients decrease with the length of the domain,
suggesting interpolation. Lastly, note that patterns A, /L(LH)/,
and D , /L(HL)/ are neutralized on single syllables, where both
show up as [213].

Leaving aside the neutralization of A and D for now, an analysis in
which the melodic units can be level or contour tones, and in which
they associate to the two ends of the domain with phonetic
interpolation controlling the pitch of any intervening syllables
accounts quite directly for the observed tone patterns. I will
discuss them one by one in order.

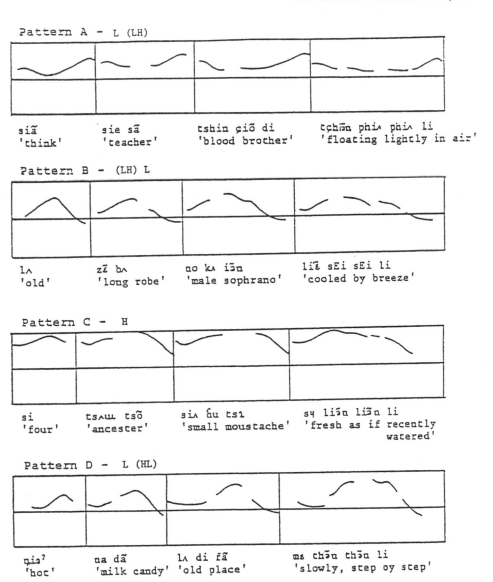

Pattern A - L (LH)

siã
'think'

sie sã
'teacher'

tshin çiõ di
'blood brother'

tçhᴚn phiᴧ phiᴧ li
'floating lightly in air'

Pattern B - (LH) L

1ᴧ
'old'

zĩ bᴧ
'long robe'

ɑo kᴧ iᴣɑ
'male sophrano'

liĩ sEi sEi li
'cooled by breeze'

Pattern C - H

si
'four'

tsᴧɯ tsõ
'ancester'

siᴧ ɦu tsı
'small moustache'

sч liᴣɑ liᴣɑ li
'fresh as if recently
watered'

Pattern D - L (HL)

ɋiɘ?
'hot'

ɑa dã
'milk candy'

1ᴧ di fã
'old place'

mᴚ thᴣɑ thᴣɑ li
'slowly, step by step'

The four tone patterns in Wuxi on mono- to
quadrisyllabic forms.

(Adapted from Chan and Ren : 1986, Fig 7)

. (14)

354 / Yip

Pattern A:

```
       o-      o- o-    o-o- o-     o- o- o- o-
      / \      |  |     |    |      |        |
     L (LH)  L (LH)    L   (LH)    L       (LH)
```

There is a rise on the final syllable, otherwise the domain is low throughout, since interpolation from L to L will give continuous low pitch.

Pattern B:

```
       o-       o- o-    o- o- o-      o- o- o- o-
      / \       |  |     |  |  |       |        |
    (LH) L    (LH) L    (LH)  L      (LH)       L
```

There is a rise on the first syllable, followed by a gradual fall to the end. The gradient of this fall depends on the length of the span, as expected given phonetic interpolation from H to L. Note that there cannot be any default L insertion, since the fall to low pitch is not immediate, nor is it followed by level low pitch. Instead, it is non-binary, as is typical of phonetic rules.

Pattern C:

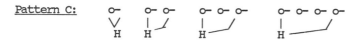

This pattern is mainly high throughout. The gradual drop off, more pronounced at the end, is the result of what Chan and Ren call "intonational factors", and is speaker-variable. (The same factor presumably accounts for the lower peak in Pattern A at end of the long span.) This is the only underlying melody consisting of a single unit, and it raises the question of what happens with a single unit and two edges. I shall assume that, in Wuxi at least, Edge-In association is literally to domain edges, and that each edge must have a tone, so that if only one tone is present it associates to both edges. Note that single syllables are also domains with two edges, and each edge must get a tone here as well. This issue arises with all level tones that occupy a whole domain: either they have two underlying tones, /HH/, in violation of the Obligatory Contour Principle (Leben 1973, McCarthy 1986, Yip 1987a), or the single tone must occupy both edges, or phonetic interpolation must be stated so as to continue the last tone of a domain unchanged to the end of that domain. Insertion of a default tone, Mid or Low, on the unassociated right edge would wrongly predict that all level tones should end up at the default pitch.

Pattern D:

```
       o-      o- o-    o- o- o-     o- o- o- o-
      / \      |  |     |  |         |        |
     L (HL)  L (HL)    L   (HL)     L       (HL)
```

This pattern is low at the start, and has a gradual rise up to the fall fixed on the final syllable.[11]

In this section I have argued that the tones of Wuxi can only be understood if contour tones can associate as melodic units. I now turn to a second consequence of a unitary analysis of contour tones: their behavior in spreading.

4. Spreading of Contours
4.1 Segmental Affricates:
Before discussing tone spreading, let us consider what happens to
segmental branching structures. The consequences of spreading, say,
an affricate apparently depend on whether it is spreading to two
string-adjacent slots (ie a geminate affricate), or to non-adjacent
slots, as in template morphology.[12] In (15) I illustrate the case
of a true geminate:

(15)   C C   [ttss] [tss] [tts] [ts]
                  V
                 root
                 / \
            [-cont][+cont]

The obvious interpretation of a structure like (15) is that there
is a single change in [continuant], and that this change is
instantiated over two timing slots. This leaves the four
possibilities given in (15), and it appears that the usual result
is [tts] . Hausa is an example of this type. Note that true
geminate affricates are never realized with two changes in
continuancy: [tsts] is not found.

In contrast, non-adjacent but doubly-linked affricates are always
realized with two changes, that is as [ts...ts], not as [t..s]. For
example, Hebrew kicec 'he cut'. Given the interpretation of
adjacent geminates, how can we account for the different
interpretation here? The simplest answer is to assume that Tier
Conflation automatically induces copying (McCarthy 1986:227) and
that this feeds phonetic realization. The situation is shown in
(16). :
    (16)   C V C   -->   C   V   C   [tsVts]
               \ / | | |
               root   root root root
               / \   / \ / \ / \
           -cont +cont   -cont +cont -cont +cont

We are now ready to look at tone contour spreading.

4.2 Tonal Affricates:
The equivalent of a true geminate in tone is a long vowel, and the
expectation here is that a contour tone will remain a simple
contour on a long vowel in all cases. As far as I know this is
true. For example, Cantonese has a vowel length contrast (although
underlyingly the distinction may be tense/lax). Both long and short
vowels realize contour tones as a single contour over the entire
rhyme: lei24 'Lei, surname' haai24 'crab'.

The more usual case is spreading to a vowel in the next syllable,
parallel to the long-distance non-adjacent geminate affricates
discussed above. If Tier Conflation operates to copy tones as it
does segmental matrices, the prediction is that there should be
cases of contour tones spreading to adjacent syllables, and being
realized as a sequence of identical contours. This is shown

schematically in (17):

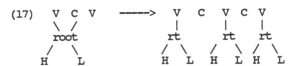

(17)   V C V   ----->   V C V C V

Cases of this sort would provide striking evidence in favor of contours behaving as melodic units, since they could not be derived in any other way. Danyang, in the next section, exhibits exactly this behavior.

4.3 Danyang

The data in this section comes from Chen (1986:10-13), who includes an interesting discussion of the problems caused by these data for most previous theories of tone. Danyang is another Wu dialect of Chinese, and like Wuxi polysyllabic domains have overall melodies covering the domain. [13] Three of these are level, L, M or H across the entire domain and three are contours. Of particular interest is Chen's Pattern 6, shown in (18):

(18)   42-24   42-42-24   42-42-42-24

All non-final syllables fall, and the final syllable rises. In a theory in which contours can associate and spread as units, and initial association is to the edges of domains, this pattern can be straightforwardly understood as an underlying HL.LH melody, associated to the two ends, rightward spreading of the HL contour, and Tier Conflation copying this contour, as in (16) above.. This is shown in (19) for the three and four-syllabled domains.

(19)
EI Assoc.
and
Rightward
Spreading

Tier
Conflation

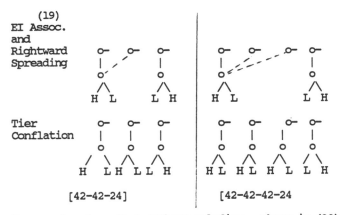

[42-42-24]   [42-42-42-24

Danyang has two other contour melodies , shown in (20):
(20)
        42-11   42-11-11   42-11-11-11
        24-55   24-55-55   24-55-55-55

These are more familiar looking, since only the last level toneme
spreads, and they show the asymmetrical character of contour
segments clearly. The spreading is shown in (21):

(21)

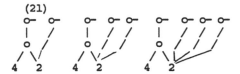

Segmental parallels to this tonal behavior are not hard to find. A
typical example would be nasalization of vowels before but not
after pre-nasalized stops. As for why the entire tonal root spreads
in (19), but only the last level toneme in (21), apparently in
Danyang the level toneme spreads if it is final, and otherwise the
tonal root node spreads, spreading the whole contour. Since
spreading is by rule, not convention, there is nothing particularly
problematic about this state of affairs, but it does leave
unanswered the question as to why spreading of the whole contour,
as in (18-19) is so rare in languages.

In sections 2-4 I have argued that the facts of three Chinese
languages require the assumption that contour tones can associate
as melodic units. Given a theory of features like that of Clements
(1985), and Sagey (1986) this is not surprising: tone contours are
exactly parallel to segmental affricates. In the final section I
discuss what this means for a typology of tone.

5. A Typology of Tonal Affricates
The first point I wish to make is that nothing I have said so far
requires that <u>all</u> contour tones be analyzed as melodic units. Just
as segmental phonology must distinguish between a cluster and an
affricate, tonal phonology may do the same. A cluster is two tonal
roots, each consisting of one level toneme. An 'affricate' is a
single tonal root dominating a branching structure of two level
tonemes. They will be indistinguishable on monosyllables, giving
[LH], but they will associate with bisyllables in quite different
ways, shown in (22):

(22) <u>Cluster</u>   <u>Affricate</u>

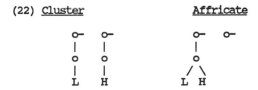

The cluster will surface as [L.H] .This is the situation found in
Mende (Leben 1973) and many other African languages. In the
affricate case the second syllable may then acquire a default tone,
say L, giving [LH.L], as in Amoy (section 2); or the root may
spread, giving [LH.LH], or the final toneme may spread, giving
[LH.H]. The spreading rules are found in Danyang (see section 4

above). The mirror-image case of a tonal affricate attaching to the right edge, followed by leftward spreading, is found in Kru (Hombert 1986:179, using data from Elimelech 1974). In addition to H and L level patterns, Kru has two contours which show up on mono-syllables and bisyllables as shown in (23):

(23) ju 'child'   [⌢] kele 'inside' [— ⌢]

su 'chicken' [⌢] kita 'coconut' [— ⌝]

These can be analyzed as /(LH)/ and /(HL)/ respectively, with association to the right edge, and spreading of the leftmost level tone:

(24)
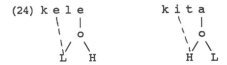

From a typological point of view, Chinese languages make widespread use of tonal affricates, whereas African languages tend to lack them. A full understanding of these issues is further complicated by the existence of phonetic interpolation, and the lack of F_0 tracings for most tone languages.

6. Conclusion

I have argued that tonal contours must be able to associate and spread as melodic units in some languages, and that this is unsurprising since it exactly parallels the behavior of segmental affricates. An understanding of feature structure allows branching representations that are on one level sequences of level tones, and on a higher level melodic units. Contour <u>features</u> are not required – indeed would yield the wrong predictions in many cases (see Yip 1980: 4-6) A full analysis of the Chinese languages in this paper has also relied on edge-in association (Wuxi, Danyang), insertion of default tones (Amoy) and phonetic interpolation rules (Wuxi).

Notes

An earlier version of this paper was given at the MIT Linguistics Club, and at the Centre de Recherches Linguistiques sur L'Asie Orientale, C.N.R.S., Paris. I would like to thank the participants in both seminars for their comments, and in particular Diana Archangeli, Francois Dell , Morris Halle, James Huang, Larry Hyman, Laurent Sagart, and Donca Steriade. All errors are of course my own.

1.There are also structures of the type shown in (i)a-b, which are true clusters, but these will not concern us here:

(i) a   V V   b.   C C
         | | | |
         L H   t s

2. See also Huang (1980), Clements (1981) on hierarchical tone structures.

3. The effects of spreading will be discussed in section 5.

4. Thanks to James Huang for help with the data in this section.

5. The notation used is that of Chao (1930). 5 denotes high pitch, 1 denotes low pitch , and so on. Thus 35 is a tone rising from mid to high, and 21 is a low falling tone.

6. The segmental parallel here would be melodies such as /ĵt/, /dⁿd/, /dnd/. All these are uncontroversial.

7. Rialland (1985) independently reaches similar conclusions in a paper on the tone patterns of Bambara nouns. She calls this the "accordion effect".

8. The analysis in Chan and Ren (1986:1) is based on Ren (1982) , and has in common with my analysis the insight that association must be to the two ends of the domain, but they do not treat contours as units, and medial syllables acquire tone by spreading. This leads them to encounter a variety of problems, both phonological (as they admit, their LLH and LHH melodies violate the OCP) and phonetic (they wrongly predict level plateaux in the middle of every long span).

9. The groupings here are Chan and Ren's, but the underlying melodies are mine.

10. The relevant environments include reduplicated verbs, verbs plus directional complements, resultative verbs, and number plus classifier sequences. In reduplicated nouns, compounds, and phrases different tone patterns are found, called pattern substitution by Chan and Ren.

11. For reasons unknown to me, the fall begins on the third instead of the fourth syllable in four syllable domains.

12. For an interesting discussion of the relationship between true geminates and long-distance geminates see Steriade (1987). See also Hyman and Pulleyblank (1987) on tonal geminates and segmental geminates.

13. Chen says, (p.13) that (unlike in Wuxi) the choice of melody on the domain is not predictable from the citation tone of any of the syllables making up the domain, so the melody must be taken as a property of the word as a whole.

360 / Yip

References

Chan, M. and Hongmo Ren 1986a Wuxi Tone Sandhi: from last to first syllable dominance. Paper presented at the XIXth International Conference on Sino-Tibetan Languages and Linguistics, Ohio State University.

Chan, M. and Hongmo Ren 1986b Wuxi Tone Sandhi: from last to first syllable dominance. In UCLA Working Papers in Phonetics, 63: 48-70

Chao Y-R. 1930. A System of Tone Letters. Le Maitre Phonetique 45:24-47

Chen, M. 1986 An Overview of Tone Sandhi Across Chinese Dialects. Paper presented at Conference on Languages and Dialects of China, Oakland, California.

Cheng, R. 1973 Some notes on tone sandhi in Taiwanese. Linguistics 100:15-25.

Clements, G.N. 1981 The Hierarchical Representation of Tone. in G.N. Clements, ed., Harvard Studies in Phonology 2: 50-108

Clements, G.N. 1985. The Geometry of Phonological Features. Phonology Yearbook.2:225-52

Elimelech, B 1974 On the reality of underlying contour tones. UCLA Working Papers in Linguistics 27: 74-83

Goldsmith, J 1976 Autosegmental Phonology. Doctoral Dissertation, M.I.T. Garland Publishing.

Halle, M. 1986. On Speech sounds and Their Immanent Structure. ms. Dept. of Linguistics and Philosophy, MIT, Cambridge, MA.

Halle, M. and K. Stevens. 1971. A note on laryngeal features. MIT, RLE Quarterly Progress Rpeort. 101:198-213

Hashimoto, O-K. Y. 1972. Phonology of Cantonese. Studies in Yue Dialects 1. Cambridge University Press, Cambridge.

Hombert, Jean Marie 1986 Word Games: Some Implications for Analysis of Tone and Other Phonological Constructs. In J. Ohala and J. Jaeger, ed Experimental Phonology. Academic Press.

Hualde, J. 1987 "On Basque Affricates" To appear in Proceedings of W.C.C.F.L. VI.

Hualde, J. (1988 "Affricates are not Contour Segments" To appear in Proceedings of W.C.C.F.L. VII.

Huang, C.T.J. 1980 The Metrical Structure of Terraced Level Tones in Proceedings of NELS 10:257-70

Hyman, L. and D. Pulleyblank 1987 On Feature Copying: Parameters of Tone Rules. To appear in L. Hyman and C. Li, (eds). Language, Speech and Mind: Studies ion Honor of Victoria A. Fromkin.Croom Helm, Ltd.

Leben, W. 1973. Suprasegmental Phonology. Doctoral Dissertation, MIT, Cambridge, MA. (Distributed by Indiana University Linguistics Club)

Marantz, A. 1982. Re Reduplication. Linguistic Inquiry 13:483-545.

McCarthy, J. 1986. OCP Effects: Gemination and Antigemination. Linguistic Inquiry 17.2:207-264.

McCarthy, J and A. Prince 1986 Prosodic Morphology. Unpublished ms., Brandeis University and University of Massachusetts at Amherst. MIT Press, to appear.

Pierrehumbert, J. and M. Beckman 1986 Japanese Tone Structure. Unpublished ms., AT&T Bell Labs, and Ohio State University.

Pulleyblank, D. 1986 Tone in Lexical Phonology D. Reidel, Dordercht, Holland.

Rialland, A. and M. Sangara, 1985 Tons lexicaux et tons flottants dans les noms de Bambara: Principes d'association. To appear in Actes de Comptes de Phonologie Nonlineaire de Lyon.

Ren, Hongmo 1982 A Multi-level mapping tone system in Wuxi Chinese. Unpublished ms, UCLA

Sagey, E.C. 1986. The Representation of Features and Relations in Non-linear Phonology. Unpublished Ph.D. Dissertation, MIT, Cambridge, MA.

Steriade, D. 1987. Vowel Tiers and Geminate Blockage. Unpublished ms, M.I.T.

Wang, W. S-Y. 1967 The Phonological Features of Tone. IJAL 33.2: 93-105

Woo, Nancy. 1969. Prosody and Phonology. Ph.D Dissertation., M.I.T. Distributed by Indiana University Linguistics Club, Bloomington, Indiana.

Yip, M. 1980 The Tonal Phonology of Chinese. Doctoral Dissertation, M.I.T., and Indiana University Linguistics Club.

Yip, M. 1988a. The Obligatory Contour Principle and Phonological Rules. To appear, Linguistic Inquiry 19.1

Yip, M. 1987b. Edge-In Association. To appear in Proceedings of NELS 18.

Argument Drop and <u>pro</u>

Shi Zhang
The Univeristy of Arizona

0. Introduction

This paper is organized into three parts. First, I show that null objects in Chinese function like pronouns, and they meet some of the diganostic tests for pro object given by Rizzi in his 1986 article. Second, I will compare both pro objects and pro subjects in Italian and Chinese. I show that little pros in Italian are restricted, while pros in Chinese are not restricted in the same manner. Third, I propose that the differences between Italian and Chinese regarding pro subjects and pro objects be traced back to the different licensing conditions in each language.

1.1. Null Object in Embedded Clause

Let's start by looking at (1) and (2).

(1)a. Bill   says that Tom doesn't believe   him.

   b. Zhangsan shuo   Lisi   bu   xiangxin ta.
            say   not believe   him
       Zhangsan says that Lisi doesn't believe
       him/her/it

Note that <u>ta</u> `him/her/it' in Chinese has no gender, no nominative or accusative markings. It could stand for pronouns <u>he/him</u>, <u>she/her</u> and <u>it</u>.

(2)a.*Bill   says that Tom doesn't believe   ec

   b. Zhangsan shuo Lisi   bu   xiangxin **ec**
           say   not believe
       Zhangsan says that Lisi doesn't believe
       him/her/it

In (2), we see that it is perfectly OK for the Chinese sentence (2b) to have a null object, a phenomenon which has been noticed by Huang (1982, 1984). In (2b), in addition to the possibility that a pronoun "ta" can be null in the object position, there are two possible interpretations for the null object. The null object of (2b) is free in reference with respect to the BINGIND THEORY (Chomsky 1981, 1982) just like <u>him</u> in English which is free in its GOVERNING CATEGORY (henceforth GC). The interpretation of this null object has been a topic of dispute (cf. Huang 1984, 1987; Xu 1986). I am not going to review the arguments, but simply emphasizes the fact that if we look at some more sentences, the null pronominal

reading is very easy to obtain in neutral contexts.
Sentences (3)-(5) are a few examples.

(3) Zhangsan zhidao Lisi genben bu hui tongyi
        know   at all not will agree

    ta/**ec**
    him/her/it

    Zhangsan knows that Lisi will not agree with
    him/her/it at all

(4) Zhangsan huaiyi Lisi kanjian le ta/**ec**[1]
        suspect   see   Asp him/her/it
    Zhangsan suspects that Lisi has seen him/her/it

(5) Lixiaojie haipai Zhangsan bu xihuan   ta/**ec**
    Ms. Li   worry   not like   him/her/it
    Ms. Li worries that Zhangsan does not like
    him/her/it

The coreference relations of the null object in (2-5)
is shown in (6) by the dotted lines, where the null object
is linked to the argument of the matrix clause NP1 and X.
However, the null object cannot be NP2.

(6) [$_S$ NP1 V [$_S$' [$_S$ NP2 V **ec**]]]
    |_ _ _ _ _ _ _ _ _ _ _ |
                           |
    X ------------------------

I am using X to stand for a unspecified noun phrase. Note
this unspecified NP does not have to be confined to a
human NP. It could be an inanimate NP. The coreference
relations in (6) are similar to those when a pronoun is
present in object position, as in (7).

(7)   [$_S$ NP1 V [$_S$' [$_S$ NP2 V Pron]]]
        |_ _ _ _ _ _ _ _ _ _ _ |
                            |
    X ------------------------

The fact that null objects in these sentences are
coreferential with matrix arguments suggests that they can
be taken as null pronominal objects, not as variables
bound by an operator, which is Huang's position.

1.2. Null Object in Relative Clause

---

[1] Asp stands for Aspectual Marker. Le indicates
completed action.

A similar property holds of null objects in the relative construction given in (8) and (9). The object pronoun <u>him</u> of (8a) must be present after the verb <u>believe</u>, otherwise we would have an ungrammatical sentence (9a). However, from the Chinese counterparts (8b) and (9b), we see that in (8b) the pronoun <u>ta</u> after the verb <u>xiangxin</u> `to believe' can be null in (9b).

(8)a. John couldn't find a man who believes him[2]

   b. Zhangsan zhao-bu-dao xiangxin ta de ren
              find not   believe him MM man
      Zhangsan couldn't find a man who believes
      him/her/it

(9)a. *John couldn't find a man who believes **ec**

   b. Zhangsan zhao-bu-dao xiangxin **ec** de ren
              find not   believe   MM man
      Zhangsan couldn't find a man who believes
      him/her/it

What we are interested in these examples is the coreferentiality of the null object of (9b) with the matrix clause argument and a discourse reference. This is given in (10) where the null object is free in its GC, referring either to the matrix subject NP1 or X.

(10) [$_S$ NP1 V [$_{NP}$ [$_S$' [$_S$ V **ec** DE] NP]]
           |_ _ _ _ _ _ _ _ _ _ _ |
      X ------------------------

In (10) we see that the null object has a similar coreference relation as that in (6). Sentences (11)-(13) are some more egs demonstrating the structure given in (10).

(11) Lisi zai zhao zhichi **ec** de ren
      Lisi Asp look support   MM mam
      Lisi is looking for a man who supports
      him/her/it

(12) Zhangsan peng-bu-zhao tonging **ec** de ren
              can-not-meet sympathize MM man
      Zhangsan cannot meet a man who sympathizes with
      him/her/it

---

   [2] MM stands for Modifer Marker. <u>De</u>, as a modifer marker, marks the relative heads which are preceded by the relative clauses.

(13)   Lisi bu xuyao bangmang **ec**   de ren
       not need help   MM man
       Lisi does not need a man who helps him/her/it

1.3. Null object as Controller

On the basis of the above discussion I would like to assume that null pronominal objects are possible candidates in Chinese, we would, therefore, expect to find cases where the syntactic activeness of a null object is observed. Now I show that the null object observed in object control structures in Chinese meets the diagnostic conditions for a null object. The tests in Rizzi 1986 include a null object being a controller, being a binder and being productive.

Generally no structurally represented null object is possible in English as shown in (14). (14a) is grammatical but (14b) without the object <u>people</u> is unacceptable. Italian, on the other hand, allows a missing object interpreted as an arbitrary plural noun. Compare (15a) which has the overt object <u>la gente</u> `the people' with (15b) which has a null object.

(14)a. This leads people [PRO to conclude what
       follows]

   b.*This leads ____ [PRO to conclude what
       follows]

(15)a. Questo conduce la gente a [PRO concludere
       quanto segue]

       This leads people to conclude what follows

   b. Questo conduce ___ a [PRO concludere quanto
      segue]
      This leads (people) to conclude what follows

                              (Rizzi 1986: 503)

If the analysis of pro object in Chinese given earlier is correct, one expects null objects in control structures in Chinese. Indeed, it is the case in (16).

(16) Zhangsan taoyan [bieren bi   zhe   __ [PRO
                       hate   others force Aspect
     xuexi]]
     study

     Zhangsan hates other people force __ to study
     Zhangsan hates it that other people force ___ to
     study

In (16), the object control verb <u>bi</u> `to force' can have a null object. This null object acts as the subject of the embedded clause <u>xuexi</u> `to study'. Sentences (17)-(18) are more examples, which show that the null object can be a controller. Object control verbs in Chinese include: <u>bi</u> `to force', <u>yaoqui</u> `to request', <u>mingling</u> `to order', <u>rang</u> `to let', <u>yaoqing</u> `to invite', <u>yunxu</u> `to permit' and etc., which all exhibit the same property of permitting a structually active null element.[3]

(17) Zhengfu yaoqui ___ [PRO zhi sheng yige xiaohai]
     government request ___ only bear one   child
     The government request ___ to have only one child

(18) Dahui   zhuxi   yunxu ___ [PRO ziyou fayan]
     conference chairman permit   free talk
     The chairman of the conference permit ___ to talk freely

1.4. Productivity

Rizzi shows that syntactically active null object is productivity in Italian. We see that it is also true in Chinese.

2.1 Differences Between pro Objects

So far, we've seen that null objects in Chinese are (i) free in GC (ii) meet the diagnostic condition for **pro**. Now I will examine the different characteristics associtated with the interpretation of pro objects between Italian and Chinese, and also the different characteristics associated with pro subjects.
The difference between the Italian and Chinese types of pros that I'd like to emphasize is captured by the terms RESTRICTED/NON-RESTRICTED. In Italian, as we will see, pros are restricted in that pro subjects require that phi-features be overtly fixed, and pro objects must be an arbitrary human plural interpretation restricted to a generic time reference. This is not the case in Chinese.
According to Rizzi 1986, in Italian an object controller can always be phonetically null if the sentence has a generic time reference. This is shown by (19)&(20).

---

[3] It is not necessarily that a null object which can be an object controller should be a <u>pro</u>. Traces can be object controllers too in sentences such as "Who do you want t [PRO to go to LA]?". The point is that the null object in the above construction is a syntactic entity. If this syntactic entity--null object--may have pronominal interpretation, it should be a <u>pro</u>.

(19) Un general puo costringere__a [PRO obbedre ai
a   general can   force   to   obey

suoi ordini]
his orders

* A general can force__ to obey his orders

(20) In questi casi, di solito Gianni invita__ a[PRO
in these   cases generally   invites to

mangiare con lui
eat   with him

*In these cases, generally Ginni invites___to
eat with him

Compare (19-20) with (21). In (21), a specific time at
five occurs and the sentence is unacceptable.

(21) * Alle cinque il generale ha costretto __ a [PRO
at   five   the general   forced   to

obbedire]
obbey

* At five the general forced __ to obey

(Rizzi 1986: 503-4)

Chinese is not affected by the generic time
limitation, as in (22-23). In (22) we have at five o'clock
yesterday afternoon as a specific time. Sentence (23)
illustrates the same point.

(22) zuotian xiawu wu dian, Lisi zhudong yaoqing__qu
yester. after 5 o'clock   willing invited go

ta jia   chi fan
his house eat meal

At 5 yesterday afternoon, Lisi invited __ to go
to his house to eat meal.

(23) Zuotian   zhanchang shang, duizhang mingling __
yesterday battle field on, commander order

[PRO liji   chetui]
immed. withdraw

Yesterday on the battle field, the commander
ordered___to withdraw immediately

In addition, pro objects in Italian must have arbitrary interpretation. Rizzi defines ARBITRARY (henceforth <u>arb</u>) as the feature set [+human, +plural, +generic], for example <u>people</u> in earlier examples.

(24) <u>Italian pro object</u>: [+human, +plural, +generic]

But a null object in Chinese is not restricted to arbitrary interpretation, feature associ012 is flexible, as given in (25)

(25) Zhangsan taoyan [bieren bizhe __ [PRO xuexi]]
          hate   others force   study
     Zhangsan hates other people force __ to study
     Zhangsan hates it that other people force (him) to study

In (25), the null object after <u>bizhe</u> `to force' can be specific, <u>Zhangsan</u> or someone else either singular or plural. The same is true of (26).

(26) Lisi shuo dahui zhuxi yunxu __ [PRO ziyou
        say conference chairman permit free
     fayan]
     talk

     Lisi said that the chairman of the conference permit__to talk freely

In (26) the missing object can be a specifiec third person singular <u>Lisi</u> [-plural, -arbitrary] or can be either a singular or plurual noun [-plural, +arbitrary], [+plural, +arbitrary].
     Besides all this, we see in structures (6) and (10) given earlier, a pro object in the embedded and relative clauses can refer either to a specific noun phrase--NP1 or with a unspecific X. Italian pro object lacks such flexibility.
     The point to be emphasized is that the interpretation of pro objects in Chinese is not at all restricted to values fixed in the feature set (24). Similar properties are observed on pro subjects between Chinese and Italian.

2.2. Differences Between pro Subjects

Compare (27) with (28). The <u>a</u> sentences are English. The ungrammatical sentence (28a) shows that the subject of the embedded clause has to be present like (27a). The <u>b</u> sentences are Chinese. The embedded subject <u>ta</u> `he' in (27b) can disappear and becomes null in (28b) (This has been noticed in Huang 1982).

(27) a. Bill   says that he doesn't believe Tom.

    b. Zhangsan shuo   **ta** bu xiangxin Lisi.
             say   he not believe
        Zhangsan says that he doesn't believe Lisi

(28) a. *Bill   says that **ec** doesn't believe Tom

    b. Zhangsan shuo **ec**   bu   xiangxin Lisi
             say   not   believe
        Zhangsan says that he doesn't believe Lisi.

The disappearance of the subject in a tensed clause in Italian, Spanish and so on is familiar to us (Perlmulter 1970, Jaeggli 1982, Rizzi 1982, Chomsky 1981). But what is interesting is the referential ability of the null subject in (28b). The null subject functions like an overt pronoun, referring either to matrix subject NP1 <u>Zhangsan</u> or an unspecified X outside the sentence. As far as I know, there is no disagreement on this issue (cf. Huang 1982, 1984, 1987).

Although Italian and Chinese all allow pro subjects, pro subjects in Italian are restricted in the sense that they must be limited to the overt phi-features in Infl, later attached to the verb, hence pro subjects are identified as to person, number and gender. However, a pro subject in Chinese in (28b) has the coreference relations shown in (29).

(29) [S NP1 V [s' [s **ec** V NP2]]]
           |_ _ _ _ _ _ _ _|
     X--------------------|

In (29), NP1 is the matrix subject, X is the unspecified noun phrase. These are familiar to us, because we have seen similar relations that I have given in (6) and (10) regarding pro objects.

That is, if we compare (6), (10) and (29), we see in Chinese both pro objects and subjects are similar in referentiality regarding their antecedents outside GC: pro has a range of references like an overt pronoun.

3. Licensing Conditions

I will propose an account of differences between Italian and Chinese regarding the interpretations and licensing of pro subjects and pro objects.

Rizzi 1986 proposed a formal licensing condition for pros and their interpretations, as in (30).

(30)   **pro**$_i$ Infl   V **pro**$_j$
              | |
            Agr$_i$ [Theta$_j$]

That is a pro subject is licensed by INFL and the content is identified by [Agr] while a pro object is licensed by verb, the content is identified by assigning an <u>arb</u> interpreation to the direct theta-role of the verb (as a syntactic process applying on theta-grids). This <u>arb</u>, which is [+human, +generic, +plural], must be transferred to the pro object.

But, as we have seen earlier, Chinese does not have similar constraints on the interpretation of **pro** with respect to either pro subjects or pro objects. A pro just needs to satisfy the following condition in (31): it must be free in its GC whether it is in subject or object position.

(31)   *$[_{GC}$ ... NP_i ... pro_i ...]
         NP_i ... $[_{GC}$ ... pro_i ...]
         X_i

Therefore, to capture the restricted vs non-restricted properties of pros. I maintain that pro subject in Italian is licensed by Infl containing Agr. Hence it follows that pronominal features can be recovered, it is in this sense that null subject interpretion is restricted to phi-features encoded in INFl.

(32)   **pro**$_i$ Infl
                |
               Agr$_i$

It has been assumed that pro subject in Chinese is also licensed by Infl (Huang 1982, 1984).

(33) Infl (in Chinese) = proper governor

If this is so, then we must ask why do pro subjects behave differently in Italian and Chinese if both are licensed by Infl? In addition, why do pro objects behave differently as well in both langagues, if both are licensed by V (as suggested by Rizzi)? And we may further ask why in Chinese pro subjects and pro objects behave the same if they are licensed differently?

As is well known, there is nothing similar in Infl in Chinese to Infl in Italian. There is no system of inflectional suffixes which pattern with Italian or English, either for tense or agreement. So, I take the position and emphasize the position that an Infl containing no Agr cannot play the same function as an Infl containing Agr. Hence, Infl cannot be the licensing head in Chinese. Instead, I suggest that V licenses pro sujects in Chinese, and it also license pro objects. Let's see what advantages we gain from this assumption. If both pro subjects and pro objects are licensed by V in Chinese, we can explain why pro subjects and pro objects have similar referential properties noted earlier in (6), (10) and

(29). It also follows that neither pro subjects nor pro objects are restricted to phi-features in Infl or to the arb interpretation noted in Italian, because in Chinese INfl is not relevant, and null object interpretation is not a fixed feature set.

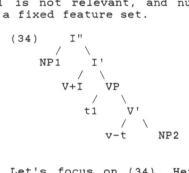

(34)   I"
        / \
     NP1   I'
          / \
       V+I   VP
            / \
          t1   V'
               / \
             v-t   NP2

    Let's focus on (34). Here I follow the proposal of Koopman & Sportiche (1985), Fukui & Speas (1986) that subjects are generated in VP. For pro subjects in Italian, V raises to Infl, forming V+I. Subject NP1, which is generated within VP, moves to Spec to meet Spec-head agreement. So, V+I properly governs NP1, hence licenses pro subject. It follows that pro subjects can be recovered by phi-features in Italian.
    Regarding pro objects, I depart from Rizzi by assuming that verb trace (henceforth v-t) in Italian in (34) licenses pro objects. Because v-t, in the first place, is substantially different form V+I, then the pro licensed by v-t should be also different from pros licensed by V+I. This is exactly what we have noticed in Italian regarding pro subjects and pro objects.
    How do we account for the arbitrary interpretation associated with pro objects? I assume that v-t in (34) forms a chain with the raised V. ie. a chain [V+I, v-t] (35a). This verbal chain, due to its heavy inflections within V+I and the intimate relation between V+I and v-t, enforces a default phi-feature interpretation onto pro objects. This default and invariant phi-features are [+human, +plural, +generic]. Therefore, the null object it licenses has a fixed arb interpretation (35b).

    (35)a. [V+I ... v-t]

        b.   v-t pro_{arb}
               |
            [V+I...v-t]$_{arb}$

    Turning to Chinese, shown in (36), I assume that V-raising is unavailable since there is no amalgamation process which requires V-raising in Chinese. In (36), I assume that NP1 needs to raise to Spec to receive ABSTRACT

CASE (Li 1985),[4] leaving t1. I assume that the raised NP1
and its trace t1 [NP1, t1] froms a chain, satisfying
antecedent government. VP in Chinese is not a barrier for
the antecedent government, for the lexical status of Infl
elments could siffice to L-mark VP.

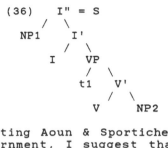

(36)

Adopting Aoun & Sportiche 1983 's definition of proper
government, I suggest that V properly govern t1 which
forms a chain with NP1 in Spec, hence V licenses pro
sujects. It follows that pro subjects do not need to be
specified by phi-features.

In addition, in Chinese, V also licenses pro object,
it follows that pro objects do not have a default arb
interpretation as Italian does. Therefore, both pro
subjects and pro objects behave alike w.r.t their
references. This is exactly what we noticed in (6), (10)
and (29) in Chinese.[5]

(37) a. **pro** ... V ... **pro**

b. **pro** has a range of references in Chinese like
a pure pronoun

4. Conclusion

To sum up, I have made two proposals. The first
proposal asserts that Chinese allows **pro** in the object
position regarding the data brought out here. I contrast
pros in Chinese and Italian; pro has a range of references
in Chinese like a pure pronoun while pro has a number of
restrictions in Italian. The second proposal claims that
Infl cannot be taken as a licensing head for pro
universally; I suggest that the differences between
Chinese and Italian regarding either pro subjects or pro

---

[4] For detailed arguments for Abstract Case in
Chinese, please see Li (1985).

[5] A reasonable assumption is that the thetas of verb
are acturally the licensing heads for pros in a language
like Chinese which does not have agreement. In other
words, the thematic structure of a verb could play a role
in allowing null elements.

objects be traced back to the licensing heads in each language, therefore providing an explanation for the similarities between pro subjects and objects in Chinese, and the disimilaries between pro subjects and pro objects in Italian.

* I am grateful to Ann Farmer, Dick Oehrle, Doug Saddy and Susan Steele for helpful discussions. I'd like to thank Marc Authier for his detailed comments. All errors are mine.

References

Aoun, J. and D. Sportiche (1983) "On the Formal Theory of Government", Linguistic Review 2, 211-236.

Chomsky, N. (1986) Barriers. MIT Press, Cambridge.

Fukui, N. and M. Speas (1987) "Specifers and Prejection" MIT Working Papers in Linguistics 8, MIT, Cambridge.

Huang, C.-T. J. (1982) Logical Relations in Chinese and the Theory of Grammar. Doctoral Dissertation, MIT.

Huang, C.-T. J. (1984)"On the Distribution and Reference of Empty Pronouns" LI 15, 381-416.

Huang, C.-T. J. (1987) "Remarks on Empty Categories in Chinese" LI 18, 321-327.

Jaeggli, O. (1982) Topics in Romance Syntax. Foris, Dordrecht.

Koopman, H. and D. Sportiche (1985) "Theta Theory and Extraction" GLOW Newsletter.

Li, Y.-H. A. (1985) Abstract Case in Chinese. Doctoral Dissertation, USC, Los Angeles.

Rizzi, L. (1982) Issues in Italian Synatax. Foris, Dordrecht.

Rizzi, L. (1986) "Null Objects in Italian and the Theory of pro". LI 17, 501-557

Xu, L. J. (1986) "Free Empty Categories" LI 17, 75-93.

Zhang, Shi (1988) "Towards a Solution of pro-Drop". Qualifying Paper, University of Arizona, Tucson.

Prosodic Constraints on Syntax: Hausa 'fa'

Sharon Inkelas

Stanford University

The distribution of conversational particles has often proved useful in diagnosing the constituent structure of various languages.[1] In this paper I analyze the distribution of one such particle (*fa*) in Hausa, a Chadic language of Nigeria, and argue that it provides evidence for a special type of constituent — the phonological phrase — that thus far has not been demonstrated to exist in the language. Moreover, the data show that the process responsible for ordering words in Hausa makes crucial reference to phonological phrases, thus threatening the hypothesis of a universal phonology-free syntactic component.

Section 1 introduces the data, gathered from two native speakers of the Kano dialect of Hausa (the standard dialect).[2] The analysis, articulated within the framework of prosodic phonology (Selkirk 1978), follows in section 2. The paper concludes with a section on the several theoretical implications of the proposal.

1. Fa

Fa is an emphatic particle which highlights the word or constituent that it follows. Never allowed at the beginning of an utterance, *fa* can always occur utterance-finally, and is inseparable by pause from the preceding word. *fa* is also found utterance-medially, but it cannot show up just anywhere. In the rest of section 2 we will take a close look at exactly which utterance-medial environments support this leftward-attaching emphatic particle.

Fa can occur between a transitive verb and following object NP iff one of the following conditions holds:

(1)

    a.   The NP is emphasized (intonationally)

    b.   The NP is branching (i.e. contains more than one word)

---

[1] Because this paper was submitted late in the editorial process, it appears out of alphabetical order with respect to the other papers in the volume. The fact that it came about at all is due largely to the generous contributions of Lawan Danladi Yalwa, co-discoverer of the data, and to the helpful comments of Mark Cobler, Kathryn Henniss, Larry Hyman, Will Leben, Bill Poser, Russ Schuh and Draga Zec.

[2] It should be noted that the distribution of emphatic particles appears to vary somewhat across speakers, even within the same dialect.

Examples (2)-(3) illustrate the effects of emphasis on the occurrence of *fa*;[3] in the (a) examples, the direct object NP contains only a single word and is unemphasized. *fa* is not allowed to precede. But in the (b) examples, where the same NP is emphasized,[4] *fa* is good.

(2)

    a.   *Ya sayi **fa** tebur.
            he bought table
            'He bought a table'

    b.   Ya sayi **fa** *teburin*.
            he bought table-def.
            'He bought the *table*'

(3)

    a.   *Ya sayi **fa** riga.
            he bought shirt
            'He bought a shirt'

    b.   Ya sayi **fa** *rigar*.
            he bought shirt-def.
            'He bought the *shirt*'

In example (4), the contrast between the starred and unstarred sentences is that of branchingness. The (a) and (b) sentences feature object NP's consisting of a single word (pronoun or noun). Neither of these NP's is branching or emphasized, and neither allows the intrusion of *fa* on the left. But the situation is different in examples (c) through (e), where each object NP contains more than one word. *fa* is permitted to precede the object in these cases.

---

[3] In this and following examples, *fa* will not be glossed in English.

[4] Intonational emphasis involves one or more of the following effects: increase in amplitude; rise in pitch; slight pause before the emphasized word. In these examples, the emphasized noun is also made definite (for pragmatic reasons) by means of the definiteness suffix. But definiteness and emphasis do not go hand in hand; though emphasized nouns tend to be definite, they need not be. Moreover, it is not the case that every definite noun is emphasized.

(4)

    a.   *Ya saye **fa** ta.
           he bought it-fem
           'He bought it.'

    b.   *Ya sayi **fa** riga.
           he bought shirt
           'He bought a shirt'

    c.   Ya sayi **fa** babbar riga.
           he bought big shirt
           'He bought a big shirt'

    d.   Ya sayi **fa** rigar Audu.
           he bought shirt-of Audu
           'He bought Audu's shirt'

    e.   Ya sayi **fa** riga da wando.
           he bought shirt and pants
           'He bought a shirt and pants'

To prove that the appropriate right-hand context of *fa* is indeed a branching constituent and not just a string of more than one word, consider the examples in (5).

(5)

    a.   *Ya sayi **fa** abinci
           'He bought food'

    b.   *Ya sayi **fa** abinci jiya
           'He bought food yesterday'

In both sentences, the object *abinci* 'food' is nonbranching; in (b), the object is followed by an adverb *jiya* 'yesterday'. Now, if *fa* was sensitive only to the number of words on the right, we would expect *fa* to be possible in the (b) example — since two words follow — but it is not. Only if those two words belong to the same constituent, as in (6), is *fa* allowed.

(6)

           Ya sayi **fa** abincin rana
           He bought food-of day
           'He bought lunch'

Conditions identical to those in (1) hold on the occurrence of *fa* between the two complements of a verb. *fa* is possible there iff at least one of the following conditions is met:

(7)

    a.   The second NP is emphasized

    b.   The second NP is branching

In the (a) sentences in (8)-(9), the direct object NP is non-branching and unemphasized; each direct object is preceded by *fa*, and each sentence is ungrammatical.

But in the corresponding (b) examples, the direct object NP is emphasized intonationally — and *fa* is good.

(8)

    a.   *Ta siffanta wa Audu **fa** riga.
           she described to Audu shirt
           'She described a shirt to Audu'

    b.   Ta siffanta wa Audu **fa** *rigar*.
           she described to Audu shirt-def.
           'She described the *shirt* to Audu'

(9)

    a.   *Ta ba wa Mani **fa** wannan.
           she gave to Mani this
           'She gave this to Mani'

    b.   Ta ba wa Mani **fa** *wannan*.
           she gave to Mani this
           'She gave *this* to Mani'

When emphasis is factored out, as in examples (10)-(12), it becomes clear that between indirect and direct objects as well, the condition of branching on the right determines the existence of a potential *fa* site. *fa* cannot precede non-branching constituents, such as the pronoun *ita* 'her' in (10a) — but is licensed before any branching constituent, e.g. the conjoined NP in (10b).

(10)

    a.   *Sun siffanta wa Tanko **fa** ita.
           they described to Tanko her
           'They described her to Tanko'

    b.   Sun siffanta wa Tanko **fa** ni da ita.
           they described to Tanko me and her
           'They described me and her to Tanko'

(11)

    a.   *Sun ba wa Audu **fa** riga.
           they gave to Audu shirt
           'They gave a shirt to Audu'

    b.   Sun ba wa Audu **fa** babbar riga.
           they gave to Audu big shirt
           'They gave a big shirt to Audu'

    c.   Sun ba wa Audu **fa** wake da shinkafa.
           they gave to Audu beans and rice
           'They gave beans and rice to Audu'

(12)

    a.   *Na bayyana wa Lawan **fa** sabuwar.
           I described to Lawan new
           'I described the new one to Lawan'

    b.   Na bayyana wa Lawan **fa** sabuwar mota.
           I described to Lawan new car
           'I described the new car to Lawan'

    c.   Na bayyana wa Lawan **fa** mota shida.
           I described to Lawan car six
           'I described six cars to Lawan'

The data in (13)-(14) underscore the point discussed earlier, namely that it is the property of branchingness — not total number of words — to which *fa* is sensitive on the right. In both examples below, tacking on the adverb *jiya* 'yesterday' after a non-branching NP has no effect on the (un)grammaticality of *fa* to the left of the NP:

(13)

    a.   *Mun ba wa Sani **fa** ita.
           we gave to Sani it-fem.
           'We gave it-fem. to Sani'

    b.   *Mun ba wa Sani **fa** ita jiya.
           we gave to Sani it-fem. yesterday
           'We gave it-fem. to Sani yesterday'

(14)

    a.   *Mun ba wa Sani **fa** riga.
           we gave to Sani shirt
           'We gave a shirt to Sani'

    b.   *Mun ba wa Sani **fa** riga jiya.
           we gave to Sani shirt yesterday
           'We gave a shirt to Sani yesterday'

Of course, adding an adjective to that same NP has the effect of licensing a preceding *fa*, regardless of the presence or absence of the adverb *jiya*.

(15)

    a. Mun ba wa Sani **fa** sabuwar riga.
       we gave to Sani new shirt
       'We gave a new shirt to Sani'

    b. Mun ba wa Sani **fa** sabuwar riga jiya.
       we gave to Sani new shirt yesterday
       'We gave a new shirt to Sani yesterday'

The distribution of *fa* within prepositional phrases headed by the prepositions *a* 'at, in' and *da* 'with, at' fits the pattern described by the preceding data; *a* and *da* can be separated by *fa* from a following NP complement iff at least one of the conditions is (16) is met.

(16)

    a.   The NP is emphasized

    b.   The NP is branching

(17)

    a.   *Mun sauka a **fa** Kano.
        'We arrived at Kano'

    b.   Mun sauka a **fa** *Kano*.
        'We arrived at *Kano*'

    c.   Mun sauka a **fa** birnin Kano.
        we arrived at town-of Kano
        'We arrived at the town of Kano'

(18)

    a.   *Sun zo da **fa** yamma.
        they came in afternoon
        'They came in the afternoon'

    b.   Sun zo da **fa** can yamma.
        they came in far afternoon
        'They came that afternoon'

    c.   Sun zo da **fa** ƙarfe takwas.
        they came at o'clock eight
        'They came at eight o'clock'

The last set of data we will look at involve initial constituents. These provide, at first glance, a direct counterexample to the observed constraints on *fa*. Take for example the noun phrase *yaron alaramma* 'boy of the alaramma'. Appearing as an object following the verb in (19a), *yaron alaramma* will not admit the intrusion of *fa*, as we have come to expect; *alaramma* is neither emphasized nor part of a branching constituent. But note what happens when *yaron alaramma* occurs as the subject in (19b): *fa* is all of a sudden possible in the interior.

(19)

    a.   *Ya nemo yaron **fa** alaramma.
        He looked-for boy-of alaramma
        'He looked for the boy of the alaramma'

    b.   Yaron **fa** alaramma ya nemi nama.
        Boy-of alaramma he looked-for meat
        'The boy of the alaramma looked for meat'

(20)

    a.   *Hadiza ta sayi sabon **fa** littafi.
            Hadiza she bought new book
            'Hadiza bought a new book'

    b.   Sabon **fa** littafi ya yi tsada.
            new book it does expensiveness
            'The new book is expensive'

(21)

    a.   *Ta siffanta wa Lawal tebur **fa** babba.
            she described to Lawal table big
            'She described the big table to Lawal'

    b.   Tebur **fa** babba yana waje.
            table big it-masc.-cont. outside
            'The big table is outside'

Before we rush to attribute special properties to subjects in Hausa, however, an important fact must be taken into account. This is that the alternations observed in the noun phrases in (19)-(21) are not true only of subjects. The generalization is, in fact, that the constraints noted earlier on possible *fa* sites within NP's and PP's are uniformly suspended in every utterance-initial constituent. The following examples illustrate pairs of sentences where a particular NP or PP occurs in final position (the (a) sentences) and is then fronted for emphasis (the (b) sentences). In each case, *fa* is allowed inside the NP/PP in (b) but not in (a).

(22)

    a.   *Na sayi babbar **fa** riga.
            I bought big shirt
            'I bought a big shirt'

    b.   Babbar **fa** riga na saya.
            big shirt I bought
            'A big shirt, I bought'

(23)

    a.   *Mun rubuta guda **fa** shida.
            we wrote unit six
            'We wrote six of them'

    b.   Guda **fa** shida muka rubuta.
            unit six we wrote
            'Six of them, we wrote'

(24)

    a.   *An haife shi a **fa** Kano.
            one gave-birth-to him in Kano
            'He was born in Kano'

    b.   A **fa** Kano aka haife shi.
            in Kano one gave-birth-to him
            'In Kano, he was born'

Although in each of the above cases *fa* happens to follow the first word of the utterance, that is not necessary, as demonstrated by the following example:

(25)

    a.   *Mun rubuta wasiƙa guda **fa** shida.
        we wrote letter unit six
        'We wrote six letters'

    b.   Wasiƙa guda **fa** shida muka rubuta.
        letter unit six we wrote
        'Six letters, we wrote'

2. Analysis

Because virtually all of the conditions on the occurrence of *fa* have been stated in syntactic terms, a logical starting point for the account is in the syntax. Below are the constraints such an account would have to incorporate:

(26)

    a. No utterance may begin with *fa*.

    b. If *fa* immediately precedes any material, then that material must be (i) a branching constituent or (ii) emphasized.

    c. Condition (b) is suspended within the initial constituent of an utterance.

We can reduce the arbitrariness of this list somewhat by isolating a common thread connecting two of the four post-*fa* environments where branching is irrelevant, i.e. within the initial constituent (c) and immediately preceding any emphasized material (b). I suggest that there is a good reason these two environments should pattern together: initial constituents in Hausa share with emphasized words the property of prominence.

(27)   Prominent constituents:

    a. Initial
    b. Emphasized

Locating a constituent at the beginning of the utterance alternates with special uses of intonation as a means of emphasis in Hausa. The intuition that the syntactic and intonational methods are just different manifestations of the same entity, which I call here 'prominence', is supported by the fact that when speakers highlight a word or phrase by fronting it, they do not have to employ any intonational tactics to get the emphatic effect across. Special intonation is by contrast obligatory for non-initial prominent material.[5]

Even if we find a way of representing prominence syntactically, however, the 'account' in (26) would still amount to little more than a description of the facts;

---

[5] Although Hausa does exhibit quite complex intonational phenomena, it fits the general pattern of lexical tone languages in providing syntactic outlets for some of the effects that are expressed intonationally in languages like English.

it lists environments without capturing their relationship. Among the unexplained generalizations are the following:

(28)

    a.   Why *fa* should care about emphasis on the right — when its function is to highlight the material on the left

    b.   Why branching constituents, prominence, and utterance-final position pattern together as the possible right-hand environments for *fa*

    c.   Why the utterance-initial element does not share whatever property connects the positions enumerated in (b)

    d.   Why *fa*, an element whose semantic effect is felt on the left, and which is prosodically bound to the material on the left, should be conditioned by any material on the right at all

The severity of these problems for a purely syntactic account of the distribution of *fa* suggests that perhaps syntax is not the proper arena in which to seek a solution. I will now turn to a quite different approach, one which makes crucial reference to prosodic structure.

2.1. A Prosodic Account

The growing literature on the prosodic hierarchy (e.g. Selkirk 1978, 1986, Nespor and Vogel 1982, 1986, and Hayes 1984) has motivated the existence of a type of prosodic constituent called the phonological phrase. Typically the domain for several phonological rules in a language, phrases are constructed in part by some syntactically conditioned algorithm operating on the X^1 hierarchy. Phrases thus mediate between syntactic structure and those phonological rules which apply only within specific syntactic configurations.

It is crucially assumed in this theory that phonological phrases, and indeed each constituent in the prosodic hierarchy, will exhaustively cover each utterance (Selkirk 1986).

(29)   Exhaustive Parsing: Utterances are parsed exhaustively into phonological phrases.

The hypothesis that the prosodic hierarchy has universal status (see Nespor and Vogel 1986 for discussion) is supported by growing evidence that the same sorts of properties are relevant for the construction of phrases across quite different languages. We will take a brief look at two such properties here: syntactic branching, and emphasis.

Branching as a condition on phrasing

In a number of languages, the head of a maximal projection will form a phonological phrase with its complement if, and only if, that complement is nonbranching. If the complement is branching it will phrase on its own. Perhaps the best known examples of this phenomenon come from French, where the phrase-bounded rule of Liaison

384 / Inkelas

applies to the final consonant of a head only when a nonbranching complement follows, as in (30):[6]

(30)   Il   est   très   intelligent.   [trez]
        He   is   very   intelligent
        'He is very intelligent'

(31)   Il   est   très   intelligent   et   modest   [tre]
        He   is   very   intelligent   and   modest
        'He is very intelligent and modest'

The conclusion drawn by Nespor and Vogel 1986 is that Liaison applies within the phonological phrase — and that branching is a crucial factor in determining whether a constituent will form a phrase. In (31) the branching AP is a separate phonological phrase, but the non-branching AP of (30) is not. Because we take utterances to be parsed exhaustively into phrases, the adjective in (30) gets phrased with what precedes — and the environment for Liaison is set up.

(32)

    a.   Il est [très intelligent]$_\phi$.

    b.   Il est très [intelligent et modest]$_\phi$.

Examples like these are by no means limited to English and French; (33) contains a partial list of other languages in which syntactic branching is relevant to the phonology. On the assumption made in the literature on the prosodic hierarchy that phonological rules refer only to prosodic structure, this evidence shows that syntactic branching must be relevant to the algorithms creating prosodic cosntituents.

(33)

        English (Selkirk 1972, Selkirk 1978, Hayes 1984, Nespor and Vogel 1986)
        Italian (Napoli and Nespor 1979, Nespor and Vogel 1986)
        Kinyambo (Bickmore 1988)
        Mandarin Chinese (Liu 1980, cited in Kaisse 1985)
        Mende (Cowper and Rice 1987)
        Serbo-Croatian (Zec, forthcoming)

Emphasis as a condition on phonological phrasing

The effect of emphasis on phonological phrasing has not been studied as extensively as that of branching, although work is beginning to be done on this topic. For example, Cho 1987 argues that focus is relevant for phonological phrasing in Korean, and Zec and Inkelas 1987 have proposed that in English, focused constituents phrase on their own even when the regular phrasing algorithm would predict otherwise.

We are fortunate in this case to have evidence from Hausa itself. Recent work on intonation in Hausa (Inkelas, Leben, Cobler 1986) has argued on the basis of four

---

[6] These examples come from Kaisse 1985, p. 113. For more on Liaison, see e.g. Selkirk 1972, Rotenberg 1978, Kaisse 1985, and Nespor and Vogel 1986.

intonational rules that Hausa has intonational phrases — and, most importantly, that emphasized words begin their own intonational phrase. Now, by 'intonational phrase' ILC mean the unit which is one step up the prosodic hierarchy from the phonological phrase; intonation phrases (Selkirk 1978, Nespor and Vogel 1986) are composed of one or more phonological phrases. It therefore follows that every word which begins a new intonational phrase must also begin a new phonological phrase.

(34)   In Hausa, emphasized words begin a new phonological phrase

With this background on phonological phrases, I will now present an account of the distribution of *fa* in Hausa which makes reference only to the structure of phonological phrases. First, I propose that in Hausa, like in French, English, and other languages, the first element of a branching structure begins a new phonological phrase. We have already concluded that emphasized words begin their own phrase. It now requires only the assumption that all prominent elements are phrased on their own to reduce (a)-(c) in the stipulative list of syntactic conditions on *fa* down to the following more elegant account:

(35)

    a.   No utterance may begin with *fa*.

    b.   If *fa* is non-final then it must immediately precede a phonological phrase.

Of course, here too we are placing restrictions to the right of *fa*, a disadvantage previously attributed to the syntactic account. But to resolve this inelegance all we have to do is recognize that the beginning of every phonological phrase is also the end of the preceding phrase (if any) — and the list in (35) collapses into one extremely simple condition on the occurrence of *fa*:

(36)   *fa* must follow a phonological phrase.

In formal terms, I assign to *fa* a prosodic subcategorization frame of the type proposed in Inkelas 1987: *fa* is a clitic, and subcategorizes for leftward attachment to a phonological phrase. The subcategorization frame given in (37) ensures that *fa* will be incorporated into the phonological phrase which it follows, satisfying the requirements of the Exhaustive Parsing constraint — and explaining why it is impossible to pause before *fa*.[7]

(37) $[\; [\quad]_\phi \; \text{fa} \;]_\phi$

The simplicity of the condition in (36) presupposes an explicit algorithm for generating phonological phrases in Hausa, and it is to this task that we turn now. I propose that Hausa phrasing has two sources. The first is a general algorithm for mapping elements into phrases on the basis of relations holding on the X^1 hierarchy.

---

[7] I am operating under the general assumption that bracket erasure automatically applies to any nested prosodic constituents of the same type, causing the innermost brackets to be invisible to rules. This assumption is independently needed for other languages; see, for example, the phrasing algorithms of Nespor and Vogel 1986, which requires the incorporation of certain material into a neighboring phonological phrase before phonological rules apply.

(38)   Hausa Phrasing Algorithm:

    a. From the bottom up, branching nodes are mapped into phonological phrases.
    b. No two phonological words on opposite sides of an XP boundary may be phrased together to the exclusion of any material in either XP.

Part (a) accounts for all of the simple branching conditions to the right of *fa* which we observed in section 2. For example, it explains why *fa* can precede the branching NP in (39):

(39)

    $[Ta]_\phi$ $[[sayi]_\phi$ $fa]_\phi$ $[babban\ tebur]_\phi$.
    'She bought a big table'

Part (b) deals with those words left unphrased by the more specific clause (a). By grouping together adjacent unphrased elements it explains why, for example, a non-branching NP direct object like that in (40) will phrase with the preceding verb:

(40)

    $[[Ya]_\phi$ $fa]_\phi$ $[sayi\ tebur]_\phi$.
    'He bought a table'

It correctly predicts that non-branching objects in double object constructions will phrase together:

(41)

    $[[Mun]_\phi$ $fa]_\phi$ $[biya\ Audu\ kuɗi]_\phi$.
    'We paid Audu money'

and that they will phrase with a following adverb, if any:

(42)

    $[[Mun]_\phi$ $fa]_\phi$ $[biya\ Audu\ kuɗi\ jiya]_\phi$.
    'We paid Audu money yesterday'

    The proviso in (38b) against allowing a phonological phrase to straddle only one of the edges of a maximal projection is designed to handle the phrasing of words dominated by maximal projections that themselves already contain a phonological phrase. Take, for example, the NP *tebur guda shida* 'table unit six = six tables'. *guda shida* is itself an NP (see (23)), and will be mapped into a phonological phrase by part (a) of the phrasing algorithm. The question now is, will the head noun *tebur* phrase with the preceding verb, as in (42), or will it constitute its own phonological phrase? The answer is the latter. As the algorithm predicts, *fa* is possible before any branching NP, regardless of the details of that NP's internal constituent structure.

(43)

[Ya]$_\phi$ [[sayi]$_\phi$ fa]$_\phi$ [tebur]$_\phi$ [guda shida]$_\phi$.
he bought table unit six
'He bought six tables'

The same is true of prepositional phrases which contain branching NP's: *fa* is always allowed to precede, indicating that the head preposition itself forms a phonological phrase, as in (44). As clause (38b) predicts, the phonological phrase containing the preposition is bounded by the left edge of the PP, and does not group the preposition together with the preceding element.

(44)

[Mun]$_\phi$ [[sauka]$_\phi$ fa]$_\phi$ [a]$_\phi$ [birnin Kano]$_\phi$
we arrived in town-of Kano
'We arrived in the town of Kano'

Clause (38b) is motivated not only in Hausa but also in a number of other languages for which phrasing algorithms have been proposed (including English); see e.g. Nespor and Vogel 1986, Selkirk 1986, and Zec and Inkelas 1987.

The phrasing algorithm in (38) is not, however, sufficient to characterize the phrasing of all Hausa utterances; in particular, it fails to capture the distinction between prominent nonbranching constituents, which always phrase by themselves, and nonprominent ones, which are phrased according to the algorithm.

We must thus introduce an additional clause into the phrasing algorithm, which says that prominent elements (members of initial constituents, and emphasized words) always begin a new phrase. The revised algorithm is stated in (45). Each clause operates only on unphrased material. Thus they are disjunctive, and the Elsewhere Condition determines that where two clauses would produce different results, the more specific overrides the more general.

(45)   Hausa Phrasing Algorithm (final version):

    a. Prominent elements are mapped into their own phonological phrases.
    b. From the bottom up, branching nodes are mapped into phonological phrases.
    c. No two phonological words on opposite sides of an XP boundary may be phrased together to the exclusion of any material in either XP.

4. Conclusion

By attributing the constraints on the syntactic distribution of *fa* to the presence of a phonological phrase break at each potential *fa* site, we capture several important generalizations:

(46)

    a.   The constraint in (82) refers only to the the left-hand context of *fa*, consistent with *fa*'s leftward syntactic and prosodic attachments.

    b.   We explain why intonational emphasis, branching constituents, and zero pattern together as the possible right-hand contexts for *fa*; these are exactly the environments which can follow the end of a phrase.

    c.   We correctly predict that *fa* is blocked utterance-initially — as no phonological phrase precedes.

Thus on both descriptive and explanatory grounds, the prosodic account for the distribution of *fa* is supported over a nonprosodic account. The analysis also has a number of important implications for the prosodic hierarchy theory.

Category-blind phrasing algorithm: The fact that the phrasing algorithm for Hausa makes no reference to the syntactic category of words or constituents supports the hypothesis — implicit in much of the prosodic hierarchy literature — that the parsing of utterances into phonological phrases can be accomplished by referring only to the geometrical structure of the X^1 hierarchy. Together with the assumption that phonological rules see only prosodic structure (Selkirk 1986), a category-blind phrasing algorithm greatly constrains the power of the prosodic hierarchy theory.

Phrases are constituents: The above analysis of Hausa *fa* requires us to view phonological phrases as real constituents in the representation, supporting the claim that the members of the prosodic hierarchy are indeed constituents. A complaint that one could level at past work on the prosodic hierarchy is that phrases have served in the literature only as abstract domains for rules. And rule clustering of this sort is not incontrovertible proof of phrasal constituency. One could imagine some theory of boundary symbols which could derive the same result. However, the striking evidence from Hausa that phrases are units to which other components of grammar may refer provides important evidence for the existence of phonological phrases as actual entities in the grammar.

Phonology-sensitive word order: The third consequence for linguistic theory is the evidence that the syntactic distribution of an element, *fa*, is conditioned by prosodic factors. While it has long been recognized that phonological rules are subject to syntactic constraints, restrictions going in the opposite direction have rarely been demonstrated. It is true that I have proposed to account for the prosodic constraints on *fa* by means of a lexical subcategorization frame, but even so it is still the case that the component of the syntax responsible for ordering words must pay attention to both the syntactic and the prosodic demands of *fa*.

References

Bickmore, L. 1988. "Branching Nodes and Prosodic Categories: Evidence from Kinyambo." Paper presented at WCCFL 7, University of California, Irvine.

Cho, Y. 1987. "The Domain of Korean Sandhi Rules." Paper presented at the 1987 LSA meeting, San Francisco.

Cowper, E. and K. Rice. 1987. "Are phonosyntactic rules necessary?" *Phonology Yearbook 4*, pp. 185-194.

Hayes, B. 1984. "The Prosodic Hierarchy and Meter." To appear in P. Kiparsky and G. Youmans, eds., *Rhythm and Meter*, Academic Press, Orlando.

Inkelas, S. 1987. "Prosodic Subcategorization." Paper presented at the 1987 LSA meeting, San Francisco.

Inkelas, S., W. Leben, and M. Cobler. 1986. "Lexical and Phrasal Tone in Hausa." Proceedings of NELS 17.

Kaisse, E. 1985. *Connected Speech: The Interaction of Syntax and Phonology.* Academic Press, Orlando.

Liu, Feng-hsi. 1980. "Mandarin Tone Sanhi: a Case of Interaction between Syntax and Phonology." Paper presented at the LSA summer meeting.

Napoli, D.J. and M. Nespor. 1979. "The syntax of word initial consonant gemination in Italian." *Language* 55, 812-841.

Nespor, M. and I. Vogel. 1982. "Prosodic Domains of External Sandhi Rules." In H. van der Hulst and N. Smith (eds.), *The Structure of Phonological Representations, Part 1*. Dordrecht: Foris.

Nespor, M. and I. Vogel. 1986. *Prosodic Phonology*. Dordrecht: Foris.

Rotenberg, J. 1978. *The Syntax of Phonology*. Doctoral dissertation, MIT.

Selkirk, E. 1972. *The Phrase Phonology of English and French*. Doctoral dissertation, MIT.

Selkirk, E. 1984. *Phonology and Syntax*. MIT Press.

Selkirk, E. 1978. "On Prosodic Structure and its Relation to Syntactic Structure." In T. Fretheim, ed., *Nordic Prosody II*, Trondheim, TAPIR.

Selkirk. E. 1986. "On Derived Domains in Sentence Phonology." *Phonology Yearbook 3*, pp. 371-405.

Zec, D. (forthcoming). "Sonority Constraints on Prosodic Structure." Doctoral dissertation, Stanford University.

Zec, D. and S. Inkelas. 1987. "Phonological Phrasing and the Reduction of Function Words." Paper presented at the 1987 LSA meeting, San Francisco.